So stay awake and be prepared,
because you do not know the day or hour of my return.

MATTHEW 25:13 NLT

He who descended is none other than he who ascended far above
all heavens, so that he might fill the universe.

EPHESIANS 4:10 REB

Watch and pray, the Lord Jesus is coming!

CHRISTOPH BLUMHARDT

Hell is only a spot in the universe of God.
Compared with heaven, hell is narrow and limited.
The kingdom of Satan is insignificant in contrast with the kingdom of Christ.

WILLIAM G. T. SHEDD

People of our time have become insensitive to the Last Things. . . .
Secularization and secularism promote this insensitivity and
lead to a consumer mentality oriented toward the enjoyment of earthly goods.

POPE JOHN PAUL II

· CHRISTIAN FOUNDATIONS ·

THE
LAST
THINGS

RESURRECTION, JUDGMENT, GLORY

DONALD G. BLOESCH

INTERVARSITY PRESS
DOWNERS GROVE, ILLINOIS 60515

InterVarsity Press
P.O. Box 1400, Downers Grove, IL 60515-1426
World Wide Web: www.ivpress.com
E-mail: mail@ivpress.com

InterVarsity Press® is the book-publishing division of InterVarsity Christian Fellowship/USA®, a student movement active on campus at hundreds of universities, colleges and schools of nursing in the United States of America, and a member movement of the International Fellowship of Evangelical Students. For information about local and regional activities, write Public Relations Dept., InterVarsity Christian Fellowship/USA, 6400 Schroeder Rd., P.O. Box 7895, Madison, WI 53707-7895, or visit the IVCF website at <www.intervarsity.org>.

Scripture quotations, unless otherwise noted, are from the Revised Standard Version of the Bible, *copyright 1946, 1952, 1971 by the Division of Christian Education of the National Council of the Churches of Christ in the U.S.A., and are used by permission.*

Chapter ten, "Israel's Salvation: The Supersessionist Controversy," is an expanded version of an earlier article by the author, "All Israel Will Be Saved: Supersessionism and the Biblical Witness," published in Interpretation *43, no. 2 (1989): 130-42.*

Images: Guy Wolek

ISBN 0-8308-1417-5

Printed in the United States of America ∞

Library of Congress Cataloging-in-Publication Data

Bloesch, Donald G., 1928-
  The last things: Resurrection, judgment, glory / Donald G. Bloesch.
    p. cm.—(Christian foundations)
  Includes bibliographical references and index.
  ISBN 0-8308-1417-5 (alk. paper)
  1. Eschatology. I. Title
  BT821.3.B58 2004
  236—dc22

2003027941

P	16	15	14	13	12	11	10	9	8	7	6	5	4	3	2	1
Y	16	15	14	13	12	11	10	09	08	07	06	05	04			

Dedicated to
Reformation and Revival Ministries

Acknowledgments

I wish to thank the following persons for helping me procure needed information on the great themes of eschatology: Gary Deddo, Jim Hoover, Bradley Longfield, John Armstrong, Alan Crandall, Craig Nissan, Elizabeth Platt, Gabriel Fackre, David MacLeod, Charlene Swanson, Paul Waelchli, John Rush and Ethel Bloesch. As always, I am indebted to my wife, Brenda, for her careful copyediting and research.

Abbreviations for Biblical Translations

KJV	King James Version
NASB	New American Standard Bible
NKJV	New King James Version
NIV	New International Version
JB	Jerusalem Bible
NJB	New Jerusalem Bible
NRSV	New Revised Standard Version
ESV	English Standard Version
REB	Revised English Bible
GNC	God's New Covenant
GNB	Good News Bible
NEB	New English Bible
LB	Living Bible
NLT	New Living Translation

(Note: Bible references not otherwise indicated are from the Revised Standard Version.)

Preface

It is fitting that this last volume of the Christian Foundations series should focus on eschatology, the doctrine of the last things. Theology is not reducible to eschatology, but it culminates in eschatology. I make clear in this volume, however, that eschatology pertains not exclusively to the future or even to the near future. It deals not only with the kingdom that is coming but with the kingdom that is already here through the power of the resurrection of Christ from the grave and the gift of the Holy Spirit to the church. Eschatology is neither futurism nor preterism (the promises of God completed in the past), but instead the revelation of the future in the present—wherever the Word of God is proclaimed, believed and obeyed.

In this volume I explore themes that are generally overlooked in the contemporary discussion on eschatology. Among these is the communion of saints—the interaction between the communities of faith on this side and on the other side of death. A related theme is the intermediate state of the dead, which comprises both paradise and the nether world of spirits. With some of the biblical writers and many of the church fathers, I hold that this underworld is not beyond the reach of God's grace but instead is invaded by the light of his grace. In this same discussion I explore the possibility of deliverance beyond the grave (postmortem salvation). I take vigorous exception to the Roman Catholic doctrine of purgatory on the grounds that it tends to undercut the all-sufficiency of Christ's atoning sacrifice on the cross. Other themes that I examine at some length are the millennium and hell, and in both of these I offer new and sometimes controversial interpretations, which I nevertheless believe stand in continuity with the biblical message.

I also underscore in this volume the inseparability of eschatology and soteriology. My aim is to steer a middle course between a postmodern eschatology of constructive ambiguity, where everything remains hazy, and a traditionalist eschatology, which presumes to know too much about what transpires on the other side of death. God still remains hidden in his revelation in holy Scripture, but we can know something of the mystery of his self-condescension in Jesus Christ and the return of Christ in glory.

On the pivotal question of the ultimate destiny of sinful humanity, I propose a fresh alternative to both traditional and contemporary theories. I warn of the allurement of universalism—the belief that every person will eventually be saved through the grace of God. I also take issue with restrictivism, which limits God's redeeming grace to only the few who are specially favored by God. Again, I have difficulties with annihilationism, which argues for the extinction of hardened unbelievers as opposed to their condemnation to a life of eternal torment. Needless to say, I unequivocally reject self-determinism or semi-Pelagianism, which makes the human will the final arbiter in salvation. In that position hell is a product of human miscalculation and heaven a product of human merit. Finally, I examine the alternative of a Christian agnosticism, which regards hell as a possibility that confronts all people at the beginning as well as at the end of their spiritual pilgrimage. This position has appeal because of its modesty, but it tends to neglect the incontrovertible biblical affirmation that there is no salvation apart from personal faith in Jesus Christ.

In contradistinction to all of the above positions I propose a theology of divine perseverance based on the belief that God continues to pursue fallen humankind even in its sin and depravity, even beyond the barrier of death. God's grace knows no limits in its outreach to a lost world, but it always directs both people in sin and people of faith to the cross and resurrection of Christ, for only there does God meet us as redeeming Savior and Lord.

The many divisions spawned by eschatological disputes are traceable in part to the inability of humans to grasp the poetic language of Scripture, particularly with regard to the spirit world beyond death and the return of Christ in glory. Instead of bowing before mystery and paradox we want to resolve mystery in a logic that the human mind can master. Here as in my other volumes I seek to combat a rationalistic spirit that reduces revelation to propositional truth and elevates rational coherence as the final criterion in theology. The unfailing source of Christian wisdom is not the objectified divine declaration in the Bible—the Bible as it stands by itself—but the paradoxical unity of the scriptural word and the illumination of the Holy Spirit, which brings the written Word of God to life in a divine-human encounter.[1]

---

[1]The Bible as a book or compendium of books can, of course, be considered a proximate source of Christian wisdom, but the ultimate source is the living Christ himself who speaks and acts in the power of the Spirit as believers seek for the truth hidden and revealed in Scripture.

·ONE·

INTRODUCTION

The Kingdom of God is a foreign country,
so foreign that even the saints must pray:
"Almighty God, I acknowledge my sin unto thee.
Reckon not unto me my guiltiness, O Lord."

MARTIN LUTHER

Christ came to found a Kingdom, not a School;
to institute a fellowship, not to propound a system.

DALLAS WILLARD

The living Spirit of Christ is today causing countless small focal points to arise,
where not only community of gathering and building up is to be found,
but real community of life.

EBERHARD ARNOLD

As we proceed from a discussion of ecclesiology (vol. 6 of the Christian Foundations series) to eschatology, it will be seen that these two subjects belong inextricably together. Their indissoluble unity is readily apparent in the unfolding of doctrine, but it is also strikingly present in the social forms that faith assumes.[1] In this chapter sociology functions somewhat as a preamble to theology, though not in the sense of a natural theology. God's truth is not uncovered through social analysis, but God's church is given heightened significance through such an analysis.

As it stands by itself, social analysis is inadequate for defining the role of the church in the plan of salvation and its status in the eyes of God, but it can shed light on the social dynamics of the church in a particular cultural setting. A purely sociological inquiry cannot determine whether the church is the mystical body of Christ or an integral arm of the kingdom of God, but it can ascertain the impact on society of a church that makes such claims. When combined with a faith commitment, sociological investigation can yield a fuller and deeper grasp of the social scene.

In the theological method I espouse, sociological inquiry is subordinated to theological reflection. Social analysis is done through the eyes of faith and is made to serve the cause of faith. It is an important element in faith seeking understanding. It does not set the foundations for faith, but it does clarify the road that faith must take in the search for a deeper and wider understanding of the social situation. In the context of a theological discussion, social inquiry both proceeds out of faith and prepares the way for a more knowledgeable faith, but it is never carried on as something independent of faith.

Troeltsch's Typology

In the light of Ernst Troeltsch's pioneering typology of religious association, one can surmise that eschatology and social formation are intimately related.[2] Troeltsch makes a convincing case that church and sect, the two principal types of religious association, have divergent views on the coming of the kingdom of God. The church presumes that the kingdom is already realized in its own rites and ceremonies. The sect views the kingdom as fundamentally futuristic and apocalyptic. The church sees the hope of the world in its ministry and sacraments, whereas the sect possesses "a passionate hope for the future."[3] The church is bent on being culturally pervasive, whereas the sect is invariably countercultural. The church projects itself as an institution endowed with grace; the sect is a voluntary society that is intent on demonstrating the grace of God in daily life. Troeltsch also speaks of the mystical society in which religion is reduced to "a purely personal and inward experience."[4] Like the church, the mystical society teaches a realized eschatology, but the eschaton is realized not in the drama of the liturgy but in the interior depths of the human soul.

In my opinion the sects are to be applauded for rediscovering the eschatological vision of the Christian faith, but they do so at the price of sundering Christian unity and failing to perceive the opportunities and promise in nature and society. Christianity can thrive only when it recovers its eschatological dimension and sees both church and world in the light of the crisis or judgment upon humanity that takes place in Jesus Christ, the full implications of which will be revealed at the time of his second advent. An eschatological Christianity is a serious Christianity and is the antidote to what Kierkegaard called "playing at Christianity."[5] Jesus came to bring not simply moral precepts but the reality of a new world order that revolutionizes the whole of life.

Alternate Pathways

Building on Troeltsch's insight on the interrelation of theology and sociology, I propose a typology of religious association that continues the discussion on a new level. First it should be noted that this is basically a sociological typology, but one laden with theological implications.[6] It is a delineation that has relevance to various religious traditions, though its primary concern is with the religious situation in Christendom.

Following Troeltsch I view the church in this context as a culturally incarnate religion. It is inclined to be both formalistic and hierarchical. Salvation rests on making contact with the means of grace. Grace, moreover, is at the disposal of the clerics of the church, who supposedly possess the keys of the kingdom. The church sees its mission as expanding its influence in society and transmitting its teachings to each new generation. It is a pancultural entity in which we are included by virtue of being born in the covenant community or being baptized as infants and confirmed when we have reached the proper age.

A sect, by contrast, is an excursus religion. It calls people out of the parent body into "the true church." Salvation rests not on the rites of the church but on personal decision and obedience. The precepts of religion are designed to shape Christian character and produce a lifestyle that is radically divergent from the surrounding cultural ethos. A sect sees the kingdom of God as being unfolded in climactic events at the end of history, some of which may well be taking place in the present time.

A third model of religious association is the cult, which here denotes a syncretic religion that strives to open up the parent body to a more inclusive vision.[7] It sees the kingdom of God as realized within us rather than as the promise of a new society in the distant future. Whereas the church tends to be a ritualistic religion intent on creating an enclave of righteousness on earth, the cult is an amorphous religion that focuses on individual self-fulfillment and esoteric wisdom. While the sect is intolerant because of its conviction that it has a corner on the truth, the cult gives the appearance of being tolerant because of its supposition that truth lies within every person.[8] A cult is oriented toward the occult, the higher realm hidden from the senses, rather than toward history. It tends to be introspective and individualistic. Like the sect the cult is an excursus religion, but whereas the former calls people into an exclusive fellowship of true believers, the latter calls people into a new religious ethos.[9]

All three of these forms of religious association have a restrictive side because of their unwillingness to submit to correction by the transcendent Word of God. The church as an institution gives a prominent place to Scripture, but it willingly subordinates Scripture to its own traditions and creeds. It reads Scripture through the lens of its own confession of faith. A sect is necessarily constrictive, since it adamantly refuses to let itself be taught by the wider church. A cult is equally resistant to instruction from the wider Christian community, since it believes that truth lies not in sacraments, creeds and confessions but within the human soul. The true church will allow itself to be taught and corrected by the living Word of God, who abides within the church as a purifying leaven. This kind of church is an eschatological, not merely a historical, reality.

Still another form of religious association in this schema is the denomination, which here signifies a transition from church to sect or from sect to church. A denomination is a compromise solution—seeking to bring together the inclusive vision of the church and the exclusive claims of the sect.[10] It is a cultural or accommodationist religion intent on preserving its theological and social identity in a pluralistic milieu. It is noneschatological, since its focus is on preserving the institution rather than on heralding a definite message that the kingdom is at hand and thereby calling for a radical decision of faith. The rise of denominations presages the eclipse of eschatological faith and ipso facto the end of a Christianity that makes rigorous demands on its people.

Finally, I wish to give attention to a fifth model of religious association—what I choose to call the renewal fellowship. This is a strategy that calls for reform within the church rather than separation from it. A renewal fellowship is a reformist religion that seeks to pour the new wine of the gospel into new wineskins but always in the service of the wider Christian community. Like the sect the renewal fellowship is nonconformist, but its goal is to strengthen rather than weaken the parent body. The renewal fellowship is a movement of revival rather than an institution. It is what Emil Brunner calls "the ecclesia," which bursts through all outward forms and structures.[11] It is the church as *Gemeinde* (community) rather than *Kirche* (institution). It may take the form of a religious order or religious community (like Lee Abbey and Jesus Abbey);[12] a missionary training center (like the Basel Mission or the Chrischona Pilgrim Mission); a class meeting (as in original Methodism);[13] or a transdenominational fellowship of the Spirit (like the Oxford Group movement).[14] A renewal fellowship is a church within the church (*ecclesiola* in *ecclesia*) rather than a company of dissenters who set out to begin their own church.

A vibrant renewal fellowship will necessarily be eschatological, for it will focus on the parousia of Christ, which includes both Pentecost and the second Advent. It will be open to correction by the wider church, since it does not regard itself as the true church to the exclusion of other churches and religious bodies. The danger in a renewal fellowship is that it so easily becomes ephemeral, for it rests on the free movement of the Spirit, not on rites, ceremonies and creeds. It must also resist the temptation to pharisaism, regarding its own way of life as higher or more meritorious than that of ordinary life in the world.

It should be kept in mind that these types of religious association are ideal types, and no particular body or group completely exemplifies any one of them. Troeltsch himself recognized that any particular historical manifestation includes dimensions of all types.[15] A typology such as this is intended to cast light upon ways of mission and worship that mirror basically different understandings of Christianity.

While these types are fundamentally sociological categories, they have immense significance for theological reflection. The sect tends to be heretical, for it represents a palpable imbalance in Christian understanding that is heightened rather than lessened by withdrawal from the parent body. A cult verges on apostasy, since it is quick to deny the exclusive claims of the parent faith. A church in this context represents a mixture of orthodoxy and heterodoxy; this is why a church invariably engenders protest movements that so often become sects.[16] A denomination irremediably weakens the Christian witness because truth is prone to be sacrificed to pragmatic considerations. A renewal fellowship contains promise, but unless it is organically related to the parent body or to the wider Christian communion it tends to become an amorphous body possessing no clear marks of distinction. It readily lapses into a mystical society oriented to satisfying personal spiritual needs, whereas ideally it should be a missionary arm of the wider church having a definite message that calls for conversion and obedience. The lines that separate a renewal fellowship from a cult or a sect are very thin indeed, and those who are active in renewal movements must be alert to these dangers.

Toward a Renewed Church

What is needed in our day as in days past is a church that both corrects the imbalances of the sect and overcomes the aridity of the established religious institution. Doctrinal purity must be united with the passion for inwardness if the church is to maintain continuity with the apostolic tradition and present a credible message to a secularized culture.

The hope for Christian renewal in our time lies in recovering the prophetic role of the church—bringing the judgment of God to bear upon both church and society. A prophetic church is the biblical alternative to an acculturized church, one that accommodates to the zeitgeist in order to ensure its survival in a secular world. A prophetic church keeps alive the distance between the already and the not yet.

The church of God must be prophetic but not exclusively so. It must also be kerygmatic—centered in the apostolic proclamation that God was in Christ reconciling the world unto himself (2 Cor 5:18-19). A church that is rooted in both law and gospel will comfort the despairing and disturb the comfortable. It will be both a source of consolation and a prod to heroic action again the forces of unrighteousness unleashed by the devil and his hosts.

In a biblically oriented church, worship will be centered not in preaching as such nor in praise nor in liturgy but in the living Word of God, who sanctifies our proclamation and purifies our supplications and intercessions. True worship does not begin until Jesus Christ himself enters the worship service and speaks *with, in* and *under* the words and ceremonies of the worshiping community. Jerome was right when he declared that our worship is truncated unless we hear "not preaching as such but *the word of truth*."[17] This transcendent dimension to worship was also acutely perceived by the venerable church father Origen: "We, the heralds and preachers of Christ, would not be able to preach, nor would we have any power to proclaim, if he who sent us were not also present with us."[18]

The sermon, like baptism and the Lord's Supper, will be sacramental in an apostolic and renewed church. It will re-present the dramatic events surrounding the life, death and resurrection of Christ. Yet it does this not through its own power but through the power of the Spirit of God. The sermon like the sacrament will ideally be a reenactment of the passion and victory of the Lord Jesus Christ.

The key to the renewal of the church lies in bringing the church into the service of the eschatological kingdom of God. The church as a historical institution must never be identified with the kingdom, but at the same time it must also not be separated from the kingdom. The church is the gateway to the kingdom, but it is not the pillar that supports the kingdom.[19] We as Christians take our stand in the church, but we wait for the kingdom. The kingdom is revealed through historical forms and structures, but it is not limited to these.

I take strong exception to Nicolas Berdyaev, who envisioned a kingdom that is basically outside of history:

> The absolute revelation of the Gospel about the Kingdom of God cannot be expressed by any social and historical forms, which are always temporal and relative. . . . There never has been and there can be no Christian state, Christian economics, Christian family, Christian learning, Christian social life. For in the Kingdom of God . . . there is neither state, nor economics, nor family, nor learning, nor any social life determined by law.[20]

In the biblical view the kingdom is not purely spiritual but is historical as well. It does not arise out of politics, but it has far-reaching political ramifications. It gives rise to new historical and social forms. It represents the sanctification of the material rather than its dissolution. While highly critical of the relativistic bent of Troeltsch's theology, I appreciate his efforts to maintain the eschatological character of the kingdom without divorcing it from the temporal and material concerns that engulf human existence.[21] Despite the Hegelian trappings Troeltsch's pregnant words invite serious reflection:

> The idea of the future Kingdom of God, which is nothing less than faith in the final realization of the Absolute . . . does not, as short-sighted opponents imagine, render this world and life in this world meaningless and empty; on the contrary, it stimulates human energies, making the soul strong through its various stages of experience in the certainty of an ultimate, absolute meaning and aim for human labour.[22]

The church as a social and historical institution can be a vessel and conduit of the kingdom, but it can also be an impediment. Sometimes churches as institutions have to die so that the kingdom can go forward. I can appreciate Kierkegaard's keen observation on the dichotomy that now and again develops between the church and the kingdom:

> The established Church is far more dangerous to Christianity than any heresy or schism. . . . There is something frightful in the fact that the most dangerous thing of all, playing at Christianity, is never included in the list of heresies and schisms.[23]

Yet Kierkegaard did not sufficiently grasp that individualism can be as dire a threat to Christianity as institutionalism and formalism. Dialectical theology calls for moving beyond the polarity of individualism and institutionalism to the synthesis of communitarianism in which *koinonia* (fellowship) is united with *kerygma* (proclamation) and *diakonia* (service). As Christians we are not solitary followers of Jesus Christ but members of his body, with responsibilities to one another as well as to the King of kings and Lord of lords. The church, theologically considered, is an organism that binds its members together in holy communion. Membership in the visible church does not guarantee membership in the mystical body of Christ, but the latter cannot exist without the former or at least without some kind of close relation between the individual and the church as a historical institution.

A communitarian vision of the church does not exclude the need for periodic withdrawal from the frenetic busyness endemic to both church and world in order to draw close to God and be spiritually recharged.[24] In an age when academic theology is in revolt against the individualism nurtured by existentialism,[25] we should keep in mind that individual decision is still highly important, indeed indispensable, for life and growth in the community of faith. I heartily agree with John Mackay, former president of Princeton Theological Seminary:

Solitary communion with Deity is a timeless imperative for Christians. This is true whatever be the human situation in which our lot is cast. Corporate worship at its best can never be a substitute for the soul's personal encounter with God.[26]

The saints are not the confraternity of the blessed who live above the tawdriness of the world (as in some kinds of mysticism), nor are they the enclave of the righteous on earth (as in sectarianism). Rather they are those in whom the future glory of the kingdom is now manifest. Saints in this discussion constitute an eschatological category: through the gift of the Spirit they participate in the mystery of the last day. The saints are the transforming leaven within the institutional structures of the church that enable the church to rise above the pressures of the culture and become a vanguard of the ever advancing kingdom of Christ. A renewed church will be an eschatological community but one that always stands in need of purification and renovation by the Holy Spirit.

As I see it, the principal theological options today are the following: a liberal latitudinarianism that regards the Christian way as only one among others; an evangelical sectarianism that focuses on issues that no longer rivet the theological imagination; and an evangelical catholicity that seeks continuity with the church of the past, with its liturgical traditions and confessions, but only in order to bring all of humanity into submission to the claims of the gospel. An evangelical catholicity should by no means be confused with a restorationism that encourages the church to retreat into the past rather than grapple with the issues that presently confront both the church and the wider culture. An evangelical catholicity will respect church tradition but will always subordinate tradition to the witness of holy Scripture. Likewise it will make a place for preaching and sacraments but strive to bring these things into the service of the coming kingdom of God, which is both wider and narrower than the boundaries of the earthly church. It is wider because God's Spirit is acting and working outside as well as inside institutional structures and social forms though never apart from the proclamation of the word.[27] It is narrower because not all who claim membership in the institutional church have been born anew by the Spirit of God into a living faith in the Lord Jesus Christ.

An evangelical catholicity will not be triumphalistic in the sense that it seeks to impose its own interpretations upon the wider church and the culture. But it will be uncompromising in its witness to the gospel of Christ apart from which there is no salvation. What I am proposing is an eschatological Christianity that is anchored in the transcendent and serves the transcendent but always through the scriptural witness and the ministrations of the believing community. The coming of the kingdom does not mean the collapse of the church but its renewal and regeneration through a fresh appropriation of the gospel and the law as this is communicated to us in church tradition. Earthen vessels point beyond themselves to spiritual reality, but spiritual reality sends us back to earthen vessels for continual nourishment in the Spirit.

·TWO·

CONTROVERSIAL THEMES IN ESCHATOLOGY

With the arrival of Jesus Christ we have
the ultimate eschatological event!
LARRY D. HART

In the sense of the concept that a part of man
continues beyond death in an unbroken way,
the idea of immortality cannot be held.
WOLFHART PANNENBERG

Resurrection hope is a total hope
that embraces the future of society and the world.
Its scope is universal and cosmic.
CARL E. BRAATEN

To claim that Jesus rose from the dead is a way of confessing that
Jesus . . . caught a glimpse of eternity.
ROBERT FUNK (OF THE JESUS SEMINAR)

E schatology, perhaps more than any other branch of theology, is laden with divisiveness, and this is particularly true in conservative evangelical circles. One reason is that the older confessions of faith, including those of the Reformation, did not deal adequately with eschatological issues. In Reformation times the overriding concern was with the doctrine of salvation. A second reason for the lack of unanimity in this area is that eschatology focuses on events beyond the parameters of space and time, events that can only be described in poetic or figurative language. The literalizing of the language of faith creates insuperable barriers in forging a comprehensive understanding of the events that constitute the last things.

The Coming of the Kingdom

Theologians in the past and the present have been glaringly incapable of arriving at a consensus on the coming of the kingdom of God. In the first several centuries of the church the apocalyptic vision of the kingdom was dominant. In this view the kingdom of God bursts into history from above in a cataclysmic rather than a gradual manner. Apocalyptic signifies divine intervention and imminent expectation of the kingdom. It lays claim to a knowledge of divine mysteries that are hidden from ordinary mortals. It promotes a pessimistic attitude toward the present age. Theologians in modern times who interpret the New Testament as teaching this understanding of the kingdom of God include Johannes Weiss, Albert Schweitzer, James Kallas and Lewis S. Chafer.[1]

Also appealing to holy Scripture are those who embrace a realized eschatology. For these scholars the kingdom of God is already manifested in the life, ministry, death and resurrection of Jesus and in the sending forth of his Spirit. The kingdom of God has already come, and what remains is for people to acknowledge this fact and to live in the freedom that the Spirit brings to us. The kingdom has already redirected the course of world history, but this fact needs to be revealed to the nations. Jesus is already victor over the powers of death, sin and hell, but this momentous truth has to be proclaimed so that its implications for daily life can be realized. Theologians who embrace some form of realized eschatology include Karl Barth, Dietrich Bonhoeffer and C. H. Dodd. We might also mention the so-called preterists who contend that all of the promises of Christ were fulfilled in the fall of Jerusalem in A.D. 70.[2]

Then there are those who envisage the kingdom as predominantly spiritual, concerning a realm outside or beyond history. In Origen, who leaned heavily on Neoplatonic philosophy, the kingdom is manifested in the soul of the believer rather than in the world. The focus is on the spiritual rather than the historical. For Nicolas Berdyaev, whose theology has a noticeable gnostic thrust, the noumenal is the only real world and the phenomenal—the world accessible to sense perception—is but an appearance. Paul Tillich distinguishes between a transcendent and an inner-historical kingdom of God.[3] The kingdom of God in its eternal fulfillment is above history, but we can hope that it will time and again break into history. History itself, however, will always be ambiguous and marked by conflict. Tillich's accent was on eternal life, not on the end of world history.

For Reinhold Niebuhr the kingdom is a regulative ideal which we can approximate but never encompass. The kingdom is "always at hand in the sense that impossibilities are really possible, and lead to new actualities."[4] According to Niebuhr the kingdom is basically otherworldly, but it has far-reaching social and political implications for this world. He saw his theology as a corrective to both the liberal error of confounding the kingdom with the progress of civilization and that segment of church tradition that depicts the kingdom as purely spiritual, removed from the perils and struggles that engulf humanity.

Other theologians have proffered an existential eschatology in which the kingdom is realized anew in the decision of faith. Rudolf Bultmann internalized the kingdom and saw it as the "presence of eternity" in time. The kingdom is never established in history, but its reality can help shape individual and moral life. There is no cosmic redemption, but there is personal freedom. There is no second coming of Christ, but there are repeated breakthroughs into freedom through the power of God's Spirit. The end of the world is the end to inauthentic existence in the crisis of repentance and faith.[5] A number of theologians, including Emil Brunner and New Testament scholar John Knox, have sought to combine an existential approach with a futuristic eschatology.[6]

Against an eschatology that is predominantly otherworldly, some Christian thinkers have been attracted to a millenarian eschatology that envisages God's kingdom being partially realized in temporal history—the millennial age—but then fully realized in an eternal kingdom that follows the millennium.[7] Some of these theologians envision an apocalyptic intervention of Christ into earthly history to establish a millennial kingdom as a precursor to the eternal kingdom. The former is identified with the visible reign of Christ on earth between his second coming and the last judgment. In dispensationalism there are two stages in the second coming—the secret rapture of the saints and Christ's appearing visibly to rule over the whole of creation. Theologians who stand in the original Puritan tradition are likely to be postmillennial, envisaging a transfiguration of worldly history through the preaching of the gospel prior to Christ's second advent.[8]

Still another option is an ecclesiastical eschatology, which identifies the kingdom with the visible church on earth between the first and second comings of Christ. This is what is sometimes called an amillennial position. It is found to a degree in Augustine and Aquinas and also in Eastern Orthodoxy and some segments of Anabaptism.

A position that appears to accommodate to the winds of modernity is a progressive eschatology. Walter Rauschenbusch envisioned the kingdom of God as humanity organized according to God's will, resulting in the transfiguration of the social order.[9] People of faith are given a share in building the kingdom of God on earth.[10] Jürgen Moltmann stands in this same tradition, seeing the eschatological hope as "the humanizing of man," "the socializing of humanity" and "peace for all creation."[11] Moltmann draws a sharp distinction, however, between *futurum* (the earthly future) and *parousia* (the presence of Christ). Our efforts in improving society cannot precipitate the coming of the kingdom, but they can prepare the way for Christ's return.[12]

Also bearing a decidedly this-worldly thrust is a theocratic eschatology. Here the kingdom is identified with a theocratic order on this earth. Spiritual leadership coalesces with political leadership. We see this approach in the radical Spiritualist Thomas Müntzer and in some utopian communities that followed the Reformation. It is also apparent in the ultra-Calvinist Christian Reconstructionist movement and in the mainstream of dispensationalism, which envisages the millennium as a Jewish theocratic kingdom in which Christ reigns visibly from Jerusalem.[13]

Much more in keeping with a progressive evangelical theology is an inaugurated eschatology in which the kingdom has already come in Jesus Christ but is still to be finalized and perfected. The ministry and atoning sacrifice of Christ constitute not a preparation for the kingdom but the actualizing of the kingdom in history. Yet this is a process that continues and will be consummated only in the return of Christ in glory. This position strives to maintain the tension between the "already" and the "not yet." Among those who can be placed in this category are Oscar Cullmann, Anthony Hoekema, Larry Hart, Adrio König, R. H. Fuller, J. A. T. Robinson and Peter T. Forsyth.[14]

My own position, which will be developed more fully in the subsequent chapters, might be designated a realizing eschatology in which the kingdom of God bursts into history and advances in history as an invading force of righteousness. Whenever the powers of evil are unmasked in history we see the dawning of the millennium, the sign of Christ's lordship, which is both present and future. I am here combining elements of apocalyptic, realized eschatology and millenarian eschatology. But more will be said about this later! The focus is not on the progressive realization of the kingdom in history but on the invasion of history by a heavenly city whose goal is to bring history into submission to eternity.

Our task as Christians is to proclaim and celebrate the coming of the kingdom, but we cannot build the kingdom of God on earth. We can hasten the kingdom by our prayers (2 Pet 3:12) but only to the degree that God permits. As soldiers of Christ we can battle by the side of our Lord and in the power of his Spirit, but only he—Jesus Christ—is the real conqueror and victor. We can hope for the future because the kingdom of God is in his hands.

The Return of Jesus Christ

All of the major branches of Christendom firmly hold to the return of Jesus Christ to the abode of humanity, but how this return takes effect has been a matter of debate, sometimes acrimonious. The mainstream of Christian orthodoxy has envisaged this return as visible and bodily, accompanied by a general resurrection and a final judgment. The epistle to the Hebrews puts it very succinctly: "Christ, having been offered once to bear the sins of many, will appear a second time, not to deal with sin but to save those who are eagerly waiting for him" (Heb 9:28). This theme is staunchly affirmed by the apostle Paul:

> The Lord himself will descend from heaven with a cry of command, with the archangel's call, and with the sound of the trumpet of God. And the dead in Christ will rise first; then we who are alive, who are left, shall be caught up together with them in the clouds to meet the Lord in the air; and so we shall always be with the Lord. (1 Thess 4:16-17)

Anabaptist theologian Eberhard Arnold powerfully gives voice to the hope that has sustained the church through the ages:

> The present age is facing its end. The greatest turning point which can occur in the history of the world and in the order of creation is imminent. Jesus will come for the second time with authority and glory. Then the rule of God shall be established over the whole earth.[15]

In dispensational theology the return of Christ is said to occur in two stages: the rapture of the saints and then after seven years the coming of Christ to set up the millennial kingdom.[16] In contradistinction to the consensus of the ancient church as well as the Reformation churches the blessed hope proves to be the secret rapture of the saints rather than the second advent of Christ.

In spiritualistic and mystical circles the return of Christ is spiritual rather than historical. His return is identified with his resurrection from the dead or the outpouring of his Spirit upon the church. Eberhard Arnold seeks to bring together the spiritualistic motif and the testimony of the mainstream of church tradition: "Through the coming of Christ to the Church in the presence of the power of the Spirit, the first historical coming of Christ and His future second coming are confirmed."[17]

Christian tradition has also generally taught the return of Christ to individual believers at the time of their death (Lk 12:20; Jn 14:2-3; Heb 9:27). This return will be a foretaste of his advent at the end of the historical age when Christ comes as victorious king to rule over the new heaven and the new earth.

Postmillennial preterists speak of the "judgment-coming of Christ," the visitation of his wrath upon disobedient Jews manifested in the destruction of Jerusalem by the Roman army in A.D. 70. Preterism, based on the idea of the fulfillment of Christ's promises in the past, stands in remarkable contrast to dispensationalism, which locates the return of Christ in an apocalyptic future.[18] Both positions contain certain imbalances.

We should, of course, include in this discussion the visitation of Christ to the church in every generation. Such a visitation brings an infusion of power to the church as well as the purifying fire of judgment. The German Reformed Pietist Johann Christoph Blumhardt here expresses a note of holy optimism with regard to Christ's coming:

> Not only has the Savior come; He will still come in God's glory in today's world. The future bears the name of Jesus Christ; it is our future and the future of the world, of all creation. The Savior is coming. He will reveal His glory, and will help us, so that we may walk in His light, to His honor and praise.[19]

In Roman Catholic theology it is quite common to speak of the eucharistic coming of Christ.[20] Not only will Christ return at the end of world history, but he returns now to his church and makes himself present in the holy Eucharist. We can find Christ by partaking of the bread and wine of holy Communion. The Eucharist becomes an eschatological banquet in which we celebrate the end of the age in which Christ's victory over the powers of darkness will be revealed to all of creation.

The Life Hereafter

The cleavage in the church concerning the life hereafter is almost as great as the split over the millennium. Part of the problem lies in the philosophical legacies that inform the various Christian traditions. Neoplatonism, which furnished the philosophical basis for Catholic and Orthodox mysticism, has a radically different picture of life after death than that found in modern existentialism and neonaturalism.[21]

In the traditional Roman Catholic view, judgment takes place immediately at death. The soul goes to heaven, hell or purgatory. The beatific vision is possessed already by souls in heaven. Those in mortal sin go directly to hell. At the final judgment the soul is reunited with the body, and the sentence of the first judgment is confirmed. The suffering in purgatory, the abode of deceased Christians not yet fully sanctified, is both cleansing and penal. One strand in Catholic tradition speaks of limbo as a level in hell without pain. The *Limbus Patrum* is for the souls of Old Testament saints and pious heathen. The *Limbus Infantum* constitutes the abode of the souls of all unbaptized children. This kind of distinction was widespread in the scholastic period.

Protestant views on the hereafter tend to reflect the impact of the Catholic tradition. For Luther, at least in one stage of his thinking, the dead fall asleep in Christ and are raised to life at the second advent of Christ. At the last judgment humankind is separated. Hell is the outcome of God's justice, heaven is the outcome of God's love and grace. Both hell and heaven contribute to God's glory. Calvin made a place for the immortality of the soul and therefore for an intermediate state between death and the final resurrection. He also acknowledged that Christ preaches to spirits in prison, the elect who have not had an opportunity to decide on earth.[22] John Wesley likewise adhered to the immortality of the soul. The saved go to paradise, the forecourt of heaven, and the damned end in an eternal hell. In Karl Barth's theology all people are saved de jure in Christ. No person has inherent immortality, but everyone has immortality in Christ. Our judgment and redemption has already taken place in Christ, but this will be certified and confirmed at the final judgment.

New Age theology reintroduces the concept of reincarnation—implied in Origen and affirmed by modern philosophers like Giordano Bruno and Gotthold Ephraim Lessing. It was also adopted by many Gnostics and their later counterparts—the Cathari or Albigenses. Others in more recent times who espouse some form of reincarnation include Emanuel Swedenborg, Leslie Weatherhead, Nicolas Berdyaev, Gerald Heard, Hannah Hurnard, Geddes MacGregor, John Masefield and Quincy Howe Jr.[23] In this view the soul returns to earth and is reborn in a new body in order to complete its purification and education.[24] Reincarnation stands in fundamental contradiction to the doctrines of the resurrection of the body and the all-sufficiency of Christ's sacrifice for sin.

In my view eternal life and eternal death begin now, depending on our response to God's self-revelation in Jesus Christ and his offer of salvation.[25] There will be degrees of glory and also of darkness. Yet even the darkness has a luminosity that reflects God's glory. We will experience a bodily resurrection following death, but we will be further clothed at the second coming when Christ consummates the redemptive process. I strongly uphold an intermediate state for both the saved and the damned, but the state of condemnation (the nether world of spirits) is not impervious to the redemptive rays of God's goodness. The gulf between heaven and hell (the final destiny of the saved and the lost respectively) is irrevocable and final only from the human side. I flatly reject the doctrines of both purgatory and reincarnation, since they undercut the gospel as the good news of God's unconditional grace going out to all peoples.

The Invisible Communion

Still another controversial area in eschatology is the communion of saints. Catholic and Orthodox spirituality gives a prominent place to the communion between earth and heaven, but Reformation Protestantism and even more neo-Protestantism have on the whole ignored or underplayed this doctrine. Even in the circles of evangelical revivalism the emphasis is on the future of world history rather than the empowering of the saints on earth by the prayers of the saints on the other side. John Wesley had a poignant awareness of the invisible church in heaven that impinges on the church below, but he nowhere developed this doctrine systematically.

Karl Barth downplayed earthly mediators in our salvation, partly in order to give all the glory and credit to Jesus Christ. Yet he recognized that the Christian community can produce signs and parables of God's redemptive work in Christ. The people of God through their words and actions can point others to Christ, though they cannot in any literal way bring Christ to others. Barth was too much of a theologian of the church to deny the doctrine of the communion of saints, but it did not play a pivotal role in the development of his theology. He was unwilling to dismiss the work of the saints in our salvation, yet he was painfully aware of the deformations of this doctrine in Catholicism in which the saints virtually usurp the role of Jesus Christ in their work of intercession.

> I am not so sure that the saints of the Church are unable to come to our aid. . . . We live in communion with the Church of the past, and from it we receive help. Yet, one fact is certain: that neither the living nor the dead can be for us what God himself is to us, namely, a help in that great distress which is ours in the face of the Gospel and the Law.[26]

Pierre-Yves Emery, a Reformed theologian and brother in the Taizé community, an ecumenical renewal fellowship in Burgundy, France, has called the church to reaffirm the ancient Catholic doctrine of the communion of saints because it is solidly anchored in Scripture and also because it can be a potential source of comfort to the church militant in its trials and struggles under the banner of the cross. According to Emery, "We are truly surrounded by the prayers of the saints; we are the object of their love, an efficacious love because it is incorporated in prayer."[27]

It is well to bear in mind that the doctrine of the saints includes much more than communion, though this particular motif is the focus of my discussion in this volume. For a full doctrine of the saints we need to consider the imitation of the saints, the canonization of saints, the relation of sanctity and heroism, and the meaning of personal holiness. It cannot be denied that the doctrine of the communion of saints is the missing dimension in contemporary eschatology.

With the rise of the New Age movement and the burgeoning interest in spiritualism and necromancy, the life hereafter is becoming a pivotal theme in modern spirituality. It is incumbent on the church again to make clear the salient differences between the communion of saints and spirit communication as conceived of in the cult of Spiritualism. It is equally important to highlight the irrevocable gulf between the Christian vision of the invisible world and channeling as we find this in New Age shamanism.

The challenge facing the church today lies in reclaiming the viability of the Christian worldview in the face of the alien worldviews that are now threatening the spiritual integrity of Western culture. It is imperative that we see through the veneer with which pagan and cultic movements mask their sinister identity so that we can successfully preserve the values of our religious heritage.

Humanity's Final Destiny

The catholic tradition of the church has consistently asserted a double outcome for humanity—heaven and hell—but this position has been contested within that tradition, and even those who affirm this truth are divided on what is the best interpretation of it. Some of the traditions listed below are overlapping, so it is therefore possible for a theologian to be placed in more than one category.

The traditionalist position can be labeled restrictivism, since it sees the grace and salvation of God as restricted to the elect or the community of faith.[28] Some in this category hold to double predestination, the view that God foreordains some to damnation and others to salvation even before their creation. Other theologians are content to say that God elects only some to salvation but chooses to pass by others, leaving them in their sins. Among those who subscribe to some form of restrictivism are Augustine, Thomas Aquinas, Martin Luther, John Calvin, Harry Buis, James Leo Garrett, J. I. Packer, Gerald Bray, Don Carson, Robert A. Peterson and Ronald Nash.[29]

Inclusivism sees the whole of humanity included in the plan of salvation, but not all respond to God's saving initiative in a positive way, and therefore not all actually come to salvation. Inclusivists strongly challenge the catholic doctrine first enunciated by Cyprian that outside the church there is no salvation. They say that God reaches out to humanity not only through the preaching of the Word but also through general revelation, reason and conscience. We are judged on the basis of how much knowledge of God's mercy we are allowed to have in the years that are assigned to us. Inclusivists point to premessianic believers in the Bible, such as Cornelius in Acts 10. Some inclusivists speak of the hidden Christ, who relates himself to people in other religious traditions but under other names and guises. Persons who might be classified as inclusivists in this technical sense are the early Ernst Troeltsch, Clark Pinnock, Karl Rahner, Paul Tillich, John B. Cobb Jr. and John Sanders.[30]

Universalists believe that God's grace will ultimately encompass the whole of human creation, and therefore all people will eventually be restored to a salvific relationship with God. Among those in the history of the church who have posited some form of universalism are Origen, Evagrius of Pontus, Gregory of Nyssa, Ephraem Syrus, Moïse Amyraut, Nels Ferré, J. A. T. Robinson, Jacques Ellul, Carl Braaten and Jan Bonda.[31] Some teach an attenuated universalism in which all are saved except those whom the Bible explicitly declares to be lost.[32] Others propound a universalism of hope based on the conviction that Christ's atoning sacrifice is not limited (as in orthodox Calvinism) but intended for all humanity (Heb 2:9 NJB). Karl Barth approaches this position and appears to endorse it at times.[33] Theologians who share this general stance include Hans Urs von Balthasar, Carl Braaten, Richard John Neuhaus and Gabriel Fackre. For these scholars universalism is not so much an article of faith as an "article of hope."

4. Annihilationism, also known as conditional immortality, has a long history in the Christian church. According to this view God does not force his grace upon anyone, but he allows some of his subjects to reject the truth of the gospel and thereby fall into damnation, which consists not in everlasting punishment but in exclusion from the kingdom of God that ends in annihilation or ontological destruction. Among those in modern times who have espoused this view are Horace Bushnell, Henry Ward Beecher, Lyman Abbott, John Stott, Philip Edgcumbe Hughes, Michael Green, Edward Fudge, John Wenham, Ellen White, Edward White, Stephen Travis and Clark Pinnock. Both Jehovah's Witnesses and Seventh-day Adventists adhere to some form of annihilationism.

5. Then there is the position known as divine perseverance, which holds that God in his love does not abandon any of his people to perdition but pursues them into the darkness of sheol or hell, thereby keeping open the opportunity for salvation. It is said that God's grace penetrates the barrier of death, thus kindling the hope of conversions beyond the pale of death. Proponents of divine perseverance are divided as to whether all will eventually accept Christ's salvation. Some speculate that God will grant willful unbelievers some kind of status within his kingdom but glaringly inferior to that of his sons and daughters, who are adopted through faith in Christ's promises. Among those now and in the past who are identified in some sense with this general position are Cyril of Alexandria, Clement of Alexandria, Ambrose, Hilary of Poitiers, George MacDonald, P. T. Forsyth, George Lindbeck, Stephen Davis, Gabriel Fackre and Donald Bloesch.[34] These theologians strive to do justice to the scriptural affirmation that Christ descended into hell and led a host of captives with him into heaven (Eph 4:8; 1 Pet 3:19; 4:6).

It is also necessary to consider the view of process theology called "objective immortality," which denies that people have self-conscious life after death; instead they have immortality in God. The memory and impact of their deeds are kept alive through God's assimilation of these values into his own life. The communion of saints becomes a communion with the memory of the departed. Norman Pittenger has given cogent expression to this point of view.[35]

Also reflecting a clear deviation from Christian tradition is radical existentialism, which we find in Rudolf Bultmann and Paul Tillich, among others. In this perspective our hope lies not in personal survival beyond the pale of death but in personal freedom that can be realized in this life through decision and obedience. Our goal and hope is not for a prolonged existence in some other world but for a transformed existence in this world. Bultmann speaks for many when he declares: "I don't know anything about immortality. The only thing we can know is that our earthly life ends with death. Whether there is another life after this one, we don't know."[36]

Finally, we would do well to give serious attention to a point of view that can be labeled evangelical agnosticism, of which Karl Barth is the prime representative.[37] Barth upholds the universality of Christ's atonement—that Christ died for all of humanity—yet the efficacy of Christ's death and resurrection is partially dependent on how we respond to the proclamation of the gospel.[38] Barth is adamant that God's grace is more powerful than human sin, but we cannot surmise how long God will allow human sin to continue. We can hope for all because all are included in God's outreach of mercy in Jesus Christ; yet this is not universal salvation, since we cannot assume that all will finally enter the kingdom of heaven. Barth indeed explicitly rejects the doctrine of *apokatastasis*—the restoration of all things.[39]

In my restatement of humanity's final destiny, which I expand on later in this volume, I wish to say that I stand with Barth in upholding the universal scope of the atonement, but I resist the inference sometimes drawn from Barthian theology that everyone is therefore saved.[40] There is no salvation apart from faith, though there is an offer of salvation before faith. Faith does not simply follow salvation (as Barth sometimes alleges), but faith is an integral element in salvation. I agree with Emil Brunner that faith and salvation are correlative, just as are unbelief and damnation. As I see it, there is a particularism within a universalism, a hell within heaven. Yet hell signifies not exclusion from God's presence but continued opposition to God's presence. Moreover, if God is present in hell, if the gospel can be proclaimed to the dead (1 Pet 3:19; 4:6), then we can hope for the conversion of many on the other side of death. Even those irreversibly cut off from full participation in the glory of heaven at the last judgment will still be encompassed by this glory. In the final consummation God will "unite all things in him, things in heaven and things on earth" (Eph 1:10). In the eschatological denouement we need to remember that God is "above all and through all and in all" (Eph 4:6).

We can look to the future with hope because all people are under the sign of God's unconditional love. God takes no pleasure in the death of the wicked; he wants sinners to turn from their way and live (Ezek 18:23). God is "not willing that any should perish, but that all should come to repentance" (2 Pet 3:9 KJV). Paul also is animated by a vision of universality: "God has consigned all to disobedience, that he may have mercy on all" (Rom 11:32 ESV). Yet the apostle is equally firm that we can be assured of our salvation only on the basis of personal faith in the Lord Jesus Christ (Gal 3:22).

There are indeed many scriptural passages that can be enumerated in support of particularism, especially in the four Gospels. Yet the fuller biblical vision is that of a particularism within a universalism. All people are under the sign of God's gracious election, but not all will realize their election in the same way. All have been included in God's act of forgiveness revealed in the cross of Calvary, but the benefits of this forgiveness can be blocked by the hardness of heart that God may permit to continue in the life of the sinner, at least for a time. The future is open, but we must also contend that the future belongs irrevocably to Christ. "He who descended is none other than he who ascended far above all heavens, so that he might fill the universe" (Eph 4:10 REB). Human sin and perdition must be finally seen in the light of this eschatological promise. We can still speak of human stubbornness and lostness but in the knowledge that God's grace is more powerful than human sin, that even when we are faithless "he remains faithful—for he cannot deny himself" (2 Tim 2:13).

The Mission to Israel

For some years there has been a profound disagreement within the World Council of Churches regarding the role of Israel in the plan of redemption. Whereas the Orthodox churches of the Middle East have insisted that the prophecies of the Old Testament regarding Israel have their fulfillment in Jesus Christ alone, churches in the West have come to see Israel as comprising "the other half of God's people" and therefore as a potential viable partner in ecumenical relations. Evangelical churches have continued to endorse missions to the Jews, whereas an increasing number of churches and theologians see the Jews as having their own way to God, a position that contains a measure of validity in light of the overall biblical witness.

From my perspective we as Christians must still uphold a mission to Israel, but it is a special kind of mission. It is based on the biblical thesis that the Jews belong to the one covenant of grace that unifies the two testaments, but they have misunderstood this covenant as one of law. Except for a remnant within the Jewish community who believe in the crucified and risen Christ, they have rejected the New Testament vision of a Messiah who came as a suffering servant—not to fulfill nationalist aspirations but to call all the nations to actualize the age-old dream of a universal brotherhood that breaks down all ethnic and national barriers. Yet even in their unbelief the Jews are still claimed by the God of our Lord Jesus Christ, for his gifts and call are irreversible (Rom 11: 29). When we evangelize among the Jews we invite them to be true to their own heritage and lay hold of the promises that have their fulfillment in Jesus Christ. It is awkward to speak of ecumenical dialogue with the Jews, for both parties do not claim to find their unity in Jesus Christ. Nor is our stance to the Jews to be one of conversation only, since mission involves much more than sharing information. Instead our goal is "to make Israel jealous" (Rom 11:11), to share the story of salvation but in the demonstration of the power of the Spirit, manifesting the fruits of righteousness, love, peace and joy.

While Paul sternly believed that the church constitutes the true Israel (Phil 3:3; Rom 2:29; 9:6; 1 Cor 10:1-12), he also held that the true Israel includes the remnant among the Jews who acknowledge Jesus as the Son of God. It is a matter of debate among scholars as to whether Paul in Galatians 6:16 is identifying "the Israel of God" with the church or with the remnant of the faithful among the Jews or even with the wider Jewish community. Herman Ridderbos echoes the voice of Christian tradition when he interprets this text as referring not to empirical, national Israel but to "all believers whatsoever, the new people of God."[41] I am persuaded by Raymond T. Stamm and Hendrikus Berkhof that Paul is praying for peace and mercy for both the church and the wider company of Israel who have not yet accepted Christ.[42]

Basically there are three positions concerning the relation of the church to Israel. The first is supersessionism, which holds that the church supersedes Israel as the covenantal community of faith. This is the view that is most firmly established in Christian tradition. The second position is dispensationalism, which holds to the literal fulfillment of Old Testament prophecy in the modern state of Israel and in the forthcoming millennial kingdom. Dispensationalists make a radical distinction between the church and the kingdom, subordinating the first to the second. In their view the church is extraneous to the kingdom rather than being the pivotal element in the kingdom (as in both Catholic and Reformation traditions). Finally, there is what might be called reunionism, in which Israel will be ultimately reunited with the church as a sign of the end of the age. The promises of God to Israel are fulfilled in its unity with the one holy and apostolic church.

While identifying with the third position, I am close to Hendrikus

Berkhof's view that the modern state of Israel cannot claim the blessing of eschatological promise because of its militant nationalism, its commitment to the ideology of Zionism, which excludes the prophetic witness of Martin Buber and other pathfinders who challenge the appeal to ethnocentrism. The repossession of the land of Israel is quite another question, since biblical prophecy gives credence to this particular hope. Yet unless the return of Israel to the land of Zion leads to the acceptance by Israel of the Messiah who is now Lord of both church and world, it cannot really be embraced as a sign of the coming of the kingdom. Berkhof makes a convincing case that the Jews in the diaspora can also be regarded as an eschatological sign because their loyalty to the nations in which they live is united with their loyalty to the worldwide community of Israel, and thus serves as a check to the pretensions of modern nationalism.[43]

The church must learn to incorporate the promises of God to Israel within its own life and mission. It should not see itself as the exclusive fulfillment of the promises of biblical prophecy but recognize that Israel too has a key role in the plan of salvation. These words from the prophet Amos have special bearing on this discussion:

> "I have promised that I will never completely destroy the family of Israel," says the LORD. "For I have commanded that Israel be persecuted by the other nations as grain is sifted in a sieve, yet not one true kernel will be lost." (Amos 9:8-9 NLT)

We would do well to pay serious attention to the report "The Church and the Jewish People," which was accepted by the Faith and Order Commission of the World Council of Churches meeting at Bristol in 1967. Berkhof approvingly cites these words of the document:

> We are convinced that the Jewish people still have a significance of their own for the Church. It is not merely that by God's grace they have preserved in their faith truths and insights into his revelation which we have tended to forget. . . . But also it seems to us that by their very existence in spite of all attempts to destroy them, they make it manifest that God has not abandoned them.[44]

The report goes on to say:

> We believe that in the future also God in his faithfulness will not abandon the Jewish people, but that his promise and calling will ultimately prevail so as to bring them to their salvation. This is to us an assurance that we are allowed to hope for the salvation of all who do not yet recognize Christ.[45]

Berkhof rightly urges us to see Israel as

> the nucleus and the mirror of mankind in both its estrangement and its acceptance, so the land has to reflect God's meaning for the earth as a whole. Both owe their particular existence to their universal meaning. Therefore, Israel's calling is not fulfilled as long as its state is one among many others. Israel is not only meant to be coexistent but proexistent. God's promises will be fulfilled when this state will reflect his will for the fellowship of mankind as a whole, as it is most clearly expressed in Is 19:24: "In that day Israel will be the third with Egypt and Assyria, a blessing in the midst of the earth."[46]

The fundamentalist churches that are heralding the return of Israel to Palestine as a harbinger of a universal Jewish theocratic state are doing a distinct disservice to the prophetic tradition of Israel that envisions Israel as a leaven for human decency and peace within the wider global community. The triumph of Israel must be integrally related to the triumph of the cross of Christ—the victory of the powerlessness of suffering love over the powers of death and destruction that still seem to prevail in our fallen world.[47]

·THREE·

LIGHT AGAINST DARKNESS

The light shines in the darkness,
and the darkness has not overcome it.
JOHN 1:5

Through the devil's envy death entered the world.
WISDOM OF SOLOMON 2:24

Evil begins with personality:
without personality the worst there can be is disorder.
EMMANUEL MOUNIER

With the increase of the power of the Kingdom of God,
the demonic realm also becomes stronger and more destructive.
PAUL TILLICH

Sacred tradition has consistently discerned the inseparable relationship of eschatology to angelology and demonology. This truth became muted in the Enlightenment, but it is increasingly being rediscovered in our time. Thadikkal Verghese, a Syrian Orthodox priest, declared at the World Council of Churches assembly at New Delhi, India (1961): "We need to recover the cosmic dimension. . . . Angelic beings should be reinstated in our theology, even though it might be incompatible with the modern scientific mind. We must recover both the angelic and the demonic."[1] In a similar vein Eduard Thurneysen urged people of faith to "count on an abundance, a host, of good heavenly beings (cf. Genesis 32:1-2), forces and powers, serviceable to God and therefore helpful to us."[2]

Scripture teaches not only the creation of the visible world but also the creation of the invisible worlds, including the realm of the angels. Angels are not at the margin of Scripture but belong to its center. They are deemed the rulers of the nations and the guardians of the church. They have an indisputable role in the three pivotal events of salvation history: the birth of Jesus Christ (Mt 1:20; 2:13; Lk 1:26-56), his death and resurrection (Lk 24:23; Acts 1:10), and the consummation (Rev 8:2). In Isaiah's vision (Is 6) and in Job "they form the heavenly court and sing the praises of God."[3] They are incorporeal, but they can take bodily form. They are immortal but not all-powerful. They are still creatures and thereby vulnerable to sin and temptation. In Job 4:18 we read: "Even in his servants he puts no trust, and his angels he charges with error."

The Angelic Rebellion

A prominent theme in biblical salvation history is the fall of the angels and their prodigious effort to gain control of the earth. This note is evident in both the Bible and the apocrypha (cf. Gen 6:2; Is 14:12-15; Ezek 28:14-15; Wisdom of Solomon 2:24; Jude 6; 2 Pet 2:4; Mt 25:41; Lk 10:18; Rev 12:9). Angels were originally seen in the biblical narrative as servants of God in ruling the world. It slowly dawned upon the prophets that some of these heavenly beings were in rebellion against God. At the same time, they were believed to be under God's control and indeed agents of God's wrath. Psalm 78:49 speaks of "destroying angels" sent by God to carry out his judgments on a sinful humanity. Origen identified the reference to the destroyer in Exodus 12:23 with the devil, the agent of God's wrath against the Egyptians.[4] It was the destroying angels who slew the firstborn of the Egyptians in order to force Pharaoh to let the people of Israel return to their promised land. In the book of Jubilees (Jubilees 49:2) this same slaughter is said to be carried out by the powers of Mastema (i.e., the angels of Satan). In

1 Corinthians 10:10 Paul may well have regarded the "destroyer" as a satanic agent working for God. Revelation 12 describes a battle between the angels: the evil angels are thrown down upon the earth, where they wage war against the people of God.

The reason for the angelic rebellion has been a subject of dispute among Christian scholars through the centuries. In Genesis 6:2 and *1 Enoch* 12 it appears that sensuality is the motivation for angelic sin. In the mainstream of biblical tradition it is pride that proves to be the tragic flaw in the angelic revolt (cf. Is 14:12-15; Job 41:33, 34; Wisdom of Solomon 2:24). The last text declares, "Death came into the world only through the Devil's envy, as those who belong to him find to their cost" (NJB). In the extracanonical Jewish literature of the four centuries prior to the Christian era Satan becomes the angelic adversary of God. The Dead Sea Scrolls depict Satan as amassing his forces for a final assault against the bastions of righteousness (the War Scroll).[5] In Matthew 12:24 Satan is portrayed as the leader of the evil spirits.

Biblical scholarship reveals that there are various traditions concerning the evil forces that work against God.[6] The source of spiritual darkness in Genesis 1 is the watery chaos, which later became personified in Rahab, the prehistoric dragon, also called Leviathan. Leviathan in ancient Semitic mythology is a sea monster that belonged to the world of chaos that the creator God had to subdue in order to establish a livable earth. In Job 41:33, 34 Leviathan is the king of all the sons of pride. In Isaiah 27:1 he is portrayed as an enemy of God. In Psalm 104:26 he becomes a mere plaything of Yahweh. In some texts Leviathan is seen as vanquished (Ps 74:13-14; 89:10); in others it is clear that the monster is still alive (Amos 9:3), yet to be finally conquered (Is 27:1). Leviathan was created by Yahweh (Ps 104:26), who subdues it by piercing it (Is 51:9; Job 26:13) or by crushing its head (Ps 74:14).

What occurs in the biblical panorama is the gradual merging of the myths of Leviathan and Satan so that in the New Testament these become virtually one. The chaos in Genesis 1 becomes the dwelling place of Leviathan in Job 41:31-32. In Revelation 9:11 Leviathan becomes "the angel of the bottomless pit." In Revelation 12:9 the dragon, the serpent, the devil and Satan are all equated.

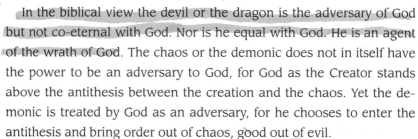

In the biblical view the devil or the dragon is the adversary of God but not co-eternal with God. Nor is he equal with God. He is an agent of the wrath of God. The chaos or the demonic does not in itself have the power to be an adversary to God, for God as the Creator stands above the antithesis between the creation and the chaos. Yet the demonic is treated by God as an adversary, for he chooses to enter the antithesis and bring order out of chaos, good out of evil.

We must bear in mind that the Bible employs mythopoetic language in describing the forces of darkness that are arrayed against the kingdom of light. This language does not imply that the devil is a mythical concept. Instead, it means that his actions can be captured only in the language of poetry, since they are more accurately regarded as super-historical rather than simply historical.

In the biblical worldview the demonic is not simply the negation of the divine. Rather it participates in a distorted way in the holiness and power of the divine.[7] The demonic represents not merely a negation of being but a perversion of being. It is not a negative principle (as in Platonism) but "perverse and powerful affirmation" (Tillich).[8] As Luther phrased it, "His craft and power are great."[9] The demons signify not simply discreativity (Edwin Lewis) but a compound of creativity and discreativity.[10] In biblical tradition the devil as a cosmic force or world power is made to serve the power of God. He can be effective only if some of the potencies of the divine are in him (Reinhold Niebuhr). The demons are called powers of darkness because they seek to direct mortals to the darkness. Darkness in this context connotes not so much the absence of light as a revolt against the light. Because the demonic contains both form-creating and form-destroying strength, "it can be a counterpositive to the divine and it can thus appear in the very sphere of the holy. Hence it exhibits an ecstatic, overpowering, creative quality."[11]

In the ongoing debate on when the demonic rebellion took place I side with those who claim that it occurred prior to the creation of humanity. This indeed was the view of Ambrose and Jerome and is reflected in *2 Enoch* (see chaps. 29—30). The serpent in Genesis 3 is the symbol of the devil, which here connotes prehuman evil. The angels fell from their heavenly glory even before the advent of humanity. This partially explains why there was suffering and pain in the world prior to humanity. The battles of the dinosaurs take on Christian significance if we believe that there was something radically wrong in God's good creation prior to the sin of Adam and Eve.

Scripture is clear that the whole world was subjugated by demonic incursion. According to 1 John 5:19 the entire earthly creation lies under the rule of the evil one (cf. Mt 4:8-9; Rev 17:18). Therefore Luther can equate the kingdom of this world with the dominion of the devil. It is the devil who is the prince or ruler of this world (Jn 12:31; 14:30; 16:11; 2 Cor 4:4; Eph 2:2; 6:12). The whole of creation stands in need of liberation (Rom 8:20-22; Col 1:20). Bonaventure claimed that evil has tainted creation itself, and this is why all of nature groans in travail as it awaits the coming of the Son of Man.

The original habitation of the devil was the angelic heaven. Then the devil was cast upon the earth; yet he was consistently viewed by sacred tradition as an unwelcome intruder. His proper habitation is the desert, the sea or the darkness. His destination is the lake of fire—God's final judgment upon angelic rebellion.

The demons in the biblical vision signify the angelic hosts under Satan. They are not wandering, disembodied spirits, as in primitive religion. Nor are they the spirits of the offspring of angelic marriages (as in *Enoch*). Jesus did not affirm but corrected the mythology of that time when he portrayed the demons as united under a superhuman intelligence, Satan or the devil, and therefore involved in a conspiracy to extend the empire of wickedness.[12]

Paul Tillich had many insightful things to say about the demonic, but his commitment to religious naturalism prevented him from treating the devil as a supernatural being with a power and intelligence of its own. The demons are not simply sociological or transpersonal forces, for one cannot be tempted by the impersonal. I agree with the twentieth-century French personalist philosopher Emmanuel Mounier: "Evil begins with personality: without personality the worst there can be is disorder. Evil can take shape only in a conscience, or in a conspiracy of consciences."[13]

The devil is better thought of as the occasion for sin than as the cause of sin. Humans cannot wholly blame the devil for their misadventures, but they may recognize the devil as making a powerful contribution to their misery. Sin is a state of bondage both to self-will and to the will of transhistorical powers of darkness. We allow ourselves to listen to the voice of temptation, but no outside force can bend our will to succumb apart from our free assent. Once we succumb we become more and more bound so that our emancipation finally rests on the action of a power or force superior to the devil and his legions—Almighty God.

Scripture postulates two kingdoms—light and darkness. God is ruler over both, but he is Savior only in the former. This present world is a battleground between light and darkness, Christ and Satan. When we are brought into union with Christ by divine grace we are delivered "from the dominion of darkness" and transferred "to the kingdom of his beloved Son" (Col 1:13). Scripture teaches not a metaphysical dualism of nature and spirit but a moral dualism of good and evil. Nathan Söderblom rightly observed that "all attempts within Christianity to escape from or to overcome dualism have weakened the fearless sense of reality within the gospel or else have led to the incredible result of locating dualism in the very nature of God."[14] I heartily concur with Philip Watson that "the fundamental biblical opposition is not between flesh and Spirit, creature and Creator, but between the Creator of the flesh and its destroyer, between God and the devil, Christ and Satan, the Holy Spirit and the Unholy."[15]

The two kingdoms in biblical perspective are spiritual or invisible, and the conflict between them is spiritual. Paul reminds us of this implacable fact: "We are . . . contending against . . . the spiritual hosts of wickedness in the heavenly places" (Eph 6:12). The exorcism of demons was not on the periphery of Jesus' mission but at its very core (R. Otto).[16] This is made abundantly clear in 1 John 3:8: "The reason the Son of God appeared was to destroy the works of the devil." Bultmann claimed that the one genuine saying of Jesus is found in Luke 11:20: "If it is by the finger of God that I cast out demons, then the kingdom of God has come upon you." Bultmann can be faulted for doubting the genuineness of many other scriptural texts, but at least he recognized that the conflict with the demons was integral to Jesus' ministry.[17]

The Victory of Jesus Christ

The conflict between the kingdom of light and the kingdom of darkness existed already at the time of creation. Indeed, the first victory over the demonic adversary took place at the creation of the world when the light was separated from the darkness (Gen 1:4). It was then that the head of Leviathan was crushed (Ps 74:13, 14).[18] The monster was mortally wounded but not destroyed. It is always trying to escape from its bonds and subdue the habitable earth.

The powers of darkness built up a kingdom in the world of fallen humanity, but their kingdom always lacked the substantiality and promise of the kingdom of Christ, which was inaugurated in the ministry of Christ. Jesus gives this enigmatic pronouncement: "From the days of John the Baptist until now the kingdom of heaven has suffered violence, and the violent take it by force" (Mt 11:12 NRSV). The kingdom of heaven suffers violence because the tyrannical powers of darkness strive to seize it for their own purposes. But surely another reason is that the kingdom of Christ powerfully establishes itself in earthly history despite all obstacles.[19] The kingdom of heaven is forcefully advancing, and the violent attack it in order to slow its advance. One possible translation is: "The kingdom of Heaven clears a way for itself by violence."[20]

Through the cross and resurrection victory of Christ the powers of darkness were dethroned. On the way to the cross Jesus declared, "I saw Satan fall like lightning from heaven" (Lk 10:18). At the cross Satan was forced out of heaven (Jn 12:31; Rev 12:7-9), and Jesus Christ is now Lord of the powers that still strive to subjugate the world (cf. Lk 10:18; Eph 1:22). The rulers of this age were shorn of their earthly power (Col 2:15). Satan's rights of rulership were taken away, yet Satan refused to abdicate. Moffatt's translation of 1 Corinthians 2:6 is apropos—"the dethroned Powers who rule this world." The powers have been dethroned, but they continue to rule on the basis of a lie—that they still have real power.

The locus of Christ's incomparable victory is twofold: the cross and the community of faith. His redemption is both objective and subjective. It occurred in his cross and resurrection victory, and it continues to occur in the decision and obedience of faith. Christ's redemption is not complete until he enters the world of flesh and blood and establishes his kingdom in history. Demonic exorcism is a sign of the advance of the kingdom of God on earth.

The decisive battle has already taken place in Christ's cross and resurrection victory. The outcome of the spiritual war has been decided, yet the warfare continues because the devil persists in fighting on. The day of total victory is still ahead of us and will not take place until Christ comes again in glory in order to consummate his kingdom.[21] The kingdom of darkness still retains a hold on humanity because of its capacity to beguile, but its wound is fatal. It is on the verge of collapse though it presents a façade of towering strength. I cannot subscribe to Gustaf Wingren's analysis of the situation: "Man's position 'before preaching' is . . . determined by the undecided and stern struggle between God and the Devil."[22] The outcome of the war is not undecided, for the devil has already been conquered. Barth and Cullman err in the other direction when they view the principalities and powers as servants of Christ after his resurrection. Bonhoeffer also too readily underplays the continuing warfare between Christ and the devil: "The world is not divided between Christ and the devil, but, whether it recognizes it or not, it is solely and entirely the world of Christ."[23]

Presenting a palpably different perspective, Paul refers to the "world rulers of this present darkness" (Eph 6:12). John writes that "the whole world is in the power of the evil one" (1 Jn 5:19). The demons are not reconciled servants or ministering spirits of Christ (as Cullmann claims) but hostile forces opposed to the reign of Christ. Their resistance and antagonism become more virulent as the kingdom of God advances. Helmut Thielicke perspicaciously observes that "the nearer the returning Christ comes to this aeon . . . the more energetically the Adversary mobilizes his last reserves."[24]

The kingdom of light or the kingdom of Christ refers not to the world but to the church—the earthen vessel of the kingdom.[25] Not all people are children of God, only believers. Scripture teaches that the sons of the kingdom are never to be confused with the sons of the evil one (Mt 13:37-43; cf. Jn 8:44-47; Lk 16:8; Rom 9:6-8; Eph 5:6-8). The sons of the kingdom or the children of light can still succumb to the devil (Heb 6:4-6). There is no eternal security apart from daily obedience under the cross.

Even after Christ's glorious resurrection the devil has real, objective power (2 Cor 2:11), though this power is significantly curtailed. 1 Peter 5:8 warns: "Be sober, be watchful. Your adversary the devil prowls around like a roaring lion, seeking some one to devour." His power is restricted but by no means innocuous. Augustine gave the analogy of mad dogs that bark but are chained and thereby cannot really hurt the people of God so long as we stay out of their reach. The devil has no real power over Jesus Christ (Jn 14:30). He cannot snatch Christians from the arms of Christ (Jn 10:28-30), but he can tempt Christians to disobey Christ. He can cast Christians into prison (Rev 2:10) and afflict them with all kinds of maladies. Yet the devil can be routed when we look to Christ as the source of our strength, and call on his name in faith. Luther phrased it well: "Christians must have . . . the vision which enables them to disregard the terrible spectacle and outward appearance of death, the devil, and the might, the swords, the spears, and the guns of the whole world, and to see Him who sits on high and says: 'I am the One who spoke to you.'"[26] As Christians we are not spared the suffering of sickness, death and persecution, but we are given the power to remain at peace amid conflict and to be fearless in the face of tribulation. This note is resolutely sounded by the apostle Paul:

> What can separate us from the love of Christ? Can affliction or hardship? Can persecution, hunger, nakedness, danger, or sword? 'We are being done to death for your sake all day long,' as scripture says; 'we have been treated like sheep for slaughter'—and yet, throughout it all, overwhelming victory is ours through him who loved us. For I am convinced that there is nothing in death or life, in the realm of spirits or superhuman powers, in the world as it is or the world as it shall be, in the forces of the universe, in heights or depths—nothing in all creation that can separate us from the love of God in Christ Jesus our Lord. (Rom 8:35-39 REB)

The Banishment of the Evil Powers

The powers of darkness have been defeated in Christ's cross and resurrection victory, and they are continuing to be defeated through the outpouring of the Holy Spirit on the church. The overcoming of the devil by Jesus Christ is perceptible only to the eyes of faith, but even non-Christians can sense that there is a power for good in history that is greater than the forces of evil. The devil continues to rule in the world even though he has been dethroned de jure. He has received a lethal wound but is not yet destroyed.

When Jesus declares that he has come to bring not peace but a sword (Mt 10:34), he is alluding to the warfare between the company of the saints and the powers of darkness, which his coming precipitates. Christ does not call us from the battle but summons us into the very midst of the battle. The gates of hell will not prevail against the church (Mt 16:18 KJV) because Christ is more powerful than the powers that rule the world.

The messianic kingdom that Christ inaugurates is already here, but it is hidden in the visible church. The millennium is the time when this kingdom shall extend throughout the world.[27] But a universal permeation of the world by the gospel is not yet a Christianized world. In the millennial age evil is only curtailed, not destroyed. The prophecies of Isaiah and others are not finally fulfilled until the new heaven and the new earth at the end of history. Scripture seems clear that there will be no visible reign of Christ within earthly history.

The denouement of history reaches its climax in an apocalyptic intervention of the forces of light into the world of darkness. There will be one final battle between light and darkness, and the devil will then be banished, thrown into the lake of fire (Rev 20:10-15). This apocalyptic vision is given poetic expression in Isaiah 27:1: "In that day the LORD with his hard and great and strong sword will punish Leviathan the fleeing serpent, Leviathan the twisting serpent, and he will slay the dragon that is in the sea" (cf. Ps 74:13-15). God's subduing of demonic forces does not necessarily imply their annihilation. Scripture speaks of the adversaries of God and humanity being consigned to enduring torment—incarceration in hell (Rev 20:10). When the plan of salvation is consummated, even the denizens of the underworld will be made to bow before the living and holy God (Phil 2:9-11).[28]

Liberal theology was profoundly mistaken when it envisaged a progressive Christianizing of the world. The biblical view is that the kingdom of light will be unfolded in a cataclysmic intervention by Christ into earthly history. The old world will not be refurbished but will disintegrate by fire (2 Pet 3:12). The old order will not be reformed or fulfilled but transformed. I say this against Emmanuel Mounier who describes history and civilization as the mediator and sacrament of the kingdom of God.[29] We need to pay heed to the prophetic words of our Lord: "When the Son of man comes, will he find faith on earth?" (Lk 18:8).

Scripture does not equivocate concerning the reality of hell, the threat of eternal banishment from the glory of heaven. Yet Scripture is equally firm that Christ has taken the punishment of hell upon himself for all of humanity. The threat of the outer darkness has been dispelled, but there remains an inner darkness, not separation from God's side but from our side. All of humanity will be in the sphere of the kingdom of light, but the possibility of a subjective blindness will persist due to our own recalcitrance and hardness of heart. Christ wills to unite himself to the whole of creation; but there will be an estrangement within this union. The kingdom of darkness will be destroyed, but the shadow of its former power will linger on. Sin, death and hell will be cast into the lake of fire. The sea passes away, but the lake of fire remains. The light that will inundate the unbeliever is the fire of God's wrath, but his wrath is the other side of his love.[30]

In this whole discussion of the triumph of good over evil we must steer clear of the gnostic heresy that evil is a metaphysical principle coeternal with good, or that this world was created by a being inferior and alien to the one true God. In the biblical view evil is to be located not in the web of materiality but in the perversion of creaturely will. Its source lies not in the intractability of matter but in the implacability of sin—the conscious turning away from God by the human and the angelic creation. A church council at Braga in 563 decreed: "Whoever denies that the devil was originally a good angel created by God, contending instead that he arose from the chaos and the darkness and has no Creator but is himself the principle and the substance of evil . . . let him be anathema."[31] Karl Barth, who freely used the language of Platonic philosophy in his discussion of evil, was adamant that evil is not coeternal with God, nor is it the shadow side of his creation. It is the revolt of the creature against the Creator, but a revolt that is made to serve God's plan for humanity. Even though Barth's emphasis was on the objective overcoming of evil in Jesus Christ, he was acutely aware of the continuing threat that the powers of darkness pose to the children of light. In his little book *Prayer* he says: "There exists a superior, ineluctable enemy whom we cannot resist unless God comes to our aid."[32]

Against the gnosticism of the New Age movement we must be very clear that the devil is not the shadow side of human striving, nor is it the materiality in which spirit is entangled.[33] The kingdom of light is not outside of history but is being realized within history. Christ does not call us out of the world (Jn 17:15) but invites us to join with him in bringing the world into submission to the will of God. The world is not the prison house of the soul but the theater of God's glory (Calvin), and though ravaged by sin it is at the same time being converted and redeemed through Christ's resurrection and ascension and the outpouring of his Spirit. The message of faith is one of hope and confidence that the One who incarnated himself in human flesh is coming again in power and glory to set up the eternal kingdom that is even now in the making.

An Excursus on Angelology

While angelology is a prominent theme in the popular culture of our time, it has little in common with the biblical view. Under the impact of the New Age movement, angels are conceived of as either departed spirits or as ascended masters who have progressed through their own spiritual acumen to a higher level of existence. In the Bible angels are servants and emissaries of the living God (Ps 103:20-21; 148:2; Acts 5:19; 7:53; Heb 1:14). The "angel of the Lord" is one in whom God himself is present (cf. Gen 16:7-13; 22:11-17; 31:11-13; Judg 13:2-3; Ps 34:7). Angels are variously called "sons of God" (Job 1:6) and "the hosts of heaven" (1 Kings 22:19), and are viewed as divine servants or attendants. Later in Old Testament thought angels were intermediaries between God and humanity (Dan 4:13-17; 7:10). They also came to be regarded as rulers and guardians of nations (Dan 10:13, 21). In the Apocrypha and Pseudepigrapha angels are portrayed as being in hierarchies. Their task is to present the prayers of the saints to God (*1 Enoch* 99:3; Tobit 12:12).

In the New Testament angels have an important role in communicating the message of salvation. They are present in the three great events of salvation history: Jesus' birth (Mt 1:20; 2:13; Lk 1:26-56; 2:8-20); his death and resurrection (Lk 24:4, 23; Acts 1:10); and the eschatological consummation (Rev 7:1-3, 11-12; 8:2). There is no suggestion of equality between angels and Christ (Heb 1:4). Saints are equal to angels (Rev 19:10; 22:8-9) and in their union with Christ they are even greater than angels (Heb 1:4). They will finally even judge the angels who have erred (1 Cor 6:3). At the same time, the saints are richly blessed by the ministry of angels (Heb 1:14). Paul stressed the lordship of Christ over angelic beings (Phil 2:9-10; Eph 1:20-21; Col 1:15-16; 2:18-19). The worship of angels is clearly forbidden (Col 2:18; Rev 19:10). In Isaiah (Is 6:1-4) and Job (Job 1—2) in the Old Testament and in the Apocalypse in the New (Rev 4), the angels form the heavenly court acclaiming the wondrous deeds of God and offering themselves to his service.

Thomas Aquinas made a solid contribution to angelology in viewing angels as mediators between the transcendent God and the earthly creation.[34] In his theology angels are pure forms, species in themselves. They exist in great numbers. Their very abundance is an evidence of their perfection. Angels are created at the same time as the world. Thomas postulated a hierarchy of angels and archangels. He also made a place for fallen angels who have succeeded in subverting the good creation. Angels are immaterial, immortal and incorruptible. They are created prior to humanity, but they are clearly subordinate to God.

In the twentieth century Karl Barth is distinctive by the attention he gives to angels.[35] For Barth the angelic vocation is one of service to God and Jesus Christ. They are authentic and infallible witnesses to God's self-revelation in Jesus Christ. In Barth's perspective angelology is a supplement to Christology. It is not derived from Christology in a manner similar to anthropology. The angels reside in heaven, but they are still a creaturely reality. Barth affirmed a hierarchy of angels reflecting the superiority of heaven over earth. In his theology angels and devils are never to be confounded. There are no fallen angels, only fraudulent imitators of angelic beings. Devils are not creatures of God but disrupters of his creation. They represent the chaos in its dynamic manifestation. They were liars from the very beginning (cf. Jn 8:44). Darkness is not a lesser light but the antithesis to light. In Barth's view devils or demons will ultimately be annihilated. The idea of fallen angels belongs to the margin of the Bible and does not represent the dominant theme in biblical salvation history.

From my perspective angels are real beings, not "poetic symbols of the structures or powers of being" (as in Tillich).[36] Angels have an ontology of their own and are not simply an extension of God's presence and power. They are guardians and protectors of the people of God and messengers of the kingdom of God (Ps 34:7; 91:11-12; Mt 4:6). They also are involved in intercession for both the church and the world. They form part of the communion of saints, bringing the petitions of the saints before the throne of God. They are "ministering spirits sent forth to serve, for the sake of those who are to obtain salvation" (Heb 1:14; cf. Ex 23:20; Ps 34:7). While they are incorporeal, tradition assigns them ethereal bodies and therefore visible identity— at least to the eyes of faith. They can assume human form and converse with mortals on their own level (cf. Gen 18:1-8; 19:1-11; 2 Kings 1:3; Lk 1:11-38). Both Scripture and sacred tradition attest the reality of angelic visitations that bring strength and power to people of faith. Angels also have a judging role, serving as instruments of God's wrath (Is 37:36; Mt 13: 41-42, 49-50; 24:31).

Friedrich Schleiermacher typified the skepticism of the Enlightenment when he raised the embarrassing question of whether there is any real need for angels in Christian theology. My retort is that we cannot disregard the abundant witness to angels in Scripture if we are to remain within the parameters of historic Christian faith. Again, the presence of angels reminds us humans that we are not alone in the universe. Their existence is also a powerful testimony that God acts in and through outward instrumentality. We are living in a sacramental universe in which God's grace is carried to us by his ambassadors and heralds (both earthly and heavenly). The demise of belief in angels has been accompanied by the rise of belief in flying saucers and extraterrestrial beings from outer space. The church will benefit immensely by recovering the biblical and catholic vision of a universe peopled by angels and archangels who intercede for us and minister to us as servants of the most high God.[37]

·FOUR·

THE DAY OF THE LORD

The great day of the LORD is near, near and hastening fast.
ZEPHANIAH 1:14

The day of the Lord will come unexpectedly,
like a thief in the night.
1 THESSALONIANS 5:2 NLT

The end of the world is coming soon.
Therefore, be earnest and disciplined in your prayers.
1 PETER 4:7 NLT

We cannot say for the mass of mankind
that the day of the Son of Man has come. We await this still.
But waiting demands great strength.
EBERHARD ARNOLD

The day of the Lord in both Testaments indicates the time when God acts to deliver his people and all peoples from both natural disaster and spiritual death. It is both a day of judgment and a day of grace. Indeed, God's grace is revealed through his judgments. At first in biblical history the "day of the Lord" applied only to Israel. Gradually it was extended to the whole world as the day when Yahweh would manifest himself in his power and glory. This "day" would mark the final victory of God over his enemies. In Daniel the day of the Lord signifies the "end of the world" (cf. Dan 9:26-27; 11:27; 12:13). The day of the Lord in the New Testament is also called "the day of our Lord

Jesus Christ" (1 Cor 1:8), "the day of Jesus Christ" (Phil 1:6), "the day of God" (2 Pet 3:12) and "the day of Christ" (Phil 1:10; 2:16).

In biblical and catholic tradition the day of the Lord constitutes "the fullness of time," when time itself will be taken up into eternity. The normal word for time in the New Testament is *kairos*, meaning divinely appointed time. It can be contrasted with *chronos*, which indicates clock time or time as a sequence. Jesus declared, "The time is fulfilled, and the kingdom of God is at hand; repent, and believe in the gospel" (Mk 1:15; cf. Mt 26:18). Paul referred to the day of the Lord as "the fullness of time," when God's promises come to fulfillment (Gal 4:4-5; Eph 1:10). In the words of Zechariah, "On that day the sources of light will no longer shine, yet there will be continuous day . . . for at evening time it will still be light" (Zech 14:6-7 NLT).

The day of the Lord signals the inauguration of the kingdom of light. Yet this kingdom is not yet firmly established over the world. Its appearance constitutes a beachhead in the world. We need to distinguish between the new order hidden in the community of faith and the age to come. This new order is the kingdom of Christ; the age to come is the eternal kingdom of God.

There is truth in both realized and futuristic eschatology. The two moments in the kingdom are fulfillment and consummation (George Eldon Ladd).[1] The fulfillment took place in the incarnation of God in Jesus Christ. The consummation will take place in his second advent when he comes to set up the eternal kingdom that has no end.

Karl Barth has sagaciously discerned three moments or aspects of the parousia—the resurrection of Christ, Pentecost and the second advent.[2] Any one of these can be regarded as the day of the Son of Man, the day that marks the coming of God into human history. But this day has yet to happen for all people, and therefore the proper attitude of the church is one of expectation and waiting.

Borrowing a phrase from World War II, Oscar Cullmann differentiated between D-Day and V-Day. The first indicates the landing of the Allied Forces in Normandy, which assured the utter defeat and collapse of the forces of Nazism. But the day of final victory did not occur until the German generals surrendered unconditionally to the Allied command. Without denying the appropriateness of this distinction, I deem it more biblically felicitous to speak of two V-days—the resurrection of Christ (including the imparting of his Spirit) and his second advent. The latter confirms and certifies the reality of the victory of Christ over Satan in his cross and resurrection.

It is fashionable in academic theology to draw a distinction between prophetic and apocalyptic hopes in the Bible. The prophets generally envisaged the gradual triumph of the forces of righteousness over the powers of evil that would take place within human history. The apocalyptic mentality foresees a catastrophic intervention of God into human history that brings the latter to an inglorious end. Apocalypticism posits two separate and different ages: the present age is temporal and irremediably evil whereas the new age is filled with hope and promise.[3] While apocalypticism is evident in some biblical writings, particularly Daniel and Revelation, it can be shown that the overall biblical perspective combined the prophetic and apocalyptic hopes.[4] The coming of the kingdom presages not the complete destruction of the world but its transformation. A kingdom of righteousness will be realized on earth, but not without divine intervention and assistance. Jerome declared, "We shall see the same world made glorious."[5] The coming of Christ does not transport us out of history but converts us into agents of social change within history. The fulfillment of time is not the negation of time but the moment in time when the course of world history is dramatically altered, when the powers of darkness are no longer able to impede the advance of the kingdom of light.

The day of the Lord occurs not beyond history (as in the early Barth) but at the center of history. The center of history is also the center of the kingdom of God. Christ's words are here apropos: "Now is the judgment of this world, now shall the ruler of this world be cast out; and I, when I am lifted up from the earth, will draw all men to myself" (Jn 12:31-32). The center of history is not yet the consummation of history when Christ will be in and through all things (cf. 1 Cor 15:28; Eph 1:10; 4:6).

Another salient mark of the day of the Lord is its imminence. Zephaniah put it very succinctly: "The great day of the LORD is near, near and hastening fast" (Zeph 1:14). The epistle to the Hebrews describes the day of the Lord as "approaching" (Heb 10:25 KJV). We are living in the time of the dawning of the age to come, the kingdom of glory, but it is still basically future even while it is at the same time incontrovertibly present in a rudimentary form.

Christ's Visitation to His Church

The day of the Lord happened, but it happens ever again. The time of fulfillment occurred in the past, but it also occurs in the present and will occur again in the future. In the words of the apostle Paul, "Now is the acceptable time; behold, now is the day of salvation" (2 Cor 6:2). The day of the Lord is often described in the Bible as a day of visitation (Ex 32:34; Is 10:3; Lk 19:44; 1 Pet 2:12), in which God showers his people with his mercy but at the same time subdues them by his judgments.

The coming of Christ may be manifested in a crisis of conversion or repentance and also in an experience of Pentecost in which we are empowered from within to bear public witness to God and his kingdom. Again, it may involve being called to a particular vocation like the pastorate or the mission field or to a particular state in life, such as marriage or celibacy.

God's visitation to his people will always imply judgment, for we cannot experience God without being humbled by his glorious majesty and convicted by his infinite purity (cf. Ex 32:34; Ps 17:1-5; Lk 19:44; Rev 2:5). It is indeed a terrible thing to fall into the hands of the living God (Heb 10:31; cf. Ex 34:10). The New Testament teaches that for the company of the faithful the guilt of eternal damnation has been canceled because of Christ's sacrifice on Calvary, but the sinner must still be cleansed and purified. As Christians we no longer suffer penalties for sin, but we are still subject to disciplines that keep us on the straight and narrow way.

Both the church and the world are spheres of divine visitation. We read of the visitation of the angel of death who slew the firstborn among the Egyptians (Ex 12:12-13, 21-36). The visitation of God implies grace as well as judgment, but only in the church is God's judgment perceived as a manifestation of his grace. The spurning of grace brings about the harshest condemnation. What is not forgiven is the sin against the Holy Spirit (Mt 12:31-32; Mk 3:28-30; Lk 12:10), the sin of final impenitence.

Just as the church is the beneficiary of the fullness of grace, so the church also receives the severest judgment of God. Scripture is clear that judgment begins with the household of God (1 Pet 4:17; cf. Jer 25:29). Those who know and do not act according to their Master's will shall receive the most severe beating (Lk 12:47-48). It is not outsiders but the sons of the kingdom who will be thrown into the outer darkness (Mt 8:12; 13:41-42).

The Lord God visits not only the church on earth, the church militant, but also the church triumphant, the redeemed in heaven. At the time of their visitation those who believe and are faithful unto death will shine out and judge nations and peoples (Wisdom of Solomon 3:1-9 NJB; Mt 13:43; Rev 2:26-27; 20:6). Christ also visits the realm of the dead, the souls in Hades (1 Pet 3:19-20; 4:6), bringing them the good news of reconciliation and redemption through his cross and resurrection.

I agree with Hendrikus Berkhof that we tend to view the drama of divine judgment too negatively. We see it largely in relation to condemnation, whereas it means "to establish the right order of things."[6] The day of judgment is designed to manifest "not the punitive powers of God but His all-conquering goodness" (Gleason).[7] The final judgment involves more than the reckoning of individual accounts. It resolves the ambiguities of history and establishes the divine order that shall persist forevermore.

The Encounter with Christ at Death

Besides comprising an event in history, the day of the Lord also signifies the crisis of death. Death itself ushers in the day of the Lord. Catholic theologian Alois Winklhofer reiterates a prominent biblical theme: "Whenever death occurs, there is a parousia of the Lord, a manifestation of his power and glory."[8] The idea of death as the gateway to victory is reflected in Psalm 73:24:

> Thou dost guide me with thy counsel,
> and afterward thou wilt receive me to glory.[9]

This note is also reflected in the New Testament. On the day of his martyrdom Stephen "gazed into heaven and saw the glory of God, and Jesus standing at the right hand of God" (Acts 7:55). Jesus said to the penitent thief who was crucified with him: "Today you will be with me in paradise" (Lk 23:43). John 14:2-3 also suggests a parousia at the time of death, though this interpretation is subject to debate: "I go to prepare a place for you. And if I go and prepare a place for you, I will come again, and receive you unto myself" (KJV).

The day of the Lord at the time of death is also portrayed as a time of judgment. This note is apparent in the intertestamental, apocryphal book of Ecclesiasticus:

> It is easy in the sight of the LORD
> to reward a man on the day of death according to his conduct.
> The misery of an hour makes one forget luxury,
> and at the close of a man's life his deeds will be revealed. (Ecclesiasticus 11:26-27)

The idea of the crisis of death as a day of reckoning is also found in the New Testament. In Luke 12:16-21 a purely personal parousia is suggested in the story of the rich farmer who spent his time accumulating wealth for himself. He is given this divine reprimand: "This night your soul is required of you; and the things you have prepared, whose will they be?" (Lk 12:20). In Paul's theology death and judgment are very closely related: "The sting of death is sin, and the power of sin is the law" (1 Cor 15:56). This theme reappears in the epistle to the Hebrews: "It is appointed for men to die once, and after that comes judgment" (Heb 9:27).

A particularly controversial verse is Matthew 24:40: "Then two men will be in the field; one is taken and one is left." Dispensationalists commonly understand this as a description of the rapture, when true believers will be lifted into the air to meet the returning Christ. Sherman Johnson gives this interpretation, which has ample support in church tradition: "*One is taken,* i.e., accepted and preserved, *and one is left* to his doom."[10] I believe that this text could also legitimately be applied to the hour of death, though its primary meaning appears to be the inauguration of the eschaton that will be totally unexpected.

The idea of a particular judgment at the time of death, which is to be distinguished from the general judgment at the end of time, is solidly anchored in both Catholic and Reformation traditions. Martin Luther declared, "Each of us has his own Last Day when he dies."[11] The particular judgment was a recurring theme among both the Pietists and the Puritans.[12]

The Last Judgment

While God's judging hand falls upon every facet of human history, Scripture is clear that there will be a final judgment in which human pretensions will be completely demolished. The author of Ecclesiastes declares, "God will bring every deed into judgment, with every secret thing, whether good or evil" (Eccles 12:14). Similarly in the words of the psalmist:

> He is coming to judge the earth.
> He will judge the world with righteousness,
>   and the peoples with his truth. (Ps 96:13 NRSV)

Daniel envisages a twofold outcome of human history: "Many of them that sleep in the dust of the earth shall awake, some to everlasting life, and some to shame and everlasting contempt" (Dan 12:2 KJV).

This note reappears in the Fourth Gospel, which speaks of a resurrection to life and a resurrection to judgment (Jn 5:25-29). Paul also is firm in his conviction of the coming judgment of God: "When the Lord comes, he will bring our deepest secrets to light and will reveal our private motives. And then God will give to everyone whatever praise is due" (1 Cor 4:5 NLT).

The last judgment is not a new judgment but the confirmation and ratification of the grace and judgment of Jesus Christ in his cross and resurrection. It is the revelation of the judgment of God in Jesus Christ on behalf of all humanity (Barth). It is also the working out of the final judgment on the cross (Forsyth). Again, one can say that it signifies the execution and completion of all preceding judgments. The great white throne judgment in Revelation 20:11-15 is not a new word from God but is consonant with all preceding words. Jesus judges with the Father (Jn 8:16). The last judgment is one that is definitive and irrevocable.

Scripture is unequivocal that the last day is indeed a day of judgment. It is the day of the Lord in which he pronounces judgment upon the human race (cf. 1 Cor 1:8; 1 Thess 5:2; 2 Pet 3:10; Rev 16:14). It is a day of visitation when Christ will come to judge the living and the dead (2 Tim 4:1; cf. 1 Pet 4:5). It is also "the fullness of time" (Eph 1:10) when Christ will come to establish his kingdom. We must not separate the parousia and the judgment of Christ as do premillennialists. Neither should we separate the rapture (1 Thess 4:16-17) and the great white throne judgment.

The day of the Lord will be a day of rejoicing; at the same time it will be a time for judgment. Amos described this day as one of darkness (Amos 5:18-20). We find this same note in Zephaniah 1:14-16 and Ezekiel 30:3. Joel portrayed it as a day of destruction (Joel 2:1-11). Isaiah referred to it as a "day of vengeance" (Is 34:8). Malachi saw it as a day of fire and devastation (Mal 4:1). Paul referred to the last day as a day of wrath (Rom 2:5-9; cf. Heb 10:31; Rev 6:16-17).

The prophets were convinced that a new creation and full salvation could only be attained through defeat and destruction. Light and salvation will come through judgment and devastation. Joel predicted a great outpouring of the Holy Spirit that would follow genuine repentance for sin (Joel 2:28-29). While Zephaniah described the day of the Lord as a day of wrath, one can also discern in his prophecy a note of tempered optimism:

> Act now, before the fierce fury of the LORD falls and the terrible day of the LORD's anger begins. Beg the LORD to save you—all you who are humble, all you who uphold justice. Walk humbly and do what is right. Perhaps even yet the LORD will protect you from his anger on that day of destruction. (Zeph 2:2-3 NLT)

The coming judgment of God will affect both the living and the dead. Even Christians will be judged. They are under divine grace and love, yet they are still vulnerable to God's wrath because of their continuing proneness to sin. Jesus warned, "Every one to whom much is given, of him will much be required" (Lk 12:48). We shall all appear before the judgment; yet on the basis of our union with Christ we know that mercy will triumph over judgment (Jas 2:13).

Christians are not exempt from the judgment of God, but they have the assurance that they will survive this judgment. Some theologians have held that the blessed martyrs will be exempt from judgment as a tribute to their fortitude and faith (see Rev 20:4-6). Yet all Christians who are faithful to the end can be assured that they are in the hands of a God who is not only searing holiness but also infinite mercy. For Christians the final judgment will be a day of "awful joy" (Forsyth), but for the wicked it will be a day of terror. It will be a day that will see the final vindication of goodness, a time when God will establish his righteousness on earth.

Christians are not only judged by Christ, but they are made priests and kings with Christ (1 Pet 2:5; 2 Tim 2:12; Rev 1:6; 5:10; 20:6). They not only receive the verdict of their vindication, but they are also made emissaries of the most high God, commissioned to carry the verdict of condemnation to a sinful world. They are not only saved by Christ but are also granted the privilege of reigning with Christ and thereby shaping history.

The final judgment will be a judgment of our works (Mt 12:35, 37; 25; Rom 2:6-13; 1 Cor 3:13-15; Rev 20:12). At the same time, it will be a judgment on the authenticity of our faith, for our faith will be judged according to its fruits. The final judgment will be a justification of the works of the saved, whereas the judgment of the cross was a justification of our persons. Scripture tells us that we are saved only by grace, but we are judged by our works. The deeper truth is that we are saved in spite of our works. Even though our works do not measure up to the demands of God's law, God accepts us and embraces us because our works are united with the perfect work of Jesus Christ—his work of atonement for the sins of humankind since the beginning of history.

The Advance of the Kingdom

The kingdom of God is commonly defined in Christian tradition as the rule of God in the hearts of his people. Yet in the fuller biblical understanding this kingdom is not simply the reign of God but also the realm where his reign is acknowledged. In this sense the kingdom is not something static but something dynamic. It signifies a realm that is constantly expanding until it engulfs the whole of creation. This idea of the kingdom of God advancing in the world is captured by Calvin: "As the kingdom of God is continually growing and advancing to the end of the world, we must pray every day that it may come: for to whatever extent iniquity abounds in the world, to such an extent the kingdom of God, which brings along with it perfect righteousness, is not yet come."[13]

Sacred tradition has frequently made the distinction between the kingdom of Christ, which is present, and the kingdom of God, which is future. This kind of distinction is legitimate so long as we remember that the eternal kingdom of God is already present in the historical kingdom of Christ, and that the latter will finally be taken up into the former. Jesus saw the kingdom of God commencing in his own ministry: "If it is by the finger of God that I cast out demons, then the kingdom of God has come upon you" (Lk 11:20; cf. Mt 12:28). Paul declares that the end will come when Christ subdues the kingdoms of this world. He will deliver the kingdom to God the Father "after destroying every rule and every authority and power" (1 Cor 15:24).

Another way to understand the progressive character of the kingdom of God in history is to distinguish between the kingdom of grace, which is present, and the kingdom of glory, which is future. The kingdom of grace is now present in history though only in islands of faith that point to a future apocalypsis. The church will never encompass the whole of humanity within empirical history; indeed, it will always remain a colony of heaven in a hostile world (Phil 3:20). Yet this colony of heaven is expanding as the gospel is proclaimed to peoples of every nation and tribe. We now enter the kingdom through "many tribulations" because the decision of faith entails a radical break with the hegemony of the culture (Acts 14:22).

In Ephesians 5:5 the kingdom of Christ and the kingdom of God are identified. In this text they both indicate the fellowship of the new creation. But we must not forget that most of humanity does not yet belong to this fellowship. They remain, however, under the rule of God. Even when the forces of evil conspire to take the kingdom by force (Mt 11:12), they are still under the control of Christ the king, whose sovereignty can be challenged but not subverted by the powers of this world.

I fully concur with Martin Luther that God now rules over all of humanity, yet not as Savior. He rules over the world by his left hand as sovereign Lord and King; he rules over the church by his right hand, as merciful God and Savior. Luther also made a helpful distinction between the strange work of God and his proper work.[14] God's strange work is his rule by the sword by which he keeps the rapacity of his subjects in check. His proper work is his rule by the cross, which creates an outgoing fellowship of love. The kingdom of Christ advances in the world through the power of the powerlessness of sacrificial love. Yet even where Christ's rule is not acknowledged, he is still reigning as sovereign king and providential guide and director.

The church is the external form of the kingdom of Christ. It is the vessel of the kingdom but not the kingdom itself. The kingdom of Christ is both more inclusive and more exclusive than the church. It includes many who are not formally affiliated with the church as an institution and yet who truly believe in Christ as Savior and Lord. It excludes many who are members of the empirical church but who lack real faith in Christ and his gospel.

The kingdom of Christ or the kingdom of God is the action that Scripture likens to the pulling of a net through the sea (cf. Mt 13:47). It catches not only good fish but also bad, and when the net is brought to the shore, the fish must be sorted out. Entrance into the kingdom entails participation in the church, since we come to faith through hearing the gospel preached, but entrance into the church is not necessarily synonymous with entrance into the kingdom. Now the wheat and tares grow together, but in the eschaton the wheat will be separated from the tares (Mt 13:36-43), and then we shall see the true church of God, the holy catholic church, which is also the kingdom of Christ. The kingdom of Christ is now invisible, but it will become visible in the light of Christ's revelation at his second advent when he comes to judge the living and the dead (Mt 24:30; Rev 1:7).

Signs of His Coming

While the Bible warns us not to seek for signs (Mt 12:38-39; Lk 11:16; Jn 4:48), it bids us to be alert to the signs that God is already working in order to prepare us for the great day of judgment and salvation. The day of the Lord will come as a thief in the night (1 Thess 5:2; Rev 3:3) for those who are scoffers and unbelievers, but for people of faith this day will not be a total surprise (1 Thess 5:4; Rev 3:3-6), for they are able to discern the signs of the times.

Among the signs that presage the coming of the Lord Jesus Christ is the appearance of antichrists—persons or powers that presumptuously claim to be mouthpieces of the most high God, often to the exclusion of all others. The antichrist is both one and many, for the "spirit of the antichrist" has many incarnations (cf. 1 Jn 4:3 NKJ; 2 Jn 7). Jesus warned of "false Christs and false prophets" (Mt 24:24). First John 2:18 speaks of "many antichrists." Paul described the antichrist as one who comes disguised as an angel of light (2 Cor 11:14). He also alluded to "the man of lawlessness," "the son of perdition" (2 Thess 2:3, 4). The book of Revelation predicts that in the last days there will be a world dictator, also known as the beast, who will wreak havoc in the world (Rev 13:17; 17:17; cf. Dan 7:23-26). Most commentators agree that St. John the Divine is referring to the Roman Empire or to a revived Roman Empire.

In the last days we will also see the revival of the occult—the fascination with extraterrestrial powers (1 Tim 4:1) and the desire to uncover the secrets of the universe. In Matthew 24 Jesus warns his followers against the signs and wonders associated with the ministry of false prophets that can only lead the people of God astray (Mt 24:24; 2 Thess 2:3, 9-11; 1 Tim 4:1; 2 Tim 4:3, 4; Rev 13:13; 16:14). It is well to note that divination, sorcery and necromancy are all condemned in the Bible (Deut 18:10-11, 14, 20; Ex 22:18; Lev 20:6; Is 8:19-20; 19:3; 1 Chron 10:13; 1 Tim 4:1; Rev 9:21; 18:23).

Another compelling sign of the coming of the kingdom is the ingathering and conversion of the Jews. According to the prophet Isaiah, in the last days "the LORD will extend his hand yet a second time to recover the remnant which is left of his people" (Is 11:11). The restoration of fallen Israel to unbroken communion with the living God is a prominent theme in both Testaments (Deut 4:30-31; 2 Sam 7:10; Is 27:6-9; 59:20-21; Jer 30:18-22; 31:33-34; 33:10-11, 14-16; Ezek 20:40-44; 37:11-28; Joel 3:1; Mic 7:18; Amos 9:11-15; Lk 21:24; Acts 15:14-17; Rom 9—11).[15]

Still another salient sign of the end times is an alteration of the heavens (Is 13:13; Joel 2:30; 3:14-16; Ezek 32:7-8; Hag 2:6, 21; Mt 24:29; Lk 21:26). Quoting from the prophet Joel, Luke writes: "The sun will be turned to darkness and the moon to blood before the coming of the great and glorious day of the Lord" (Acts 2:20 NIV).

Additional signs of the end mentioned in Scripture are the proclamation of the gospel to all peoples, thus fulfilling the great commission (Mt 24:14); the wholesale destruction of peoples and nations by fire (Joel 2:3; 2 Pet 3:10; Rev 8:7-8); major earthquakes and famines (Lk 21:10-11; Rev 6:12; 18:8); the startling increase in knowledge and travel (Dan 12:4, 9); devastating wars (Dan 9:26; Mt 24:6, Mk 13:7; Lk 21:9); the appearance of scoffers (2 Pet 3:3-4); the increase in lawlessness (Dan 12:10; Mt 24:12; 2 Thess 2:7; 2 Tim 3:1-5); and the widespread persecution of believers (Mt 24:9-10; Mk 13:9, 12, 13; Lk 21:12-16).

Are we in the last days now? In every period of history since the resurrection there will be signs of the last time or the end. Some times are more apocalyptic than others. In most periods of history some of the signs will be missing. We are not yet living in the golden age of the church, even though the Christian mission goes forward unabated in many parts of the world. Elton Trueblood surmised that we are still in the beginnings of Christian history. According to Barth we now are living "between the times." For Calvin the term "last days" refers to all the time between the coming of Jesus Christ and the Last Judgment.[16]

Because some of the signs are present in every age, the church is confronted by a temptation to speculate and make unwise predictions of the coming of Christ. We must remember that no person can know the day or the hour (Mt 25:13), not even the Son of Man (Mt 24:36). The day of the Lord will come suddenly like a thief in the night (1 Thess 5:2). It will come when least expected. At the same time Christians can and should be prepared for this day (cf. 1 Thess 5:4). We are given signs by the most high God, but these signs will always be to some extent equivocal. We are given enough light to arouse our expectations but not enough to know all the secrets of the kingdom.

The Blessed Hope

Jesus Christ has come to a world yearning for salvation (Rom 8:22-23), and he is coming again. The parables of Jesus in Matthew 24 and 25 all deal with a Lord, a bridegroom whom we will meet and whose coming we should anticipate with watchfuness. In Jesus' words in the Fourth Gospel: "A little while, and you see me no more; again a little while, and you will see me" (John 16:16 REB). The visible second coming of Christ is strongly attested in 1 John 3:2: "We know that when he appears we shall be like him, for we shall see him as he is." This climactic event is also the subject of Acts 3:20-21: "Then he will send you Jesus, your long-heralded Christ, although for the time he must remain in Heaven until that universal restoration of which God spoke in ancient times through all his holy prophets" (Phillips). This same theme appears in the epistle to the Hebrews: "So Christ, having been offered once to bear the sins of many, will appear a second time, not to deal with sin but to save those who are eagerly waiting for him" (Heb 9:28). The church in all ages should affirm with the book of Revelation: "Come, Lord Jesus!" (Rev 22:20).

The second advent of Christ is not simply a manifestation or confirmation of the first advent. Nor is it an entirely new work of salvation; instead it is the consummation and fulfillment of the one great work accomplished in the cross and resurrection of Christ. The second coming marks not simply the end of the old aeon but the end of world history. Karl Heim is helpful in his analogy of thunder and lightning to illustrate the inseparability of the two comings of Christ. But his analogy falls down at this point: the second coming is not simply a reverberation of the first but a new act of God, which completes the salvation begun at Calvary.

The "blessed hope" is not a secret rapture of the saints but the visible appearing of the Lord Jesus Christ at the end of time (1 Jn 3:2; Tit 2:13; Rev 1:7; Is 52:10). It signifies "the great and terrible day of the LORD" (Mal 4:5) which completes all salvific activity that has gone before. It is not a historical event as such, in the sense that it arises out of history; instead, it signifies the inbreaking of God into earthly history. It brings about the destruction of the earth, indeed of the entire universe, by fire (2 Pet 3:7, 12). It constitutes the final crisis of world history when "heaven and earth will pass away" (Lk 21:33; cf. Zeph 1:18; Mk 13:31; 1 Jn 2:17; 2 Pet 3:7, 13). It effects not the annihilation of the world but its transformation (Rev 11:15). The inbreaking of the kingdom of God in history involves more than a transfiguration of the world: it entails a reconstitution of the world. This momentous event precipitates more than a change in outward appearances; it ignites an ontological change that has vast repercussions in the whole of God's creation.

I heartily agree with George Eldon Ladd: "The consummation of the Kingdom, although breaking into history, will itself be beyond history, for it will introduce a redeemed order whose actual character transcends both historical experience and realistic imagination."[17] The glory of the holy city far surpasses that of the lost paradise. This transformation is not meant as a restoration of the beginning but as a transmutation of one order of existence into another. The renewal of the earth is also the negation of the earth, for what we will see is a new creation, a new heaven and a new earth (Rev 21:1; Is 65:17; 66:22; 2 Pet 3:13). Time and space will be altered. No sun or moon will be necessary. There will be no more night, for the Lord God will be the light in the new order of existence (Rev 22:5). The epistle to the Hebrews states that Christ will shake once more not only the earth but also the heavens. This "indicates the removal of what is shaken . . . in order that what cannot be shaken may remain" (Heb 12:26-27).

The eschaton represents not the mere future but the absolute future as opposed to history. It is not an extension of history but the taking up of history into eternity. Christ's coming signals both the *telos* and the *finis* of world history. History will be both negated and fulfilled in a grand climax initiated by the holy Trinity—the Father acting in conjunction with the Son and through the power of the Spirit.

Those who do not yet believe are not necessarily eternally condemned, but they are not yet saved. The glorious news of God's coming to earth in Jesus Christ and his promise to come again remain incomprehensible to people bereft of faith. Yet at the second coming the veil will be lifted from their eyes, and they will witness what is now beyond human imagination. As Christians our best service to people of unbelief is to announce to them the coming day of the Lord and call them to a life and death decision.

Scripture is clear that the day of the Lord is imminent, near at hand. Even though it is beyond history, it impinges on every period within history. I concur with F. F. Bruce: "Whatever the duration of the period may be, for faith 'the time is at hand' (Rev 1:3). Each successive Christian generation is called upon to live as the generation of the end-time, if it is to live as a *Christian* generation."[18]

The Christian is challenged to affirm what cannot yet be comprehended. The day of the Lord confronts us as a mystery, yet light shines through this mystery. Martin Luther put it very succinctly: "We know that the last day will come, yet we know not what and how it will be after this life, but only in general, that we, who are true Christians, shall have everlasting joy, peace, and salvation."[19]

World history is a preparation for the kingdom of God in eternity. The light that beams from the coming kingdom already impinges on history, though only those with the eyes to see and ears to hear can understand what is taking place. We now live in the tension between the already and the not yet. The shadow of God's coming judgment casts a pall over the whole of human history, but people of faith perceive a silver lining in the crisis of God's judgment—the presence of unmerited grace that is more powerful than human sin and perfidy. God's judgment will shatter the world's dream of security through human cooperation and world brotherhood, but it nonetheless contains a promise that a new world order will arise out of the chaos and destruction of the old. We can hope and pray that God's kingdom will come, that his will will be done on earth as well as in heaven because Christ has already conquered, Pentecost is a present reality, and what remains is for this glorious and incomparable salvation to be revealed to the whole creation through a final outpouring of the Holy Spirit upon all flesh (Joel 2:28; Acts 2:17).

Appendix A: The Olivet Discourse

The prophecy in the Gospels concerning the coming of the Son of Man (Mt 24; Mk 13; Lk 21) is generally known as the Olivet discourse or "the eschatological discourse." This discourse patently builds upon the book of Daniel and may also possibly draw upon then-circulating Jewish apocalyptic material.[20] What appears to be a corroborating text is Matthew 16:28: "There are some standing here who will not taste death before they see the Son of man coming in his kingdom." This text may well refer either to the transfiguration or to the resurrection experiences of the apostles. But is this the subject of the Olivet discourse?

Possible Interpretations

Preterists commonly interpret the Olivet discourse as referring to events that were then shortly to take place. The most critical of these was the destruction of Jerusalem by the Roman army in A.D. 70. For these scholars the coming of the Son of Man is his coming in judgment upon Israel. John Bray believes that "*all* the things Jesus mentioned prior to verse 34 [in Mt 24] actually took place in the first century, and more precisely, during the time ending with A.D. 70."[21] Similarly David Chilton declares, "The Olivet Discourse . . . is not about the Second Coming of Christ. It is a prophecy of the destruction of Jerusalem in A.D. 70."[22] Such a position radically challenges the mainstream of church tradition which sees these texts as prophecies of the second coming of Christ at the end of time. Part of the problem with the preterist interpretation is that the sign of the proclamation of the gospel to all the nations manifestly did not occur at that time (see Mt 24:14; Mk 13:10).[23] Nor did the universal lighting up of the whole creation take place as Scripture predicts (Lk 17:24).[24]

A quite different approach to this issue is the contention that Jesus was mistaken concerning the imminence of the coming of the Son of Man. Some biblical scholars, such as Albert Schweitzer and Johannes Weiss, have perceived Jesus as an eschatological prophet who simply had an erroneous understanding of when the kingdom of God would be inaugurated. Some of those who are attracted to this position see it as buttressing Jesus' true humanity, since if he were truly or fully human he would necessarily be limited in his understanding, but this does not make him an unreliable or unworthy moral and spiritual teacher.

Then there is the position that there might be a cleavage or at least a dissonance between Jesus' teaching and the viewpoint of the Gospel writers. According to George Buttrick, Matthew 24:34 represents Matthew's belief, while Matthew 24:36 "has authentic marks of Christ's own utterance."[25] Robert Gundry says it is salutary to "distinguish between Jesus' meaning, as evident in Mark [13:30-31], and Matthew's meaning" (reflected in Mt 24:34).[26] Here again we are confronted with the view that the Gospel writers were redactors and editors as well as authors. Granted that some difficulties can be assuaged in this way, we need to consider that faithful followers of Jesus would be fully respectful of their teacher's position and would likely submit to it rather than elaborate on it.

Again, we must give attention to the allegation that the Olivet discourse contains two or more different prophecies. The *NIV Study Bible* contains this commentary on Matthew 24: "It appears that the description of the end of the age is discussed in vv. 4-14, the destruction of Jerusalem in vv. 15-22 (see Lk 21:20) and Christ's coming in vv. 23-31."[27] The problem is that some of these verses appear to describe two different events. The possibility of a double reference is rejected, I think too quickly, by the preterist J. Stuart Russell: "There is not a scintilla of evidence that the apostles and primitive Christians had any suspicion of a twofold reference in the predictions of Jesus concerning the end."[28]

A very common attitude in conservative circles is to deny that there is any real contradiction between the sayings of Jesus and the happenings of history. Eduard Schweizer holds that "Jesus' statement is not patently false because by 'this generation' Matthew means not just the first generation after Jesus but all the generations of Judaism that reject him."[29] *The NIV Study Bible* suggests, "If the term [generation] is understood as a normal life span, it may refer either to the generation in which Jesus lived while on earth or to the generation living when these signs begin to occur."[30] According to evangelical biblical scholar Daniel Lewis, the most reasonable interpretation is that Jesus was speaking of the last generation of history.[31] Dispensationalists commonly argue that "this generation" refers to the generation that would see the sign of the fig tree—the emergence of Israel as a nation. Critical scholar S. MacLean Gilmour holds that the passing of history colored the way this text was interpreted: "When the later church adjusted its thinking to an indefinite continuance of the historical order, *this generation* was interpreted to mean either 'the race of mankind' or 'the company of the faithful.'"[32]

Toward a Fuller Understanding of Jesus' Teaching

The position I endorse is not new, but it often appears so in the context of today's discussion. With Robert Mounce, Robert H. Gundry and Joseph A. Fitzmyer, among others, I contend that biblical prophecy can have a double or even multiple fulfillment. A passage like the one we are exploring may have a preliminary fulfillment (such as the destruction of Jerusalem) and an ultimate fulfillment (the destruction and renewal of the world). Preterists resist this approach because it goes counter to their assumption that the eschatological fulfillment of God's promises took place in the past. I here heartily concur with Robert Mounce:

> Biblical prophecy is capable of multiple fulfillment. In the immediate context, the "abomination of desolation" (v. 15) [Mt 24] builds on the defilement of the temple by Antiochus Epiphanes, is repeated when the sacred temple in Jerusalem is destroyed by the Roman army in A.D. 70, and has yet a more complete fulfillment when the eschatological Antichrist exalts himself by taking his seat in the "temple of God" proclaiming himself to be God (2 Thess 2:3-4). In a similar way, the events of the immediate period leading up to the destruction of Jerusalem portend a greater and more universal catastrophe when Christ returns in judgment at the end of time.[33]

Commenting on Luke's rendition of Jesus' eschatological discourse,

Catholic New Testament scholar Joseph Fitzmyer contends that the "Lucan discourse looks back at the catastrophe in Jerusalem (A.D. 70) in a microcosmic view; it sees the crisis that the earthly coming of Jesus brought into the lives of his own generation, but sees it now as a harbinger of the crisis which Jesus and his message, and above all his coming as the Son of Man, will bring to 'all who dwell upon the entire face of the earth' (21:35)."[34]

The notes on Matthew in *The New Jerusalem Bible* reflect a similar stance:

> This eschatological discourse of Matthew combines the announcement of the destruction of Jerusalem with that of the end of the world. . . . Though separated in time, these two [events] are inseparable in the sense that the first is the inevitable forerunner and prefiguration of the second. The destruction of Jerusalem marks the end of the old covenant—Christ has thus manifestly returned to inaugurate his kingly rule. Such a decisive intervention in the history of salvation will not occur again until the end of time when God will judge the whole human race, now chosen in Christ, with the same judgment he pronounced (in A.D. 70) upon the first chosen people.[35]

The NJB notes on Mark 13 by contrast tend to give a preterist interpretation of this apocalypse, namely, that God's deliverance of his people already occurred in events of that time.[36]

With regard to the passing away of heaven and earth in Matthew 24:35, John Bray interprets this as referring to the passing away of the old Israel and therefore as something completed in the past.[37] I agree with Bray that the language is figurative or metaphorical, but it surely includes the thought that Jesus' teaching is steadfastly reliable and enduring. Here again it might be possible to find a double reference in this passage, but this approach invites the charge of subjectivism and the abandonment of grammatical-historical exegesis. In determining the revelatory meaning of any particular text in the Bible we must try to perceive this text in the context of the whole panorama of biblical history culminating in the apostolic proclamation of God's self-revelation in Jesus Christ.

Some Closing Comments

Part of the problem in assessing the significance of the Olivet discourse as well as of other apocalypses in Scripture is that we are dealing not with literal or straightforward language but instead with apocalyptic, figurative language, what I have sometimes called mythopoetic language. Dispensationalism in its insistence on a strictly literal interpretation of biblical prophecy reflects the legacy of evangelical rationalism with its appeal to historical evidences and rational consistency. While the preterists generally acknowledge the poetic or figurative complexion of apocalyptic literature, they too manifest a rationalistic bent by striving for ideas that are clear and distinct (à la Descartes). Like the dispensationalists their method is to harmonize the various texts as much as possible so that the Bible can yield a coherent and comprehensive system of truth.[38] They shrink from affirming that a text may have a double reference or a hidden meaning.

It should be made clear that in the Olivet discourse Jesus' concern is not with chronological sequence, as both dispensationalists and preterists often imply, but with the call to costly discipleship. Jesus reminds his hearers that no person knows the day or the hour of the cataclysmic termination of history, not even the Son of Man (Mt 24:36). It is a mistake, however, to insinuate that Jesus' concern is exclusively ethical and not also eschatological. Indeed, his ethics are grounded in an eschatological vision, for we are called as Christ's disciples to prepare the way for the coming of the kingdom through our prayers, preaching and deeds of mercy.

Apocalyptic literature is not easily reconciled with the human penchant for orderliness and consistency in interpretation. Robert Mounce bids us "to remember that apocalyptic literature is a genre that does not share our Western concern for orderly continuity. . . . Matthew moves freely between the coming destruction of Jerusalem and the final consummation."[39] It is important to recognize that the Olivet discourse as well as the apocalypses in Daniel and Revelation unite themes that are commonly associated with conflicting perspectives regarding the future. The tension between the already and the not yet is not overcome but heightened in this kind of literature. Christ is coming, but in another sense he is already here—through the power of his resurrection and the gift of his Spirit. The biblical message culminates not in the judgment on Israel manifested in the destruction of Jerusalem in A.D. 70 but in the second advent of Christ at the end of history and the creation of a new heaven and a new earth. The catastrophe that befell the Jewish people in A.D. 70 is a sign of the final judgment over the entire human race that will be inaugurated when Christ comes again in power and glory to set up his kingdom that shall have no end. This futuristic, eschatological perspective shapes both the proclamation of the church and the living out of the Christian faith under the banner of the cross. Let us strive for a genuinely catholic perspective that corrects the imbalances in both preterism and futurism, that does justice to both the movement of the Spirit of God in past history and to the Spirit's outpouring in present and future history.

The apocalyptic thrust of the Christian message paints a picture of the kingdom of God as something radically different from the cultural ethos in which we are formed and therefore as something that has revolutionary implications. The message of the kingdom calls us to a life that goes completely counter to the plans and hopes of people of the world. We would do well to listen to the Anabaptist theologian J. Heinrich Arnold:

> Nations are building their freedom and security on the most dangerous weapons that have ever existed. Yet we are called to build our security on something else—that which is of God. And we long that something of God might be given to all nations. It is not enough to lead even the most perfect life of peace in church community. Our longing will be satisfied only when the whole earth comes under the rulership of God, not the rulership of force.[40]

The kingdom of God advances not by the sword but by the cross. The sword cannot be dispensed with in the quest for justice, since a just social order cannot be maintained apart from the coercive power of law. Law cannot be allowed to have the final word, however, for unless it is guided and critiqued by the ideal of love it can become the occasion for new forms of tyranny. A thorough-going pacifism underplays the persistence of human rapacity, which can only be contained by the force of law. The new social order of God's kingdom has its basis not in law but in the personal transformation brought about by faith in the living Lord and Savior Jesus Christ. The final answer to the human predicament lies not in social engineering—though this has its place in God's providence—but in the gift of conversion through the power of God's Spirit. Our mission as Christians is to call attention to what God is doing as he brings a new social order into being.

There are mysteries in eschatology that cannot easily or ever be resolved by simply collating texts or by speculating on the exact time of Christ's coming because, as Arnold says, "God wishes to keep them hidden." But he goes on to say, "We can rejoice in this: the coming of the kingdom is certain, and it is a kingdom of peace, victory, and justice."[41]

The founder of the Bruderhof, Eberhard Arnold, exudes a similar confidence:

> God's kingdom is approaching over all the earth. God is near wherever the complete transformation of all things which His reign brings with it, is sought. His kingdom has no bounds in space. . . . We are heralds of the last kingdom. We stand here and go out as bearers of the cause, as envoys, as messengers of God's kingdom. The turning of all things is near; everything else must be overthrown, God's love alone shall triumph![42]

The Olivet discourse of Jesus in the context of a futuristic eschatology harbors millennial expectations, though it does not counsel withdrawal from the world. Instead it summons us to be overcomers of the world, harbingers of a new world order that will signal the collapse of the principalities and powers that now hold the world in subjection. The biblical apocalyptic is united with a prophetic vision of the dawning of righteousness and peace on earth. This hope is certain because

God is acting and moving in such a way as to give concrete realization to his purposes for all of humanity. Moreover, he has given us his promise to act in a final and extraordinary manner, bringing to fulfillment the whole panorama of human history in a kingdom that will prove to be impregnable and indissoluble.

·FIVE·

THE

MILLENNIAL

H͒PE

May your glory shine over all the earth.
PSALM 108:5 NLT

The second death has no power over them;
they shall be priests of God and of Christ,
and they will rule with him for a thousand years.
REVELATION 20:6 GNB

Jesus wants to build up a human society in God's praise and honor, here on earth.
His great goal is that the nations may yet come to Zion and worship.
CHRISTOPH BLUMHARDT

God lets us feel how He is at work everywhere and how
His cause is growing and moving forward.
The time is being fulfilled and the light shall shine,
perhaps just when it seems to us that the darkness is impenetrable.
EBERHARD ARNOLD

The final scene in the drama of history is not the emergence of a
utopia but the clash between Christ and Antichrist.
T. A. KANTONEN

Perhaps no doctrine has more divided modern evangelical Protestantism than that of the millennium, the thousand year reign of Christ depicted in Revelation 20. This doctrine is also known as chiliasm, from the Greek *chilias* (meaning one thousand). Those who adhere to a millennial kingdom in earthly history inaugurated by the cataclysmic coming of Jesus Christ in power and glory are known as premillennialists. Those who contend for a millennial period of peace and justice prior to Christ's visible coming in glory are postmillennialists. Those who conceive of a millennial kingdom already realized in history in the flowering of the church are amillennialists.

One's position on this question depends largely on the method of interpretation given to Revelation 20. Futurists interpret these texts as referring to events at the end of history. Preterists (from the Latin *praeteritus*, meaning "completed in the past") understand the whole of the book of Revelation as referring to events that were shortly to take place in the first century. Idealists bring a symbolic or allegorical interpretation to the texts in question. This is to say, Revelation does not purport to describe events in actual history but illuminates the ongoing battle with evil in the depths of the human soul.

While a millennial kingdom is explicitly propounded only in Revelation 20, it is hinted at in many places in the Bible. Paul writes in 1 Corinthians 15:24-26: "Then comes the end, when he delivers up the kingdom to God the Father, after deposing every sovereignty, authority, and power. For he is destined to reign until God has put all enemies under his feet; and the last enemy to be deposed is death" (REB). This might well be interpreted as referring to Christ establishing his millennial kingdom in history before offering it to the Father who incorporates it into an eternal kingdom. On the other hand, it can also be validly understood as Christ's victory over the powers of darkness that is progressively realized within history before his second advent when he brings all things to completion.

The millennial promise basically refers to hope within history and is therefore a penultimate rather than an ultimate hope. In this light it can be argued that there are many passages in Scripture that affirm a this-worldly dimension to the Christian hope. Jesus declared in Matthew 5:5: "Blessed are the meek, for they will inherit the earth" (NRSV).

And again: "Thy kingdom come, thy will be done, on earth as it is in heaven" (Mt 6:10). Our Lord also announced: "With all these things the birth-pangs of the new age begin" (Mt 24:8 NEB). Yet there is no reference to a millennial kingdom before the end will come. Instead, what is postulated is the spread of lawlessness. This passage could just as well be employed by postmillennialists and amillennialists. What is affirmed is that the new age will arise out of the crises and turmoils of the present age (Mt 24:9-14).

When we turn to the Old Testament, we find many passages that depict a future within history that embodies millennial expectations. The prophecies of the restoration of the Davidic kingdom and the return of the Jews to the holy land all have a distinctly millennial ring (cf. Is 2:1-4; 11:6-16; 49:7-26; 51:4-6; 52:10; Jer 16:16-21; 23:1-8; 32:36-44; Ezek 34:11-16; 36:24; Micah 4:1-5; 7:11-20; Joel 2:28-32; Zech 8:1-8; 14:16-21; Amos 9:14-15).

The paramount question in all of these Old Testament passages is whether the prophecies are intended to have a literal fulfillment (as dispensationalists claim) or whether in the light of the New Testament revelation they have their fulfillment spiritually in the New Israel, the church of the living God (as amillennialists and some postmillennialists allege).

Part of the debate today revolves around whether biblical eschatology is primarily apocalyptic or prophetic in character. Apocalypticism is the belief in "two totally distinct and different ages: this present age is temporal and irremediably evil because it is under the control of the author of evil; whereas the new age will be eternal and perfectly righteous because it will be under the direct governance of God."[1] It is well to note that early Jewish apocalypses like Daniel and Isaiah 24—27 did not include a messiah or a messianic kingdom. Yet as the idea of a messiah gained ground in later apocalyptic thinking he was envisaged as ruling over a temporal kingdom. The prophetic type of eschatology looks forward to a gradual increase in social righteousness through prophetic preaching and royal decree, though divine intervention is also deemed necessary for a full transformation of the cultural landscape. In the prophetic ethos the kingdom of God is like a leaven that slowly but surely transforms the whole of society. In the apocalyptic vision the kingdom of God is entirely future and enters this world cataclysmically. The key word in the prophetic understanding is *process*; in the apocalyptic view it is *crisis*.

Needless to say the biblical vision includes elements of both apocalyptic and prophetic strands. The kingdom is both now and in the future. It is present now in anticipatory and preliminary form. In the future it will be consummated or fulfilled. Whether this consummation will be in two stages (as in premillennialism) or one stage (as in amillennialism) is a continuing bone of contention.

Renewed Interest in the Millennium

While church tradition after Augustine has for the most part ignored the millennial hope, theologians in more recent times have manifested an increasing interest in this subject. Among these are Karl Barth, G. C. Berkouwer, Paul Tillich, Jürgen Moltmann, Raymond Bulman, Richard Bauckham, Bruno Forte[2] and Stanley Grenz.[3] The Catholic theologian Bulman is sharply critical of Augustine and Jerome for downplaying the millennium.[4] In his view the millennial vision is "neither catastrophic nor pessimistic; it is rather a vision of hope, in defiance of the negativity of the historical moment." In the words of Moltmann, "Only millenarian eschatology understands the eschaton as the goal of history, as future history, as the consummation and final condition of history. Non-millenarian eschatology can only talk about a rupture of history, which can have no relevance for present ethics."[5] Stanley Grenz voices the growing consensus among progressive evangelicals:

> The anticipation of a climax to human history—a corporate eschatology—and the resultant question concerning the millennium as a specific stage in that climax cannot be relegated to the fringes of the biblical proclamation. On the contrary, it belongs to the heart of what the Bible intends to teach.[6]

Karl Barth in his earlier years sought to make a place for the millennium. "The millennium is by no means an island of the blest, but the kingdom of saints and martyrs built over the bottomless pit in which the old dragon is chained."[7] He was convinced that "ethics can no more exist without millenarianism, without at least some minute degree of it, than without the idea of a moral personality."[8] At the same time the kingdom that comes from the hand of God must never be identified with any of the kingdoms of this world.

The millennial theme runs through Paul Tillich's theology. He viewed the kingdom as having both an "inner-historical" and a "transhistorical" side.[9] The millennial imagery preserves the first. For Tillich the millennium is never a realized goal of history but a symbol of "the victory over concrete demonic forces within history."[10] The millennium is the *kairos* or fulfillment of time when history will witness the dawning of righteousness and peace. Yet Tillich reminds us that Satan is only partially bound in Revelation 20 and that he is periodically released from his prison when he again plunges history into chaos. For Tillich the symbol of the millennium must be taken seriously but not literally.

In both the Augustinian Catholic tradition and the tradition of the Reformation the millennium is regarded as a theological aberration. Neither Luther nor Calvin wrote a commentary on the book of Revelation. The Augsburg Confession condemns premillennialism, and Protestant orthodoxy continued this aversion to millennial speculation.[11] According to James P. Martin the repudiation in orthodoxy of the millennial hope "furthered the separation of the hope of the consummation from the process of history and placed the Last Judgment completely beyond history."[12] "The cosmic and realistic soteriology and Christology of the New Testament" was replaced by "a spiritualized and individualized eschatology."[13]

The opposition to the millennium and to apocalyptic eschatology in Protestantism created a spiritual vacuum which was soon to be filled by Pietists, Puritans and later by sectarians including the Catholic Apostolic Church, the Seventh-day Adventists, the Mormons, the Christadelphians and the Plymouth Brethren. The Seventh-day Adventists, who emerged out of the Millerite revival in 1843-1844, portrayed the millennium as the rule of the saints in heaven over a desolate earth occupied by the devil.[14]

Millennial ideas also appeared in neo-Protestantism, which drew upon Enlightenment notions in its quest for righteousness and peace on earth. A millennial vision pervaded the Socialist and Communist movements as well. Friedrich Engels wrote in 1842: "The self-consciousness of mankind, the new Grail, around whose throne the nations joyfully assemble. . . . that is our profession, that we become knights of this Grail, to put the sword around our waists and joyfully venture our life in the last holy war after which the thousand years empire of freedom will emerge."[15] A secularized millennialism also dominated the ideology of National Socialism, which looked forward to a thousand-year *Reich* (kingdom) when the inferior races of the world would be ruled by the master race. In both Marxism and Nazism, as well as the communal societies spawned by the Enlightenment and pietistic Protestantism, the millennium is identified with a this-worldly utopia.

Premillennialism

Among the principal millennial options in eschatology is premillennialism, which dates back to the early Christian centuries. Like its alternatives, premillennialism is not monolithic, but it does have certain distinctive characteristics. It basically holds that Jesus Christ is coming again to inaugurate the millennial, or thousand-year, period of righteousness and peace on earth. During this period Satan will be bound in the sense that he will not be able to deceive the nations concerning the truth of the gospel. At the end of this period Satan will be let loose for a while before he is finally decapacitated. Premillennialists emphasize the discontinuity between the millennial age and the present age. This is why the millennium can even be described as being beyond history, though for many proponents of this view it is envisaged as the final stage of history. The final revelation of Christ is portrayed in terms of an apocalyptic intervention into history. Premillennialists tend to be pessimistic. They see the church losing influence in the final days of history. They also envision two resurrections: the resurrection of the saints at the inauguration of the millennium and then the resurrection of the wicked unto judgment at the end of the golden age that constitutes the millennium.

Premillennialists are known for their stress on the imminence of God's kingdom. Time and again some of their adherents have predicted the exact time of Christ's coming, only to be painfully disappointed. Various critics of premillennialism see the kingdom as imminent in every age of the church, since the Spirit moves in always new and dramatic ways.

Premillennialism can be rightly criticized for entertaining an overly pessimistic view of world history, sometimes bordering on fatalism. Reformed theologian Adrio König makes this pertinent observation:

> Chiliasts simply write off the world as incorrigible, painting a one-sided picture of total decay spreading over the entire world. Little room is left in their view for a gospel that includes the promise of victory—even in this life. So it is not strange that they fail to do justice to the coming of the kingdom in the ministry of Jesus.[16]

While they tend to be political quietists, they are certainly spiritual activists, since evangelical missions have prospered in a premillennial vision where Christians are encouraged to call people to repentance before the curtain rolls down on world history. Moreover, a premillennial outlook does not necessarily lead to political quietism.[17] If the emphasis on the second coming of Christ is united with a recognition of the social and political implications of the outpouring of the Spirit at Pentecost, the motivation to make the nations ready to receive the risen Christ becomes very pronounced.

One glaring weakness in premillennialism is its lack of a firm biblical basis. While the second coming of Christ is certainly part of the gospel, the millennial reign of Christ is only hinted at in a few places. We need to interpret Revelation 20 in the light of the wider Scriptures rather than interpret the Scriptures through the lens of Revelation 20, as do most premillennialists.

In addition an egocentric strand runs through premillennialism. The Christian goal sometimes appears to be experiencing the pleasures of the millennium rather than glorifying God in lowly service. Our service to the world should be fueled by hope in the second advent of Christ, but this hope should turn us ever more to the world in its poverty and misery rather than away from the world toward an idyllic kingdom that lies on the other side of history.

Premillennialism has certain strengths which should be acknowledged by all parties in this dispute. First it promotes "a lively interest in the futurist aspects of eschatology."[18] It reminds us that eschatology is basically about the end of the world and not about happenings in the history of the early church. It also claims the support of a number of pre-Constantinian fathers including Irenaeus, Justin Martyr, Commodian, Lactantius, Montanus and Tertullian.[19] While reduced in prominence during the Middle Ages and opposed by the magisterial Reformers, it nevertheless continued as a potent force among the Anabaptists and Spiritualists of the sixteenth and seventeenth centuries. It enlisted the support of some Reformed theologians including Johann Heinrich Alsted (1588-1638) and William Sherwin (1607-1687).[20] In the nineteenth and early twentieth centuries it experienced a resurgence in the writings of Edward Irving (1792-1834), John Nelson Darby (1800-1882) and Cyrus I. Scofield (1843-1921). Because the modern form of premillennialism tends to be dispensational, I shall expand on this innovation in the next section of this chapter. Modern exponents of the historic millennial position include W. J. Eerdman, J. Barton Payne, R. A. Torrey, Millard Erickson, Clarence Bass and George Eldon Ladd.

Dispensationalism

Without any doubt the dominant strand of premillennialism today is dispensationalism, whose immediate roots are in the late nineteenth and early twentieth centuries.[21] Among its guiding luminaries are John Nelson Darby, C. I. Scofield (author of the Scofield Reference Bible), W. E. Blackstone, and more recently Charles Ryrie, Lewis Sperry Chafer, John F. Walvoord, Arno C. Gaebelein and J. Dwight Pentecost.[22] Other proponents of dispensationalism are Gleason L. Archer, Donald G. Barnhouse, M. R. DeHaan, Charles L. Feinberg, Norman L. Geisler and Harry A. Ironside. Dispensationalism has been popularized by Hal Lindsey, especially in his bestselling *The Late Great Planet Earth*.[23] Dispensationalism constitutes a new challenge to traditional faith, but this movement is not totally divorced from church tradition. In his illustrious *City of God* Augustine divided human history into stages of God's administration of the world culminating in the seventh stage, the eternal sabbath rest of the people of God. In the seventeenth century the Dutch Calvinist and covenant theologian Johannes Cocceius perceived two covenants—works and grace—and within the latter several dispensations.[24] What makes modern dispensationalism distinctive is its literalistic hermeneutic (all prophecies in the Bible have a literal fulfillment) and its vision of a future kingdom of Israel that is only loosely related to the New Testament church.

Mainstream dispensationalism sees history divided into seven periods, the most important of which are law, grace and the millennial kingdom. In each dispensation believers are tested in order to prove their worthiness before God. The difference between the dispensations of law and grace is that for the latter "the point of testing is no longer legal obedience as the condition of salvation, but acceptance or rejection of Christ, with good works as a fruit of salvation."[25] A current controversy in evangelical theology is whether the dispensations are different ways of salvation. For the later dispensationalists like Charles Ryrie there is only one way of salvation, the way of grace, but various modes of implementing this salvation. In the millennial kingdom there will be a reversion to Jewish ceremonial rites and law which will regulate life in the new age but will not purchase or secure salvation for those who believe. The Jewish ceremonial rites in the context of the millennium are not expiatory but commemorative of Christ's atoning death and demonstrate our worthiness for inclusion in the millennial glory.

Dispensationalism is not monolithic and has undergone alterations in interpretation. Original or classical dispensationalism is represented in John Nelson Darby and C. I. Scofield. Revised dispensationalism is associated with Charles Ryrie, the New Scofield Reference Bible and the Dallas Seminary statement of faith. Progressive dispensationalism, which emphasizes the unity of the people of God, is associated with Robert L. Saucy, Darrell L. Bock and Craig Blaising, among others.

Dispensationalists generally see the second advent of Christ in two stages—the rapture and the millennial return. In the first the church will be caught up in the air and translated out of this world of gloom and despair. After a period of seven years Christ will come again in order to set up his millennial kingdom in which the chosen people of God, the Jews, will play a pivotal role. Most dispensationalists are pretribulationists, meaning that they believe Christ will come before the great tribulation that will engulf the whole of humanity except for the raptured church. In a marked deviation from classical dispensationalism the so-called progressive dispensationalists believe that Jesus began his heavenly Davidic reign at his resurrection rather than in the dawning of the millennium.[26]

Reformed Christianity has many problems with dispensationalists. Their hermeneutic of literalism compels them to envisage the millennium as a predominantly Jewish kingdom. They fail to grasp the universal implications of biblical, prophetic faith—the vision that all people are intended to belong to the family of God, that Zion is the mother of all nations (cf. Ps 87 JB; Dan 7:13-14).[27] Again, their stringent separation of law and gospel prevents them from acknowledging the unity and complementarity of law and gospel. Similarly their proneness to separate Israel and the church tends to empty the Old Testament of its Christian significance. The millennial kingdom, not the church, is considered the fulfillment of Old Testament prophecy. For dispensational-ists the church began not in the Old Testament (as with Calvin) but in the event of Pentecost. By viewing each dispensation as a period of testing, dispensationalists seem to open the door to works-righteous-ness. The later strand of dispensationalism views the dispensations not as ways of gaining salvation but as ways by which the implications and fruits of salvation are realized in daily life.[28]

Paradoxically hand in hand with the opening to works-righteous-ness is an antinomian strand that views Christians in the church age or age of grace as under the gospel only and not also under the law. The law is something that is done away with, though the moral teachings of Jesus in the New Testament continue to have force. In Reformed Christianity the Christian is saved by grace alone but for the purpose of living a holy life. Our responsibility is not simply to receive and believe but to take up the cross and follow Christ in costly discipleship.

Of particular concern to Reformed Christians is the idea that the mil-lennium will witness the reenactment of Jewish ceremonial law, in-cluding animal sacrifices. Philip Edgcumbe Hughes has these insightful comments:

> The reinstitution of the levitical system would be an anticlimax of colossal proportions; but, worse than that, it would be contrary to the true essence of the Gospel and a disastrous return to the shadowy and temporary ordi-nances which have been irrevocably superseded by the perfection of the ev-erlasting reality to which they pointed. It is futile to attempt to place the new wine of the Gospel in the old wineskins![29]

Adventist theologian Hans K. LaRondelle warns against the hermeneu-tic of literalism that loses sight of the symbolic and poetic nature of much of the biblical language. It also involves a misunderstanding of biblical prophecy:

> The hermeneutic of ethnic and geographic literalism in prophecy is based on the assumption that prophecy is nothing but history ahead of time. Conse-quently, it ascribes to the prophetic portrayals the exactness of a photo-

graphic picture in advance. This assumption allows no room for greater and better things to come, things that "no mind has conceived" but God alone (1 Cor 2:9; Is 64:4).[30]

Dispensationalism signifies a marked innovation in eschatological studies, but this does not imply that it is cultic or sub-Christian, as John Gerstner believes.[31] Dispensationalists not only appeal to the Bible, but at least some of them are willing to modify and correct some of the earlier assertions of the movement. Their greatest difficulty is in reconciling the testing in the various dispensations and the biblical doctrine of salvation by grace alone (*sola gratia*). Scofield himself as well as other early leaders perceived the dispensations as ways of salvation, and Gerstner contends that this supposition is still implicit in dispensational theology.

Where the wider evangelical community can appreciate dispensationalism is in its recovery of the biblical idea of progressive revelation, its hope for the salvation and restoration of Israel, and its futuristic orientation that today seems to be crumbling under the impact of preterism. A careful reading of the New Testament reveals the Christian hope as focused not only on the first coming of Christ but also on his second coming at the end of history, and this is something we need to affirm in a time when in academic circles the eschatological hope is increasingly internalized as an inward or existential experience. Yet we must resist the dispensationalist capitulation to mythological speculation in trying to know too much about the chronology of the last days, which Scripture resolutely warns against (cf. Mt 16:1-4; 24:36). Our focus should be not on the chronology of the events of the last days but on the certainty of God's promises, which are already fulfilled in the life, ministry and resurrection of Jesus Christ, though they still await a universal acknowledgment and confirmation.

Amillennialism

Amillennialism is the position that the millennial reign of Christ has already been realized in his cross and resurrection victory and in the outpouring of the Spirit at Pentecost. This is not a visible reign but an invisible one—hidden in the church and in history. The forces of evil are now being restrained, thereby allowing for a heavenly imprint on history. This age of expectation and waiting will be fulfilled when Christ returns in glory.

In the history of the church this strand of interpretation has generally taken two forms: an ecclesial millennium and a heavenly millennium, in which the saints rule from above. Its most illustrious proponent is Augustine, who spiritualized the millennium, identifying it with the period between Christ's ascension and his second advent. Amillennialism was anticipated in the early church in the epistle of Barnabas, who applied to the church the Old Testament promises given to Israel.[32] An amillennial stance can also be detected in Thomas Aquinas, Martin Luther, John Calvin and in modern times G. C. Berkouwer, Floyd E. Hamilton, Stanley Grenz, Anthony Hoekema, Louis Berkhof, William E. Cog, Abraham Kuyper, Stephen Travis, Leon Morris, Michael Wilcock, G. K. Beale and Philip Hughes. Despite his remarkable openness to chiliasm there are strong amillennial motifs in Karl Barth.

According to amillennialists we are now living in "the end of the ages" (cf. 1 Cor 10:11). Christ has come to set up his kingdom through the agency of the church. The first resurrection has already occurred through the gift of faith, which constitutes a spiritual rising from death to life. Amillennialists appeal to such verses as John 3:34-35; 5:24; Romans 6:4-5, 13; Ephesians 2:5-6; Colossians 2:13; 3:1.

Amillennialists as well as some postmillennialists adhere to the theory of progressive parallelism when dealing with the book of Revelation. This hermeneutic discerns an emerging pattern in which various chapters return to a common theme—God's incomparable gift of salvation in Jesus Christ—and then build upon this theme on the basis of further illumination from the Spirit of God. From this perspective, Revelation 20 does not chronologically follow Revelation 19 but constitutes a redescription of the unfolding eschatological panorama.[33]

The "thousand years" in Revelation 20 is treated as symbolic of the resurrection victory of Christ and its continuing resounding impact on world history. According to amillennial theologian G. C. Berkouwer the thousand years do not indicate time but symbolize power, a position endorsed by Adrio König: " 'A thousand years' symbolizes the absolute defeat, binding, and total subordination of Satan and his forces which are clearly taught by the rest of the New Testament. 'Thousand' does not refer to time at all; it demonstrates the completeness of Christ's victory over Satan."[34]

In Berkouwer's theology the vision of Revelation 20 "is not a narrative account of a future earthly reign of peace . . . but is the apocalyptic unveiling of the reality of salvation in Christ as a backdrop to the reality of the suffering and martyrdom that still continue as long as the dominion of Christ remains hidden."[35] For this theologian the magnitude of Christ's victory over the powers of darkness will not be fully grasped until the final consummation.

After a careful investigation of the various theories on the millennium Stanley Grenz, who was once a premillennialist, now opts for an "amillennial realism" that

> lifts our sights above the merely historical future to the realm of the eternal God. It reminds us that the kingdom of God is a transcendent reality that can be confused with no earthly kingdom prior to the final transformation of creation. No earthly city can ever hope to become the New Jerusalem, except through a radical transformation both of human nature itself and of the universe that through the Fall unwillingly participates in the human predicament.[36]

While close to Grenz's amillennial vision, I must take exception to a consistent and thorough-going amillennialism. Whereas amillennialism inclines toward a realized eschatology in which the kingdom has already been established in history, I see the kingdom of God progressing within history. It is neither fully implanted within history nor wholly beyond history. Moreover, I hold to the outpouring of millennial glory within various periods of history, not just at the end of history or on the boundary of history. Furthermore it seems that realized eschatology fails to account for the continuing presence of the powers of darkness within history and their ability to thwart the mission of the church. Can we honestly claim that Satan is bound when events like the Holocaust take place? If we are already in the millennium, then why do the demonic powers still seem so threatening? Amillennialists try to give an answer to these questions, and I shall speak to these questions in the last section of this chapter.

Postmillennialism

A credible alternative to both amillennialism and premillennialism is postmillennialism, the view that Christ's kingdom is progressing in history and will culminate in a Christianized world prior to the second advent of Christ. Whereas amillennialists and premillennialists tend to be pessimistic regarding the outcome of world history, postmillennialists are inclined to be optimistic, but this is an optimism based on the outpouring of the Holy Spirit and the forward advance of the church in history through the power of the Spirit. Postmillennialists speak of the harvest of history in which the gospel is preached to all nations, and after that the end will come (Mt 24:14). Theonomic postmillennialists believe that Christians empowered by the Spirit can bring changes in cultural life that will result in a modicum of justice and peace here on earth.[37] The Puritan ideal was that of a "holy commonwealth" in which church and state work together to bring about a Christian social order, though this must not be confounded with the kingdom of God. The binding of Satan is envisaged not in static but in progressive terms, as something that is being accomplished through the advance of the church on earth. David Chilton voices this holy optimism characteristic of Calvinism and Puritanism: "Satan is bound *progressively* as Christ's Kingdom grows throughout history, extending its influence to transform every aspect of life."[38] In contrast to dispensationalists, postmillennialists see the fulfillment of Old Testament prophecies in the church rather than in a future, restored Israel.[39]

Postmillennialism has been present throughout Christian history, though in certain periods it has been overshadowed by amillennialism and premillennialism. In the early church, Eusebius of Caesarea interpreted the victory of the church under Constantine as the beginning of the "millennium." Postmillennialism was also evident in Montanism, which posited a great outpouring of the Spirit before the second advent of Christ, preparing the way for his advent.[40] The postmillennial vision was rekindled in utopian and spiritualistic movements in the Middle Ages and in modern times. Especially significant is Joachim of Flora (c. 1132-1202), who divided history into three overlapping stages—those of the Father, Son and Spirit.[41] The age of the Father was to be directed by married men. The age of the Son was to be governed by priests. The age of the Spirit was to be led by an order of monks. Joachim saw himself as living in the dawn of the third or final period of history. There was nothing said, however, about a visible reign of Christ after the dispensation of the Spirit.

Postmillennialism emerged as a potent force in the church in the age of the Puritans and Pietists who believed in a triumph of the kingdom of God within history through the preaching of the gospel.[42] The conquering rider on the white horse in Revelation 19 symbolizes the conquest of the world by the risen and ascended Christ working through the power of the Spirit. Among those who have embraced a postmillennial vision are Daniel Whitby, Jonathan Edwards, Isaac Backus, Samuel Hopkins, John and Charles Wesley, Philip Spener, Samuel Rutherford, and later Johann Christoph Blumhardt, Christoph Blumhardt, Charles Hodge, B. B. Warfield, W. G. T. Shedd, Augustus H. Strong, Jonathan Blanchard (who was the founder of Wheaton College), T. A. Kantonen,[43] J. Marcellus Kik,[44] Loraine Boettner[45] and John Jefferson Davis.[46]

The holy optimism characteristic of postmillennialism is voiced by Johann Christoph Blumhardt: "Not only has the Savior come; He will still come in God's glory in today's world. The future bears the name of Jesus Christ; it is our future and the future of the world, of all creation."[47] And in the words of Christoph Blumhardt: "Only one desire is important: that the power and nature of Jesus may again take shape upon earth and be seen once more."[48]

Yet those who rose out of a Lutheran and Reformed ethos, including the Blumhardts, still perceived a church under the cross, one that must continue the battle against Satan and his legion of demons. Lutheran theologian T. A. Kantonen voices this element of caution in postmillennial expectation: "The church of the millennium is still an '*ecclesia militans*,' with sin and unbelief to fight, with a cross to bear, awaiting in hope the full consummation of the divine purpose."[49]

It can be shown that postmillennialism was a guiding motif among the votaries of the Social Gospel movement. At the same time they betrayed an unwarranted accommodation to Enlightenment ideology by positing a kingdom of God on earth brought about by social engineering. Shirley Jackson Case is emblematic of this secularizing trend: "Viewed in the long perspective of the ages, man's career has been one of actual ascent. Instead of growing worse, the world is found to be growing constantly better."[50] Our mandate is not to look vainly for "a catastrophic end of the world" but instead to throw ourselves "heart and soul into the task of improving the existing order."[51]

Postmillennialism can be criticized for its sometimes naïve optimism that overlooks the incontrovertible fact that Satan continues to mount unrelenting attacks upon the church, though he cannot take away from Christians their faith in Jesus Christ. Loraine Boettner contends that Christ will return to a world that is virtually Christianized.[52] This flatly contradicts Jesus' intimation that when the Son of Man comes, faith on earth will be hard to find (Lk 18:8).

Postmillennialism tends to lose sight of the two-sidedness of the millennial hope—hope *within* history and hope *beyond* history. We need to fasten our eyes not only on what the Spirit accomplishes through the church in history but also on a new climactic divine intervention into history that will establish a kingdom that is eternal. We are called as Christians not only to change the world but also to herald a new world that is anticipated now in fellowships of outgoing love (koinonia) that exist both within and outside the institutional church.

The strength of the postmillennial position is that it magnifies the work and power of the Holy Spirit. It also forcefully reminds us that the kingdom of Christ is already present in the church and that this kingdom is expanding and advancing in world history. It bids us not to give up on the world in its pride and obtuseness but to place confidence in him who overcomes the world through his glorious resurrection and his mighty deeds of justice and mercy realized through the outpouring of the Holy Spirit (cf. Jn 16:33).

Idealist-Symbolic Views

While the three previous positions all make a place for pictorial language in the depiction of the millennium, there have been many scholars who virtually reduce the millennium to symbolism. Among these was the church father Origen, who presented the kingdom as "an event which would take place not in space or time but only in the souls of believers."[53] Another symbolist was the religious philosopher Emanuel Swedenborg (d. 1772), who espoused a theosophical millennialism in which the second coming of Christ was reinterpreted as the influx of a new spiritual energy in the world.[54] Immanuel Kant (d. 1804) envisioned an era of eternal peace through the harmonizing of the social order and the moral order. In our day Harry Boer contends that the martyrs are the only ones who will share the glory of the millennium, but even this is symbolic: "While wronged innocence will always cry out for justice and vindication, we have no reason to believe that there is a heavenly reality corresponding to this symbolism."[55] For the liberal theologian Shailer Mathews the kingdom of God is "an ideal . . . social order" that is progressively approximated in the forward advance of humanity.[56]

Without succumbing to the optimism rooted in the Enlightenment, Reinhold Niebuhr identifies the kingdom with the power of the moral ideal of sacrificial love. By locating this ideal at the edge of history rather than in the midst of history, he effectively challenges both the millennial and catholic traditions in Christian faith. In his view the kingdom is not a supernatural realm but a transcendent goal. It is "the picture of what this world ought to be."[57] It is an ideal that both lures history forward and judges history's pretensions. The church is the community where "the Kingdom of God impinges most unmistakably upon history."[58] The antichrist may be understood as that evil which "appears at the end of history" in the form of "the assertion of selfish ends in the name of Christ or in the name of God."[59] Niebuhr speaks not of actual events in history but of "eschatological symbols"—the antichrist, the new Jerusalem, the Last Judgment and so on.[60] Niebuhr believes the goal of the community of faith should be a just world, not a Christianized world. The kingdom is basically "beyond history," though we can make progress toward it by uniting the wisdom of the church and the wisdom of humanistic culture.[61]

Those, like Niebuhr, who define the kingdom of Christ as a moral ideal grasp only one aspect of the biblical vision, since the Bible depicts the new age as inaugurated in history by divine intervention. The kingdom in the biblical view is not progressively realized through humanitarian action but is introduced into history as a new world order by the surprising work of the Holy Spirit. This fulfillment of time (*kairos*) has already occurred in Christ's death and resurrection, but it will occur again when Christ comes again (literally, not merely symbolically) in order to bring his kingdom to fulfillment in a transformed heaven-earth.

Reinhold Niebuhr exploded the modernistic myth of the moral progress of humanity and sedulously tried to distinguish between the kingdom as the ideal of sacrificial love and a just social order. Yet he could not bring himself to accept the plain teaching of Scripture that the kingdom has already been inaugurated by supernatural incursion and that it will be fulfilled in a dramatic apocalyptic unfolding at the climax of world history. For Niebuhr the kingdom remains above the vicissitudes of history, though it always relates to history.[62] It impinges on history without ever becoming relativized by history. In my catholic evangelical perspective the kingdom is a vital force within history that signifies both the *telos* and *finis* of history.[63] Niebuhr is to be commended for his astute recognition of the role of symbolism in the depiction of the kingdom of God, but like his mentor Augustine he is too ready to spiritualize the millennial realities and thereby sacrifice the biblical prognostication of a temporal kingdom in the historical future for an eternal kingdom in the absolute future that never quite enters into the maelstrom of history.

Moltmann's Millennial Explorations

Jürgen Moltmann is significant for this discussion because of his endeavor to incorporate traditional chiliastic motifs into a theology of hope with its emphasis on social liberation and ecological sensitivity. Moltmann brings together themes from postmillennialism and premillennialism in order to construct a socio-dynamic view of the future that heralds justice and peace for the whole creation.[64]

In stark contrast to Augustinian orthodoxy Moltmann resists the tendency to reduce the millennial reign of Christ to his reign in the institutional church. Moltmann accuses traditional theology of undercutting the struggle for justice and peace on the grounds that these things have supposedly been attained, at least in part, through the dawning of the new age in Jesus Christ. He vigorously opposes the idea of a realized millennium because it legitimates the privileged status of both the clerics of the church and the rulers of the state. He looks with cautious favor on chiliasm because it fans a revolutionary spirit that is bent on overthrowing the oppressive structures of the world in its quest for a new heaven and a new earth.

Moltmann speaks of two kinds of millenarianism: the historical and the eschatological. The first is an ideology of power that envisions the millennial goal as already realized in church and state. The second is "an expectation of the future in the eschatological context of the end, and the new creation of the world."[65] For Moltmann the eschaton has not yet occurred except in anticipatory form. It is now being realized as people of goodwill combat the stultifying principalities and powers that hold countless numbers in bondage.

With Joachim of Flora, Moltmann posits three stages or ages in the human struggle for justice, revolving around first the Father, then the Son and then the Spirit. These ages are overlapping rather than occurring in strict chronological sequence. The kingdom of the Spirit has already begun, bringing with it a revolutionary impetus that heralds a new kingdom that stands over against the oppressive kingdoms of the world. Eschatology means an expansion of the horizon of human freedom. In the age of the Father we have the freedom of servants; in the age of the Son the freedom of children; and in the age of the Spirit the freedom of God's friends. The kingdom of the Spirit is not, however, the eternal kingdom of glory, but it is a foretaste of the glory that lies ahead.

What Moltmann endorses is a transitional or messianic kingdom that prepares the way for the eternal kingdom of the new heaven and the new earth. He sometimes portrays Christ's rule in two stages: his messianic rule in the present and his millennial reign in the future[66] A realized millennialism, in his view, is a theology of glory; a futurist millennialism is a theology of the cross. While appreciating the protests of chiliasts against oppressive structures, he is critical of dispensationalism for its apolitical quietism, for its "apocalyptic flight from the world."[67] "Revelation was not written for 'rapturists' fleeing from the world, who tell the world 'goodbye' and want to go to heaven; it was meant for resistance fighters, struggling against the godless powers on this earth."[68]

Interestingly Moltmann envisions a resurrection *from* the dead that ushers in "a reign of Christ *before* the universal raising of the dead for the Last Judgment."[69] "That is to say, it leads into a messianic kingdom in history before the end of the world, or into a transitional kingdom leading from this transitory world-time to the new world that is God's."[70] As a millenarian Moltmann sees the goal of history within history—the millennial reign of Christ. In his view "the millennium

consummates history; the eschaton ends history."[71] "In the eschatological new creation it is not something different which replaces creation;
it is *this* creation which will be made new."[72]

My principal criticism of Moltmann is that he fails to see that the
goal of history is not some breakthrough to social justice within history
but the new heaven-earth, time taken up into eternity (cf. Is 65:17;
66:22; 2 Pet 3:13; Rev 21:1). A second criticism is that he envisions the
mission of the church in terms of the ideal of ecofeminism, the renewal
of the earth through God-directed social planning.[73] It seems that *theos*
in his theology is subordinated to *bios*. He describes the mission of the
church as a "mission of life."[74] A perusal of his sermons indicates that
the kerygmatic proclamation of what God has already done for us in
Jesus Christ is overshadowed by a call to realize human potentiality as
guardians of the earth.[75] Still another difficulty I have with Moltmann is
that he tends to underplay or ignore or even deny the supernatural dimensions of Christian faith. For him the goal of history is not eternity
but a transfigured earth and just society. Nothing is said of the communion of saints, the role of the believing departed in the progression
of the kingdom.

Where I appreciate Moltmann is in his vigorous attempt to recover a
biblical millennialism—one that calls people not out of the world but
into the world as shapers and builders of a just society. I also com-
mend him for differentiating the eschatological hope from futurism:
the parousia is not to be confounded with human attempts to bring in
the kingdom of God but is a gift of grace that is being unfolded now in
history and that will be fulfilled in a messianic kingdom within history
(I here prefer to say "beyond history"). Finally, I applaud Moltmann for
his resolve to maintain an open view of history. Not everything has
been predetermined, nor has salvation been fully realized. We are free
agents, though paradoxically God realizes his goal through human decision and struggle. For Moltmann the Christian hope must not be confused with either pessimism or optimism. It is closer to what William
James called meliorism, in that it constitutes a challenge to reshape re-

ality and history in the light of God's self-revelation in Jesus Christ.[76]

Moltmann takes pains to differentiate his position from the Enlightenment faith in progress:

> Eschatology is not a doctrine about history's happy end. In the present situation of our world, facile consolation is as fatal as melancholy hopelessness. No one can assure us that the worst will not happen. According to all the laws of experience: it will. We can only trust that even the end of the world hides a new beginning if we trust the God who calls into being the things that are not, and out of death creates new life.[77]

In my opinion Moltmann's position belongs primarily to the postmillennial tradition of Christian faith, though he would prefer to be known simply as a millenarian or as one who seeks to incorporate the millenarian vision in a world-transforming eschatology.[78] His major contribution is to demonstrate the integral relation between eschatological hope and the battle for social justice. We need to join Moltmann in this effort but without losing sight of the biblical truth that the church's mission is primarily spiritual, for its message is supernatural regeneration through the outpouring of the Spirit whereby people are baptized into the death of the Lord Jesus Christ through faith in his atoning work at Calvary.

Toward a New Understanding of the Millennium

It is my belief that the time has come for a new statement of the millennium, if for no other reason than to bring a semblance of unity to the evangelical churches. Part of the problem lies in the literalizing of the biblical language, in failing to understand the nature of apocalyptic, figurative language. The millennium in Revelation 20 must be understood as a symbol of divine manifestation in history, not a literal thousand-year period within history. The binding of Satan in Revelation 20 does not mean the decapacitation of the devil and his legions but seeing through his subterfuges and thereby reducing his power to deceive (cf. Is 24:21-22; Rev 20:1-3). This binding, moreover, is to be construed not as an act fully realized in the past but as a process that will be completed in the future. Satan is dethroned not only by the crucified and risen Christ (Rev 12:10) but by the preaching of the gospel by the church under the cross (Rev 12:11).

I propose a realizing or unfolding millennium. The millennium is the kingdom of Christ that is now hidden in the crises and turmoils of history. It is a kingdom that is ever advancing but always meeting with renewed opposition by the principalities and powers that still wreak havoc in the world. Our mandate is to bear witness to this advancing kingdom of Christ, which does not yet include the whole of humanity. Pentecost is a continuing reality, for it indicates an empowering by the Spirit of the Christian community in its unremitting struggle to hold up the banner of the gospel in the darkness and dereliction of the world.

The millennium belongs to both history and superhistory. Its goal is a transfigured earth, an earth transformed by the light of the Word of God. The fulfillment of the millennium will be realized in the second coming of Christ. Its inauguration has already occurred at his first coming. Now we have the millennium in its preliminary phase; then we shall see it in its manifest or consummate stage. Now it is hidden except to the eyes of faith; then it shall be visible to the whole creation. The millennial kingdom is not yet the eternal kingdom, but when Christ comes again he will deliver his kingdom to the Father, and it will become the kingdom of God in its fulfillment (1 Cor 15:24-25). This is not a purely triumphalist model of the kingdom, for its triumph lies not in the worldly power of the institutional church but in the suffering of the persecuted people of God.

While I appreciate dispensationalists for holding to the futuristic side of eschatology, I oppose any view that depicts the kingdom as exclusively future, thereby turning this world over to the powers of darkness. Our mandate as Christians is not to flee from the world but to bring the world into subjection to the advancing kingdom of Christ.

The millennium is a fluid symbol representing any period in the history of the world where the victory of Jesus Christ becomes manifest.

But its manifestation is a reality only for those with the eyes to see and the ears to hear. The millennium is a symbol of the earth in a stage of transition from history to eternity. It is a symbol of the world in the process of being transfigured by the glory of God.

I oppose a premillennialism that makes the kingdom of Christ wholly future and in effect abandons this world to the devil. But I uphold that part of the millennial vision that includes the promise of a transfigured earth anticipated in Christ's resurrection and powerfully carried forward at his second advent. In the millennium Christ with the glorified saints proceeds to extend his rule over the kingdoms of this world, but this rule is hidden and will become manifest in the period of millennial glory following the return of Christ.

What I am presenting might be labeled a historical-symbolic view. It must not be confounded with the idealistic position. The symbols of apocalyptic eschatology refer not to timeless truths but to the penetration of the kingdom of God within history. This view can also be described as transmillennial, for the millennium points beyond itself to the new heaven and the new earth, which constitutes the fulfillment of the millennium.

I differ from the amillennial position because I see the kingdom of Christ surging forward within history. I do not envision the kingdom as simply beyond history, though it indubitably has a transcendent dimension. Moreover, I perceive the dawning of millennial glory within history, not just at the end of history.

Against the postmillennialists I reject the idea of a steady progression of righteousness in history. The kingdom of God is advancing, but its triumph within history is always partial, never complete. I here wholeheartedly agree with Reinhold Niebuhr: "The antinomies of good and evil increase rather than diminish in the long course of history."[79] We live in "the best of times" and "the worst of times" (Charles Dickens). There is incontestable technological progress, but such progress creates new opportunities for evil as well as for good.

In contrast to preterists, who are both amillennial and postmillennial, I do not see a millennium realized in the past. Instead I view the millennium as being realized in the present and consummated in the future. I hold to both partial fulfillments and final fulfillments of biblical prophecy. Although some prophecies have already been partly fulfilled, their final fulfillment is still to occur.

We must not view the millennium as the core of the Christian hope, since this hope is directed to the eternal kingdom of God in eternity. We should heed this timely admonition of the evangelist Dwight L. Moody: "The word of God nowhere tells me to watch and wait for the coming of the millennium, but for the coming of the Lord."[80] Stanley Grenz here fully expresses my own sentiments:

> Because of the cosmic dimensions of the vision of corporate eschatology, our ultimate goal is not a golden age on earth, whether preceding or following the return of Christ. Rather, we await with eager anticipation a glorious eternal reality, the new heaven and new earth. This alone forms the complete fulfillment of the promises of land and physical blessings given to the ancient people of God and the promise of the fullness of our participation in eternal life proclaimed in the New Testament. Only with the coming of the gloriously re-created cosmos will God make his dwelling with us. And only on the redeemed and transformed creation will we experience full community with nature, with each other and, most important, with God our Creator and Redeemer.[81]

Our mission as Christians is not to build the kingdom of God but to herald its coming—not only in the future but in the past and the present.[82] We are also given the opportunity to demonstrate its power as we put into daily practice the spiritual gifts that form the legacy of faith. Hans Urs von Balthasar trenchantly articulates this biblical vision: "We do not build the kingdom of God on earth by our own efforts (however assisted by grace); the most we can do, through genuine prayer, is to make as much room as possible, in ourselves and in the world, for the kingdom of God, so that its energies can go to work."[83]

In our discussion of the millennium and the last things in general we need to keep in mind that the Bible presents not a finalized system of truth but a multiform witness to truth. It sets us on the way but does not give us a perfected vision of truth. The Bible yields not total consistency in all of its assertions but various viewpoints that can be partially reconciled when taken symbolically, not literally. I vehemently disagree with one dispensationalist author that "there is no essential difference between the language of the Bible and a medical dictionary."[84] It seems that for biblical literalists "the Biblical language is like the language of a science textbook; that is, that its terms have a fixed meaning from beginning to end."[85] Once we acknowledge that biblical language is for the most part poetic or symbolic rather than straightforward—yielding precise history (the view of naïve realism)—we must allow for a healthy dose of agnosticism in our assertions, and this is especially true in the area of eschatology.[86] Now we see through a glass darkly, but then face to face (1 Cor 13:12). The glory that God is preparing for us cannot be contained in human imagination (1 Cor 2:9). We must wait for it in simple faith and go about performing our daily tasks undergirded by the hope that God's grace will conquer in the end. Our real hope is not in history, nor in the millennial unfolding of history, but in the revelation of eternity that will be inaugurated by Jesus Christ in his glorious second appearing at the end of history.

·SIX·

THE RESURRECTION OF THE DEAD

Thy dead shall live, their bodies shall rise.
O dwellers in the dust, awake and sing for joy!
ISAIAH 26:19

I am the one who raises the dead and gives them life again.
Anyone who believes in me, even though he dies like anyone else, shall live again.
JOHN 11:25 LB

Since the day when the Savior rose from the dead,
death is no longer a fearful thing.
ATHANASIUS

With his resurrection the general resurrection begins.
ADRIO KÖNIG

I
n the history of the church the Christian teaching of the resurrection of the body has again and again been challenged by the mystical notion of the inherent immortality of the soul, which has its roots in Platonism and Neoplatonism. Many mainstream theologians have tried to affirm that our immortality is located in resurrection from death. Origen typifies those who emphasize immortality at the expense of resurrection. In his view at the end of the human pilgrimage there will be a complete destruction of the body, "for wherever bodies are, corruption

follows immediately," so the end of all things will be incorporeal.[1] In clear contrast to this position is the Jewish apocryphal book 2 Baruch, which teaches the restoration of exactly the same body that was laid away (2 Baruch 50:2). In the prophetic tradition of Christian faith "soul" does not mean a divine spark within humanity but the totality of a human being in its individual, personal existence (Karl Barth). The whole person can be described as both soul and body at the same time.

The Resurrection of Jesus

The doctrine of the resurrection has its basis in the bodily resurrection of Jesus from the grave. This event has been interpreted in many different ways, and the controversy that it has engendered is still with us. In naturalistic philosophy the very idea of a resurrection miracle is called into question. John Dominic Crossan, one of the leaders of the Jesus Seminar, declares, "I do not think that anyone, anywhere, at any time brings dead people back to life."[2] The apostle Paul voices a strikingly different understanding:

> Now if this is what we proclaim, that Christ was raised from the dead, how can some of you say there is no resurrection of the dead? If there is no resurrection, then Christ was not raised; and if Christ was not raised, then our gospel is null and void, and so too is your faith. . . . If it is for this life only that Christ has given us hope, we of all people are most to be pitied. (1 Cor 15:12-14, 19 REB)

Contemporary theologians are painfully divided on this question. In line with traditional faith some interpret the resurrection of Jesus as a historical occurrence. Among these are Wolfhart Pannenberg, Walter Künneth, N. T. Wright, Michael Horton, Carl Henry, Avery Dulles and Millard Erickson. While by no means disputing the historicity of the resurrection, Erickson reminds us that the evidence we have of Christ actually rising from the dead is not direct but indirect. This evidence includes "the empty tomb and the appearances of Jesus following his crucifixion and burial."[3]

Other theologians prefer to describe Jesus' resurrection as an eschatological event, an encounter with the inbreaking power of the new aeon. Such an event interrupts the course of history and cannot be explained by the causal sequences of history. Karl Barth and Rudolf Bultmann sometimes use this terminology, but their meanings are vastly different. Barth affirms the objective reality of Jesus rising from the dead, but this event, though *in* history is not *of* history. It is not verifiable by historical investigation. Bultmann on the other hand denies an objective, corporeal resurrection and reduces the resurrection to the transforming power of the cross.

Then there are those who interpret Jesus' resurrection as the dawning of a new religious consciousness on the part of the disciples. The resurrection is explained as the experience of a new horizon of freedom. Among religious thinkers who embrace this position, which in effect bows to modern skepticism, are Willi Marxsen,[4] Carl Jung, Gerd Lüdemann,[5] John Shelby Spong[6] and most of the theologians of the Jesus Seminar. Reflecting a concern to maintain the objectivity of the resurrection, Edward Schillebeeckx views Jesus' resurrection as a postmortem revelation of Jesus as living.[7] At the same time he underlines the necessity to participate in "the Easter experience" in order to apprehend the significance of Jesus' death and resurrection.[8]

My own position is that Jesus' resurrection is both historical and eschatological.[9] It occurs in history but is not accessible to historical investigation. It represents an encounter with the One who ushers in the eschaton, the day of glory. Tillich says the resurrection is not a fact but a symbol based on fact. I prefer to say that the resurrection is both factual and existential. It is not only fact but truth that reaches out to us through fact.

Theologians go astray when they either physicalize Jesus' resurrection or spiritualize this event. We are not talking about the resuscitation of a corpse but of the renewal of a self. Nor can this resurrection be reduced to the appearance of a ghostly apparition. Jesus did not rise as spirit only but as a whole person—body, soul and spirit.

The resurrection concerns not simply the risen Christ but the risen Jesus Christ. It signifies not just the preservation of the historical Jesus but the victory of Jesus over sin, death and hell. He conquered death and did not simply reverse death. Faith is not merely assent to his resurrection but union with him in his resurrection. As people of faith we participate in his resurrection (cf. Rom 6:5-10; 1 Pet 1:3).

The resurrection of Christ is first and foremost an event of redemption. It represents the completion of the cross. Forsyth phrased it well: "The Cross alone is no solution without the solution for the Cross itself, the Resurrection, and all its train beyond Christ's death."[10] Jesus' resurrection entails humanity's deliverance from the power of death and not simply an individual survival of death.

Again, Jesus' resurrection is an event of revelation. It is through the power of the risen Christ that we are enabled to see and understand the mystery of Jesus as the living God incarnate. Through God's self-revelation in Christ Thomas was persuaded of the authenticity of Christ's mission and the reality of his deity (Jn 20:26-29). Similarly Paul was converted through being confronted by the risen Christ, and Paul viewed this meeting as a resurrection appearance of Christ.

Finally, the resurrection of Jesus brings us the gift of assurance of our salvation (Acts 17:31). This was one of Calvin's emphases.[11] Yet it is not a rational certainty but an inner conviction that needs to be deepened and renewed through our bearing of the cross in imitation of Christ.

This brings us to the basis of the truth of Jesus' resurrection. My position is that this truth does not rest on historical analysis, for history yields only an approximation, not certainty. The New Testament does give us evidences of Jesus' resurrection, among which are the empty tomb and the appearance of Jesus to his disciples after his death. Yet these are not proofs that can compel reason, because they leave too many unanswered questions. They are evidences, however, that ratify faith. The empty tomb is a sign of the reality of Jesus' resurrection, but divine revelation alone is the cause of our acceptance of belief in this resurrection. The women at the tomb of Jesus believed not because they saw a tomb that was empty but because an angel appeared to them and announced Jesus' resurrection (Mt 28:1-7; Mk 16:5-6). Similarly Paul believed not because he was persuaded by the testimonies of eyewitnesses but because he was personally visited by the risen Christ and heard the voice of Christ with his inner ears (Acts 9, 22).

I agree with Pascal that the Christian faith has many evidences in its support, but it is not these evidences that make us believe.[12] Faith comes as a gift of God through the power of his Spirit in its unity with the evangelical proclamation. This does not imply that an appeal to miracles and evidences has no effect or is always counterproductive. If such an appeal leads one to hear the message of salvation through the cross and resurrection of Christ, then it has some benefit. But if the whole question of faith is made to rest upon attempts to harmonize the data of the four Gospels concerning Christ's resurrection, then the skeptics are aroused to mount counter arguments that sometimes are persuasive to those who reflect on them.

Kierkegaard perhaps minimized the role of faithful reasoning in explicating the truths of divine revelation. Yet his words of caution are worth pondering: "The so-called proofs for the divinity of Christ that people claim Scripture sets forth—his miracles, his resurrection, his ascension—are not, when you think about it, in harmony with our reason. On the contrary, they demonstrate that believing in Christ's works is a matter of faith."[13]

While freely acknowledging the inconsistencies in the resurrection narratives, Karl Barth affirmed that they nonetheless give ample support to the historicity of Christ's resurrection:

Unquestionably, the resurrection narratives are contradictory. A coherent history cannot be evolved from them. The appearances to the women and apostles, in Galilee and Jerusalem, which are reported by the Gospels and Paul, cannot be harmonized. . . . The evangelical theologians of the nineteenth century . . . were wrong in trying to arrange things so as to prove the historicity of the resurrection. Their intention deserved praise. But they should have remembered that even the early Church had not tried to harmonize the resurrection stories. She has really felt that about this unique event there was something of an earthquake for everybody in attendance. The witnesses attended an event that went over their heads, and each told a bit of it. But these scraps are sufficient to bear witness to us of the magnitude of the event and its historicity.[14]

Reformed theologian Michael Horton represents the older view by calling the resurrection "a public event, open to the usual tests for determining the historicity of reports."[15] Like Pannenberg he contends that "if Christianity really is public truth, it must live and move and have its being in the real world and stand up to real challenges in the wide-open spaces."[16] "Unlike the world's religions, Christianity rests its case upon an empty tomb, not on universal reason, experience, morality, values, or the like."[17] In contradistinction to Horton I claim that the truth of our faith rests on the Word and Spirit, not on the outward sign of the empty tomb, though this sign becomes part of the testimony of faith concerning the reality of Christ's resurrection from the dead.

Liberal theologians occasionally argue that the stories of the empty tomb constituted an apologetic for the resurrection devised by church leaders to gain adherents to their faith. In my opinion, the fact that these stories contain numerous discrepancies attests their genuineness as real history, since historical reporting is seldom if ever flawless.

I agree with Calvin that faith rests not on tangible proofs but on the willingness to make a venture of obedience in answer to the command of Christ. We only "know Christ in the right way when we experience the meaning of his death and resurrection within us and as they become effective in us."[18] Calvin insisted that our being willing involves our being made willing by the Holy Spirit. In his theology the truth of the resurrection of Christ is not external or cerebral but existential and spiritual.

James Denney astutely reminds us that the resurrection "is not attested in the gospels by outside witnesses who had inquired into it as the Psychical Research Society inquires into ghost stories; it is attested—in the only way in which it can be attested at all—by people who are within the circle of realities to which it belongs, who share in the life it has begotten, and who therefore know that it is, and can tell what it means."[19]

Yet we must not fall into the spiritualistic error of separating the truth of the resurrection from its historical matrix. Torrance is here surely on target: If "we consider the gospel at its decisive point, in the resurrection of Jesus Christ from the grave, it must be insisted that we empty it of any real or final significance when we think or speak of the resurrection without an empirical correlate in space and time such as the empty tomb."[20]

The Christian proclamation includes wondrous events such as the virgin birth and the empty tomb, but its power does not rest on these things. The Christian message is not that Christ came back to life from beyond the grave but that he rose from the dead for our justification (Rom 4:25). It is possible to believe in the empty tomb and still not believe that Jesus is the Savior from sin.[21] Faith is necessary to perceive the mystery of our salvation accomplished by Christ in his cross and resurrection victory, but this faith is deepened and renewed when we consider the evidences that the Bible itself produces concerning the reality of Christ's resurrection.

Resurrection as Event and Process

The resurrection of the dead constitutes both an event and a process. This is also true of Jesus' resurrection, in which we who believe are included. Jesus rose from the dead at one particular point in history, but the impact of his resurrection resounds throughout history. Resurrection entails in both Jesus' case and ours not simply a coming back to life but a surge of new life. It gives us who are redeemed from sin not only a new spiritual horizon but also a new nature. Through faith we have the assurance that we are now resurrected because we participate in Christ's resurrection. We are also granted the certainty that we will be resurrected because Christ has given us victory over the grave.

The underlying concern of this chapter is with the final destination of humanity, particularly the new humanity in Christ. These are the saints—those who believe and obey through the power of grace. Sanctity is integrally related to the mystery of predestination. Just as "the Father raises the dead and gives them life, so also the Son gives life to whom he will" (Jn 5:21).

When we speak of the resurrection of the dead, we have in mind first of all those who are dead in sin. We need to gain victory over sin before we gain assurance of life beyond the grave. "From sin to righteousness" precedes "from death to life." (cf. Rom 6:18; 1 Pet 2:24; Jn 5:24; 1 Jn 3:14).

Resurrection in its deepest sense involves the whole person—spirit and body. We are raised from the dead through faith, and we are granted assurance of our resurrection as faith works through love. Paul declared, "You also must consider yourselves dead to sin and alive to God in Christ Jesus" (Rom 6:11; cf. Jn 5:24; Eph 2:4-6; Col 2:12-14; 1 Jn 3:14). The process of rebirth and inner renewal occurs when the Holy Spirit applies the fruits of Christ's resurrection to our lives. In Luther's words, "This is done by the Holy Spirit who sanctifies and awakens even the body to this new life, until it is completed in the life beyond."[22]

The resurrection of the dead begins with Jesus Christ—with his coming into the world of sin and death and triumphing over these powers. "I am the resurrection and the life," said our Lord. "He who believes in me, though he die, yet shall he live, and whoever lives and believes in me shall never die" (Jn 11:25-26). Christ's incarnation in human flesh was already a sign that creative and redeeming power was at work in history. The climax of his resurrection occurred in his rising from the grave after his crucifixion. It was then that he became the first fruits of the community of resurrection, which includes all who believe on this side and on the other side of death.

Jesus rose from the dead for our salvation, but we must share in his resurrection if we are to know eternal life. Our resurrection must be a present experience, but it is grounded in a past event in history. Our goal as Christians is to be as he is—risen from the grave and ascended into heaven. Focusing on his triumph over sin, death and the devil, we look forward to the resurrection of our bodies on the last day, the event of the parousia when Christ will be present with us visibly in the new world (cf. Rom 8:18-25; Phil 3:11).

Our resurrection as a present reality begins in faith and repentance. In faith we pass from death to life (Jn 5:24; 1 Jn 3:14; Eph 2:4-6). In faith we already partake of the powers of the age to come (Heb 6:5). Even at our baptism we were buried and raised with him. In the mystical union effectuated by baptism and faith we are united with the risen Christ. In the power of faith we participate in both his sufferings and his resurrection power (Phil 3:10).

Resurrection in reference to both Jesus and the saints involves transformation. We are not only turned in a new direction (converted), but we experience a re-creation in the image of Christ. We become a "new creation" (2 Cor 5:17). We participate in the glory that is still to come. Sanctification as a present experience leads into glorification as a new reality. We are baptized into the regenerating power of the risen Christ, which sets us on the road to future glory. Paul describes it as an ongoing process in which we already experience eschatological glory: "And we all, with unveiled face, beholding the glory of the Lord, are being changed into his likeness from one degree of glory to another" (2 Cor 3:18).

Evangelical theology speaks not of the resurrection of the flesh but of the resurrection of the person. It entails both soul and body. The inner person who persists after death includes the somatic as well as the psychic part of humanity (Pierre Emery).[23] Karl Rahner urges us always to bear in mind that "given the substantial unity of man, which takes ontological precedence over the pluralism of his constituent principles, a statement about the 'body' is also one about the 'soul' and vice versa; that the dead man can neither be thought of as wholly departed nor yet as subject to space and time in the same way as those still living."[24] According to C. H. Dodd, Paul does not mean by "body" anything material, but "the organic principle which makes a man a self-identical individual, persisting through all changes in the 'substance' through which he realizes himself, whether material or non-material."[25]

The body is under the promise of resurrection, but the "flesh" is the power of death that must be destroyed (Cullmann). While soul and body must be distinguished (cf. Mt 10:28; 1 Thess 5:23), the soul always seeks and needs some kind of bodily form. Soul and body are therefore inseparable. The body is necessary for a restored humanity as a means of fellowship, communication and identification.

Both soul and body participate in the drama of the new birth (Rom 8:10-11). The healing process touches both, as is amply demonstrated in the miracles of Jesus. When Jesus forgives sin, those ensnared in sin are frequently healed in body as well. Yet the renewal of the body is provisional and temporal. The renewal of the inner person, on the other hand, is permanent. Our outer nature is wasting away, but our inner nature is being renewed daily (2 Cor 4:16). The physical body must finally be discarded (2 Pet 1:14). Yet it serves as the vehicle for the new body, the spiritual body.

Jesus is the first fruits of the new humanity (1 Cor 15:20). We shall be like him in the eschatological culmination (Phil 3:21). Our body will be like his glorious body. His bodily resurrection is a sign of our future resurrection—when we will receive the gift of an incorruptible body. We need to remember that Jesus too was given a new body. He appeared to his disciples but "in another form" (Mk 16:12). In his case there was perfect continuity between the old body and the new because his body was not corrupted by sin. In our case there will be a substantial but not exact identity between the old and the new. Yet even in Jesus' case there was no exact identity. His appearance was markedly altered after his resurrection. Mary Magdalene, his disciples on the seashore and the two men on the way to Emmaus did not at first recognize him (cf. Jn 20:11-18; 21:4; Lk 24:13-43).

We must refrain from drawing the conclusion that only the spirit of

Christ was resurrected. Our Lord declared, "A spirit has not flesh and bones as you see that I have" (Lk 24:39). Yet his new body was at the same time spiritual, and it steadily became more spiritualized in his postmortem encounters with his disciples. He ate food on the Emmaus road (Lk 24:13-35), but he also passed through closed doors (Jn 20:19, 26). He broke bread with his disciples (Jn 21:13), but at his ascension he was elevated into heaven and became invisible (Acts 1:9). Nor was he visible to the naked eye on the Damascus Road where he confronted Paul (Acts 9:7).

Even in the case of Jesus we can surmise that the resurrection was a process as well as an event. His body was not resuscitated but transformed. Even in his earthly ministry his body was being renewed and strengthened. His soul was not abandoned to hades nor did his flesh see corruption (Acts 2:31).

Because of his sinless perfection only Christ has the perfectly developed spiritual body. After our deaths as sinful mortals, the soul is not in nakedness, but there is a lack of completeness or wholeness in the spiritual body as it exists. For a perfect and complete spiritual corporeality we must wait for the eschatological fulfillment of all things in the risen and ascended Christ who will then be all in all.

The idea of resurrection as a process of inner transformation completed only on the other side of death will strike many of my readers as novel. While it resonates with certain themes in Christian mysticism, this notion is understandably not prominent in circles that stress crisis over process in Christian conversion. Interestingly it is fully endorsed by Catholic theologian Romano Guardini, who contends that after baptism and faith

> life is a mysterious interchange of becoming and ceasing to be. In all actions, in all happenings, the death of the old man and the resurrection of the new are in continuous process. Dying consists in continuous turning to God, in obedience, self-conquest, renunciation, effort and struggle, in all that we call the imitation of Christ.[26]

The Crisis of Death

The Christian can be said to die two deaths—the death of the "old man" at the time of conversion and then the last death. In Paul's theology death is not a friend or brother but "the last enemy" (1 Cor 15:26; Rom 6:23). The sting of death can be overcome only in Jesus Christ. Death is a sign of past judgment on sin. It is also the doorway to particular judgment.

In the light of Christ's resurrection, death acquires a positive as well as a negative connotation. Death is no longer a barrier to eternal happiness but now a passageway to eternal happiness. Whereas once it was a curse, it now becomes a blessing.[27] For the one who believes, death is no longer a payment for sin but now a dying to sin and entering into life eternal.[28] Bonhoeffer could even describe death as "the supreme festival on the road to freedom."[29] Yet there is still pain in death, and this pain reminds us of God's judgment on sin.

The Christian message, which announces victory over death, stands in palpable contrast to the verdict of philosophy that death is inimical to human destiny. Aristotle spoke of death as that which is most to be feared because "it appears to be the end of everything."[30] Sartre asserted that death "removes all meaning from life."[31] The church father Athanasius brings a new perspective on death: "Since the day when the Savior rose from the dead, death is no longer a fearful thing. All those who believe in Christ know that in dying they no longer perish and that the resurrection will render them incorruptible."[32]

Does the inner person or the spirit die? Jesus declared, "He who hates his life in this world will keep it for eternal life" (Jn 12:25). In 2 Timothy 1:10 we read that Christ "abolished death and brought life and immortality to light through the gospel." In the idealistic and mystical traditions in philosophy the core of the soul is held to be indestructible. As Spinoza phrased it, "The human mind cannot be absolutely destroyed with the body," for "there remains of it something which is eternal."[33] By contrast Lutheran theologian T. A. Kantonen rightly observes that the Bible knows nothing of an immortality of the person but only of an enduring personal relationship with Christ.[34] The Psalmist confesses, "My flesh and my heart may fail, but God is the strength of my heart and my portion for ever" (Ps 73:26). Not only the flesh, the bodily structure, of the human person is destroyed at death but also the heart—the center of the personality (Kantonen). Yet the whole person is immediately revived and restored by the Spirit of God after the interruption of death. In the Christian understanding death is not annihilation but the suspension of consciousness and radical suffering.

In one sense the Christian already experiences the power of the resurrection and therefore cannot die. Jesus was adamant that the one who eats of the bread from heaven will "not die" (Jn 6:50). "If any one keeps my word, he will never see death" (Jn 8:51; cf. Jn 11:25-26). Assuredly the human spirit tastes death but is then revived and carried to a new and higher level (cf. Heb 11:35). Thomas Aquinas held that the soul experiences death as the form of the body but lives on in a new form.[35] Jesus himself was put to death in the flesh, but he was then made alive in the Spirit (1 Pet 3:18). Flesh and blood cannot inherit the kingdom (1 Cor 15:50), but the mortal does put on immortality (1 Cor 15:53-54).

At death we fall not into nothingness but into the hands of the living God. Death is not a rupture in the ascent of spirit to God but only a temporary break. It marks not the end of life but the transition from this life to the life to come. To depart from this world is to be with Christ (Phil 1:23). The first martyr Stephen was received by Christ at death (Acts 7:54-60). In Luke 16:22 we read the "the poor man died and was carried by the angels to Abraham's bosom." As he was dying on the cross, Jesus assured the thief who was crucified with him: "Truly, I say to you, today you will be with me in Paradise" (Lk 23:43). In John Bunyan's *Pilgrim's Progress* the passage through the river of death leads immediately to the heavenly city.[36]

Scripture makes clear that even unbelievers will be carried through death (cf. Dan 12:2; Jn 5:28-29; Acts 24:15). But they are resurrected not unto life but unto judgment. They find themselves in the shadowy existence of sheol or hades. Their soul is translated not into paradise but into the nether world of spirits.[37]

Even in the interim state the human spirit is not disembodied. Indeed, we who die in Christ will be further clothed (2 Cor 5:1-5). At death we put on a heavenly dwelling. Paul may be thinking in this context of the last day, but the day of our death is also a last day for us. At the time of our death we are raised up to new life. We will be invested with glorified bodies and will be like angels (Lk 20:34-36).[38] Angels are clothed in heavenly garb, though they have the appearance of mortals (Dan 8:15).

Paul declared, "It is sown a physical body, it is raised a spiritual body. If there is a physical body, there is also a spiritual body" (1 Cor 15:44). And again in Philippians 3:21: "He will transfigure the body belonging to our humble state, and give it a form like that of his own resplendent body, by the very power which enables him to make all things subject to himself" (NEB). The resurrected state beyond death can be aptly described as a "spiritual corporeality" (Emil Brunner).

Oscar Cullmann errs by denying any continuity in bodily existence in the immediate hereafter.[39] Even Samuel in sheol was portrayed as being wrapped in a robe (1 Sam 28:14). The saints on the Mount of Transfiguration were in bodily form, since Peter wished to make booths for them (Mt 17:3-4; Mk 9:4-5). The saints in paradise are pictured as being "clothed in white robes" (Rev 7:9; cf. 6:11). The two witnesses in Revelation 11 are raised bodily into heaven (Rev 11:12). A bodily assumption into heaven is also associated with Enoch and Elijah and, of course, with Jesus himself. The common understanding in biblical times was that the dead are clothed in some kind of body (1 Cor 15:35).

The earliest Christian tradition speaks of the faithful passing straight from this bodily death to Christ. This idea is also expressed in the Second Helvetic Confession. It is ably defended by W. D. Davies in his *Paul and Rabbinic Judaism*.[40] In Roman Catholicism the assumption of Mary is interpreted as a revelation of what will happen to all believers at the time of their deliverance from death.[41]

The resurrection body, which is being built up within us now and which we will receive in fuller form at death, is a new creation. It stands in both continuity and discontinuity with the natural body. The natural body undergoes corruption, not annihilation. By analogy the seed is not annihilated but is changed substantially into the plant which springs from it (Winklhofer).[42] This is only an analogy and must therefore be treated with caution. Note that in this analogy the hull or outer covering of the seed is discarded. Death can also be likened to a plant taken out into the scorching sun. The plant soon wilts and decomposes, but then it emerges as a vision of delight when rain (grace) falls upon it. Still another analogy, found in church tradition, is that of the caterpillar that is encased in a cocoon and then rises up as a beautiful butterfly.

In 1 Corinthians 15 Paul speaks of a celestial body and a terrestrial body, a spiritual body and a physical body. He also refers to different kinds of seed. To each kind of seed is given its own body (1 Cor 15:38). It is sown a physical body and raised a spiritual body (1 Cor 15:44). The important thing is that nothing of significance is really lost. The inward person who persists after death includes the somatic as well as the psychic part of the human creation. The Bible teaches not the rehabilitation or resuscitation of the physical body but its transformation as well as its elevation. What Lazarus, the son of the widow of Nain and Jairus' daughter experienced was resuscitation through the power of the Spirit. What Jesus and the saints who follow him experience is victory over death and the passage to a glorified state beyond the pale of death.

In the resurrection we will not have the very same body that we have now. I state this against a rationalistic form of orthodoxy. There is no material identity, for the two disciples on the road to Emmaus did not recognize Jesus. I would argue for a formal identity. What we have is a body that corresponds to the physical body, indeed is rooted in it. There is a material continuity but not a reduplication. We should note that though Jesus rose bodily from the dead it is also true that "he appeared in another form" (Mk 16:12). This will surely hold true for all who are in Christ as well.

We can say that at death the *soma* (body) of the believer is changed from *sarx* (flesh), which by its very essence decays, into *doxa* (glory)—the divine element.[43] The new body will be characterized by solidity, denseness and substantiality. Paul is quite emphatic: "Flesh and blood cannot inherit the kingdom of God, nor does the perishable inherit the imperishable" (1 Cor 15:50). Luther shares this enduring insight: "Because flesh and blood cannot enter into the Kingdom of God it must cease, die and pass away and rise in a new spiritual being in order to reach heaven."[44] Alan Richardson concludes that in the glorified or raptured state we shall possess means of expression, identification and recognition.[45]

The state of those in the beyond is often characterized as one of sleep. Those who sleep still live with Christ (1 Thess 5:10). For Calvin this means rest from our worldly labors. This should not be confused with the sleep of death, which is equivalent to being dead in sin (Ps 13:3; Eph 5:14). Resurrection means awakening from this sleep and rising from the dead (Eph 5:14). To fall asleep in Christ is something better than remaining in the flesh (1 Cor 15:17-19; Phil 1:21). It is "to depart and be with Christ" (Phil 1:21-24). To be "away from the body" is to be "at home with the Lord" (2 Cor 5:8).

The state of the dead is not a sort of "soul-sleep." Rather the term "sleep" is a euphemism for death—one that indicates the manner of dying to some extent and also the meaning of death for the Christian. Those who die in Christ (1 Thess 4:16) have the terror of death behind them—they are at rest (Rev 14:13). Because the dead are in Christ they may be said to be "asleep," though outwardly death retains its character as the enemy. Because Christ is risen, the dead in Christ do not perish in death (1 Cor 15:16-23). The term "asleep" in its biblical context is therefore theological and eschatological, not anthropological.

What Paul means by being asleep in Christ corresponds to what Hebrews means by entering God's rest (Heb 4:1-11). I would agree with

Robert Bailey that "sleep" is not the most felicitous term for the interim state.[46] It is well to note that Jesus speaks of "falling asleep" as a name for death (Jn 11:11). Jeremias avers that "the idea of soul-sleeping is foreign to the entire New Testament as well as to late Judaism."[47] The view of antiquity was that in sleep the soul leaves the body. In the Christian worldview we are resurrected from the state of sleep into active service in the kingdom of God.

The Final Resurrection

The resurrection of the dead has its *telos* and *finis* in the parousia, the second advent, final glorification. Christ will come to judge both the living and the dead (Jn 5:25-29; 6:39-40). According to the apostle Paul, "There is an order to this resurrection: Christ was raised first; then when Christ comes back, all his people will be raised" (1 Cor 15:23 NLT).

The final resurrection is both the culmination of a process and the crisis of world history. It is both the renewal of the world and an event or series of events that marks the end of the world. It is both the fulfillment of the millennial hope and the realization of the eternal hope.

The idea of two resurrections is alluded to several times in the New Testament (cf. Jn 11:23-26; 1 Cor 15:20-23; Rev 20:4-6). The first resurrection is the spiritual resurrection of the dead through faith. The second is the physical or bodily resurrection at the consummation of world history. The final resurrection indicates the elevation of those who believe to the glorious presence of the Lord Jesus Christ.

We are resurrected now by virtue of being made participants in Christ's resurrection through the power of the Holy Spirit. We will be resurrected then when Christ comes again to set up his kingdom that shall have no end. The last day is not to be confused with the moment of death (cf. 2 Tim 2:18; 4:6-8), but the moment of death marks a transition to what is final and ultimate in the eschatological panorama.

Some scholars hold that the eschatological day of the Lord will comprise the revelation in bodily or earthly form of what we already are in Christ. The parousia will in other words also be an *apocalypsis* (revelation). At the same time the unfolding of the eschatological drama will involve a new creation, the fulfillment of the process of glorification. It will constitute a resurrection not only from the state of sin but also from historical time.

In Christian tradition, at the last day the spirit will be united with the natural body. The truth in this idea is that nothing of significance will really be lost. The untruth is that it denies that the final body is a new creation. There will be a substantial though not material identity between our resurrected bodies and our natural bodies.[48] At the moment of death we are clothed with an incorruptible body. When Christ comes again, we will be reclothed with a glorified body that is eternal. We can also say that on that final day of judgment the saints in Christ will be revealed in bodily form.

The general resurrection involves a transformation of matter itself. Irenaeus declared, "Not only is matter susceptible of salvation but the salvation of man, the resurrection, implies the salvation of matter."[49] We look forward not only to a heavenly eternity but to a new heaven-earth in which the material will be taken up into the spiritual.

At the moment of death when we are taken up into glory, the earthly garment is discarded, but our resurrection is both bodily and spiritual. Käsemann phrases it well: "Redemption naturally takes place ultimately when the earthly body is put off, but it also involves the conferring of a new corporeality."[50]

We can say that in the general resurrection what is now hidden will be made public. There will be a materialization or making visible of what is now invisible. The events that comprise the eschatological consummation can only be described in metaphorical language, for their glory transcends the human imagination (1 Cor 2:9).[51]

Church tradition has attested that the various dimensions or poles of the reality of the resurrection are manifested in the celebration of the eucharist. In John 6:54 our Lord says, "He who eats my flesh and drinks my blood has eternal life, and I will raise him up at the last day." To "raise up" in this context means to be elevated into the presence of

God. We now participate in the body and blood of Christ as we eat of the bread and drink of the cup, and at the same time we proclaim the Lord's death till he comes (1 Cor 10:16; 11:26; Mt 26:26-29).

The final goal of the resurrection process has been variously described as glorification, deification and entire sanctification. Already in faith we participate in the divine energies. But on the last day there will be a deepening of faith, a fuller and richer participation in the energies of God. In the words of K. E. Kirk: "The final revelation of God's greatness will not merely engross our vision, but transform our characters . . . so that we ourselves become a part of the manifestation of His true nature."[52] God will be glorified in us, and we will be glorified in God.

Finally we should note that resurrection in its biblical context is a cosmic hope. We hope not simply for our own salvation but also for the redemption of the cosmos. We look forward not only to heavenly glory but also to the renewal of the world. Paul speaks of the whole creation "groaning in travail" as it awaits the glorious coming of Christ (Rom 8:22). In the words of one interpreter, "The hope of the created order is bound up . . . with 'the revealing of the sons of God' (vs. 19)."[53] For Paul "the resurrection of the dead was no mere symbol of openness to the future but the end of earthly pain."[54] This means that the gospel "is good news not only for humanity but for the entire world of nature and history."[55] "Resurrection hope is a total hope that embraces the future of society and the world. Its scope is universal and cosmic. On account of Christ crucified and risen in the end God will be all in all, totally present in everyone and everything."[56]

Our immortality is not something inherent in our natures but something conferred upon us by a gracious God. We have our immortality in him who was crucified on our behalf and who rose from the dead for our redemption. We already have a glimpse of this immortality through faith, but we will be given tangible proof of its reality when we shall appear before Jesus Christ who is both our Judge and our Savior and receive the invitation to "drink the water of life without charge" (Rev 22:17 NLT).[57]

·SEVEN·

THE INTERIM STATE

The souls of the upright are in the hands of God,
and no torment can touch them.
To the unenlightened, they appeared to die
. . . but they are at peace.

WISDOM OF SOLOMON 3:1-3 NJB

The souls of Christ's disciples go to the invisible place
determined for them by God and there dwell awaiting the Resurrection.

IRENAEUS

In the interim, the soul does not sleep but is awake
and enjoys the vision of angels and of God, and has converse with them.

MARTIN LUTHER

Paradise is only the porch of heaven. . . .
It is in heaven only that there is fullness of joy;
the pleasures that are at God's right hand for evermore.

JOHN WESLEY

I n the early centuries of the church it was quite common to postu-
late an interim state of partial happiness and mitigated suffering
between death and the final resurrection on the last day. This belief was gradually edged out by the belief that the souls of the righteous
at their death go directly to heaven and the souls of the imperfect go to
purgatory. The very ungodly end in hell. This view was given official
sanction by Pope Benedict XII in his bull *Benedictus Deus* (1336). In my

opinion this development marked a significant break with the biblical and apostolic consensus in which the interim state of hades played a major role. Nevertheless, in their discussion of Christ's descent into hell the doctors of the medieval church made a place for an interim state of rest within hell for those earmarked for salvation.[1] In popular evangelicalism today the only worlds beyond seem to be heaven and hell (the place of the damned). We need a new statement on this subject that does justice to the biblical and apostolic witness to the reality of various worlds beyond.

The Worlds Beyond

Among the worlds beyond is the heavenly world of the angels, which is duly acknowledged by the mainstream of church tradition. There are visible heavens but also invisible heavens, and both are created by God. The angels form a link between the invisible God and the visible creation. This earth is also the realm of angelic visitation, for angels are active in both the church militant and the church triumphant.

Another world beyond is the nether world of spirits called in biblical and ecclesiastical tradition by various names, including sheol, hades and limbo.[2] It is also referred to as "the pit" (Ps 30:3), "the grave," "corruption" and "the depths of the earth." In Hebraic spirituality sheol was originally a vague subterranean place where souls live a grim life, sometimes pictured as devoid even of consciousness. It was an endless dwelling place for good and bad alike. But in later Old Testament history sheol became a temporary dwelling for the dead before the resurrection and judgment. In the apocrypha and in apocalyptic literature hades is sometimes pictured as an intermediate state where the dead await the resurrection.[3] It is variously portrayed in Scripture as a place of darkness (Job 10:21-22), a place of silence (Ps 94:17) and a place of forgetfulness (Ps 88:12). It is a place without knowledge of what transpires on earth (Job 14:21). What is important to keep in mind is that God is present in sheol or hades and in absolute control (cf. 1 Sam 2:6; Job 26:6; Ps 86:13; 139:8). Peter in Acts 2:31 proclaims that Jesus was not left in hades, thereby implying a visit to the underworld. This idea is also present in Ephesians 4:9 and 1 Peter 3:19; 4:6.

Another supernatural realm testified to in Scripture is the unworld of the demons, variously called the desert (*midbār*) and the watery chaos (*tehôm*). It is also depicted as the sea, the nether darkness, the bottomless pit and the depth. In Ephesians 2:2 it is described as the air as over against the sky. In Daniel 7:3 the four great beasts are pictured as coming from the sea. Originally the heavens were the habitation of the demons. But when they conspired in rebellion against God they were cast out of heaven into the outer darkness. This darkness is not an eternal realm as is the heaven of God, but darkness came into being through angelic sin. In the Old Testament the origin of evil was a primordial chaos or nether darkness, but it became personified as Rahab, Leviathan, the dragon and then finally Satan.

In Scripture this world is the temporary abode of the demons. But they are intruders, for they belong to another realm—antithetical to justice and order. Yet through their schemes they have captured control of this world (cf. Mt 11:12). They have even infiltrated heaven and have lured other angels into following their example (cf. Eph 6:12). It is in light of this fact that we can understand Job 15:15: "Behold, God puts no trust in his holy ones, and the heavens are not clean in his sight" (cf. Job 4:18).

The demons are consigned to the lowest place in sheol-hades (cf. Jude 6-7; 2 Pet 2:4; Rev 20:1-3). The abyss and "Tartarus" (2 Pet 2:4) could be equivalent to the "lowest Sheol" (cf. Deut 32:22; Ps 86:13). Hades is sometimes identified by the church fathers with Tartarus and sometimes distinguished from it. Tartarus is occasionally portrayed as a different and lower region than hades. I believe that it is more in keeping with the unfolding of biblical revelation to distinguish the abyss or Tartarus from the general abode of the dead. The proper abode of the demons is the nether gloom, but they do not remain there. They have allies or collaborators in the heavens, and they have captured the earth. Calvin Schoonhoven differentiates between "the wholly demonic" (Eph 6:12; 1 Cor 15:24) and the essentially loyal but imperfect powers (cf. Job 15:15).[4]

Some of the fathers, though not the earliest ones, associated the binding of Satan in Matthew 12:29 with the triumph of Christ over the devil as the ruler of hades. Christ triumphed in his descent into hades, thereby breaking the rule or power of the devil. In the new age Satan is bound (Rev 20:2), but he can still menace God's good creation through the power of the lie. He cannot deceive the chosen of God, who see through his subterfuges through the gift of the discerning of spirits.

The apostle Paul is adamant that Christ will eventually bring all things in subjection to him, things "in heaven and on earth and under the earth" (Phil 2:10). The saints, who are now united with Christ, will be his emissaries and will take part in the judging of angels (1 Cor 6:3).

It is well to keep in mind that the language Scripture employs in describing the drama of redemption is for the most part figurative and poetic, not literal or univocal. We must not confuse scriptural metaphors with spiritual realities; on the other hand, we are able to grasp the latter only by means of the former. Our grasp is not comprehensive, however, but partial and broken. We look forward to a more complete understanding when God becomes all in all.

We must also consider paradise as a world beyond—the present abode of the glorified saints. This is the interim state of the blessed. Like hades it pertains to "the near hereafter" as opposed to "the far hereafter."[5] This distinction corresponds to one made in late Jewish thought between the heavenly paradise and the final paradise of the world to come.[6] Like the angelic heavens, paradise belongs to the realm of created light as opposed to uncreated light. But whereas there is darkness in the angelic heavens because of the angelic rebellion, there is no darkness in paradise.

Paradise has been variously described as "Abraham's bosom" (Lk 16:22), "the second heaven" and "under the altar" (Rev 6:9). Purgatory might be depicted as the forecourt of paradise or the gateway to paradise. John Wesley relegated paradise to the upper section of hades.

Biblical scholar Joachim Jeremias doubts whether Abraham's bosom in Luke 16 refers to a part of hades. It may be more felicitous to describe it as an interim heaven. In Luke 10:15 Jesus makes a distinction between hades and heaven.

Still another world beyond is hell—the future state of the damned. It is not simply the state of the dead (as is hades). It is gehenna, the inferno, the lake of fire. It is a thoroughly eschatological concept. Admittedly gehenna was sometimes seen in Hebraic thought as a part of sheol. In *The Book of Enoch* gehenna was portrayed as the lowest section of sheol (*1 Enoch* 18:11-16; 27:2-3; 90:26). In late rabbinic (post-Christian) thought gehenna and hades came to be identified. Another strand regarded gehenna as a kind of purgatory. I believe it is consonant with the deepest insights of both Scripture and tradition to distinguish between gehenna and hades, hell and the so-called nether world of spirits. Scripture is clear that hades itself will eventually be cast into the lake of fire (Rev 20:14). It is possible to speak of those who reject the gospel as being in hell now insofar as their condemnation is sealed, but the final rejection lies before them.

Finally, there is the eternal heaven, the abode of God himself. This heaven signifies the very presence of God. According to Barth, eternity is God's spaciality. This spaciality is identical with his being. There is a spaciality that belongs to him. God's heaven is therefore distinguished from the creaturely heavens (both visible and invisible). God is also present in the angelic heavens. Yet he himself is beyond the highest heaven (1 Kings 8:27). The eternal heaven is at the same time the new heaven, which includes the new earth. This has been variously described as the holy city, the kingdom of God, Mount Zion, the new Jerusalem and the state of glory. The new heaven-earth is earth taken up into heaven, God's eternity. It participates in the realm of uncreated light. It constitutes both an earthly heaven and a heavenly earth. God's eternity suffuses the new heaven-earth. It is a new creation, but it exists for eternity.

The new heaven-earth and hell are future realities. Paradise and hades are present realities. They have their existence in the perspective of eternity, but they are temporal or provisional rather than everlasting. The new heaven-earth is an extension of the presence of God. It is also a new creation of God.

Paradise is a kind of interim heaven, just as hades is a kind of interim hell. These are fluid concepts where the meaning is not always fixed. Paradise will eventually merge into heaven, and hades into hell.

The saints or the people of God are already seated "in the heavenly places" (Eph 2:6). Our glorification begins now in the struggle of faith. We are continually being changed from one degree of glory to another (2 Cor 3:18). When Christ appears at his second advent, we will be taken up into his glory and made to reflect his image.

In the strict sense, the interim state constitutes the world of spirits (hades) and paradise. But these realities are not the intermediate state of much traditional theology. At this juncture I am saying little or nothing about purgatory, though this concept will be considered in the last section of this chapter. We as the people of God are already in God's presence. Yet we look forward to the consummation of his kingdom when millennial glory will become eternal glory.

Paradise

I concur with ancient church tradition that the interim state of the blessed is paradise, though it can also be described by other names. Jesus assured the thief on the cross: "Truly I tell you: today you will be with me in Paradise" (Lk 23:43 REB). Paul testifies that at his conversion he was "caught up into Paradise" (2 Cor 12:2-3). Paradise is not the realm of the dead but a place of superabundant life, of resurrection life. The dead in Christ have been made alive by the Spirit of Christ. They constitute the church triumphant, though they are also involved in the church militant.[7]

In his retort to the Sadducees Jesus implied that Abraham, Isaac and Jacob are not dead but living (Mt 22:32). He also contended that Abraham saw the day of the Lord and rejoiced (Jn 8:56). Again, Jesus insisted that the dead are equal to angels (Lk 20:34-38) and therefore cannot die anymore.

Against Cullmann I hold that the saints on the other side are not in a state of nakedness but are clothed in a resurrection body. They have not disembodied life but newly embodied life. They are clothed in a spiritual corporeality. Paul referred to them as "the saints in light" (Col 1:12).

The beatific vision begins in paradise (Jn 17:24; Acts 7:54-60). It can nevertheless be anticipated now (cf. 2 Cor 12:3). In his *Commentary on Genesis* Luther categorically stated: "In the interim, the soul does *not* sleep but is awake and enjoys the vision of angels and of God, and has converse with them."[8] Yet the sojourn of the saints is not fulfilled in perfect beatitude until the parousia of Christ on earth or the eschaton (1 Cor 13:12). Only then will we see the plan of God in its full manifestation. Only then will the kingdom of Christ be consummated in the eternal kingdom of God.

The eminent Reformed theologian P. T. Forsyth was convinced that the dead in Christ are not in some subterranean sheol but in the very presence of Christ:

> The dead in Christ see a more wondrous Christ than we do—the same, indeed, yesterday, today and for ever, yet another. There is a new departure for them in Christ's work, which is greater than when their eyes were opened to Him here, even as the second creation is greater than the first. Christ's contact with the dead is a new and greater phase of the new creation.[9]

Paradise is not a state of vulnerability as is hades. It is not the underworld but a preliminary realm of glory. In Acts 7:54-60 we are told that Stephen already beheld the glory of God at his death. Jesus was standing ready to welcome him into his immediate presence. Paul spoke of being caught up into the rapture of paradise (2 Cor 12:3). It is in light of his firm conviction of life after death on a higher level that we can understand his otherwise enigmatic words: "To live is Christ, and to die is gain" (Phil 1:21).

Although they still do not possess their final resurrection body, the spirits of the dead in Christ are nevertheless clothed in heavenly garments. Some are depicted as being in white robes (Rev 6:11), a symbol for bodily existence. It is well to note that Samuel in his visitation from the dead was also clothed in a robe, giving him the appearance of a god (1 Sam 28:13-14). I believe Loraine Boettner is in error in his assertion that in the intermediate state we have no body and no sense.[10]

In Revelation 14 the 144,000, the symbol for the company of the redeemed, are pictured as being in the very presence of Christ. These are the ones who have experienced the "first resurrection" (Rev 20:5). We are indeed closer to God in paradise than in our earthly, bodily existence (2 Cor 5:6-8).

Originally in Hebraic and churchly speculation paradise was located in hades. This notion continued in the church for many centuries.[11] There was already a change of thought, however, in the intertestamental and early church periods. The Wisdom of Solomon speaks of the righteous dead as being in the immediate presence of God (Wisdom of Solomon 3:1-3; cf. 4 Maccabees 7:19; 13:17; 16:25; 17:18).[12] This idea steadily gained ground among the church fathers. Tertullian contended that although paradise is not in heaven, "it is yet higher than hell . . . and is appointed to afford an interval of rest to the souls of the righteous, until the consummation of all things shall complete the resurrection of all men with the 'full recompense of their reward.'"[13] John Wesley presented this picture of the interim state of the blessed: "We cannot tell, indeed, how we shall then exist or what kind of organs we shall have: the soul will not be encumbered with flesh and blood; but probably it will have some sort of ethereal vehicle, even before God clothes us 'with our nobler house of empyrean light.'"[14]

It is important to recognize that only Jesus has attained the incorruptible, eternal body. Enoch, Elijah, Samuel and the saints who rose with Jesus (Mt 27:52-53) have new bodies, but they still await the glorious consummation of God's kingdom. Enoch and Elijah had passed through death without undergoing the decomposition of their bodies, though we can surmise that their bodies were transfigured. Their assumption into heaven anticipated the resurrection of Christ, but it played no role in the procuring of our salvation. Only Jesus was raised for our justification (Rom 4:25), only he conquered death and banished the powers of darkness.

In Roman Catholic tradition we encounter the dogma of the assumption of Mary, the mother of Christ. This may have some basis in Revelation 12:1-2 which speaks of the heavenly mother, though most scholars agree that these verses refer to the church, not to Mary. Mary's assumption has no solid grounding in either Scripture or patristic tradition, but it does speak to the yearnings of the human soul for the redemption of our material bodies. From my perspective it should be treated as no more than a pious opinion, never as a dogma of faith. At the most it can be regarded as a revelation of what happens to all Christians at the time of their death. It means not that we are exempt from death but that we shall come through death into victory. In evangelical perspective Mary's assumption is not a special privilege that pertains only to her but a special disclosure of what is in store for all faithful believers in Christ.[15]

There is much speculation but also abiding truth in the notion that the saints grow or progress in paradise. Even in a state of perfect sanctification one is still able to grow "in wisdom and in stature," as did Jesus himself (Lk 2:52). Scripture speaks of degrees of glory (1 Cor 3:18), the lowest levels beginning in this life (cf. Heb 12:23). Scripture also holds out the promise of a final incorruptible or eternal body. This is not a refurbished natural body but a body that has been transformed and recreated (1 Cor 15:35-49).

All the saints, on this side and the other side of death, exist in a state of expectation and waiting (cf. Heb 11:40; Rev 6:11). The "time of their visitation" is still ahead of them (Wisdom of Solomon 3:7).[16] Calvin envisioned the interim state as one of *beatitudo* and *expectatio*. In Christ and beyond death we have the vision of God, but we still await the final resurrection of the body.

The saints on the other side are depicted in Scripture and holy tradition as being in a state of sleep or rest—but only from worldly labors (Rev 14:13). They are now engaged in the new work of intercession in which they rest neither day nor night (Rev 4:8). The biblical "rest" is not "the suspension of work, but the untroubled fructification of work."[17] With a "quickened sense and heightened joy" they serve God still.[18] The *rest* of the saints is analogous to the sabbath rest, which Jesus reaffirmed but also reinterpreted. Our mandate as followers of Jesus is to depart from the routines of daily living on this day and devote ourselves to the work of kingdom service; we are to subordinate all other concerns to this end.

In paradise there will be perfect love and perfect holiness but not perfect peace or perfect joy. Neither will there be perfect knowledge. In the words of John Wesley, "Paradise is only the porch of heaven. . . . It is in heaven only that there is the fullness of joy; the pleasures that are at God's right hand for evermore."[19] The glorified saints will have perfect fellowship with God but not perfect fellowship with the children of God, since the church militant still battles against death and oppression. The martyrs under the altar continue to cry, "How long?" (Rev 6). The saints on the other side pray that God's justice might be revealed and vindicated.

Scripture is clear that the saints in the state of glory have still not received all that had been promised (Heb 11:39). Apart from us they shall not be made perfect (Heb 11:40). Their happiness is dependent on our redemption. In the words of Bernard of Clairvaux: "Many among us are already in the courtyards waiting until the number of their brethren shall be complete; into this blessed house they shall not enter without us, that is to say: no saints without the whole body."[20] According to Taizé brother Pierre-Yves Emery, the departed saints "will wait until the end of the world for us, the believers still on earth, to fulfill their ministry, their works, their crown, their joy."[21]

During the messianic age, in which we now live, the martyr saints rule with Christ over the kingdoms of the earth. They rule not from an earthly Jerusalem but from heaven (as does Christ). They will also accompany Christ in the final battle against Satan. Moreover, they will take part in judging the rulers on earth. Paul intimates that all of God's saints will have a role in ruling and judging (cf. 1 Cor 6:1-3; 1 Thess 3:13; cf. Wis of Sol 3:7-8; Jude 14-15; Rev 19:14; 20:4).

Paradise is the church triumphant, but the church triumphant is still engaged in the ongoing struggle against death and darkness. In the new heaven-earth the church triumphant will be transmuted into the eternal kingdom of God. Now we as believers proceed from one degree of glory to another (2 Cor 3:18), but we shall not reach the pinnacle—uninterrupted joy and peace—until we are joined with all our brothers and sisters in Christ in the grand finale of Christ's cosmic victory over chaos and unrighteousness.

The Nether World of Spirits

Both Scripture and early church tradition lend support to the notion of a nether world of spirits as a place of waiting for the parousia at the end of time. In the Old Testament this place is called sheol, and in the New Testament it is known as hades. The two are virtually identical in Acts 2:27 where Peter quotes from Psalm 16:10. Hades originally had two levels—one for the good and one the bad—but as Christian thought developed, paradise was ever more differentiated from hades. Irenaeus, Justin and Tertullian still held that hades was a twofold state, of preliminary bliss for the righteous and preliminary woe for the ungodly. Ignatius and Cyprian and later Augustine separated hades and paradise. They believed the souls of the righteous go immediately into the presence of the glorified Christ, and this would make paradise a kind of interim heaven.[22] Purgatory was not taught by the early fathers, though it has its roots in ideas of purification after death circulated by Augustine and others.[23] In later Roman Catholic theology hades becomes hell—a place of unending torment.

What is not so well known is that a considerable number of the fathers and teachers of the early church held out the possibility of redemption in hades. They based their appeal, moreover, on holy Scripture as well as on apocryphal books that supplement Scripture. It is well to examine some of the texts that tend to support the view that redemption extends to the nether world of spirits.

The Scriptures have much to say on this important question. Psalm 49:15 speaks of the ransoming of the soul from sheol (cf. Ezek 37:12; Hos 13:14; Jon 2:2, 6). Isaiah declares, "Thy dew is a dew of light, and on the land of the shades [sheol] thou wilt let it fall" (Is 26:19). In the apocryphal 2 Maccabees 12:43-45 intercession and sacrifice are offered so that those who have fallen in battle may be delivered from their sins.[24] The dead in hades are said to profit and find deliverance by the intercession of the living. In Matthew 27 we read of the saints who were raised with Jesus and who went into the holy city and appeared to many (Mt 27:51-54).[25] Matthew here refers to the opening of the tombs, a pregnant symbol of the underworld or hades. This same note is found in John 5:25-29, which affirms that those who are in the tombs will hear the voice of the Son of Man at his coming, and "those who hear will live" (Jn 5:25). Another text that supports the idea of redemption beyond the grave is Matthew 12:31-32, where Jesus speaks of forgiveness in this world and in the world to come (cf. Mt 5:26).

Of special significance are the texts in 1 Peter that envisage Christ preaching to spirits who are in prison (1 Pet 3:19-20; 4:6). The teaching that Christ descended into hell (hades) after his crucifixion was also seized upon by the church fathers to support their position on the harrowing or plundering of hell (cf. Acts 2:31; Eph 4:9-10; 1 Pet 3:19-20).[26] In the words of Paul: "When he ascended on high he led a host of captives, and he gave gifts to men." Previously Christ had "descended into the lower parts of the earth" (Eph 4:8-9). Jesus' words about the gates of hell not prevailing against the church portray the church on the offensive emptying hades of its denizens (Mt 16:18 KJV). The notion of baptism for the dead entertained by some of the early Christians also attests the perduring hope that salvation extends beyond death (1 Cor 15:29).

In the apocryphon cited from Jeremiah by Justin and Irenaeus we find a further confirmation of the idea of redemption from hades: "The Lord, the Holy One of Israel, remembered His dead ones who slept in the dust of the earth, and descended to them to preach His salvation and save them."[27] Similarly in a Latin text of Ecclesiasticus (24:32) Wisdom says: "I will penetrate all the lower parts of the earth, and will visit all that sleep, and will enlighten all that hope in the Lord."[28]

The earliest patristic reference to the descent of Christ to the nether world of spirits is found in the epistle of Ignatius around the beginning of the second century. Tertullian believed that Christ descended into hades "to make the patriarchs and prophets partakers of Himself."[29] Clement of Alexandria included the righteous pagans as well as the saints of the Old Covenant as benefiting from the descent. According to Athanasius Christ rescued more than the patriarchs and prophets: his grace extended to all those who cried out continually to God. In the opinion of Ambrose Christ spoiled hades when he led away the captives who were held there because of Adam's transgression. Cyril of Alexandria spoke of Christ "emptying the insatiable recesses of Death" and "leaving the devil desolate and alone."[30] Gregory of Nazianzus was convinced that all mortals in hades were rescued, except the worst sinners who were left in a lower region of hades. Others in the early church who address this subject include Polycarp, Justin Martyr, the Shepherd of Hermas, Origen, Irenaeus, Cyprian, Hippolytus, Augustine, Cyril of Jerusalem and Jerome.

In contrast to the mainstream patristic tradition Thomas Aquinas taught that Christ descended to the underworld not to convert unbelievers but to put them to shame for their unbelief.[31] Even the souls in the limbo of children were not delivered by Christ's descent, but the fruits of his passion were given to the just and holy souls in the limbo of the patriarchs.[32]

It is interesting to note that the Gnostics in the early centuries of the church had little if any place for the underworld of the dead.[33] Christ descended not to hades but to one of the lesser heavens occupied by the imperfectly righteous souls. For the gnostic mainstream, hades indicates this present world. Marcion was an exception, for he taught an actual descent of Christ to the underworld of hades.

I believe there is a firm basis in both sacred Scripture and sacred tradition for affirming sheol-hades or the nether world of spirits as the interim state for the great majority of people who remain outside the circle of faith at the time of their death.[34] The souls in hades await the final judgment, the great assize, and some may even look forward to possible deliverance. A number of residents of hades will take part in the judging of others. We are told in Matthew 12:38-42 that the people of Nineveh and the Queen of Sheba will rise at the judgment to judge Israel. Sheol-hades is a temporary abode, for it will be cast into the lake of fire after giving up its dead (Rev 20:13-14). The final and irrevocable separation of the just and the unjust has not yet occurred. Heaven and hell are still in the future—not only for us but also for the souls in hades.

Salvation is fixed at death for those who are in Christ, but the condemnation of those who have never known about Christ is not yet decided at death. They are not necessarily eternally condemned, but they are not yet saved. I am teaching not a doctrine of a second chance but the universality of opportunity for salvation. In this context it is best not to speak of chance but of universal Providence. Luther declared, "God forbid that I should limit the time of acquiring faith to the present life. In the depth of the Divine mercy there may be opportunity to win it in the future."[35] This statement was more of a passing hope, however, than an integral part of Luther's creed. The idea that Christ's salvation penetrates the realm of the dead was tacitly assumed if not thoroughly embraced by various followers of the Reformation. According to Peter T. Forsyth, there may well be more conversions on the other side of death than on this side.[36]

It is my contention that a change of heart can still happen on the other side of death. In the parable of Lazarus and the rich man, the latter shows some change of heart, though this was probably remorse, not repentance (Lk 16:19-31). I concur with Gerald C. Studer in his *After Death, What?* that the parable of Lazarus and the rich man is not strictly a parable but an actual description of life in the immediate hereafter.[37] This story makes clear that a great chasm exists between the saved and the unsaved in the world beyond (Lk 16:26); yet God can bridge this chasm (Eph 4:8-9). Nothing can separate us from the love of God, not even sin and damnation (Rom 8:38-39), and God's love goes out equally to all (Mt 5:45; Jn 3:16).

In Protestant orthodoxy the idea of a descent of Christ into hades to convert the lost was considered questionable, though it found a place in later Lutheranism.[38] Matthias Flacius and Abraham Calovius as well as a number of other Lutheran theologians regarded the descent of Christ as bringing a verdict of judgment against the rejected. Luther and Lutheran orthodoxy in general viewed the descent as the first stage in Christ's exaltation. Reformed theologians for the most part held that the descent into hell was a figurative expression of the incomparable sufferings of Christ in his humanity. It poignantly revealed the depth of his humiliation and dereliction.[39]

I believe it is more in keeping with the tradition of the church catholic to view the descent as opening the door to the salvation of those who are not yet in the family of God. Not all will believe when they hear the gospel for the first time, but it is not impermissible to surmise that many will come to faith in Christ. In a sermon preached at Torgau in April 1533 Luther spoke of the descent as if "the Lord Christ—the entire person, God and man, with body and soul, undivided—had journeyed to Hell, and had in person demolished Hell and bound the Devil."[40] Granted that Luther's views on this subject shifted, he was nonetheless hopeful at least on occasion that God's grace can penetrate the barrier of death and reclaim those who are now lost and rejected.[41] The risen Christ himself assures us that he is now alive for evermore and that he has the keys to death and to hades (Rev 1:18). Our hope is based not simply on Christ's descent into hell but also on his ascent into heaven and the outpouring of his Spirit on earth. The nether world of spirits is not outside the reach of God's grace, and this is why the intermediate state of the spiritually deprived and forsaken can be preached as part of the gospel—the good news that Christ has come to save the lost and that his grace is irresistible and invincible. Not even the gates of hell can impede its advance (Mt 16:18).

Purgatory

An intermediate state that appears in later Christian tradition but is remarkably absent from both the scriptural witness and the early church fathers is purgatory. In Roman Catholic theology purgatory is a place of cleansing and punishment for believers who have not yet made adequate reparation for their sins and who are therefore not yet ready for entrance into heavenly glory. It is based on the view that the eternal penalty for sin has been taken care of by the atoning sacrifice of Christ, but temporal consequences of sin still have to be endured if one is to be received into heaven. Catholic theologians point to Matthew 5:8 which states that only "the pure in heart . . . shall see God." A similar notion is found in Hebrews 12:14, which urges us to strive for holiness, "without which no one will see the Lord." Another relevant text is Revelation 21:27, which declares that nothing unclean shall enter the holy city. The point is that sinners not only need to be forgiven of their sin but also purified of their sin if they are to dwell in the presence of the living God.

Still another key text is 1 Corinthians 3:13-15: "Everyone's work will be put through the fire to see whether or not it keeps its value. If the work survives the fire, that builder will receive a reward. But if the work is burned up, the builder will suffer great loss. The builders themselves will be saved, but like someone escaping through a wall of flames" (NLT). This passage affirms the need for inward purification before enjoyment of the glories of heaven, but nothing is said about a place of punishment for misdeeds that are not covered by Christ's atonement.

A more explicit basis for the doctrine of purgatory is to be found in the apocrypha, books of spiritual repute that are not included in the Hebrew canon. In the Wisdom of Solomon we are told that "after a little chastisement they will receive great blessings" (Wis of Sol 3:5 NEB). Second Maccabees asserts that Judas Maccabaeus made "an expiatory sacrifice" for those fallen in battle "so that they might be released from their sin" (2 Macc 12:45 NJB). In the kind of evangelical theology I espouse, prayers for the dead are permissible, but salvation is located not in our expiatory offerings but in Christ's sacrifice alone, and this is communicated to us only through the hearing of the gospel (Rom 10:17; Col 3:16; Gal 3:2, 5).

While the doctrine of purgatory is relatively late in the Christian panorama, the idea of purification after death is already to be found among the church fathers. Clement of Alexandria (c. 150-c. 215) held that those who repented of their sins on their deathbed and who had therefore had no time to do works of penance were sanctified by purifying fire after death.[42] According to Origen (c. 185-c. 254), "If a man depart this life with lighter faults he is condemned to fire which burns away the lighter materials, and prepares the soul for the kingdom of God, where nothing defiled may enter."[43] The Catholic Catechism quotes from John Chrysostom (c. 347-407) in its defense of purgatory: "If Job's sons were purified by their father's sacrifice, why would we doubt that our offerings for the dead bring them some consolation? Let us not hesitate to help those who have died and to offer our prayers for them."[44]

The Catechism also appeals to Gregory the Great (c. 540-604), who builds upon Jesus' words in Matthew 12:31:

As for certain lesser faults, we must believe that, before the Final Judgment, there is a purifying fire. He who is truth says that whoever utters blasphemy against the Holy Spirit will be pardoned neither in this age nor in the age to come. From this sentence we understand that certain offenses can be forgiven in this age, but certain others in the age to come.[45]

Augustine is sometimes referred to as the father of purgatory, since he alluded to both cleansing fire and temporary punishments after death.[46] He also allowed that it was proper to pray that some of the dead might be granted remission of sins. Yet he nowhere postulates a place of purgation alongside heaven and hell; nor does he imply that Christ's atonement is insufficient to cleanse from all sin. He also taught that all of the just go directly to heaven at death. They "do not have to wait for the end in some indeterminate place."[47]

As the doctrine developed, purgatory became a place of fire and judgment and was conceived of as the abode for those whose lives fall drastically short of the perfection demanded by Christ from all his disciples. It became ever more associated with a legalistic understanding of salvation, which took root already in the early church. According to Thomas Aquinas (c. 1225-1274) and other scholastic theologians, the pain in purgatory is greater than any pain experienced in this life. Both Thomas and Bonaventure taught that the fire in purgatory is the very same as the fire in hell. Catherine of Genoa (1447-1510) held that the fire of purgatory is God's love burning away whatever in us has not been purged by God prior to death. Purgatory was endorsed at the Council of Lyons (1274) and the Council of Florence (1445) and reaffirmed at the Council of Trent (1545-1563).

The doctrine of purgatory also carries with it the notion of indulgences—benefits that the church can impart to those willing to make sacrifices in order to gain assurance of salvation.[48] Indulgences are based on the idea of a treasury of merits, the superabundant merits of Christ and the saints that supposedly can be transferred to those lacking in worth before God. According to Karl Rahner, an indulgence is effectual "only where the individual is prepared for an ever deeper purification of his whole being—an indulgence is no substitute for penance."[49] The efficacy of an indulgence therefore rests partly on the performance of the good works enjoined by the church.

Eastern Orthodoxy has generally opposed purgatory as a place of punishment, though it has been open to the idea that the purifying work of the Spirit continues beyond death. The Confession of Dositheus ratified by the Synod of Jerusalem in 1672 admitted a third category of souls—those in hades whose punishment is ameliorated by the prayers of the church. This Confession has not found acceptance in the mainstream of the Eastern Church and was withdrawn by its author at a later time.[50]

In the contemporary period purgatory is being rethought by many Catholic scholars and spiritual writers. The idea of punishment is downplayed, and the emphasis is on purification as a gateway to paradise (or heaven). Mother Mary of St. Austin suggests that Christians have their purgatory here: "Love itself is the fire which attacks and devours the impurities of the soul, and that with a greater violence proportionately to its greater intensity and consequent hostility to them."[51] Ladislaus Boros views purgatory as the "point" of intersection between life and death. The encounter with Christ at death is our purgatory.[52] Bernhard Bartmann suggests that we think of the pain in purgatory as a pain of loss rather than external affliction.[53] The fire in purgatory is increasingly being viewed as figurative, symbolizing a process of interior cleansing.

As an evangelical Christian I reject the doctrine of purgatory for several reasons. First, it is demonstrably not a biblical teaching, though it draws upon certain biblical insights, notably, that salvation involves inward purification. But this inward purification already takes place in this life. The thief on the cross was assured by Jesus that on that very day he would be with his Lord in paradise (Lk 23:43). Nothing is said of a period of waiting and cleansing in purgatory. Second, purgatory is a vital component in a spirituality of works-righteousness that rests upon the attaining of merit rather than justification by free grace. Again, the implication is that Christ's sacrifice is insufficient to cleanse from all sin and that his work of reparation needs to be completed by works of penance on the part of believers who have not broken free from all sin. Furthermore, purgatory fosters a churchly imperialism in which the clerics of the church arrogate to themselves the power to forgive sins and ensure salvation.[54] Finally, the doctrine of purgatory induces unnecessary anxiety about one's salvation. Whereas evangelical Protestants have assurance that they will be with Christ at the moment of death because of faith in his atoning blood, Catholics can only hope that eventually they will see the glory of heaven. Unless they are already saints, they must expect to experience new suffering in purgatory. The fact that purgatory is not really taught by the early church, even by St. Augustine, should make the serious Christian reluctant to affirm it.

In our criticisms of purgatory, which are shared by a growing number of Catholic theologians, we must try to ascertain the truth in the doctrine. This is indeed an ecumenical imperative if we truly seek the unity of the church. Salvation does entail purification by the Holy Spirit, but we must insist that this purifying work takes place in the daily life of the Christian. We can surmise that it is consummated at death or in the very brief transition from death to paradise. Purgatory is not a place inhabited by "suffering souls" or "poor souls," but there is a purgatorial element in the living out of Christian salvation. The life of faith is depicted in the Bible as "the valley of the shadow of death" (Ps 23:4), and we must expect a certain degree of suffering as part of the Christian walk. This suffering, however, does not atone for sin, nor does it render us acceptable before God. We are justified and redeemed only on the basis of Christ's righteousness, which is imputed to us by faith and which motivates us to be righteous in life through acts of sacrificial love.

There appears to be a real divide between Catholic and evangelical theologians on the subject of purgatory, though this divide should not be regarded as insurmountable. I believe that the restoration of hades as an intermediate state in which we wait and hope for Christ's salvation may speak to some of the concerns of those who embrace purgatory. We must, however, continue to resist the allegation that the debt of punishment that one incurs through sin has "not necessarily been cancelled" by Christ's sacrifice on the cross and that it can be paid for by the "expiatory suffering" of still struggling believers.[55] Evangelicals can never accept the view that the temporal penalty for sin is remitted "by the willing bearing" of penances and disciplines imposed by the church.[56] But they can be persuaded to make a place for the daily suffering of inward purification as Christians take up the cross and follow Christ in daily obedience.

Jerry Walls of Asbury Theological Seminary has made a noteworthy contribution to the ecumenical discussion in a pioneering study designed to break down barriers between various Christian traditions on the last things.[57] Walls shows an openness to the Eastern view in his reconceiving of purgatory as essentially a purgative and sanctifying process on the other side of death culminating in eternal joy. In his theology it seems that heaven is what humans deserve through moral action on their pilgrimage to perfection. Not surprisingly he rejects the Reformation doctrine of salvation by faith alone (*sola fide*) and substitutes a synergy in which God and humanity work together in redeeming the cosmos. Walls's book highlights rather than overcomes the abyss that still separates Christians on this vital issue.

As an ecumenical gesture, I affirm not purgatory but a purgatorial dimension in the pilgrimage of faith leading to glory. Our focus as people of faith should be not on making ourselves acceptable to God through works of reparation, but on holding up Christ as the only mediator between God and sinful humanity and rejoicing in what he has done for us on the cross. We are indeed summoned to live a Christian life that redounds to the glory of God, but we must never cease to confess that our strength and confidence lies not in our merits but in God's grace available to all who repent and believe.

·EIGHT·

THE COMMUNION OF SAINTS

Seeing that we have so great a host of witnesses encompassing us like a cloud,
let us clear every obstacle out of our way,
divesting ourselves of sin by which we are so prone to be ensnared.

HEBREWS 12:1 GNC

And you have come to the spirits of the redeemed in heaven
who have now been made perfect.

HEBREWS 12:23 NLT

All the martyrs that are with Christ intercede for us.
Their prayers never cease, so long as we continue in our sighs.

AUGUSTINE

When we suffer and die, we should bravely believe and be certain
that not we or we alone, but Christ and the church suffers and dies with us.

MARTIN LUTHER

The saints are not our way to God;
he is our way to them.

ROBERT W. JENSON

I f there is any doctrine that has been abysmally neglected in evangelical Protestantism, it is the communion of saints. While we blithely mouth the words of the Apostles' Creed "I believe in . . . the communion of saints," we generally fail to take this particular affirmation with the seriousness it deserves. We need to reclaim the ethos of the apostolic church that we are surrounded by "a cloud of witnesses"

(Heb 12:1), that we are in contact with the "spirits of the righteous made perfect" (Heb 12:23 NRSV).

By the saints I mean in this context the whole company of the faithful—on this side and on the other side of death. The church has also included under this designation the angelic hosts who fight on the side of righteousness and who are called in the Bible "the holy ones." The communion of saints encompasses both the visible and the invisible church. The latter is hidden in the visible church and in heaven. This communion is veiled to the empirical eye, but it is sensed by the believing heart. While it is "impalpable" and "intangible" (Luther) it nevertheless has empirical manifestations. It is a communion in spirit linking believers from every tribe and nation. Empirically the church is a community of sinners. This is why the communion of saints, like the incarnation and resurrection of Christ, can only be believed.

Witness of Sacred Tradition

While its roots are incontrovertibly in biblical faith, the doctrine of the communion of saints is given additional sanction by the enduring witness of sacred tradition. The ties that bind the company of the faithful on earth to the departed in heaven came to be expressed in the liturgies of the church (both East and West) and were a growing source of comfort to both laity and clergy. In a letter to Cornelius, bishop of Rome, when both were expecting martyrdom, Cyprian pleads, "If one of us goes before the other, let our love for one another be unbroken, when we are with the Lord; let our prayers for our brethren and sisters be unceasing."[1]

In later church tradition the saints on the other side became points of contact with God and were even viewed as mediators of redemption. Mary especially was elevated to the role of a dispenser of grace and advocate for sinners, and thereby became a source of spiritual consolation to the faithful, sometimes supplanting the Holy Spirit in this regard.[2] It was said that we come to Jesus through Mary, though official Catholic theology cautioned that the intercession of Mary and the saints is ineffectual unless it is united with and undergirded by the intercession of Jesus Christ.

Though protesting against the cult of the saints, which attributed to individual saints special powers, Martin Luther and the other Reformers did not deny the reality of the mystic communion that binds earth and heaven. According to Luther the "spirits of departed ones could be conscious of those left behind in the physical world."[3] In 1546 he wrote to a clergyman in Bremen:

> I shall pray for you, I ask that you pray for me. As little as I doubt that your prayer is effective for me you should not doubt that my prayer will be effective for you. If I depart this life ahead of you—something I desire—then I must pull you after me. If you depart before me, then you shall pull me after you. For we confess *one* God and with all saints we abide in our Savior.[4]

Joseph Hall, Anglican bishop of Exeter in the seventeenth century, was convinced that we receive help from both angels and saints in the heavenly realm. The glorified saints are now "partners of those heavenly Angels" as they plead for their brothers and sisters on earth before "the throne of grace." The help that we receive from the good spirits in the invisible world is not discernible by the senses; yet it has concrete effects that create a lasting impression on our lives.[5]

Both John and Charles Wesley were firm believers in the communion of saints, and for them this was something to be celebrated, for it gives additional comfort to those who are struggling on this side of death. John Wesley acknowledged that God may work immediately upon the human soul, but he often chooses to make use of "subordinate means," and one of these is the prayers of the departed in Christ. The saints after death are not only translated into the very presence of God, but they are permitted to minister to those whom they have left behind.[6]

In the twentieth century Congregational theologian P. T. Forsyth stands out as a stalwart defender of the mystical communion that binds the saints together on earth and in heaven. "In Him the other world acts on this, and this world on the other. But our chief action from this world on the other is prayer."[7] And again: "The dead in Christ see a more wondrous Christ than we do—the same, indeed, yesterday, today and for ever, yet another."[8]

Another voice in the twentieth century calling for a renewed appreciation of the doctrine of the communion of saints was Eberhard Arnold, founder of the Anabaptist brotherhood known as the Bruderhof. He was convinced that "in the flame of the Spirit there is living unity between those who have gone and those who remain on earth."[9] "The unanimity of the people gathered to full community in the house of God" reflects "the unity of the Church above," the saints who live in the perfect light of God's presence.[10]

In both liberal and neo-orthodox theology the communion of saints is sometimes interpreted as a communion with the memory of the departed. The realistic interaction between the saints on earth and in heaven is downplayed in favor of a solitary communion between the individual soul and the living God. It is occasionally said that we pray with the saints who have gone to glory rather than for the saints and they for us.[11]

In Catholic tradition the distinction developed between the church militant and the church triumphant, and this was reaffirmed by the churches of the Reformation. The church militant refers to the struggling church on earth. The church triumphant signifies the church in repose, the church in heaven with God. In Roman Catholic teaching there is also a church expectant—comprised of the poor souls in purgatory. In my opinion there is need for a new articulation of these distinctions if we are to remain true to the total biblical witness and the most profound insights of church tradition. Instead of separate churches we should affirm one holy catholic church—triumphant, militant and expectant at the same time. The church triumphs through suffering and combat, and the holy ones on the other side continue in battle but now with the added certainty of final victory.

Testimony of Hymns

While evangelical Protestants have been almost mute on the subject of the communion of saints in their excursions in systematic theology, their hymnody presents a somewhat different picture. The hymns of evangelical Protestantism are permeated by allusions, even explicit references, to the saints, including the departed saints. Gerhard Tersteegen, the German Reformed mystic (1697-1769), was profoundly aware of the invisible reality of saints and angels who buoy us up by their prayers:

> See the crowds the throne surrounding!
> "Holy, Holy, Holy,"
> Hear the hymn ascending,
> Angels, saints, their voices blending![12]

William Walsham How's (1823-1897) celebrated hymn "For All the Saints Who from Their Labors Rest" includes these words:

> O blest communion, fellowship divine!
> We feebly struggle, they in glory shine;
> Yet all are one in thee, for all are thine.[13]

Samuel John Stone (1839-1900) reveals his staunch commitment to the communion of saints in his much loved hymn, "The Church's One Foundation":

> Yet she on earth hath union
>   With God, the Three in One,
> And mystic sweet communion
>   With those whose rest is won.[14]

A similar note is sounded by William Dalrymple Maclagan (1826-1910):

> Grant us thy grace till life shall end;
>   That with all saints our rest may be
>   In that bright Paradise with thee![15]

The Anglican hymn writer John Athelstan Riley (1858-1945) includes an invocation of the saints in his famed "Ye Watchers and Ye Holy Ones":

Respond, ye souls in endless rest,
Ye patriarchs and prophets blest,
    Alleluia, Alleluia!
Ye holy twelve, ye martyrs strong,
All saints triumphant, raise the song,
    Alleluia![16]

This hymn also contains a special eulogy for Mary, the mother of our Lord:

O higher than the cherubim,
More glorious than the seraphim,
    Lead their praises, Alleluia!
Thou bearer of the eternal Word,
Most gracious, magnify the Lord,
    Alleluia![17]

Finally there is Charles Wesley's well-known hymn, "Come, Let Us Join Our Friends Above":

Come, let us join our friends above
    That have obtained the prize,
And on the eagle wings of love
    To joys celestial rise:
Let all the saints terrestrial sing,
    With those to glory gone:
For all the servants of our King,
    In earth and heaven, are one.

One family we dwell in him,
    One Church, above, beneath,
Though now divided by the stream,
    The narrow stream of death:
One army of the living God,

To his command we bow;
Part of his host have crossed the flood,
    And part are crossing now.

Ten thousand to their endless home
    This solemn moment fly;
And we are to the margin come,
    And we expect to die;
Ev'n now by faith we join our hands
    With those that went before,
And greet the blood-besprinkled bands
    On the eternal shore.

Our spirits too shall quickly join,
    Like theirs with glory crowned,
And shout to see our Captain's sign,
    To hear his trumpet sound.
O that we now might grasp our Guide!
    O that the word were given!
Come, Lord of hosts, the waves divide,
    And land us all in heaven.[18]

Martin Luther once observed that the two most enduring sources for the life of faith are Holy Scripture and the hymns of the church. Especially in those hymns that cross denominational lines we can perceive the work of the Spirit bringing the Word of God to bear on the way people worship and believe. The hymn writers of the church, together with great preachers, people of prayer, renowned theologians and other luminaries of faith and holiness, belong to the second circle of witnesses after the prophets and apostles of biblical history. Their hymns do not constitute an absolute norm for faith, but they celebrate this norm, and they lead people to this norm. Hymns, too, can be a means of grace, particularly if they exalt Jesus Christ and retell the story of salvation through his life, death and glorious resurrection.

Mystic Communion Between Earth and Heaven

In a time when supernaturalism is eroding in the mainline churches it is incumbent on us to reaffirm the communion of saints—the mystic communion of the people of God that bridges the barrier between earth and heaven. According to the Second Helvetic Confession, "the Church Militant . . . still wages war on earth, and fights against the flesh, the world, and the prince of this world, the devil; against sin and death."[19] But the Church Triumphant "triumphs in heaven immediately after having overcome all those things and rejoices before the Lord. Notwithstanding both have fellowship and union one with another."[20] As has already been made clear, we must not separate these two churches, for we are speaking basically of two dimensions of one church. It is important to acknowledge, as did the Reformers, that the saints on earth and the saints in heaven are linked together in a mystic communion that can never be shaken or terminated.

We Christians on earth share in the inheritance of the saints in light (Col 1:12). We are undergirded by a cloud of witnesses and are in contact with the spirits of the just made perfect (Heb 12:1, 23).[21] We have "come to the assembly of God's firstborn children, whose names are written in heaven" (Heb 12:23 NLT). The account of the saints who rose with Christ and appeared before many (Mt 27:52, 53) is an affirmation of the penetration of God's grace beyond the pale of death. Another text that lends support to the communion of saints is Revelation 6:9-11, which describes the saints under the altar pleading for the vindication of God's justice for those who have endured persecution—those who shine in heaven and those who struggle on earth (cf. 16:7). The angelic sealing of the servants of God gives them "protection in and through death," showing the impact of the invisible agents of righteousness upon the church in its earthly pilgrimage (Rev 7:1-8; 8:1-5).[22] In Revelation 11 we read of the two prophets who descend to earth to give guidance to the saints. The accounts of the transfiguration of Christ, which depict the visitation of Moses and Elijah to Jesus and his disciples (Mt 17:1-13; Mk 9:2-13; Lk 9:28-36), also constitute a powerful witness to the belief of the early Christians that they were linked to the saints in paradise through a common faith in the Lord Jesus Christ.

Jesus likened the communion of saints to the vine and the branches (Jn 15:1-17). Christ is the vine, and all believers in Christ are the branches. The branches bear fruit only insofar as they abide in the vine. The vinedresser is the Father, and we are engrafted into the vine by the baptism of the Spirit. Branches that do not bear fruit are cut off from the vine (Jn 15:6). Those that bear fruit are given special recognition in the kingdom of God.

Another graphic metaphor for the communion of saints is found in the apostle Paul, who referred to one body and many members (1 Cor 12:12-30). All members must work together for the good of the whole. We attain our goal of perfect beatitude in Christ only by helping one another to realize a common vocation. "If one member suffers, all suffer together; if one member is honored, all rejoice together" (1 Cor 1:26). Christ is the head of the body, and the Spirit is the catalyst that energizes the members in giving honor and glory to Christ (1 Cor 12:12-13; Col 1:18).

While it is unclear whether the two preceding discourses include the dead in Christ, there can be no doubt that this is the implication when viewed in the context of the developing consciousness of the Christian community concerning life after death (cf. Rev 5:8-14; 6:9-11; 14:2-5; Heb 12:22-24). The communion of saints is founded on the belief that we are related to others in the faith not directly but indirectly—through the intercession and mediation of Christ. And this holds true for the communion on this side of the grave as well as the other side.

What This Communion Involves

The communion of saints involves remembrance, mutual intercession and conversation. This communion must be sharply distinguished from "spirit communication" or necromancy, which is clearly forbidden in Scripture (Lev 19:26, 31; Deut 18:9-14; Is 8:19-22; 19:3; Acts 16:16-18). Spirit communication as promulgated by the cult of Spiritism or Spiritualism is a direct communication, and it also takes place by means of the senses. According to Scripture this kind of activity pertains to the realm of shadows, phantasy and also darkness. We do not really make contact with the spirits of the dead in the world of spirits, though we might be deceived into thinking so. "The dead know nothing, and they have no more reward" (Eccles 9:5; cf. Ps 88:11-12).[23] The communion of saints concerns real interaction between the faithful in heaven and the faithful on earth. The incident recorded in 1 Samuel 28:3-19 where the medium at Endor supposedly brings back Samuel from the dead does not validate the Spiritualist position, for the medium herself is surprised, even alarmed, when she sees a "god coming up out of the earth" and recognizes him to be Samuel.[24] This incident attests the reality of a spirit world that cannot be tapped into either by mediums or by shamans, but that nevertheless impinges on those in spiritual pilgrimage, those who believe in Christ. We who believe have both "friends on earth" and "friends above" who see us through our trials by directing us to Jesus Christ, the one fount of all mercy.[25]

Sacred tradition is firm that we reach the saints not directly or even through earthly channels, such as mediums, but through Christ himself.[26] Heavenly spirits always behold the face of God (Mt 18:10), and therefore they hear us through God or through Christ. We also hear them by the mediation of Christ. It is generally an inward hearing and seeing that is not available to others. Yet on occasion some persons are granted a special dispensation of grace and see and hear more directly.[27] This sometimes occurs at the time of death, as in the case of Stephen, the first martyr (Acts 7:54-60). It may also take place during some life crisis, as with Samuel Rutherford, the Westminster divine, who sought to minister to a family who had just suffered the loss of their daughter. Rutherford relates that on one occasion while he was "in the Spirit" he was "caught up into Paradise to see the beauty of his Lord, and to hear his [own] little daughter singing Glory." He wrote to the father of the stricken family, "I give you my word for it. . . . I saw two . . . children there [in Paradise], and one of them was your child and one of them was mine."[28] Similarly, in a time of acute distress J. B. Phillips, author of *The New Testament in Modern English* and whose integrity is beyond dispute, was consoled by words of encouragement from C. S. Lewis, who had then only recently been translated into glory but who appeared visibly to Phillips on two occasions.[29]

What about the age-old practice of petitions *to* the saints? If the saints can help us, may we then invoke them for aid? Because of the excesses of the cult of saints, the Reformers sternly warned against this practice. They were especially vehement in their critique of the then-popular view that some saints have special influence with God. This is an idea that probably has its origin in the patron saints of Greek folk religion. We recognize, of course, that saints on this side of death can help us. Paul declares, "I know that through your prayers and the help of the Spirit of Jesus Christ this will turn out for my deliverance" (Phil 1:19; cf. 1 Cor 9:22; Jas 5:13-18). But can we receive help from departed spirits, those who have gone before us? We know that the spirits in sheol cannot help us, for they themselves stand in need of the salvation offered in Christ. In Isaiah 8:19 we read, "Should they consult the dead on behalf of the living?" Yet Scripture is clear that angels can help us and can pray for us (cf. Gen 48:16; Dan 9:20-23; Zech 1:12; Lk 1, 2; Acts 1:10-11). We also have grounds for believing that glorified saints can help us (2 Pet 1:15; Rev 5:8; 6:9; 8:3-4). It is to "our mother" "the heavenly Jerusalem" (Gal 4:26 NLT) that St. Paul refers the Galatians in their difficulties. Malachi says: "I shall send you the prophet Elijah before the great and terrible day of the LORD comes. He will reconcile parents to their children and children to their parents, lest I come and put the land under a ban to destroy it" (Mal 4:5 REB; cf. Rev 11:1-13).

Popular Catholicism inculcates devotion to the saints as sources of divine mercy and favor. Official Catholic theology has been more circumspect in this regard. Father John Sullivan declares: "We honor them, and they pray for us; but neither they nor the Blessed Virgin Mary can give us any grace or show us any mercy. They can simply present our prayers to the Almighty and unite them to their own."[30]

The Reformers and various Reformation confessions of faith affirmed that the saints in glory pray for us and for the whole church, but they resolutely opposed the practice of invoking the saints, chiefly because this appeared to take away glory from Christ. The Apology of the Augsburg Confession allowed that the saints can be intercessors, but never propitiators.[31] Luther believed that Mary and the saints should be celebrated as examples of faith and devotion, but they should never be thought of as having a special pipeline to God.[32]

John Wesley welcomed assistance from both angels and saints, though he believed that glory and power ultimately reside in God alone. "May we not probably suppose that the spirits of the just, though generally lodged in Paradise, yet may sometimes, in conjunction with the holy angels, minister to the heirs of salvation? May they not sometimes, on errands of love, revisit their brethren below?"[33]

In my view, which I believe stands in continuity with evangelical tradition at its best, the communion of saints entails a real communion between earth and heaven. The saints (both on earth and in heaven) are intercessors, yet only insofar as they participate in the intercession of Christ, which alone truly counts in the end. Because of the inveterate temptation to view the saints as mediators of redemption, we should generally refrain from invoking the saints in glory, but we may request their aid in our prayers to God and Christ. The saints may be intercessors, but Christ alone is our Advocate, one who reaches down and redeems sinners. The saints point us to Christ, but they cannot take the place of Christ in his role as the fountain of mercy.

As a Reformed churchman I am comfortable with the Anglican position that we should honor the saints without promoting or engaging in the practice of invocation. Anglican spirituality "has avoided invocation in the strict sense of direct appeal to the saints to pray for us or to bestow gifts upon us. It remains satisfied on the whole with the inspiring sense of fellowship with the saints in prayer and praise, enforcing the power of their examples in the bond of faith."[34]

May we petition angels, since they are messengers and ambassadors of God's grace? Daniel is fortified by the consolation he receives from an angel and invites the angel to speak to him further (Dan 10:18-19). In answer to the angel Gabriel's announcement Mary uttered these words of faith: "Behold, I am the handmaid of the Lord; let it be to me according to your word" (Lk 1:38). In evangelical spirituality appeals or requests to angels should be an exception, not a rule, but we need to recover the catholic truth that the company of the faithful are aided and sustained by angelic visitors through whom Christ may reach us and teach us (cf. Ps 103:19-22; Zech 6:1-8; Rev 10:9-11; 14:6-7).

Are petitions *for* the saints ever permissible in an evangelical catholic theology? I am thinking here primarily of petitions on behalf of the faithful departed, though this practice extends to anyone claimed by the grace of God. Both Elijah and Elisha interceded for a dead child, bringing the child back to life (1 Kings 17:20-22; 2 Kings 4:32-34). First Corinthians 15:29 alludes to the early practice of baptism for the dead, which indicates a belief that those on this side of death can help those on the other side. Paul declares in Ephesians 6:18 that we should make supplication "for *all* the saints" (italics mine). Jesus prayed for the resurrection of Lazarus (Jn 11:38-44), and Peter prayed for the resurrection of Dorcas (Acts 9:36-41).

In Protestantism the Anglican Church especially has encouraged prayer for the departed. In the words of one of the officially sanctioned prayers: "We also bless Thy holy name for Thy servants departed this life in Thy faith and fear; beseeching Thee to grant them continual growth in Thy love and service."[35] Another prayer contains the plea "Grant them your peace; let light perpetual shine upon them; and, in your loving wisdom and almighty power, work in them the good purpose of your perfect will; through Jesus Christ our Lord."[36] We should note these perspicacious comments of Archbishop William Temple:

> We do not pray for them because God will otherwise neglect them. We pray for them because we know He loves and cares for them, and we claim the privilege of uniting our love for them with God's.

Do not be content to pray for them. Let us also ask them to pray for us. In such prayers while they lived on earth they both displayed and consecrated their love towards us. Doubtless that ministry of love continues; but let us seek it, ask for it, claim it. It is in the mutual service of prayer, our prayer for them and theirs for us, that we come closest to them.[37]

Eastern Orthodoxy, appealing to the church in antiquity, supports prayer for the blessed dead, though not as an act of reparation for sin but as an act of solidarity with the whole church. According to Kallistos Ware:

> We pray for those who have died, and accept with joy the fact that they are praying for us, not for any juridical reasons, but simply because we and they belong to the same family. No other justification is either possible or necessary. Such prayer is the fruit of our love for each other: for death cannot sever the bond of mutual love and mutual prayer that links together all the members of Christ's Body.[38]

P. T. Forsyth, who espoused a catholic Puritanism, was quite adamant that Christians should pray for the dead, even for those who are not yet bound to Christ in faith, on the grounds that the Spirit may well be at work in such prayers turning people to Christ for redemption and purification. This view is entirely consonant with his hope that there may be more conversions on the other side than on this side.[39]

From an evangelical and Reformed perspective we can pray for the faithful departed, but we should not pray for their justification and redemption, since this has already been accomplished in Christ's sacrificial death and resurrection (Rom 3:24-25; 1 Cor 1:30). We may, however, pray for their progress toward final glory, since we can surmise that there is spiritual growth beyond the grave—where the Lamb, as their shepherd, "will guide them to springs of living water" (Rev 7:15-17; cf. Eph 2:6-10; Heb 11:40).[40] We may also pray for divine blessing on their intercessions.

Herman Bavinck, whose Reformed credentials are seldom questioned, is emphatic that "there is still room in the case of the blessed in

heaven for faith and hope, for longing and prayer (Rev 6:10; 22:17).
Like believers on earth, they eagerly await the return of Christ, the resurrection of the dead, and the restoration of all things. Only then has
the end been reached (1 Cor 13:24)."[41]

Just as the saints on earth are now "being changed into his likeness
from one degree of glory to another" (2 Cor 3:18), so this glory bright-
ens the portals of heaven as the kingdom of God advances under the
banner of the gospel (Lk 15:7). The bride, who comprises the entire
body of believers both on earth and in heaven, joins with the Spirit in
calling for the speedy return of the Lord Jesus Christ to claim his own
(Rev 22:17).[42]

What about prayers for the lost? We may hope for the final reunion
of all souls and even pray for this, but we should not go beyond this. It
is not wrong to pray "May God have mercy on their souls" if we fear
that the deceased have separated themselves from the love of Christ.
We must remember that we have access not to those outside of Christ
but only to those in Christ. We should hope for all, but on the basis of
Scripture we have confidence that only those in Christ are saved for
eternity. Eastern Orthodox theologian Kallistos Ware allows for
prayers for the diminution of suffering in hell. He even indicates that
for many Orthodox release from hell is possible, "for in the period between Christ's resurrection and his second coming the gates of hell
stand open, and until the last judgment no one is as yet irrevocably
condemned to remain there for eternity."[43] In my opinion we need to
keep alive the biblical hope that God's grace reaches beyond the barrier of death (1 Pet 3:19-20; 4:6), yet at the same time recognize that
one cannot finally be mystically united with Christ apart from trust and
confidence in his mercy.

The Saints in the Work of Redemption
The saints, that is, all persons who are justified and sanctified in Christ,
play a pivotal role in the work of redemption—but as witnesses, not as
redeemers. Christ alone procured the remission of sins; yet the saints

direct people to Christ so that they can find their salvation in him. The saints participate in the passion and victory of Christ through their words and deeds. By their prayers and sufferings they fill up what is lacking in the suffering of Christ (Col 1:24). They do not complement or add to Christ's atoning work, but they participate in his present passion as he battles the forces of evil in the world. I particularly like the NJB version of Colossians 1:24: "It makes me happy to be suffering for you now, and in my own body to make up all the hardships that still have to be undergone by Christ for the sake of his body, the Church." The NJB commentary on this passage is helpful:

> Jesus suffered in order to establish the reign of God, and anyone who continues his work must share this suffering. Paul is not claiming to add anything to the redemptive value of the cross (to which in any case nothing is lacking); but he associates himself with the trials of Jesus, by his sufferings in his apostolate.[44]

Reformed Christianity has emphasized the all-sufficiency and sole efficacy of Christ's atoning sacrifice for sin, but it has nevertheless made a prominent place for the work of the saints in communicating the fruits of this sacrifice to the world. According to Calvin, the saints do not contribute to the remission of sins, but they have a share in the upbuilding and extension of the church, and this involves the sanctification and salvation of the world. The Heidelberg Catechism declares that every member of the body of Christ ought to know that they are under the obligation to use their gifts for the welfare and benefit of the other members.[45]

The saints in evangelical perspective are not Saviors but helpers (Rom 16:1-2). Through the grace of Christ they are privileged to be helpers of one another and also of those outside the circle of faith. They are servants of Christ, not co-redeemers. They are intercessors but not advocates or mediators of redemption. Yet as intercessors they can contribute to the upbuilding and outreach of the kingdom of God. Bonhoeffer put it well: "Intercession, like every other form of prayer, cannot compel God, but if he himself gives the final sanction then a man can ransom his brother, by virtue of the church."[46]

In Reformation perspective there is no treasury of merit to which we gain access through indulgences, but there is a treasury of grace that is open to all Christians through their prayers and entreaties. Christ alone has the keys to this treasury, and therefore we go to him alone for salvation. The church cannot dispense or withhold grace, only announce grace and receive grace. It can serve as a channel for the outpouring of grace, but this outpouring is solely the work of the Spirit of Christ. The saints by directing us to Christ help us to gain access to this treasury. They have, however, no independent power of intercession. Apart from Christ they can do nothing (Jn 15:5).

Are the departed saints in a state of rest or activity? They are in rest from their trials on earth, but their work of intercession continues. This truth was recognized by the Lutheran Pietist theologian Count Zinzendorf, who held that the prayers of the saints in heaven directly benefit their brothers and sisters who are still on their earthly pilgrimage.[47] The injunction in the gospel hymn, "Work, for the Night Is Coming" applies to the saints in the beyond as well as to those on earth.[48] Micaiah's vision of the spirits at work in heaven refers to angels, not to departed saints (1 Kings 22:19-23), but it throws light upon the ministry of the saints, for the saints will become like the angels (Lk 20:36). The saints who are now in paradise "serve him day and night" (Rev 7:15; 4:8). I concur with Loraine Boettner that "rest" in scriptural usage carries with it the idea of satisfaction in labor or joy in accomplishment, not the cessation of activity.[49] In the Eastern Orthodox view the repose of the saints is a state of expectancy, but this expectancy overflows in works of intercession and mercy.

Both Eastern Orthodoxy and Roman Catholicism have been profoundly forthright in their vision of the departed saints helping their brothers and sisters on their earthly pilgrimage. Origen here gives trenchant expression to the sentiments of the undivided ancient church: "All those fathers who have fallen asleep before us fight on our side and aid us by their prayers."[50] In his funeral oration for his own father, Gregory of Nazianzus paid this remarkable tribute: "I am satisfied that he accomplishes there now by his prayers more than he ever did by his teaching just in proportion as he approaches nearer to God after having shaken off the fetters of his body."[51] Teresa of Ávila declared that if through her intercessions in heaven she could help a struggling soul praise God and love him more, this would be a greater consolation than to be with God in glory.[52] And in the words of Thérèse of Lisieux: "I wish to spend my heaven in doing good upon earth. . . . No, I shall not be able to take any rest until the end of the world."[53] "When the angel cries: 'Time is no more,' then I shall rest. I shall be able to rejoice, for the number of the elect will be complete." She insisted that she would not simply *look* down from heaven but *come* down and let fall "a shower of roses."[54] Protestants should not have insurmountable difficulty with these words of promise so long as the emphasis is on sacrificial service to Christ rather than a duplication or repetition of his sacrifice, which was once for all times (Heb 9:23-28).

We now come to the question of whether the departed saints suffer. Thomas Aquinas surmised that the saints know our woes but that they cannot be grieved because they are filled with the joy of glory. Luther by contrast postulated a "hell in heaven." He declared in 1520: "When I come to die, I should be confident that not I, or at least not I alone, am dying, but that Christ and the community of saints are suffering and dying with me." "If I should die, I am not alone in death, if I suffer, they suffer with me," namely Christ "with all holy angels and blessed in heaven and godly people on earth."[55]

The Bible itself alludes to a present passion of Christ that is to be sharply distinguished from his atoning suffering (cf. Acts 9:4-5; Heb 6:6; Eph 4:30). Pascal caught this note when he said, "Jesus shall be in agony until the end of the world."[56] Scripture also speaks of "the fellowship of his sufferings" (Phil 3:10 KJV) in which the whole company of the saints join Christ in his continuing passion. Paul declared, "If one member suffers, all suffer together; if one member is honored, all rejoice together" (1 Cor 12:26). Jesus told his disciples that there will be joy in heaven over one sinner who repents (Lk 15:7, 10). Although the reference is very probably to angels, the saints are comparable to angels in their mission.

The communion of saints exists only by the initiative of God in bringing together all those who believe in Christ, incorporating them into Christ's mystical body. The saints of Old Testament history only received the promises of God by being awakened to their status as sons of God in Christ. Scripture is clear that the Old Testament saints reach their perfection "only in company with us"—the saints of the New Testament dispensation (Heb 11:40 NEB). Similarly, we of the new dispensation reach our perfection only by being joined to the heavenly Jerusalem by faith in the living Christ (Rev 21:1-4).

At the final judgment and general resurrection both the quick and the dead will be judged. But prior to this event or series of events the saints are joined in an indissoluble fellowship. All Christians are in one family, the family of the Father. Racial, class and gender distinctions are superseded, for in Christ "there is neither slave nor free," neither "male nor female" (Gal 3:28). The communion of saints is already intact, but it will be realized on a new level when Christ comes again to bring in the kingdom of glory. In the eschaton pain, suffering and death will come to an end, but the work of adoration and celebration will continue. I concur with Taizé brother Pierre-Yves Emery, who contends that the departed saints "will wait until the end of the world for us, the believers still on earth, to fulfill their ministry, their works, their crown, their joy."[57] There will be a glorious and resplendent homecoming in which the saints will be united in visible fellowship with one another through a new outpouring of the Holy Spirit.

In conclusion, I emphasize again that a full-orbed doctrine of the communion of saints is possible only if we appeal to both holy Scripture and holy tradition. Tradition, however, contains erroneous as well as faithful understanding and therefore needs to be corrected by Scripture. Tradition is a subordinate norm; Scripture is the ruling norm. Tradition amplifies and clarifies Scripture but can never take its place. Our ultimate authority is the Holy Spirit who inspired Scripture and who illumines tradition. It is the Spirit who guides the church in its appraisal of Scripture. It is also the Spirit who corrects tradition in order to bring it into greater accord with Scripture. There are errors in tradition that need to be exposed so that a truer and fuller understanding of the faith can emerge. A theology of Word and Spirit not only honors the Word but also upholds the Spirit as he makes explicit what is implicit in Scripture and reveals this wider vision to the church through the centuries.

Tradition understood as the enduring witness to the faith through the ages partakes of the infallibility of both Christ and Scripture, but as the historical matrix in which faith is transmitted it is necessarily vulnerable to cultural bias. Scripture too bears the imprint of cultural and historical relativity, but when united with the Spirit it unfailingly conveys the truth of divine revelation.[58]

·NINE·

PREDESTINED
TO GLORY

The evil you planned to do me has by God's design been turned to good,
that he might bring about . . . the deliverance of a numerous people.

GENESIS 50:20 JB

God chose you from the beginning to be
saved through sanctification by the Spirit and belief in the truth.

2 THESSALONIANS 2:13

Without God we cannot,
Without us, he will not.

AUGUSTINE

The predestined must strive after good works and prayers
because through these means predestination is most certainly fulfilled.

THOMAS AQUINAS

P redestination is an eschatological and not merely a metaphysical concept. It pertains not only to the first things but also to the last things. Its ground or source is in the past; its goal and culmination are in the future. Predestination basically means to determine in advance. In the Bible it is closely related to election, which means being selected for a particular purpose—to glorify God and to serve his kingdom.[1]

In Paul's theology predestination is linked to foreknowledge. Indeed, those whom God foreknows he also predestines, and those whom he predestines he calls, justifies and finally glorifies (Rom 8:29-

30). His predestination is based not on how God knows humans will respond to his gracious initiative, but on his unconditional love that embraces us even while we are still in our sins. Predestination is not dependent on good character, but good character eventually results from predestination.

While the Bible staunchly affirms divine predestination, it shrinks from endorsing fatalism. Predestination is nearly always joined to human freedom and is realized through human free decision. At the same time, there are passages in Scripture that might imply a residue of fatalism or of causal determinism. In Ecclesiastes we read: "Everything has already been decided. It was known long ago what each person would be. So there's no use arguing with God about your destiny" (Eccles 6:10 NLT). The book of Proverbs declares, "The king's heart is a stream of water in the hand of the LORD; he turns it wherever he will" (Prov 21:1). Yet the Bible also portrays the future as relatively open and human choice as supremely important in the unfolding of human destiny. Psalm 81:10-12 is typical of many passages:

I am the LORD your God,
  who brought you up out of Egypt.
  Open wide your mouth and I will fill it.
But my people would not listen to me;
  Israel would not submit to me.
So I gave them over to their stubborn hearts
  to follow their own devices. (NIV)

Another fascinating text is 1 Peter 2:8: "They stumble because they disobey the word, as they were destined to do." The NLT puts it this way: "They stumble because they do not listen to God's word or obey it, and so they meet the fate that has been planned for them." This text has been used to argue for both conditional predestination and double predestination, the supposition that God ordains some to salvation and others to damnation. Basically it mirrors the mystery that both God's grace and God's judgment are at work in all human decision making.

We stumble because we disobey God's word, but even our disobedience is included in God's plan for our lives and is made to serve his ultimate goal—to bring God glory and to advance his kingdom.

Theological tradition has been most faithful to sacred Scripture when it has sought to hold together the announcement of God's boundless grace and God's command to his people to work out their salvation in fear and trembling (Phil 2:12). God does not expressly will everything that happens, but the whole panorama of history is under God's direction. God does not will evil, but he brings good out of evil. In the words of Ecclesiasticus: "Do not say 'The LORD was responsible for my sinning,' for he is never the cause of what he hates" (Ecclesiasticus 15:11 JB). Yet God creates darkness as well as light, he brings judgment and disaster as well as peace and security (Is 45:7).[2] God is not the infinite cause of all that comes to pass, if this be taken to mean the exclusive cause. God is not in direct control of all things, but he does wield indirect control.

Church tradition has employed philosophical concepts in order to express the mystery of how God's foreordination is realized through human cooperation with grace. The distinction is commonly made between God's permissive will and his ordaining will. He permits some things to happen that are not expressly ordained. Some things have their source in God's lesser will, but his lesser will serves his greater will. Another polarity is that between God's manifest will and God's hidden or secret will. We are in murky waters when these are regarded as two entirely different wills. Orthodox or traditionalist theologians have also differentiated between primary and secondary causes. The ultimate cause of human faith and obedience is God's grace, but this grace may be realized through human participation in God's redemptive activity. Or God may act in and with human response and obedience (*concursus*). Strictly speaking, God does not determine whatever comes to pass, but God unfailingly accomplishes his purpose according to his will (Eph 1:11-12) and against the powers of darkness that defy his will.

The specter of rationalism arises when church theologians are led to affirm double predestination. If one says that God elects only some to salvation, the logical corollary is that God elects others to damnation. To be sure, defenders of double predestination can find in Scripture a modicum of support. For example, Proverbs 16:4 declares,

The LORD has made all things for Himself,
Yes, even the wicked for the day of doom. (NKJ)

A comparable text is Jude 4: "Certain men have crept in unnoticed, who long ago were marked out for this condemnation, ungodly men, who turn the grace of our God into licentiousness and deny the only Lord God and our Lord Jesus Christ" (NKJ).

It should be noted that both the above texts say nothing about predestination to hell, only that the wicked are assured of divine retribution. Those who teach false doctrine are marked out for condemnation, but we cannot infer from these texts that this condemnation constitutes eternal separation from God.

Similarly, advocates of double predestination point to Romans 9:13: "Jacob have I loved, but Esau have I hated" (KJV). The Bible is clear, however, that God's judgment on Esau is not everlasting, for Esau is reunited with Jacob and regains the favor of God (Gen 33:1-15). Romans 9, moreover, must be interpreted in light of Romans 10 and 11, which declare that Israel's rejection is not final and that all Israel will be saved.[3]

The Calvinist or double predestinarian theory is also allegedly supported by Romans 8:29-30, which speaks of God's foreordination of those who are called by God to serve his loving purpose. Yet the intent of this passage is to show the integral relation between divine predestination and human character, not to teach that only some are predestined. The predestined here constitute an indefinite number, which may well be very high. The passage by no means detracts from Paul's universal vision—God consigning all people to disobedience that he may have mercy on them all (Rom 11:32). We are faithful to Paul if we affirm the universal outreach of God's election but not necessarily the coming to faith of the whole of humanity.

It is true that election contains the idea of rejection. There is a negation within God's affirmation, as both Schleiermacher and Barth duly recognized. Yet this negation serves God's affirmation as it is worked out on the plane of history. Part of the problem with Origen and Augustine, as Pannenberg deftly shows, is that their view "makes the divine decision timeless, in abstraction from the concrete historicity of the divine acts of election as the Bible bears witness to them."[4] The same criticism can be leveled at Calvin and Luther, who at times lapsed into the monergistic heresy that God does all and humanity does nothing with regard to the attainment of salvation. In his seminal work *The Bondage of the Will* Luther posited a disjunction between God hidden and revealed.[5] God is hidden not only in his revelation but also behind his revelation. According to Eberhard Jüngel the possibility of "God's having a different character from that which is disclosed in Christ is abhorrent" and must be rejected.[6] As Luther developed his theology, however, he came more and more to subordinate predestination to justification and made salvation correlative with personal faith and repentance.[7]

In Reformed theology a rigid predestinarianism tended to eclipse human responsibility and accountability in both sin and salvation.[8] Calvin himself, however, warned against speculation concerning the secret will of God and the mystery of reprobation. The theme of his celebrated *Institutes of the Christian Religion* was not predestination but regeneration. While predestination remained an enduring motif in his thought, it was not the center of gravity.[9] T. F. Torrance's observations are very apropos:

> One of the calamities of traditional exposition and interpretation of Calvin's theology has been, by means of arid logical forms, to make Calvin's own distinctions too clean and too rigid. This has resulted in an over-simplification which obscured the flexibility as well as the range and profundity of his thought.[10]

In contrast to Emil Brunner, Karl Barth made a significant place for double predestination and reprobation in Christian theology. In Barth's view God takes our reprobation upon himself in the person of Jesus Christ so that Christ becomes both the elect and the reprobate. Pannenberg criticizes Barth on this point.[11] For Pannenberg Christ was not rejected by his Father but was obedient to the mission he received. He was rejected by the world. Pannenberg does not appear to grasp or appreciate the subtlety in Barth's reasoning. If substitutionary atonement means that Christ was made sin for us so that we might become the righteousness of God (2 Cor 5:21), then it also entails Christ suffering the torments of hell in our place (Is 53:4-6; 1 Pet 2:23-24), a position heartily endorsed by the mainstream of evangelical theological tradition. According to Brunner it is more biblical to affirm that predestination is correlative with faith and thereby avoid speculation on the eternal destiny of those outside the circle of faith.

Barth and Brunner also clash in their views on the wrath of God.[12] For Brunner God is wrath outside of Christ, but in Christ he is love and forgiveness. Barth by contrast sees the wrath of God as one form of his love. The wrath of God is indeed revealed in his love for us in Jesus Christ, for Christ signifies both God's grace in the face of sin and God's judgment on sin. In my opinion Barth's position is more consistently biblical, since the Bible seems to indicate that God's judgment on sin cannot be known and appreciated except in the light of his grace that overcomes sin.[13]

Barth is also more profoundly biblical in his perception of the universal outreach of God's predestinating grace. Not all are predestined to have faith in God, but all are claimed by faith and are destined to serve the cause of faith. Brunner limits predestination to the company of the faithful; yet if God is in control of history, if he is directing the course of history, then predestination surely pertains to all humankind and becomes indeed good news for everyone, since it means unconditional grace to undeserving sinners revealed and fulfilled in the cross and resurrection victory of Jesus Christ.

The Unfolding of Predestination

There can be no denying the striking divergence between philosophical theology and biblical religion regarding the unfolding of predestination. In the first predestination is reduced to an eternal decree whose effects in world history are automatic and irreversible. Causality is collapsed into logical necessity (as in Spinoza and Schleiermacher). In biblical religion predestination is the providential overseeing of world history guiding the historical process toward its fulfillment in the new heaven and the new earth. God is envisaged not so much as the infinite cause of everything that happens but as the creative, providential hand that directs the course of world history. All things are not directly caused by God but are under the will of God. God does not directly determine whatever comes to pass, but God accomplishes his purposes in and through everything that happens.

In biblical perspective predestination is both an event and a process. It is dynamic rather than static. Predestination, like salvation itself, has a past, present and future. It is not completed until the eschaton when God will be in all things. Predestination is the working out of the plan of God but in and with human effort and collaboration. This dynamic side of predestination is powerfully attested in Isaiah 48:3, 5 (REB):

> Long ago I announced what would first happen.
> I revealed it with my own mouth;
> suddenly I acted and it came about. . . .
> I told you of these things long ago,
> and declared them to you before they happened.

Predestination in the biblical sense is not an arbitrary fiat but the creative expression of divine planning and willing that has its source in divine love. God's decisions are fully consonant with his nature. He does not arbitrarily redeem and condemn, but he does all things out of his love for a lost and failing humanity. He acts to insure the very best outcome for his children and for the whole human race. But God does not force people to bend to his will. He lures them into cooperating with his will to advance his kingdom on earth. His grace is irresistible in the sense that once we are fully convicted of our sin and convinced of God's gratuitous pardon we will invariably grasp the hand outstretched to save us.

Predestination is both conditional and unconditional. His election is not dependent on our works and merits but flows out of his unconditional grace. At the same time, the efficacy of his predestination depends partly on how we respond to his invitation to take up the cross and follow Christ. Predestination unfolds not apart from human willing but in and through human willing—sometimes even against human willing.

Scripture is clear that the children of God are elected in Christ. Jesus Christ is chosen to be "the first-born among many brethren" (Rom 8:29). In him we have our election and our salvation (Is 28:16; Rom 8:29-30; Col 1:15-20; 1 Pet 2:6). As Paul declared:

> Before the foundation of the world he chose us in Christ to be his people, to be without blemish in his sight, to be full of love; and he predestined us to be adopted as his children through Jesus Christ. This was his will and pleasure in order that the glory of his gracious gift, so graciously conferred on us in his Beloved, might redound to his praise. (Eph 1:4-6 REB)

In the deepest sense Jesus Christ himself is the predestined one. Our election and redemption are effected through his cross and resurrection victory and will be confirmed in his second advent. We are elected to be his sons and daughters, but his election is not realized apart from our faith and repentance.

From the biblical perspective history is a mixture of indeterminacy and determinacy. The Bible portrays an open future, but it is not entirely open. Paradoxically and mysteriously human freedom is made to serve divine freedom. Humans are guided toward their destined end by the incomparable grace of a sovereign and caring God. Joseph assured his brothers that though they meant evil against him, God "meant it for good" (Gen 50:20). God's plan for Joseph and for Israel was realized through the obstinacy and malice of Joseph's brothers who had sold him into slavery.

In the scriptural understanding predestination does not simply precede justification and sanctification but includes them and indeed every aspect of salvation. Predestination is not a fate imposed upon humanity but a plan that allows for the free cooperation of humanity. It is not so much an imposition as an invitation—to join hands with God in working out the implications of God's saving acts in Jesus Christ in our daily lives. Predestination is not causal determinism but the unfolding of triumphal grace through our faith, repentance and obedience.

In the older Reformed theology a distinction was sometimes drawn between the general call and the effectual call (F. A. Lampe). The general call to service in the kingdom goes out to all humankind, but this call does not become effectual until it meets with surrender and faith. In the theology I uphold God's effectual call is both universal and effectual, but when it meets with unbelief it becomes effectual for damnation.

Universalism and Particularism

There are both universalistic and particularistic motifs in holy Scripture. Both Testaments are united in affirming the universal triumph of the kingdom of God. The Lord declares through his prophet, "All mankind will come to bow down before me" (Is 66:23 NASB). And in Titus 2:11 we read, "The grace of God has dawned upon the world with healing for all mankind" (REB). God does not only judge his enemies but pursues them so that they will seek his name (Ps 83:13-16). Scripture does not refer only to Israel as the people of God; on occasion other nations are also given this honor (cf. Is 19:25; Zech 2:11). There will not only be a separation between righteous and unrighteous (Mt 25:31-46), but both righteous and unrighteous will be united with Christ who will be in and through all things (Eph 1:10; 4:6). Jesus said, "No one comes to the Father, but by me" (Jn 14:6). But at the same time he extends his grace to all (Rom 11:32). I agree with Paul Althaus that there is both a universal restoration and a particular redemption.[14] There is "salvation in no one else" (Acts 4:12 NRSV), yet Jesus reaches out to all and claims all for his kingdom. We must avoid both universalism in which all things are destined to return to their original divine source (as in Origen), and particularism in which Christ's atoning work is limited only to the elect (as in Calvinism).

Both Karl Barth and Emil Brunner tried to affirm both dimensions in Christian salvation—the universal and the particular. Brunner contended that salvation is correlative with faith and that we must avoid speculation on how many will finally be saved. Barth was convinced that Christ's salvation is designed to reach all people and that all are objectively saved by reason of Christ's universal atonement. All are saved in principle (de jure), and through the outpouring of the Spirit this salvation will be made concrete and effective in daily life (de facto). Both of these Reformed theologians present biblical alternatives to Calvinistic orthodoxy, which consigned a significant part of the human race to damnation.

I contend that divine election is both universal and particular. It is universal in its outreach and particular in its efficacy for faith. All are elected to be in the service of Christ, but only some are destined for fellowship with Christ. The invitation goes out to all, but adoption is only for some. Unbelief is the reason for being barred from fellowship with Christ. God is the cause of our salvation; unbelief is the cause of our damnation. Whether human unbelief is final and irreversible will be discussed in a later section of this book.[15]

The mistake in the older liberal theology was to see the Word of God as a message of love only, not also as a word of judgment. Scripture is clear that the Word of God is a sword with two sharp edges. It cuts with an edge of life and with an edge of death. It always cuts with one side or the other—in a saving or a judging manner (cf. Is 49:2; Jn 12:47-48; 2 Cor 2:15-16; Heb 4:12; Eph 6:17; Rev 1:16; 2:12, 16-17; 19:15). God's Word is also likened to a fire which devours all that stands in its path and to a hammer "which breaks the rock in pieces" (Jer 5:14; 23:29).

In medieval theology it was sometimes said that all are predestined to grace, but only some are predestined to glory. I think it more biblical to contend that God's grace reaches out to all, and consequently all are destined to participate in his glory. Yet we will share in God's glory in different ways, depending on our response to his gracious invitation. God will be glorified in the salvation of some and in the damnation of others. At the same time, damnation is always in the service of salvation. God makes "the wrath of men" to praise him (Ps 76:10). Grace introduces even the reprobate to glory, though this will indubitably be an unsettling experience. The challenge facing the Christian church today is to recover the universal implications of the gospel without falling into universalism, which asserts that all will be saved irrespective of their faith and obedience.

A Theology of Paradox

Predestination is best understood in the light of the paradox of divine sovereignty and human responsibility. God is in control, but humans are still accountable for their actions. They are responsible for fulfilling the requirement of a godly life that God demands from all of his children.

Rationalists are not at home in the world of paradox, since they prefer ideas that are clear and distinct (à la Descartes). Their goal is to resolve or dissolve the paradox in order to make the truth of its assertions comprehensible. Pannenberg urges us to think through the paradox so that mystery does not entirely eclipse rationality.[16] For rationalists paradox does not overturn the laws of logic; instead these laws enable us to penetrate through paradox and mystery to rational ultimacy.[17]

The biblical view is quite different. Meaning is not reduced to logic nor is meaning dissolved in mystery. Instead, meaning shines through mystery. God truly reveals himself, but he remains hidden in his revelation. Paradox is involved in both the drama of human salvation and the mystery of divine incarnation.[18] Kierkegaard called the latter "the absolute paradox," since it constitutes the source of everything that is enigmatic and inscrutable in Christian faith.

Despite his immersion in philosophy Augustine astutely discerned the unfathomable and paradoxical character of divine revelation:

> Without God we cannot,
> Without us, he will not.[19]

Indeed, "He who created you without your help, will not save you without your cooperation."[20] The paradox lies in the biblical truth that we cannot cooperate without being enabled to do so by divine grace. Yet God will withhold his grace if we refuse to cooperate.

Perhaps more than any other thinker in the modern era, Søren Kierkegaard made paradox fashionable in theology.[21] Yet he was adamant that there is no paradox in God, and therefore paradox is an appearance, not reality in itself. Paradox is the logical form of truth that excites passion, inwardness and faith.

Another seminal thinker who acknowledged the pivotal role of paradox in Christian thought was P. T. Forsyth, who affirmed the kingdom of God as a free gift to undeserving sinners and yet who held to the necessity of working out our salvation.

> Only by moral effort, discipline, and experience does the believer become the Christian he is. He must acquire his legacy. This, of course, is a paradox. But then paradox, where mystery is not only dark but aggressive, not only dim but absurd, is the very nature of Christianity as spiritual. Christ's is not the religion of common sense and mother-wit. The great practical problem of Christianity is to incarnate the paradox, and reconcile these two ideas of the Kingdom in a working fashion for experience.[22]

The theme of paradox is also conspicuous in the theologies of Emil Brunner, Paul Tillich, Reinhold Niebuhr and Paul Jewett. Brunner remains close to Kierkegaard when he contends that "the object of faith is something which is absurd to reason, i.e. paradox; the hallmark of logical inconsistency clings to all genuine pronouncements of faith."[23] For Brunner, paradox is not simply a logical difficulty in the process of communicating the faith, for it inheres in the very nature of faith. Tillich affirms paradox but does not wish to say that paradox offends rationality. "Paradox points to the fact that in God's acting finite reason is superseded but not annihilated; it expresses this fact in terms which are not logically contradictory but which are supposed to point beyond the realm in which finite reason is applicable."[24] Niebuhr's basic stance is that "in all matters of rationality . . . the complexity of the data forbids premature systematization."[25] Jewett differentiates between paradoxes that are the outcome of fallacious reasoning and those that mark the limits of human reason.[26]

As I see it, paradox in the biblical milieu is an event, not a proposition. It may be contradictory to reason but not to experience. The incarnation of God in Jesus Christ is not a contradictory event but an extraordinary event that escapes human comprehension. Paradox in the context of Christian faith is not a logical riddle nor a verbal puzzle but the inbreaking of a new reality into human thought and experience. Yet it carries a meaning that illumines the facts of human existence. We should not glory in paradox but rejoice in the reality that comes to us in the form of paradox.

Theology under the impact of rationalism has often succumbed to the fallacy of false alternatives—the view that in the mysteries of faith human logic allows for only two options and these are mutually exclusive.[27] On the subject of divine sovereignty and human freedom it is alleged that the only alternatives are monergism (God does all) and synergism (God does his part and mortals do theirs). The affirmation of one means the exclusion of the other. But Christian faith discerns another alternative—one that includes the truth in both monergism and synergism. We might call it the mystery of double agency in which God does all but in and through human action. I fully agree with Berkouwer: "There is no place for a divine *Alleinwirksamkeit*, a divine sole activity, that sees all human activity as a threat to God's own glory."[28] All the creative and salvific power lies in God (*Allwirksamkeit*), but God grants humans a role in the salvific undertaking, though our role is not to determine but to follow. God acts prior to and in conjunction with the human subject, but God is not the exclusive actor in the drama of salvation. God's action does not cancel human agency but empowers human agency.[29] The ontological change within humanity is effected by God alone, but the psychological change involves human cooperation.

The laws of human logic are not annulled by God but instead are superseded by God. Both Ernst Troeltsch and Paul Tillich used the term "metalogic" to refer to the reasoning that takes into consideration the arational, tragic and fateful element in human history.[30] Both thinkers were unhappy with Hegel's panlogism that threatened the dynamic character of history. Emil Brunner used the term "alogic" to indicate the mysterious working of God in human life that cannot be captured by rational deliberation.

Protestant orthodoxy endeavored to avoid the peril of determinism by positing primary and secondary causes in which God acts, but in and through outward means. Some scholars also drew a distinction between natural and moral ability, holding that sinful humans have lost only the second. A parallel distinction was sometimes made between moral and metaphysical freedom. Through sin we have lost the freedom to do the good, but we retain the freedom to follow our own desires. As Luther put it, "We are free in the things below but not in the things above."[31]

Our works of faith and obedience do not help to procure Christ's redemption, but they do communicate the fruits of his redemption to the world. They are not causal agents in our redemption, but they are signs that Christ's redemption is being carried forward by the Spirit. They give substance to our vocation, but they do not insure our reconciliation and redemption. These last works belong to God;[32] yet through his Spirit God makes us active in receiving and acknowledging them. We cannot save ourselves, but we can demonstrate our gratefulness to God for what he has done for us in Jesus Christ.

Openness and Mystery

In contrast to the fathers of the ancient church, evangelical rationalists link faith with clarity—almost to the exclusion of mystery. The legacy of Descartes remains in both liberal and conservative Protestantism, but especially in the latter. Descartes gave utterance to the ethos of modernity: "I am determined to accept nothing but what I can clearly and distinctly perceive to be true."[33] For Edward John Carnell, who unites Descartes' rationalism with Lockean empiricism, faith "is a resting of the mind in the sufficiency of the evidences. Saving faith may go beyond this general expression, but it does not exclude it."[34] Hugh Ross manifests a similar orientation: "Biblical faith, like the faith exercised by scientists, must be . . . rooted in testable facts and logic."[35] Vincent Brümmer argues against a theology of paradox in favor of an "internally coherent" theology.[36] David Basinger regards "the law of noncontradiction" as a tool by which we identify biblical truth.[37] Against the above views and in keeping with the deepest intuitions of the catholic faith, Thomas Torrance argues that there is no logical bridge between concepts and reality. With the modern empiricists he affirms an epistemological realism, but it is a realism in which the object makes itself known rather than being under the control of the subject.[38]

What this means for the doctrine of predestination is that faith must resist the pull of human logic to portray predestination as causal determinism. In contrast to this rationalistic mentality, faith views predestination as part of the good news effecting human liberation, not as a threat that casts a pall over all human endeavor. The challenge in our day is to make predestination preachable once again, and it can be preachable only as good news (James Daane).[39] Predestination means that grace is not only sovereign but also irresistible, for when one becomes convinced of the depth of Christ's love, how can one resist Christ's gracious invitation? Martin Luther put it succinctly: "Since God is dependable—his predestination cannot fail, and no one can withstand him—we still have hope in the face of sin."[40]

We cannot plumb the mystery of God's working in our lives, but we can know something: his will is gracious and his promises are certain. Building upon an illustration from Charles Finney, I see the natural person in a canoe paddling obliviously toward a gigantic waterfall, which would mean certain death.[41] Finney says someone on safe ground cries "Stop!" thereby motivating us to change our course and paddle toward the shore. In Calvinism, by contrast, the current proves too strong. We are headed inexorably toward our doom. Our hope resides in a helicopter or something similar from the beyond that suddenly appears and lifts us out of the canoe, which capsizes and finally breaks apart on the rocks at the base of the falls. In my judgment the Calvinist vision is more true to Scripture and experience; yet it may dim the biblical truth that we are not altogether passive in our redemption but are made active by a will superior to our own.

Another illustration that illumines the mystery and paradox of salvation is a man sinking in quicksand. The more he struggles the more precarious is his situation. A Savior figure then appears and lassoes him with a rope. He is pulled safely to solid ground as he clings to the rope as his only hope. The Bible does indicate that we can cut the rope and in our absurdity sink into oblivion (Heb 10:26-29; 2 Pet 2:20-22). No person in their right mind would do such a thing, but the very nature of sin is that it is irrational and absurd.

The mystery of divine sovereignty and human liberty is further illumined by an illustration from John Polkinghorne in which he likens world history to a dramatic production of which God is both author and producer.[42] History is not a puppet theater, for God allows the actors to realize their roles in their own way. God becomes part of the process when he appears as one of the visible actors—Jesus Christ. Yet I contend that God foreknows how each actor will respond, and he guides the actors in their response. Herein lies the inscrutable mystery of how providence coincides with human freedom.

As has already been noted, Peter Forsyth was poignantly aware that human salvation is both a gift and a task: "The believer already belongs in Christ to the future, and the future is already his. He has the redemption. But on the other hand it is also the Christian's *moral ideal*. It needs time to come home. Only by moral development is its perfection projected."[43]

A theology of paradox takes us beyond the polarity of rationalism and mysticism. The truth of faith cannot be made rationally comprehensible, but it can throw light on the ambiguities of human existence. It cannot be assimilated into a rational system, but it can give coherence and intelligibility to the church's proclamation. It is not antirational but suprarational. It leads us beyond the parameters of human reason, but it is not an absurdity. The Word of God invites us to use our reason responsibly: "Come now, let us reason together, says the LORD" (Is 1:18).

John Sanders takes issue with my position that God's logic is not identical with human logic. He accuses me of not demonstrating how one "knows this to be the case."[44] He also objects to my conclusion "that no final rational solution of this issue is possible."[45] My reply is that holy Scripture plainly indicates that there is a disjunction between divine revelation and human reason.[46] Isaiah is adamant that God's thoughts are qualitatively different from human thoughts (Is 55:8-9). The mystery of God's saving love is inscrutable and unsearchable (Rom 11:33; Eph 3:8). The knowledge of revelation is too high to be captured by human reason (Ps 139:6). Yet in the eschaton we will come to know what is presently veiled to us. Now we know in part; then we shall know fully (1 Cor 13:12-13; 2 Cor 5:7). Now we can speak of God only by analogy and simile; then we shall be able to speak univocally, for faith will have been replaced by sight. We are predestined to share in a knowledge that now escapes our comprehension. Yet we can now have a foretaste of this knowledge sufficient to give guidance and direction to our earthly endeavors.

In summary, predestination does not cancel the human will but sets this will free to believe and obey. Human freedom is not overturned but placed on a new foundation. This mystery was not only enunciated by the Reformers and newly appreciated by Protestant neo-orthodoxy but also anticipated by many of the church fathers. I have already alluded to Augustine's concept of the will liberated by grace for service.[47] John Chrysostom declared, "Even the act of faith is not self-initiated. It is . . . *the gift of God*."[48] And in the words of Jerome, who emphasized human accountability: "Even this very freedom of choice has God as its author, and all things are to be referred to his generosity, in that he has even allowed us to will the good."[49] In biblical faith this mystery becomes credible only when we strive to believe, only when we act upon the announcement of God's unfathomable grace, only when we participate in his passion and victory over sin, death and the devil. God *for* us can be grasped only on the basis of God *in* us, but God does not reside within us apart from our faith and obedience.

Appendix B: Theology's Emancipation from Rationalism

The rationalist legacy of the Enlightenment has made an indelible imprint on both evangelical and liberal theologies, but it seems to be especially pronounced in the former.[50] Whereas the mainline Reformers advocated a theology of Word and Spirit, their successors in the age of Protestant orthodoxy sought to bring reason to the aid of faith. This in itself can be laudable, but there is a thin line between reason in the service of faith and faith depending on reason for its credibility. In Protestant orthodoxy the "doctrinal" and "conceptual" came to overshadow the "inexpressible."[51] Faith was translated into assent to propositional truth as opposed to trust in the mystery of God's providence and redemption. Whereas Protestant orthodoxy still made a place for mystery in faith, modern fundamentalism is inclined to hold to univocal knowledge of God and of his revelation in nature and history.[52] Whereas Protestant orthodoxy affirmed the incomprehensibility of God and the transcendence of God over his revelation, modern evangelical rationalism tends to equate divine revelation with holy Scripture and thereby makes revelation directly accessible to natural reason.[53]

Rationalism in this discussion is the appeal to human cognitive powers in the quest for knowledge of ultimate reality. For evidentialists these powers include sense perception, and the method is induction from experience. For the pure rationalists the goal is logical consistency and comprehensiveness.[54]

In evangelical rationalism, whether of the empiricist or apriorist hue, reason can validate the claims of faith and prepare the way for faith, though it cannot procure or induce faith. Faith is always a gift of God, but reason can show that faith is necessary for a right understanding of God and the self. In a theology of Word and Spirit, as I conceive it, reason can clarify and amplify the claims of faith, but it cannot of itself lead to faith or establish faith.

Against rationalism I contend that God is not exclusively or exhaustively rational (as in Gordon Clark's philosophy).[55] God is indubitably rational, but he is much more: he is indomitable will and creative energy.[56] He is not only a God who thinks but also a God who acts. God is not thought-thinking-upon-thought (as in Aristotle) but redeeming love reaching out to the unlovable.

Carl Henry is an example of an evangelical theologian who seeks to undergird the claims of revelation with an appeal to the rigors of logical thinking that includes the law of noncontradiction.[57] There is much in his theology that can be appreciated by a Word and Spirit theologian such as myself. I need only mention here the pivotal role of propositions in the explication of faith and faith's undeniable social and political consequences. He rightly reminds both the evangelical and the wider Christian communities that the overriding issue in theology is the meaning of truth, not any strategy for evangelism or church growth. Yet Henry defines truth in predominantly conceptual and propositional terms, not in terms of a divine-human encounter. He also subsumes faith under an apologetic agenda rather than allowing faith to defend itself through the power of the Holy Spirit.

What we find in Henry is a qualified rationalism that assigns reason a major role in coming to faith but recognizes that reason cannot compel obedience except through faith.[58] For Henry revelation is the communication of knowledge concerning the nature of God, his deeds and promises—knowledge given to us preeminently in holy Scripture. Scripture is the source of salvific knowledge of God, and reason is the instrument by which we grasp this knowledge. I would say that the source of our knowledge of God is the living Jesus Christ who speaks to us by his Spirit through the instrumentality of holy Scripture but also through preaching, sacred tradition, works of mercy, and so on. For Henry the authority of Scripture is also the authority of reason, since Scripture embodies the rationality of God. He insists that "the truth of revelation" can be known "prior to commitment to Christ." "An unbeliever can know the meaning of revelation and the meaning of life and history if only he will heed what the Bible teaches."[59] In Henry's view the role of the Spirit is to assist us not in knowing the propositional content of Scripture but in committing our lives to the truth of Scripture. The Fall did not impair our rational competence to recognize truth, but it did impede the will to pursue truth.

Henry does not deny the residue of mystery in revelation, but basically God's secret is now "an open secret," since God has truly though not exhaustively revealed himself to all who will make an effort to heed the scriptural witness. With the Reformers I contend that even in his revelation God remains the hidden God (*deus absconditus*).[60] God can be known only as he gives himself to be known by his Spirit speaking in conjunction with the written and proclaimed word of God. Henry acknowledges an extraverbal side of revelation, but it belongs to the rim of revelation, not its center.[61]

I stand with Henry in his reservations concerning arguments from empirical evidences that somehow bolster the authority or credibility of revelation. I also endorse his warning against a biblical obscurantism that denies the findings of science concerning the age of the earth, the poetic nature of some biblical stories, and so on.[62] Yet I take strong exception to his virtual reduction of Christianity to a logical system that rests on undemonstrated axioms (presuppositionalism) rather than a fellowship of faith whose witness is always reformable and open-ended.[63]

In a Word and Spirit theology Christianity is both a way and a doctrine. It is a way of life that authenticates the doctrinal affirmations of faith and also a doctrine that leads directly into a way of life. Kierkegaard made a signal contribution in his contention that our principal adversary as Christians is not shoddy reasoning (though this must always be combated) but human vanity, which insists that there is practically nothing that we are not capable of understanding.[64] He declared, "The fight of faith is not a fight without doubt, thought against thought, but a fight for character."[65] For Kierkegaard our task as people of faith is not to prove the rational superiority of Christianity but to demonstrate its moral power to remold and reclaim broken lives.

Against evangelical rationalism I see the language of faith, including the language of Scripture, as second-order language. It is not itself revelation but a human witness to revelation. It is therefore open to critical investigation and even reformulation in the light of a higher criterion—the living Word of God who speaks in and through and sometimes over and against his witnesses. We must never confuse our language and interpretations with God's self-interpretation in Jesus Christ, for this would be idolatry. First-order language belongs to God alone; yet we can really know God and his plan of salvation only when his Spirit illumines the second-order language of faith. God speaks to us not only indirectly through the words of the prophets and apostles but also directly and immediately by his Spirit. Yet his direct speaking is always in conjunction with the witness of the church and of the Bible.[66]

We cannot be disciples at first hand unless we hear the personal address of God in Jesus Christ. If our faith consists only in intellectual assent to the traditions of the church, it is not yet saving faith. It becomes saving faith when Christ encounters us personally and directly. Then we become disciples at first hand, for we now know and perceive what God has in store for us.[67]

This discussion has immense implications for eschatology, since Christian faith is founded on the assumption that now we walk by faith, not by sight (2 Cor 5:7). In this earthly pilgrimage we still see—

yet only through a glass darkly (1 Cor 13:12). The light and truth of God's self-revelation in Jesus Christ is being unfolded in history, and we can participate in this truth through faith and obedience. Yet we cannot comprehend this truth in all of its sublimity and majesty while we are still in mortal flesh. We are now living in the age that Scripture calls the fulfillment of time, but its realities can be only dimly grasped by human reason, even a believing reason. Historical time is being invaded by eternal time, a mystery that can only be captured in the language of poetry and myth—never divorced from fact but always united with fact.[68]

The central task of theology is neither biblical summarization (as in biblicism) nor a synthesis with cultural wisdom (as in modernism); instead its mission is to herald a message that is always the same, yet always new. Theology reaches its goal not in exegesis but in application—relating the promises and demands of faith to the existential situation in which people find themselves. We cannot truly sense the impact of the incomparable victory of Jesus Christ over the powers of darkness until we translate this victory into a style of life that runs counter to the values and pressures of the cultural ethos. The new way of life that Christianity upholds will always entail a spoken witness, but this witness lacks depth and viability unless it is suffused with the power of Christ's resurrection from the dead and the expectation of his return in glory to set up the kingdom that shall have no end.

The Current Debate

The controversy that presently rages within evangelicalism over the doctrine of God raises again the specter of rationalism penetrating into the domain of theology.[69] Open theism (also known as the openness of God theology) posits a God who is ever changing and whose perfection lies not in self-sufficiency (as in classical theism) but in a dynamic relationship to a struggling humanity.[70]

Interestingly both sides in this conflict appeal to logical demonstration as well as evidential corroboration in support of their position.

The defenders of open theism argue that the poetic accounts in the Bible of God changing his mind must be read univocally to describe metaphysical changes within the very being of God. On the other side, the argument is made that such language remains on the level of poetry and cannot be used to argue for the passibility and changeability of God. I propose that we learn to think dialectically. The thesis is that God does not change in any respect; the antithesis is that God necessarily changes as he interacts with mortals; the synthesis is that God wills to interact with mortals but without changing in the integrity of his being or in his overarching will and purpose for humankind. The synthesis proves at the same time to be a paradox, since its truth cannot be contained within the parameters of reason.

Open theists are wrong to claim on the basis of either the Bible or logic that God knows the future only in part. I concur with the judgment of J. I. Packer that much of the current theological confusion is due to "the intruding of rationalistic speculations, the passion for systematic consistency, a reluctance to recognize the existence of mystery and . . . a consequent subjecting of Scripture to the supposed demands of human logic."[71] Yet we must not relegate reason to a secondary role; as Christians we are called not to repudiate reason but instead to harness reason in the service of faith seeking understanding (Packer would agree). Reason by itself cannot bring us to faith, but it can clarify what faith affirms; yet this clarification can only be partial because reason can never encompass either the mystery of God's inner being or the paradox of God's sovereign will working concurrently with human decision and obedience.[72]

·TEN·

ISRAEL'S
SALVATION

The Supersessionist Controversy

And even those of Israel, if they do not persist in unbelief, will be grafted in, for God has
the power to graft them in again.
ROMANS 11:23 NRSV

Is the church ever really the "saved" People of God until the Jews too find salvation?
GEORGE A. F. KNIGHT

The faithlessness of Israel cannot nullify God's faithfulness.
MARKUS BARTH

In the past several decades the paradoxical relationship between
the church and Israel has been painstakingly reexamined in the
mainline Protestant denominations as well as in the Roman Catholic Church. The tragically horrendous event of the Holocaust has been
the catalyst for the new interest in this problem. A growing number of
theologians have argued that the church cannot be considered the
saved people of God without the inclusion of Israel, to whom the covenant of grace was originally given. It is further maintained that the ancient covenant with Israel is still in force and that Israel has therefore
not been superseded by the church in the plan of salvation. The con-

tinuing validity of Judaism is affirmed not simply as a preparation for the realization of the covenant promises in Christianity but as "a viable, integrated, and fully adequate response to God's call for faithfulness as found in the Hebrew Scriptures."[1]

Franklin Littell sees the myth of supersession, which he claims originated in the early church, as having two foci: "(1) God is finished with the Jews; (2) the 'new Israel' (the Christian church) takes the place of the Jewish people as carrier of history."[2] In the revisionist schema, Israel has its own unique contribution to be a light to the nations; and the church is another light, but not one that surpasses or supersedes Israel.

In defense of the traditional position, the Lutheran scholar Johannes Aagaard argues that the church is the new and only Israel.[3] Because ethnic Israel has become secularized, the Jews have the same calling as other nations—to acknowledge the Messiah of God. The church is the people of the New Covenant and the sole eschatological reality. To the traditionalist H. H. Rowley it is clear that in Paul's thought the church was not co-elect with the synagogue but had inherited the synagogue's election. Therefore "the Jews who would not accept Christ had forfeited their election, and were branches torn out of the tree."[4]

In revisionist theory, both Judaism and Christianity are looking forward to an ultimate redemption, and their unique witness to this redemption should command mutual respect. One implication is that the Jews' non-acceptance of Jesus as the Christ is to be viewed as an act of obedience to God, not disobedience.[5] Another is that Christianity must surrender or at least qualify its exclusivistic claims regarding truth and salvation.

The Mystery of Israel's Election and Rejection

The mystery of the Jews as the chosen people of God is to be understood in light of the wider biblical view that God intends his covenant of grace for all humanity. All peoples are destined to serve the glory of God and participate in the kingdom of God. Scripture tells us that for the realization of this universal promise God chose Abraham and his descendants to be the light to guide the nations to true faith and loving service in his name. In the promise contained in the covenant with Abraham, it is expressly said that "in you all the families of the earth shall be blessed" (Gen 12:3 NKJ). The book of Isaiah makes clear that Israel has been elected to be a light to lighten the Gentiles (Is 42:6; 49:6; cf. Lk 2:32; Acts 13:47; 26:23). The last day, which will bring redemption to Israel, will also be the day of judgment and redemption for the nations (Is 2:2-4; 25:6-9; Mic 4:1-4). The eschatological fulfillment will see Egypt and Assyria sharing in the blessings given to Israel (Is 19:24-25). On that day the temple of Israel shall be called "a house of prayer for all peoples" (Is 56:7; Mt 21:13; Mk 11:17; Lk 19:46).

While there are various covenants articulated in Old Testament history, on close examination they prove to be dimensions or facets of the one covenant of grace, which was instituted not because of Israel's supposed righteousness but simply because of God's gratuitous, unfathomable love (cf. Deut 9:4-6; 10:15).[6] The fruits of the covenant are, however, conditional on Israel's obedience, for it is said that God will withhold his blessings if Israel tolerates injustices or turns to idolatry (Is 5:24-25; Jer 2:20-37; Amos 5:18-27).

In the midst of covenantal disobedience Israel is promised a new covenant to be written on the hearts of all believers, assuring Israel of God's unremitting faithfulness to his people (Jer 31:31-34; Ezek 34:25; 37:26-28). This covenant is not entirely new, however, for the same law is affirmed; but it has now become a law of spirit and life, sealed in the innermost depths of our being by the Spirit of God. This new covenant is to be seen as a reaffirmation of the covenants with Abraham, Moses and David. It is unconditional in that it proceeds out of the free grace and mercy of God, but its efficacy is contingent on faith and obedience. At the same time, faith and obedience are virtually assured because of the way the covenantal promises will be applied to God's people.

In the New Testament, the covenant is personified and fulfilled in the Messiah of Israel, Jesus Christ. The covenant of grace given to Israel is reenacted in the death and resurrection of Jesus Christ (Mk 14:24; 1 Cor

11:25). The followers of Christ are regarded as the members of the new covenant (2 Cor 3:6), although the covenant with Israel is not annulled (Lk 1:72; Acts 3:25; Gal 3:17). The covenant of grace made with Israel reaches its fulfillment in the outpouring of the Holy Spirit upon all flesh—Jews and Gentiles (Acts 2:17). The breaking down of the wall of hostility between Jews and Gentiles takes place in the atoning death of Christ, despite all evidence to the contrary (Gal 3:28; Eph 2:11-18).

The mystery of Israel's election to be a light to the nations is deepened in view of Israel's subsequent rejection of its Messiah, Jesus Christ. Because of this disobedience in not acknowledging Christ as the culmination of the covenantal promises, a hardening has come over Israel that prevents it from seeing the light. Paul complains, "To this day whenever Moses is read a veil lies over their minds; but when a man turns to the Lord the veil is removed" (2 Cor 3:15, 16). While some Jews, including virtually all the apostles, were ready to acknowledge the Messiah, the great majority refused to believe, partly because the messiah who came was not the messiah who was expected (Reinhold Niebuhr). Judaism looked forward to a this-worldly kingdom that would liberate the people of God from oppression, but the kingdom inaugurated by Jesus was a spiritual kingdom conquering by the power of suffering love.

In Romans 9—11 Paul delineates a theology of Israel and the church that demands careful examination. Paul identifies believing Israel with the remnant (Rom 9:27), the company of the faithful acclaimed in Isaiah 10:22. "Not all who are descended from Israel belong to Israel, and not all are children of Abraham because they are his descendants" (Rom 9:6-7). He likens unbelieving Israel to Pharaoh whom God raised up for the very purpose of revealing his power and mercy so that his holy name might be "proclaimed in all the earth" (Rom 9:17). Unbelieving Israel signifies the vessels of wrath made for destruction that are endured so that the riches of God's glory may be poured into the vessels of mercy—believing Israel and believing Gentiles (Rom 9:22-24). In discussing the inclusion of the Gentiles in the family of God, Paul cites

Hosea: "Those who were not my people I will call 'my people,' and her who was not beloved I will call 'my beloved'" (Rom 9:25). Israel pursuing a righteousness based on law did not attain it, whereas Gentiles who saw in Christ the hope of the world received a righteousness based on faith.

What is important to understand is that both Israel's rejection and the Gentiles' election are acts of God that belong to the mystery of divine providence. To be sure, Israel's disobedience provoked God's displeasure, but this very disobedience was sanctioned by God for the express purpose of opening up the blessings of the covenant with Israel to the Gentile nations. "Through their trespass salvation has come to the Gentiles" (Rom 11:11), and thus God's purposes for the redemption of the world are fulfilled.[7]

In Romans 11 we are introduced to the still deeper mystery that God's rejection of Israel is not final. The covenant made with Abraham is likened to an olive tree that does not wither and die when some branches become barren. These barren branches, representing unbelieving Israel, are broken off; but in their place are grafted in branches from a wild olive tree, representing here the Gentile believers. Moreover, the natural branches that have been discarded can be grafted in again if they do not persist in their unbelief (Rom 11:23).

Paul then goes on to confess that the gifts and call of God are irrevocable (Rom 11:29). Even if Israel is faithless, God is faithful (Rom 3:3-4). His rejection of his people is not final but only provisional. In the "No" of God's rejection is hidden the "Yes" of his election. Those whom God elected to be his witnesses will by no means be permanently discarded. Indeed, even in their rejection they continue to be signs of the mercy and power of God among the Gentiles. "As regards the gospel they are enemies of God, for your sake; but as regards election they are beloved for the sake of their forefathers" (Rom 11:28). God has consigned all peoples, both Jews and Gentiles, to disobedience so that he might have mercy on all (Rom 11:32). The way he reveals his mercy, however, will be different—depending on his own plan of salvation that has its source in his own wisdom, which defies the wisdom of humankind.

A hardening will come upon part of Israel until the full number of Gentiles comes in; then "all Israel will be saved" (Rom 11:25, 26). Paul foresees not the casting away of Israel but its final redemption in union with the redemption of all elect Gentiles. That this redemption is contingent on faith is made clear in Romans 10:5-17 and 11:23, where Paul is adamant that the way to salvation for both Jew and Greek is the way of faith in Jesus Christ as Lord and Savior of the world (cf. Zech 12:10-13).

When Paul confesses that "all Israel will be saved," he is indubitably thinking of the future restoration of ethnic Israel. Calvin erred when he interpreted "all Israel" to mean the sum total of the complete church—Gentile Christians and the remnant of believing Jews. It was the Puritans and Pietists who reclaimed the Pauline hope for Israel as a nation and through Israel hope for the world.[8] This hope was shared by our Lord himself, for Jesus looked forward to that joyous day when his people would acclaim him as the Messiah of Israel and Lord and Savior of the world: "I tell you, you will not see me again, until you say, 'Blessed is he who comes in the name of the Lord'" (Mt 23:37-39).

Karl Barth interprets Romans 11 as affirming that "God's *mercy* must and shall be revealed to all Israel."[9] This should not be taken to mean, however, that every member of ethnic Israel will finally come to faith, and the same holds true for Gentiles. God's kindness is revealed in the outpouring of his Holy Spirit upon the nations; but unless they acknowledge this salvific work, they too will be cut off (Rom 11:22). God's kindness will once again be manifested to the Jews; and while Paul foresees the nation as a whole coming to true faith, this does not mean that there will not be some who, having seen the light, go back to the old ways and crucify the Son of God anew (cf. Heb 6:4-6; 2 Pet 2:20). It is possible to quench and grieve the Holy Spirit, but God's sovereign purposes will not finally be thwarted even by human unbelief, though the result may be the humiliation rather than the exaltation of the sinner.

What is also significant in Romans 9—11 is that the church is portrayed as dependent on Israel for the fulfillment of its mission.[10] Israel is the root that sustains the church, and not vice versa (Rom 11:18). At the same time, Paul also tells us that in another sense Israel stands in need of the church, for it is through the gospel proclaimed by the church that Israel will come to appreciate anew its glorious heritage and enter into its glorious destiny (Rom 10:8-17; 1 Cor 1:21-24).

Nowhere in the New Testament is it asserted that the Jewish people as a whole are under some irremediable curse because of their rejection of Jesus Christ. Even in 1 Thessalonians 2:15, where Paul refers to the Jews as killers of Jesus Christ and of the prophets, his reference is plainly to Jews who are persecuting the church and not to Israel as such. While left desolate because of its intransigence, Israel will be enabled by God's grace to acknowledge and rejoice in the Messiah when he comes again (Mt 23:37-39). Scripture makes clear that those immediately responsible for the death of Christ, both Jews and Romans, acted out of ignorance (cf. Lk 23:34; Acts 3:17-18; 13:27-30). The real cause of Christ's death was God himself, who decreed that the Messiah must suffer.

At the same time, because of Israel's esteemed place in the plan of salvation, because Israel is "the apple of the eye" of the Lord (Deut 32:10; Ps 17:8; Zech 2:8), because Israel is the prototype of sinful humanity favored by grace but rebelling against this same grace, because Israel is beloved by the Lord even in its iniquity and rejection, other nations are provoked to jealousy and resentment. There is moreover in the people of Israel an ineradicable transparency to the living God as Lord and Savior (Is 49:16) that serves as a painful reminder to outsiders of their own guilt and condemnation by God. The Jews are a living mirror of God's judgment against unbelief but also of God's incomparable grace that confounds human sin.

The Jews are hated by the world not so much because they are thought of as Christ killers but paradoxically because they are Christ bearers. They constitute an irrevocable sign of the divine light that has come to enlighten the world in its darkness, and darkness cannot withstand this light.[11] It is their witness to Christ even in their rejection of him that aggravates the sin within people and nations and creates the suspicion and hatred known as anti-Semitism.

One text often cited to explain the precarious existence of the Jews is Matthew 27:25: "His blood be on us and on our children." It is true that the enemies of Christ among the Jews invited this kind of curse upon their own people, but God's ways are not our ways. If "the blood of Jesus comes upon the children of Israel, it comes upon them as a savior's blood,"[12] for his blood is salvific, not avenging. By means of the shedding of Christ's blood, remission of sins is brought to both Jews and Gentiles. Both are under the sign of the cross; but this is especially true of the Jews, since Christ came to give glory to the people of Israel as well as be a light of revelation to the Gentiles (Lk 2:32).

When we fallaciously make the Jews the scapegoat for the death of Christ, we are guilty of a profound misreading of the drama of redemption as presented in the New Testament. The truer picture is that Jesus Christ himself is the scapegoat for the sins of the world, that God in Christ has taken upon himself the guilt and shame of the world so that all who believe might not perish but have eternal life (cf. Is 53:5, 6; Rom 4:25; 2 Cor 5:21; Gal 3:13). The penalty for sin is voluntarily borne by Christ and not simply Christ as man but Christ as the merciful and holy God. Both the Jews and Romans were instruments of God's redemptive purpose, even though they were obviously unaware of their privileged role in the divine plan of redemption culminating in Christ.

Judaism and Christianity

While both Christianity and Judaism have common roots in the heritage of the children of Israel as described in the Old Testament, the two faiths began to diverge markedly after the resurrection of Christ and even more after the destruction of the Jewish temple in A.D. 70. Rabbinic Judaism, which originated in the Exile, became ever more a religion of law; one scholar sees in the Mishnaic materials "no trace of a tendency to effect reforms" but instead "a veneration for the letter of tradition remarkable for pedantic insistence on verbal exactitude."[13] The idea of works and merit, which has a Hellenistic as well as a Judaic base, also became more pronounced in Christianity as it developed into a religion of ritualism and formalism, though the truth of *sola gratia* was again and again rediscovered in reforming movements.

The question that engages many scholars today is whether the Judaism of the New Testament was congruous or incongruous with the gospel of the kingdom of God as proclaimed by Jesus and his disciples. While there are definitely strands of continuity between the heritage of Israel and the religion of the new covenant focused on Jesus Christ, there are also striking dissimilarities. What the two religions have in common is a respect for the revealed law of God in the Old Testament, the desire to glorify God in every area of life, the messianic hope of the redemption of the world through the intervention of the living God in history, and the celebration of the momentous events of deliverance in Old Testament history, such as the exodus and the return from the exile.

Yet the teachings of Jesus and even more the theology of Paul introduced insights that could not easily be assimilated into Jewish tradition without a drastic reinterpretation of this tradition. Jewish scholar Joseph Klausner sees the un-Jewishness of Jesus in his radical reduction of the Torah to the spirit of love, the anational character of his teaching, and the concept of a God who requires love of enemies and lets his sun shine on both good and evil.[14] The idea of the Messiah who conquers by vicarious suffering and the powerlessness of love is definitely in the Old Testament heritage (cf. Is 52:13; 53:1-12), but it could not be harmonized with the Jewish hope for a this-worldly or political liberation. The doctrines of the incarnation of the preexistent Son of God in Jesus Christ and his bodily resurrection from the grave were to an even greater degree antithetical to rabbinic Judaism. The new wine of the gospel could not finally be contained in the old wineskins (Mt 9:16-17).

Given the radical discontinuity between rabbinic teachings and the teachings of the new covenant, it is not surprising that the supersessionist idea arose that Christianity has displaced Judaism in the plan of salvation. This notion could be read into John 1:17: "The law was given through Moses; grace and truth came though Jesus Christ"; and also in Romans 10:4: "Christ is the end of the law, that every one who has faith may be justified."

Yet there are other passages that show the inseparability of law and gospel, works and grace. Matthew records these words of our Lord: "Think not that I have come to abolish the law and the prophets; I have come not to abolish them but to fulfill them" (Mt 5:17). Paul was adamant that although we are justified *by* the righteousness of Christ alone received by faith, we are justified *for* righteousness in daily living. We are called to present our bodies as living sacrifices, "holy and acceptable to God" (Rom 12:1-2), out of gratitude for what God has done for us in Christ. The ethos of the Old Testament is certainly conspicuous in this Petrine admonition: "As he who called you is holy, be holy yourselves in all your conduct; since it is written, 'You shall be holy, for I am holy.' And if you invoke as Father him who judges each one impartially according to his deeds, conduct yourselves with fear throughout the time of your exile" (1 Pet 1:15-17).

Rabbinic Judaism might be described as a covenantal nomism, in which obedience to the law fulfills the conditions of a covenant that has its ultimate origin in God's unsurpassable grace. It can also be depicted as an ethical monotheism in which the belief in one God is to be demonstrated through a life of service to the community of faith.

The Christian revelation does not necessarily call these into question, but it radicalizes the demands of faith to include love of enemies. It upholds, moreover, the justification of the ungodly based on faith in a righteousness wholly extrinsic to the sinner, whereas Judaism is inclined to speak of a justification of those who make progress toward personal righteousness.

Today the overwhelming temptation is to find points of convergence between Judaism and Christianity, especially in the sorry recognition that a churchly triumphalism that tendentiously disparaged Judaism contributed substantially to the virus of anti-Semitism culminating in the Holocaust. Yet a creative syncretism could undermine both the integrity of Judaism as a religion and the uniqueness of the Christ revelation. What we as Christians should strive for is not a synthesis of Judaism and Christianity but their mutual purification and transformation by the truth and power of the gospel of God revealed in Jesus Christ.

One can decry syncretism and at the same time acknowledge the inseparability of the two traditions. I can resonate with the Jewish scholar Franz Rosenzweig who sees Judaism as "the star of redemption" and Christianity as "the rays of that star." For Rosenzweig the church is the successor of Israel in one important respect: By virtue of the gospel the walls between Jew and Gentile are destroyed once and for all, and the covenant with Israel is now opened to the world in a way that Jewish faith could not provide.[15] As an evangelical Christian, I would see the star of redemption not as the religion of Judaism but as the covenant with Israel reaffirmed and fulfilled in Jesus Christ; the rays of the star signify not Christianity as a religion but the proclamation of the gospel in the power of the Spirit.

The revisionists are wrong and the traditionalists and supersessionists are right in this respect: The revelation of God in Christ introduces something indisputably new. It is not simply the Torah but now the Torah personified in a concrete individual that is upheld as the way to salvation. Our hope is not in obedience to the Torah but in God's gracious act of deliverance of those who could never obey perfectly because of the intractable reality of original sin (not acknowledged in Judaism).

Yet supersessionism is wrong when it denies or downplays the fact that Christianity represents not the annulment of the heritage of Israel but its fulfillment even in the midst of negation. It also fails to acknowledge that the covenantal promises still apply to Israel even though the covenantal relationship is partially broken, and that ethnic Israel still plays an important role in salvation history.

The epistle to the Hebrews could possibly be designated as a supersessionist book, since the author insists that the Old Testament sacrificial system and priesthood have been superseded by the all-sufficient sacrifice of Jesus Christ and his efficacious intercession as our one High Priest. Yet even here Old Testament heroes and heroines are celebrated as models of true faith in God. One passage intimates that the faith of Israel finally apprehends its object through the sanctifying of the church (Heb 11:40).

While insisting on the basic discontinuity between the revelation of God in Christ and Judaism as a religion, we must recognize that this discontinuity holds true for Christianity as well. The revelation of the Word of God is always a new act and never the possession of any religious institution. This revelation stands in judgment not only over the legalism in Judaic religion but also over the legalism and ritualism in the Christian religion. As Christians we must never boast of the superiority of our religion over the Judaic religion, for we too may be cast off if we do not continue in the covenant (Rom 11:22). What makes Christianity qualitatively distinct from Judaism is that in the church the lordship and saving work of Jesus Christ are openly acknowledged, whereas in Judaism these truths are denied. The church can therefore be a positive sign and witness of the redemption offered in Christ, whereas the synagogue can be at best a negative sign of this redemption. Yet the church can become the synagogue where trust in its own principles and laws overshadows the message of free grace, just as the synagogue can become the church where a perception of the unconditional character of grace and the messianic identity of Christ takes place.

Judaism and Christianity might be likened to two moons that reflect the light of the Sun of righteousness (Mal 4:2), who, in Christian perspective, is identical with the Son of God incarnate in Jesus of Nazareth. These moons do not possess any light in themselves but point to the light that resides in the living Christ. Both communities are signs of the redemptive mercy and awesome power and holiness of God. At the end of the age the Judaic moon will merge into the Christian moon, but even then the source of light will remain in God and his Word alone.

Again, the two communities might be compared to an orchestral symphony that confronts us with the beauty of the holiness of God as well as the depths of his love. Those instruments representing the heritage of Israel when played by themselves are in discord. On the other hand, there is a palpable incompletion or imbalance in the symphonic rendition when the contribution of Israel is deleted.[16] It is only when the orchestra functions as the Israel of God (Gal 6:16), the eschatological unity of the two traditions, that we have a perfect or full witness to the Wisdom of God incarnate in Christ.

Neither Judaism nor Christianity is in itself a way to salvation. The way to salvation is God's way to us revealed in Jesus Christ. Our task is to acknowledge that salvation does not lie in rites or ceremonies, in laws or traditions, even in worship that is done in spirit and in truth, but in God's miraculous act of condescension in Christ that sets all of our laws and rites on a new foundation. We should strive to live the life of godliness not to procure salvation or even to prepare the way for it, but to demonstrate and manifest a redemption already given in Jesus Christ.

Missions to the Jews?

Many theologians today argue against missions to the Jews partly on the grounds that in the light of the Holocaust such missions will seem insulting to Jews and partly on the grounds that people are already in contact with the true God in Judaism. Peter von der Osten-Sacken urges the church to give up its missionary attitude toward Israel and try to forge a fraternal relationship with the Jewish people.[17] Paul Van Buren suggests that Christian missions to Jews should be reinterpreted as protecting the Jews as a people and coming to their aid.[18]

Yet the church is betraying its evangelistic mandate if it withholds the gospel of salvation from the very people who gave us the Messiah and Savior of the world. Such an attitude could be construed as the worst kind of anti-Semitism because it means deliberately bypassing the Jews in giving out the invitation to the banquet of the kingdom (cf. Lk 14:15-24). Such an attitude could imply that the Jews are incapable or unworthy of receiving the blessings of the new covenant. Or it might suggest that they can best find God by adhering to their own laws and traditions, but this is to reinstate the dividing wall between Jew and Gentile that Christ tore down (Eph 2:14). Significantly the German Christians, those in the German church who sought to accommodate to Nazism, vigorously opposed missions to the Jews on the grounds of racial contamination.

The New Testament is unequivocal that the Jews too should be included in the Christian mission; indeed, they even have priority over the Gentiles. Paul declared that the gospel is "the power of God for salvation to everyone who has faith, to the Jew first and also the Greek" (Rom 1:16). The name of the Lord has to be carried "before the Gentiles and kings and the sons of Israel" (Acts 9:15). Our Lord said to his disciples on the eve of Pentecost: "You shall be my witnesses in Jerusalem and in all Judea and Samaria and to the end of the earth" (Acts 1:8).

I concur wholeheartedly with Markus Barth: "That the Law and the Prophets are fulfilled, that the dividing wall is broken down, that the good news is the same for every sinner and every nation—these facts cannot be kept secret by the Christians, for the Jews have as much right as do the Gentiles to hear of it, to experience it, to enjoy it."[19]

Karl Barth is even more forthright:

The whole Church of Jesus Christ needs the Jews. She needs their failure: even this has turned into riches for the world; she needs their remaining afar off: even this has enriched the Gentiles ([Rom.] 11:12); she needs their rejection: even this was the means of the world's redemption (11:15)—but she needs even more their full entrance into the faith in their Messiah (11:12), their addition to the Gentiles and Jews who already do believe in him (11:15). For when that happens, what is as yet hidden even from the Church will come to light; then she will receive those greater riches, now only promised to her: then the dead shall rise (11:15), then it will become manifest and evident, that in the death and resurrection of Jesus Christ the end and the new beginning of all things have already taken place, that the Kingdom of God on a new earth and under a new heaven has already begun in secret.[20]

Yet both father and son have profound reservations regarding missions to the Jews understood as an organized strategy of evangelizing. Their concern arises partly from the fact that the Jews are not to be placed in the same category as pagan nations and partly from the fact that only God converts.[21] What we can do is to share the story of salvation: but we cannot make it comprehensible, for it is based on the wholly unexpected and inexplicable intervention of God in the particular history of the man Jesus of Nazareth. Markus Barth cites the Constitution of the Netherlands Reformed Church after World War II in which the conversation with Israel is mentioned alongside of but not as part of the mission to the nations (Article VIII).[22]

While I empathize with the Barthian position on this question, I would retain the concept of missions to the Jews precisely because this mission differs qualitatively from missions to other peoples. It will involve a confession of indebtedness to the Jews for what they have given the church and the world (cf. Is 2:3; Jn 4:22) and also a confession of guilt for our complicity as Christians in fostering anti-Semitic attitudes through the ages. Unlike other peoples, the Jews are not called to something entirely new and unexpected but rather invited to share the fulfillment of their ancestral pledge made to Abraham.

The prophecy of Paul that "all Israel will be saved" rests on the confident hope that God himself will intervene and pour out his Spirit on Israel in an extraordinary way when the number of Gentiles is complete. Israel's restoration will depend not on the missionary expertise or apologetic strategy of the church, but on an unprecedented act of God in the last days.

Missions to Israel that result simply in the conversion of individuals should nevertheless command the support of the Christian community, for in this way we extend the hand of fellowship to those who are foreordained to be our brothers and sisters in the Lord. Such missions attest our faith in the present and future mercy of God and in the eternal validity of the covenant made with Israel. Jewish Christians have a special role in the economy of redemption, for they are a sign both of Israel's presence in the church and of the presence of Jesus Christ in Israel. They give a poignant testimony to both Israel and the church that the fullness of the Israel of God will not be realized until the eschatological day of redemption. They remind us that both Israel and the church have a common destiny just as they had a common origin. They remind us that the hope of the church and of the world rests on the Messiah of Israel who has come once but who will come again in power and glory to set up the eternal kingdom that shall have no end.

·ELEVEN·

THE TRIUMPH OF GRACE

He floods the darkness with light; he brings light to the deepest gloom.

JOB 12:22 NLT

Once more you will show us compassion
and wash away our guilt,
casting all our sins into the depths of the sea.

MICAH 7:19 REB

And when I am lifted up from the earth I shall draw everyone to myself.

JOHN 12:32 REB

Your malice may be measured, but God's mercy cannot be defined;
your malice is circumscribed, his mercies infinite.

JOHN CHRYSOSTOM

He descended into hell; the third day he rose from the dead.

THE APOSTLES' CREED

He is buried, but he rises again.
He goes down to hell, but he saves the damned.

GREGORY OF NAZIANZUS

There can be no question of God's giving up anything or anyone
in the whole world, either today or in all eternity.

CHRISTOPH BLUMHARDT

While giving serious consideration to the continuing battle between light and darkness, Scripture is unequivocally clear that light will triumph over darkness, that God's grace is more powerful than human sin. We are given the promise that "all the ends of the earth shall see the salvation of our God" (Is 52:10). And again from Isaiah: "From sabbath to sabbath, all flesh shall come to worship before me, says the LORD" (Is 66:23). In the words of Habbakuk: "The earth will be filled with the knowledge of the glory of the LORD, as the waters cover the sea" (Hab 2:14; 3:3; cf. Num 14:21; Ps 97:6). In the New Testament we are told that every knee shall bow before God and every tongue confess Jesus as Lord (Phil 2:9-11; Rom 14:11; cf. Is 45:23). When all things are subjected to God, then God will be "all in all" (1 Cor 15:28 KJV; cf. Eph 1:10).

The anger of God is but for a moment; the mercy of God is everlasting (Mic 7:18). A similar note can be detected in Lamentations 3:22: "The steadfast love of the LORD never ceases, his mercies never come to an end." This theme reappears in James 2:13: "Judgment is without mercy to one who has shown no mercy; yet mercy triumphs over judgment." The point is that the one who shows mercy need have no fear of judgment. Yet the deeper implication is that the one who judges rightly will be motivated by mercy, as is asserted in James 5:11: "You have seen the purpose of the Lord, how the Lord is compassionate and merciful."

The work of Christ on the cross and his glorious resurrection from the grave ensured the utter defeat of the powers of darkness. Death, hell and the devil will be cast into the lake of fire (Rev 20:10, 14; cf. 1 Cor 15:24-26). The sea, the symbol for the outer darkness, shall pass away (Rev 21:1). In Jesus Christ we see the glorious fulfillment of divine predestination, the concrete realization of the plan of salvation. This is the plan for the fullness of time—"to unite all things in him, things in heaven and things on earth" (Eph 1:10). "Through him God chose to reconcile the whole universe to himself, making peace through the shedding of his blood upon the cross—to reconcile all things, whether on earth or in heaven, through him alone" (Col 1:20 NEB). In our folly and sin we mortals are ready to deny the reality of God's gracious act of reconciling the whole world to himself (2 Cor 5:18-19), but God is faithful even while we are faithless (Rom 3:3-4; 2 Tim 2:13). God's grace breaks through the defenses of sinful humankind and accomplishes its purposes in and through and sometimes over and against human action.

Sacred tradition attests that God created all people for eternal life (Wis 2:23). This note was acutely discerned by Count Zinzendorf: "All human souls . . . are designed for salvation."[1] According to Zinzendorf many more persons are saved than lost. The lost are the exceptions.[2] In his theology the whole world has been set free from the curse of sin and darkness. Karl Barth, who builds on this insight, speaks of a liberated world rather than a demonized world. Barth is adamant that Christ is Savior as well as Lord of the whole human creation. First Timothy reminds us, however, that faith still makes a crucial difference: "We have our hope set on the living God, who is the Savior of all people, especially of those who believe" (1 Tim 4:10 NRSV).

God's judgment falls on all humanity in its sin and obduracy, but only to reveal the truth that God in his essence is love, not wrath. This note comes out clearly in Paul: "God has made all people prisoners of disobedience, so that he might show mercy to them all" (Rom 11:32 GNB).

What about those who have never heard the good news of God's reconciliation of humanity to himself in Jesus Christ? Jonathan Edwards echoes a theme widely pervasive in Christian tradition: "God will make all men to know the truth of those things which he speaks of in his word, one way or another; for he will vindicate his own truth."[3] Edwards is not implying that all people will be saved: rather he is affirming the scriptural dictum that all people will be exposed to the knowledge of salvation in one way or another, but always through God's providential oversight and guidance.

Tillich's depiction of the unfolding of the drama of redemption as an eschatological panentheism can be accepted with certain modifications. God will be all in all, but not all will be related to him in the same way. All things will be united in him, but this unity will be incomplete unless it rests on the mediation of Christ acknowledged by faith.

The universal triumph of Christ over the powers of darkness and evil has its basis in the universal atonement of Christ on the cross of Calvary. Christ will conquer in the end because he has already conquered in the fulfillment of time epitomized in the incarnation. Moreover, his triumph in his death and resurrection mirrors his original triumph at the beginning of all things, his victory at the creation where he brought the primordial chaos under control.[4] Creation itself is a demonstration of the power of grace over encroaching disorder, a power that is carried forward by the coming of Christ into human history. God's victory over the chaos will be given additional confirmation in his second coming, which will bring worldly history to an end and supplant the kingdoms of this world by the kingdom of God.

The Last Judgment

While the judgment of God impinges on all human history, indeed shapes the course of all history, Scripture is clear that there will be a final judgment when all people will have to give an account of their misdeeds before the throne of God. Scripture speaks of the great assize—when the company of true believers will be separated from the sons of perdition (cf. Dan 12:2; Mt 25; Rev 20:11-15). The last judgment will be not simply the revelation of all preceding judgments but their execution. Church tradition teaches that at the time of death every person will experience a foretaste of the final judgment. This particular judgment at death will be reaffirmed at the last judgment that signals the end of history.

The final judgment of the holy and righteous God upon the iniquity of humanity powerfully reveals the depth of his love toward that same humanity. Predestination has both negative and positive connotations, but the first is subordinate to the second.[5] God's predestination extends to all, but it will not be realized in the same way for all. All people are predestined to life and to the service of God's glory. God's reconciliation and predestination reach out to all mortals. Yet only those who respond in faith will be acknowledged as sons and daughters of the most high God. Only they will experience life in its fullest dimension—

characterized by joy, peace and blessedness. Those who reject the offer of God's grace are nonetheless made to serve grace. They are not sons and daughters of God but instead unwilling servants. They see Jesus only as Lord, not as Savior. For them Jesus is not the balm of Gilead but the messenger of doom. What they fail to discern is that Jesus Christ acts in mercy and love even when he executes judgment.

Thomas Aquinas was one who sought to hold together the polarities of judgment and mercy in God's dealings with humanity. "Although in justice God could deprive of existence and annihilate a creature that sins against him, yet it is more becoming justice that he keep it in existence to punish it." In the case of annihilation "justice would have no admixture of mercy, since nothing would remain to which he might show mercy; and yet it is written (Ps 25:10) that all the ways of the Lord are mercy and truth."[6] This note is also discernible in the Catholic mystic François Fénelon: "Thou grantest grace even to those who will forever experience the rigour of thy justice."[7]

From my perspective hell as the outer darkness, eternal perdition, has been destroyed by the cross and resurrection victory of Christ, since he died for all and his gracious election goes out to all. The possibility of ontological separation from God has been cancelled by Jesus Christ through his universal atoning sacrifice. This kind of hell has been excluded from God's purposes. Yet an inner darkness remains as a sign and shadow of what has been overcome. To the rejected it appears to include the horror of eternal separation from God. The truth of the matter is that the pain in hell is due to the presence of God rather than to his absence, to his unfathomable love rather than to any abysmal hatred, or what is worse, gross indifference.

Scripture tells us that the only sin that is unforgivable is the sin against the Holy Spirit (cf. Mt 12:31-32; Mk 3:28-29; Lk 12:10). This sin simply means the rejection of the great invitation to join the banquet in heaven. It consists of saying "No" to God's grace, though whether we can persist in saying "No" to a grace that is finally irresistible is something I shall consider in the next section of this chapter. P. T. Forsyth has this insightful observation: "The great sin is not something we do, but it is refusing to make ourselves right with God in Christ's Cross. We are judged in the end by our relation to the Cross of Christ."[8]

The sin against the Holy Spirit cannot be forgiven, but it can be changed—from a curse to a blessing, or from an unmitigated curse to a curse with a blessing. Our "No" to God's grace has dreadful consequences, but whether we can persist in resisting the only hope for salvation in the face of God's insurmountable grace is quite another matter. Even in our act of defiance we are upheld by God's grace. Even in our folly and hardness of heart we are never the objects of an election to damnation. We are sheep that have strayed from the fold, but the good Shepherd is pursuing us even into the darkness. Even if we make our bed in hell Christ is there ready to restore us if we will only accept the fact that he has borne the judgment on sin in our place and in the place of all humanity (cf. Ps 139:7-12).

The reality of hell must be taken seriously, but this is not a hell outside the compass of the love of God. Augustine confessed: "Why, then, do I ask Thee to come into me, since I indeed exist, and could not exist if Thou wert not in me? Because I am not yet in hell, though Thou art even there; for if I go down into hell Thou art there."[9]

In a depiction of the last things that is fully consonant with the mysteries of Christian faith, we must affirm no ultimate dualism but instead a duality within an ultimate unity. There is no coeternal evil, but an evil that has been overturned by good, though this fact has still to be realized by people. When our inward eyes are opened to the invincibility of God's grace and to the depth of his love as revealed in Christ, we then see that God's judgment is not opposed to his glory; his glory is indeed revealed in his judgment. The glory of God already fills all things, but it will be revealed as all-encompassing when Christ comes again to judge and redeem the world. I here heartily agree with Moltmann: "God's judgment in the Last Judgment is not God's last word. His last word is: 'Behold, I make all things new.'"[10] The last judgment is the opening of the doorway to the eternal kingdom of God that reaches out and includes all people, though this glorious fact remains hidden to the world of unbelief.

The Meaning of Hell

In biblical and catholic tradition hell is a place as well as a condition. It is not a physical place in the cosmos but a spiritual place. To affirm that hell is only a condition of the soul or state of mind is to separate body and soul. Greek dualism then takes priority over Hebraic holism. Even Pope John Paul II has not broken free from what I have called the biblical-classical synthesis.[11]

Both heaven and hell are dimensions of existence that transcend this present world. I cannot agree with Nicolas Berdyaev that "hell belongs to this world and not to the world beyond."[12] Surely hell begins in this world, but it is basically an eschatological category. It definitely belongs in a discussion of the last things.

Hell in the sense of an eschatological destination for those entrapped in their own iniquity is to be associated with gehenna more than with hades. Gehenna means "down there" and "in the darkness." It also carries the idea of a refuse heap upon which are tossed all the useless and corrupted things of life. Originally it designated a valley or ravine near Jerusalem, where living human victims were sacrificed. Gehenna was at one time the sanctuary of Moloch. But under the impact of divine revelation this symbol was transformed and came to mean a lake of fire.

The fire of hell is not, however, outside the compass of God's love. This insight was not lost to the church fathers. According to Isaac the Syrian: "The sorrow which takes hold of the heart which has sinned against love, is more piercing than any other pain. It is not right to say that the sinners in hell are deprived of the love of God. . . . But love acts in two different ways, as suffering in the reproved, and as joy in the blessed."[13] This note was also captured by Dante, who in his *Divine Comedy* inscribed over the gates of hell that it too was created by love.[14]

In biblical perspective mercy does not exclude punitive action or chastisement. God's mercy is not heedless, though in its spontaneity it rises above legal precept and obligation.[15] Real kindness means saying "No" as well as "Yes." Donald Baillie puts it rightly: "God must be inexorable towards our sins . . . not in spite of His love, but because of His love: not because His love is limited but because it is unlimited."[16] Von Balthasar has a similar understanding: "Crucified love is something that sears and consumes, and its two aspects—redemption and judgment—are inseparable and indistinguishable."[17] According to Thomas Merton, "If we refuse His love and remain in the coldness of sin . . . then will His fire (by our own choice rather than His) become our everlasting enemy, and Love, instead of being our joy, will become our torment and our destruction."[18]

God's compassion must not be confused with leniency. "No judgment is so terrible as that of love" (David Petander). Love has negative manifestations as well as positive. God's love is a holy love that sometimes involves being deaf to pleadings. His seeming indifference to our plight, however, is only for the purpose of preparing us for the glory of his salvation.

Hell in catholic tradition is a creation of God's love as well as of his justice. It is a manifestation of his mercy as well as of his holiness. Scripture too endorses this conception: "Execute true judgment and show mercy and compassion every man to his brother" (Zech 7:9 KJV; cf. Zech 8:16-17). If we refuse to show mercy to others, we cut ourselves off from God's mercy (Zech 7:10-14). According to Paul Tillich judgment is an act of love that allows that which resists love to self-destruct.[19] Hell or condemnation is "not the negation of love but the negation of the negation of love."[20] To phrase it another way, hell is the pain of knowing that God will eternally frustrate our inveterate desire to have our own way. Moreover, he does this for our own good and for the purpose of our conforming to his will.

A similar note can be detected in Richard John Neuhaus, who draws this daring conclusion: "Even the will to damnation is damned and thereby defeated by the One for whom and in whom damnation is not allowed the last word." From my perspective this line of reasoning does not necessitate the destruction of hell but instead calls for its radical reinterpretation, which brings hell into the light of heaven. Neuhaus and I are fairly close on this matter, but I resist following him into a quasi-universalism. Both of us from our similar yet different perspectives believe that Christians may hope even for those who will their own damnation because Christ in his incomparable love takes their damnation upon himself in his atoning suffering and death. But I would stress more than Neuhaus that our hope must be tempered by the realization that some may never see the light because of their intransigence and recalcitrance. Yet we can still rest assured that they are in the hands of a God who is all-merciful, even in his ineradicable holiness and awesome majesty.[21]

In the old theology hell signified separation from God's love, even from God's presence. The Baltimore Catechism made it clear that the denizens of hell are no longer objects of charity.[22] This idea is controverted by Psalm 89:30-33.

> If his children forsake my law and do not walk according to my ordinances, if they violate my statutes and do not keep my commandments, then I will punish their transgression with the rod and their iniquity with scourges; but I will not remove from him my steadfast love, or be false to my faithfulness.[23]

Some rigid Calvinists distinguish between God's chastisement of his children whom he loves and God's punishment of the wicked whom he hates. But this line of thinking ends in the doctrine of double predestination and drives an irreparable cleavage into the heart of God.[24]

Fire in the Bible symbolizes not the absence of God but his presence. God is depicted as "a consuming fire," a "devouring fire" (cf. Deut 4:24; 5:24-25; Ps 21:9; 29:7; 50:3; Is 29:6; 30:27, 30; Neh 9:12; Heb 12:29). Those who persist in unbelief will be tormented with fire in the presence of the Lamb and the holy angels (Rev 14:10). But Christ's presence is not acknowledged in hell as grace. Their penalty is separation from the blessings of God (2 Thess 1:9), but not from his presence, which is all-pervasive. This separation means the interruption, not the cessation, of all communion with God. Paul Althaus trenchantly defined hell as "inescapable godlessness in inescapable relationship to God."[25]

Fire in the Bible is a symbol of both God's love and God's wrath. When Scripture tells us that we must be salted with fire (Mk 9:49-50), the focus is on the positive effects of fire on the human soul. But fire can also involve the torment of purification. By love we heap coals of fire on the wicked (cf. Prov 25:21-22; Rom 12:20). Karl Barth put it this way: Where the opposition of people to God does not result "in faith in the Son given, even the love of God must itself be destructive."[26]

On the basis of sacred Scripture and sacred tradition I affirm that Christ's death benefits all people. No person is rejected by or excluded from God's love. But exclusion from salvation in the kingdom of God is quite another matter. Not all are adopted into the family of God and given the title of sons or daughters. But even those who are refused admission to the great banquet in heaven are still loved by God and called by God.

Hell in Christian tradition is often portrayed as the outer darkness, but in view of the fact that God's grace reaches out to the whole cosmos, this must be understood as basically an inner blindness. Hell is darkness, not to God, but to the sinner. The light of God indeed permeates hell as well as heaven. The Psalmist says: "Even the darkness is not dark to thee, the night is bright as the day; for darkness is as light with thee" (Ps 139:12). And again: "If I make my bed in Sheol, thou art there!" (v. 8). Sheol is not hell, but the point is that God is present in every dark and forbidding place, even in the nether gloom. The prophet Nahum declares that God will pursue his enemies into the darkness (Nahum 1:8).

Luther too affirmed that God's presence is all-encompassing. "Even hell, no less than heaven, is full of God and the highest Good."[27] To be sure in this text Luther saw only God's justice or judgment in hell. But the wider biblical view is that God himself as loving Savior dwells both in hell and in heaven, for God's justice cannot be separated from his love.

The mystical writer Jakob Boehme (1575-1624) contended that hell and heaven are inseparable. "Hell is in Heaven and Heaven is in Hell. But the angels see only the light, and devils only the darkness."[28] This stands in apparent contrast to Luther's conviction that God's mercy does not dwell in hell and hell does not praise him. Instead hell "desecrates and blasphemes Thy justice and truth."[29] Yet Luther also held out the hope that God's love "remains even in deathly and hellish pain."[30]

One reason why hell has been discounted in academic circles and also in the popular imagination is that for too many centuries it was depicted as a place of torture, where God wreaks vengeance on those whom he has consigned to damnation. Cyprian's view of hell came to prevail over Origen's, which depicted hell in medicinal terms. According to Cyprian the "ever-burning Gehenna will burn up the condemned with living flames; nor will there be . . . respite. . . . Weeping will be useless and prayer ineffectual."[31] In the Middle Ages it was commonly held that the bliss of the redeemed would be enhanced by their contemplation of the torments of the damned because they would then know that justice was being done.[32] This attitude gained ascendancy in Protestantism, as can be seen in this hymn by Isaac Watts:

> What bliss will fill the ransomed souls
> When they in glory dwell,
> To see the sinner as he rolls
> In quenchless flames of hell.[33]

We also encounter this baleful legacy in contemporary evangelicalism. In the words of Lutheran pastor Richard Wurmbrand: "One such sufferer [in hell] may storm the heavens for a million years, and God will not answer back even with a drop of cool water for a parched tongue."[34]

In the fuller biblical perspective the lake of fire proves to be none other than the ocean of God's searing love. The fire of God's wrath is the fire of God's chastising love, and therefore we can still hope for those who are lost and despairing. The error of modern fundamentalism is to separate God's love and God's wrath. Scripture itself urges us toward a more holistic interpretation.

With the rise of the Enlightenment in the late seventeenth and eighteenth centuries attitudes toward hell began to change. Within the community of faith hell was still affirmed, but it was now seen as a monument to human freedom rather than deliberate afflictions imposed by a wrathful God on the impenitent. Even the justly inflicted sufferings of other people are to be pitied rather than enjoyed.

Instead of viewing hell as a torture chamber or concentration camp presided over by the devil, I believe it is more in keeping with the deepest intuitions of biblical faith to envision hell as a sanatorium for sick, incurable souls.[35] Moreover, it is not the devil but Jesus Christ who presides. I cannot subscribe to Milton's portrayal of Satan in *Paradise Lost*, for whom it is better to reign in hell than to serve in heaven.[36] It is not the devil who is in control but Jesus himself, and this is why hell is a place of spiritual torment for those who deny and defame the name of the Son of God.

C. S. Lewis has proposed an idea of hell that is more in keeping with the express teaching of the Word of God—that "the LORD is just in all his ways, and kind in all his doings" (Ps 145:17). According to Lewis, God created hell out of his mercy in order to set a limit on how bad people can get.[37] Those who choose hell prefer the gloominess of hell to the light of heaven, for they can then hide their true status. It would appear that for Lewis hell is the last refuge for the sinner. Yet I would go on to say that what makes hell hellish is that incorrigible sinners are not permitted to flee into anonymity, for their sins are unceasingly exposed by the light that reveals the depth of their corruption and depravity.

I believe Lewis's insights are confirmed in Christian experience. We all know that many addicts to strong drink prefer the darkness of the tavern to the light of day because they wish to hide their shame. They also feel much more at home in a tavern than in a church where they have to mingle with the sometimes-condescending righteous. What turns the tavern into a place of discomfort is when Salvation Army officers or other evangelists make an appearance proclaiming the good news that there is a way out of the dereliction experienced by seemingly hopeless souls. But this is precisely what hell is: being exposed to the light that redeems even when darkness is much preferred. Hell is the incapacity to love even in the presence of love.

The catholic faith holds that there is real torment in hell, even though this suffering is alleviated by the grace that is pervasive in all of creation. It is more terrible to reject God and still be close to him than to reject God and be apart from him. As I have already noted, fire is a metaphor for God's presence, and it is in this presence that those who choose the life of sin will be unceasingly tormented.

The punishment in hell is not simply retributive and punitive but curative or remedial. Yet it includes retribution. Sin is both a sickness and a crime in the sight of God. If it were only a disease, it could not then be pardoned. One cannot sin against God with impunity; yet God afflicts sinners not to annihilate or ruin them but to show them the error of their ways, to chastise them and also to drive them to repentance. God desires that sinners feel the sting of his anger and thereby be restrained and corrected. Hell is related both to God's justice and to his mercy. The punishment of the guilty is tempered by God's mercy. This punishment is not sheer vengeance but holy love—the love that purifies, consumes and pardons.

Hell is not purgatory, however, because in hell the fire of purification is perpetually resisted. It is unending rather than temporary or provisional.[38] When I describe the punishment in hell as curative or remedial, I mean that it would eventually result in a cure if only it were not resisted. The medicine in this sanatorium for sick souls would cure if it were gratefully accepted. Nevertheless it alleviates the pain of being alienated from God and preserves the sinner from annihilation. Hell is as C. S. Lewis described it: God's last "mercy" to those who will let him do no other. This is why St. John Chrysostom could say: "We must thank God even for hell."[39] Whether there is a passageway from hell to heaven is another question, which I shall discuss later in this chapter.

We must now confront the question of who goes to hell. The patristic vision of the harrowing of hell appeared to empty it of all inhabitants. Eventually hell may be emptied, but Scripture teaches that it remains the destination of incorrigible sinners—those who are perversely and blatantly unrepentant (cf. Rom 2:12). All sins are forgiven except the sin against the Holy Spirit (Mk 3:28-30), which means outright rejection of the gospel. The specter of eternal death looms upon those who hear and understand the truth of the gospel and yet deliberately repudiate it. All of their sins send them to hell, but the sin against the Holy Spirit keeps them in hell. It is the refusal to believe that prevents mortals from entering his rest (Num 14:20-23; Heb 3:18-19). It is reprobate Christians who are to be judged the most severely (Heb 6:4-8; 10:26-27). It is sons of the kingdom who are thrown into the outer darkness (Mt 8:12). Even the servants who have been set over the household of the Lord will suffer condemnation (Mt 24:45-51). Tyre and Sidon, notorious pagan cities, will be judged less severely than some Jewish cities (Lk 10:13-14). Those who know but do not act accordingly are beaten with many stripes (Lk 12:47). The hypocritical scribes will receive the greater condemnation (Lk 20:47).

Hell is outside the bliss and rapture of the kingdom but not outside the rule of the kingdom. It is not outside the sphere of God's sovereign love. Those in hell are outside the body of Christ, the holy community, but they remain under the rule of Christ. They are not in Christ but with Christ. Or still better, Christ is with them. God's steadfast love encompasses even those who transgress God's law (Ps 89:30-33).

Even hell contributes to God's glory. Wherever God's sovereign power is acknowledged and respected, even by those who reject the Savior, there God's name is magnified, there his radiant splendor is manifested. Even the reprobate will be made to serve God and thereby give him glory. In the words of the Psalmist: "Human opposition only enhances your glory, for you use it as a sword of judgment" (Ps 76:10 NLT).

God will unite all things to himself (Rom 11:32; Col 1:19-20; Eph 1:10; 4:6), but this unity indicates a mixture, not a fusion or absorption.[40] The eschatological denouement might be likened to an orchestra that brings together disparate melodic strands in a final harmony of opposites.[41] It also might be likened to a rainbow. The colors do not fuse into one another but in their coexistence produce a picture of unspeakable beauty.

Is hell eternal in the sense of everlasting? It would be consonant with God's love and justice if this were so. Among those who seem to be hopelessly lost are the sons of perdition, false prophets and the evil one (cf. Jn 17:12; 2 Thess 2:3-12; Rev 20:10). Yet this does not preclude the possibility of some being finally restored to full health and salvation. The unbridgeable gap spoken of in Luke 16:26 is between hades and paradise, and it is a gap only in the sense that unrepentant sin constitutes a formidable barrier to salvation. The gates of the holy city are depicted as being open day and night (Is 60:11; Rev 21:25), which means that access to the throne of grace is a continuing possibility. The gates of hell are locked only from within (C. S. Lewis). Yet even when we find ourselves prisoners in the inner darkness that we have created, Jesus Christ has the keys to this hell and can reach out to us by his grace (Rev 1:18). Even when one is in hell one can be forgiven.[42]

Yet the Bible gives only hints of the harrowing or pillaging of hell. It does not teach a universal restoration of all souls, but it does teach the availability of the grace of God even for the most hardened sinner. Daniel Day Williams declares:

> There is no basis in faith or experience for concluding that every soul will finally know the peace and joy of life with God; but there is the basis in Christian experience for asserting that in the face of any evil and sin in the human spirit there is always the power of the divine mercy as our ultimate resource.[43]

I would go further than Williams in contending that the power of divine mercy reaches out to us even in our sinful condition and turns us around—sometimes even against our will and inclination.

C. S. Lewis entertains the possibility of commerce between hell and heaven, though he admits that this is fantasy more than fact. In his view the apostate and the depraved feel more at home in hell than in heaven. Those who actually leave hell for heaven were not in hell in the first place but in purgatory.[44]

Two clear distortions of faith are universalism and double predestinarianism.[45] We must not say that God loves the elect only. Nor should we separate God's love from his justice. This would make God a split personality and also introduce the spurious conception of a coeternal evil. The other danger is to assert that God must love all people in the same way. Therefore all are forgiven, all are restored, all end in heaven. We need to remember that God's love is a holy love. It signifies not empathy or even simple acceptance but judgment and chastisement—for the purpose of breaking us but also for the purpose of raising us up even in our brokenness and despair.

Jonathan Kvanvig contrasts two competing models of hell—the self-determination model and the retributive punishment model.[46] The first sees hell as the product of human choice. God in his love permits us to go the way of our own choosing, even if this means being lost to his kingdom. The second portrays a God of wrath and judgment who creates hell as a place of deserved retribution for the wicked. Without denying the truth in each of these models I propose still another—one that does justice to the themes of preservation and rehabilitation. Hell rehabilitates in the sense that it restores to constructive activity, not in the sense that it finally results in salvation. Jesus is both the Savior from sin and the Great Physician. As the latter he cures disease as well as vindicates his righteousness. In his mercy he relieves the pain of even the most hopeless in hell, but we are not permitted to say that every condemned person is finally restored to his favor.[47] We can affirm, however, that even those in the nether world of gloom will "bow" before God and "confess that Jesus Christ is Lord, to the glory of God the Father" (Phil 2:10-11; cf. Is 45:23; Rom 14:11).

The Glory of Heaven

Heaven like hell is an eschatological category and therefore points to the future. As Tertullian put it, "No one enters Heaven before the end of the world."[48] Like hell, heaven is a place as well as a condition. Our Lord said, "I go to prepare a place for you" (Jn 14:2-3). According to Tillich heaven "is not a place beside others but a place above all places; nevertheless it is a place and not spaceless 'spirituality' in the dualistic sense."[49] Tillich is speaking of the place of which God is ruler. While Austin Farrer opposes the idea of heaven as being part of our perishable universe, he contends that if heaven were completely nonspatial, the heavenly life would be "a featureless sea of feeling, a shapeless ecstasy; or anyhow, nothing you could fairly call the resurrection-state of man." In his theology heaven is "a new creation," "a created sphere" where God raises us into perfect fellowship with himself and with all the saints.[50]

It is always a temptation to claim to know too much about heaven and hell. We tend to forget that these are mysteries beyond human comprehension. Reinhold Niebuhr warned against speculating on the "furniture of heaven" and the "temperature of hell." Yet we can know some things about these future realities, for Scripture is not silent, though it is circumspect.

Scripture does not endorse a timeless, spaceless heaven, nor one that is purely spiritual. Instead it envisages a heaven-earth as the final eschatological reality. Heaven will come down to earth, and earth will be taken up into heaven (Rev 21). The goal of creation is a heavenly earth or a heavenly life on a new earth. It signifies the fullness of joy and perfect fellowship—not only with God but with the whole company of the saints. Until the lost sheep are brought into the fold, this "new heaven" will not yet exist. Its consummation will not occur before the number of the elect is complete.

The new heaven or the new heaven-earth will be a new cosmic reality (Rev 21:5). Neither sun nor moon will be needed to provide light in the city of God (cf. Is 60:19, 20; Rev 21:23-24). The light of the city will be God's own splendor shining directly within it. There will be neither night nor death in the holy city. Furthermore, there will be no temple in heaven, for God himself will be its temple (Rev 21:22).

The new heaven-earth will involve the restoration of all creation, but a restoration that involves transformation and new beginnings. It will embrace a multitude that no mortal can number (Rev 7:9). Charles Hodge says: "We have reason to believe . . . the number of the finally lost in comparison with the whole number of the saved will be very inconsiderable."[51] Concerning the destiny of those who die in infancy and the severely retarded, we can rest assured that they are in the hands of a living, loving God who will not withold his mercy from them.

The eschatological heaven will constitute a holy community in which sacred and secular are united in an enduring synthesis. This final unfolding of God's purposes involves not the rebuilding of the earthly Jerusalem (as dispensationalists assert) but the appearance of a new Jerusalem, one that is anchored in the world of spirits. The holy city already exists in heaven (Mt 27:53), but it is not yet established on earth.

Heaven entails a "new heaven" and a "new earth," but this is a spiritualized or transfigured earth. Those in heaven will feast on spiritual food and drink from the water of eternal life (Mt 26:29; Lk 14:15; Rev 21:6; 22:1-2). The purpose of food and drink is both fellowship and sustenance.

In addition, there will be real treasures and rewards in heaven.[52] Jesus alone is the priceless treasure, and simply to be in communion with Jesus is greater than any other treasure or reward. We are accepted into heaven on the basis of faith alone, but we are adorned in heaven on the basis of the fruits of our faith. There will be distinctions in heaven but not unlawful discriminations. I affirm not levels in heaven but greater and lesser lights in heaven (cf. Mt 5:19; 18:1-4).[53]

Scripture is clear that there will be no marriage in heaven (Mt 22:30; Lk 20:35). The tie that connects the saints is not blood or sex but obedience to God and self-giving love. Gender distinctions will persist (Rev

12 speaks of the woman in heaven), but sexuality will be left behind.

Heaven will be a spiritual family—a "brotherhood of man" under the fatherhood of God. This does not mean that the ties of natural kinship are abrogated in the kingdom of heaven, but it does mean that such ties are superseded and transcended. Mothers, fathers, husbands, wives, parents and children now see themselves primarily and essentially as brothers and sisters in Christ. Their love for one another is not diminished but on the contrary is heightened and raised to a new level. Their past relationships are not forgotten, but they now have fellowship as members of a spiritual family. Jesus is, of course, our prime example. He loved his parents and kinsmen dearly but was adamant that obedience to God comes first. When his mother and brothers asked to speak to him, he responded, "'Who is my mother, and who are my brothers?' And stretching out his hand toward his disciples, he said, 'Here are my mother and my brothers! For whoever does the will of my Father in heaven is my brother, and sister, and mother'" (Mt 12:48-50).

Those in the final or eschatological heaven will not have to undergo any suffering (Rev 21:4). They will have perfect love and perfect beatitude. I say this despite the fact that they will be poignantly aware of the existence of hell. But they will see hell from the perspective of eternity—as something that is already overcome. They will have the perfect knowledge that all people are taken care of and loved by God.

Roman Catholics and Eastern Orthodox Christians speak of the vision of God as the consummate eschatological reality. Evangelicals look forward to perfect fellowship with God and neighbor. The two concepts are not contradictory, for we have perfect fellowship with one another only on the basis of our communion with God. As people of faith we will have in the eschaton perfect but not inexhaustible knowledge. We will not be gods but remain creatures wholly dependent on God. Our horizons will be vastly extended. We shall see the world through God's eyes, but as creatures we shall never know literally everything.

As saints of the most high God we shall be engaged in active service to God (cf. Rev 22:3 KJV). Jesus assures his disciples that they will have positions of leadership in his eternal kingdom. In the parable of the pounds we are told that the faithful servants will be given new tasks (Lk 19:11-27). Our holy vocation for service in the name of Christ will continue on a new level. Our motivation for service will be neither the horrors of hell nor the pleasures of heaven but the compulsion of love (2 Cor 5:14 NIV). It is not the fear of hell but the fear of God that drives us to obedience, and this latter fear includes both adoring love and reverence for God (see Mt 10:24-33). Its crowning evidence is the sacrificial love of the cross, the love that goes out to the lowliest of sinners, all of whom are claimed for the kingdom of God. Even those who are seemingly incorrigible in their obtuseness are objects of his love. All mortals are claimed for the kingdom of God; all are included in some way in the plan of salvation.

To reach perfection means to be spurred on to even greater perfection. According to Gregory of Nyssa "even in heaven perfection is growth."[54] A similar notion is found in Irenaeus: "God will always have something more to teach man, and man will always have something more to learn from God."[55] Eastern Orthodox theologian Kallistos Ware envisages eternity as "unending progress, a never-ceasing advance."[56] A life of perfect love is the goal of Christian endeavor; yet this is not a static perfection but an ever expanding and abounding perfection.

Grace Invincible
The good news is that God's grace will triumph over sin, death and hell.[57] We must not say with D. James Kennedy that "hell is beyond the reach of God's grace."[58] Meister Eckhart is more true to scriptural teaching when he says, "The person who hopes to escape God . . . cannot escape him. All hiding places reveal God; the person hoping to escape runs into his lap."[59] In the glorious eschatological consummation there will be no longer two kingdoms arrayed against one another but one kingdom—the city of God.

God's grace will be triumphant, but not in the same way for all people. For believers grace means adoption into the kingdom of God as sons and daughters. For unbelievers grace means their subjugation as servants of the king. Rejection of the gospel must be taken seriously. Even Barth who affirms the universal dominion of Christ over the whole of human creation sounds a warning against persistent unbelief.[60] There is a cutoff point when God says, "Your will be done." It is possible to forfeit eternal salvation. It is not possible, however, to escape the reach of God's grace, to live apart from God in inglorious autonomy.

I have tried to balance the retributive and medicinal aspects of hell. Hell is not another kingdom that lies outside the dominion of God, for this would be to posit a co-eternal evil. I have likened hell to a hospital for sick souls within the domain of the kingdom.[61] Yet it lies outside the holy city, outside the joy and rapture of the kingdom. What sends one to hell is the disease of hardness of heart. The ultimate destiny of those who refuse to believe and accept help remains an open question. The curse on Cain is relevant here, for Cain is a type of fallen humanity. Cain was still under the sign of God's protection, that is, the sign of the cross.[62] He was still shielded against danger, even though condemned for his sin. As Tillich phrased it, "Love must destroy what is against love, but not him who is the bearer of that which is against love."[63] Paul reveals that he had received mercy because he had acted ignorantly in unbelief (1 Tim 1:13). Jesus prayed, "Father, forgive them; for they know not what they do" (Lk 23:34). If we are faithless God remains faithful, for he cannot deny himself (2 Tim 2:13). Every person is a liar in the sight of God, but God will nevertheless remain true to his promises (Rom 3:4 NIV).

John Wesley cautioned against being too quick to judge those who are without faith: "That sentence, 'He that believeth not shall be damned,' is spoken of them to whom the gospel is preached. Others it does not concern; and we are not required to determine anything touching their final state. How it will please God, the Judge of all, to deal with *them*, we may leave to God himself."[64]

The sin against the Holy Spirit is unforgivable (Mt 12:31-32; Mk

3:28-30; Lk 12:10), but will mortals forever persist in this sin? There are two strands in the Bible, a universalist and a particularist one, and they coexist in paradoxical tension. God is not bound to withhold his judgment if we persist in defying his will. God may allow us to walk by the light of our own fire and end in hell (Is 50:11). Yet hell in its deepest meaning connotes that our will has been thwarted by the love of God. This love because it is rejected condemns instead of saving us.

James Lowell, in his magnificent hymn "Once to Every Man and Nation," reminds us that the decision for life or death will come to every person in some way or other. Now is the day of decision, and if we try to avoid it the opportunity may never return. As the hymn expresses it,

> The choice goes by forever
> 'Twixt that darkness and that light.[65]

Yet Lowell sees only part of the truth, for Scripture teaches that light invades darkness, that darkness will eventually be flooded by light (Job 12:22).

May we hope for the curing of incurables? Or the overcoming of perversity? Yes, but the only cure is the cross of Christ received by faith. The Bible speaks of two realities: the universal love of God and banishment from the kingdom of God. To hope for the salvation of the condemned is surely permissible as a personal hope. It is not, however, an integral element in the Christian hope. It is not an article of faith; it is not a part of the gospel message. Yet there are theological grounds for this hope, for Scripture teaches that God is with the rejected, that his grace is triumphant and inexorable.

The eminent Catholic theologian Hans Urs von Balthasar declared, "In the light of living faith, I can never believe, fundamentally, in anyone's damnation but my own; as regards my neighbor, the light of the resurrection can never be so obscure for me, as to allow or compel me to cease hoping for him."[66] Yet Scripture speaks of the damnation and condemnation of those who dwell in unbelief, those who steadfastly reject the grace of God. Hell reminds us that we are living in a moral universe. It is a striking monument to human freedom, but it must not be divorced from God's sovereignty and goodness. A. W. Tozer warns against dismissing the idea of hell because of the belief that God is love: "The vague and tenuous hope that God is too kind to punish the ungodly has become a deadly opiate for the consciences of millions."[67] We must take seriously the threat of rejection by God as contained, for example, in this warning from Hebrews 2:3: "How shall we escape if we neglect such a great salvation?"

The important thing is that God will be glorified everywhere. All people will come to acknowledge Jesus Christ as Lord (Phil 2:10-11), even if some do it unwillingly. All people will be made to serve Jesus Christ whether in fear or in love. Evil has been vanquished; darkness has been dispelled. The light of Jesus Christ shall penetrate all things (Eph 1:10). We must therefore never give up on anyone or consign anyone to damnation. God is flexible in his judgments but inflexible in his grace (James Daane). We can prevail in prayer for the salvation of our neighbor (cf. Ex 32:32; Rom 9:3). Norman Grubb is here being true to the deepest insights of Scripture:

> Save them, or damn me with them! If I cannot go to heaven with them, I'll go to hell with them! God can never refuse a holy dispensation like that. It changes his mind. Of course it did, because it always was His mind to save them.[68]

Barth powerfully enjoins us to view every person optimistically. We should not build fences around God's grace. We must not teach that everyone will necessarily be saved, but we can proclaim that no one can escape the outpouring of the grace of God. We may perhaps allow for the possibility of a universal restoration of the lost, but we must also equally admit the possibility of the fall of unbelieving humanity into nothingness.[69] Yet even the fall into nothingness and hell cannot sever us from the love of Jesus Christ that reaches down into the depths as well as soars upward to the heights (Rom 8:38-39). Whatever else eternal life entails, it is meeting Jesus Christ, and such a meeting calls for a life and death decision.[70]

Barth is frequently contrasted with Calvin, who affirmed a predestination to damnation, but in this time of ecumenical rapprochement we need to recognize that there is also a universalistic note in Calvin. Commenting on Colossians 1:14 Calvin asserts, "By the sacrifice of his death all the sins of the world have been expiated."[71] In reference to the "Our Father" phrase in the Lord's prayer he says:

> Just as one who truly and deeply loves any father of a family at the same time embraces his whole household with love and goodwill, so it becomes us in like measure to show to his people, to his family, and lastly, to his inheritance, the same zeal and affection that we have toward this Heavenly Father. For he so honored these as to call them the fullness of his only-begotten Son. Let the Christian man, then, conform his prayers to this rule in order that they may be in common and embrace all who are his brothers in Christ, not only those whom he at present sees and recognizes as such but all men who dwell on earth. For what God has determined concerning them is beyond our knowing except that it is no less godly than humane to wish and hope the best for them.[72]

According to the eminent Baptist theologian Bernard Ramm, "Every sensitive evangelical is a universalist at heart."[73] Ramm appeals to Ezekiel 18:23: "Have I any pleasure in the death of the wicked, says the Lord GOD, and not rather that he should turn from his way and live?" Second Peter holds out a similar hope: "The Lord is . . . not wishing that any should perish, but that all should reach repentance" (2 Pet 3:9).

The Christian hope is anchored in the triumph of grace already realized in the cross and resurrection victory of Christ. Whether we are saved or lost, we are in the hands of the living God. Grace triumphs through the preaching of the gospel, importunate prayer, hymns of victory and deeds of mercy. Even the gates of hell cannot withstand the church of Jesus Christ (Mt 16:18). This does not necessarily mean universal salvation, but it does imply that God's grace and love will reign even in hell. God will punish our transgressions, but he will not remove from us his steadfast love or be false to his faithfulness (Ps 136).

Is there a way from hell into heaven? It does not seem so if one focuses only on the bleak picture of the human condition presented in the Bible. But there is a way from heaven into hell, a note that also belongs to biblical tradition (Is 26:19; Rev 1:18). Christ descended into sheol to bring good news to the captives, and he ascended into heaven leading a host of captives with him (Eph 4:8-10).[74] Jonah felt that he had been cast out from the presence of God when the fish swallowed him, but God was already there in the belly of the fish (sheol). God heard Jonah's cry and brought him out of the nether darkness (Jon 2). There is still hope if we pray, but we cannot pray unless the Spirit of God enters into us and moves us to pray. God's grace is greater than human sin, God's love reaches down to the lowest regions of hell. This is why we can hope—for ourselves and for the whole world.

Hell in its broadest connotation—every state in the beyond where people are still in their sins—has been opened to penetration by God's grace. Hell is not yet emptied, and it may never be so completely; yet it is now being emptied as the forces of light continue their march against the powers of darkness. Even in the banishment of souls to perdition after the final judgment Christ is there tempering his judgment with mercy, reaching out to the condemned with the balm of Gilead (cf. Is 26:19; Jer 8:22; 46:11).

The doctrine of hell reminds us that God is both wrath and love. God in his wrath resolutely brings down arrogant sinners from the perilous heights of self-conceit. God in his love marvelously upholds even unrepentant sinners in the depths of their despair and hopelessness. Yet wrath and love when applied to God are not parallel concepts. God in his essence is love. His wrath is the reaction of his holiness to sin. But even in his wrath God's love is active in the work of purification and discipline.

We cannot sin against God with impunity, but God does not allow us to sink into oblivion. God does not give up on any soul, and this is especially true for those who manifest sorrow over their sins (Lk 15). God will fortify his people even in their condemnation. He will snatch them from the jaws of hell and redeem them from the curse of death (Hos 13:14 NIV).[75] Those who believe can join with the apostle Paul in his hymn of triumph:

> Death is swallowed up in victory.
> O death, where is your victory?
> O death, where is your sting? (1 Corinthians 15:54-55 NLT)

Epilogue

In this section I wish to recapitulate some of the themes that have animated this discussion. In the process I shall include some new material.

1. I affirm both a twofold and a singlefold outcome to human history, but the latter is more comprehensive. In the climax of world history the elect and the reprobate will be separated, but this separation is not irrevocable. Both contribute to the glory of God in their own way. My position is a particularism within a universalism. The kingdom of God is intended to include all people, but only those with faith enjoy what it has to offer.

2. We need to hold together the sovereignty of God's grace and the inexorability of God's justice. Grace does not cancel the law of justice but fulfills it and also goes beyond it. Both heaven and hell are creations of God's love and of God's justice. Both are products of God's incomparable grace and God's unquenchable wrath. Our merits (which are really God's gifts) adorn us in heaven; our demerits send us to hell. But only the merits of Christ open the door to heaven. Only the obedience of Christ saves us from hell.

3. The polarity of heaven and hell must be radically rethought. Heaven is not beside hell but over hell and in hell. Hell is not parallel to heaven but preparatory to heaven. Hell is a penultimate, not an ultimate reality. It is a searing word of judgment before the final word of grace. At the same time, it is a means by which God conveys his grace to incorrigible sinners. Paradoxically the severity of God's judgment attests the boundlessness of God's grace. Hell is a reality in heaven, not alongside heaven. Only one kingdom will be left standing—the eternal kingdom of God.

4. Regarding the ultimate fate of the wicked, I uphold a reverent agnosticism. I here stand with G. C. Berkouwer, Herman Bavinck and Karl Barth.[76] The Bible teaches hope for the hopeless, but this is not necessarily universal salvation. Scripture does, however, affirm the universal lordship of Christ. Christ, not Satan, is the king in hell. Hell does not eclipse heaven but is made to serve heaven.

5. World history finally ends not in tragedy but in a restored paradise that goes through tragedy—the dereliction of the cross. The essence of tragedy is "a sense of injustice, permanent and unresolvable, never to be remedied."[77] Christianity has a goal that lies beyond tragedy, yet is tinctured with tragedy. The story of Christian faith constitutes a divine comedy (as Dante poignantly observed).[78] Good triumphs over evil; heaven is not limited by hell but overthrows hell.

6. We need to resist all eschatological options that have their roots in the drive for logical coherence rather than in fidelity to holy Scripture. Annihilationism meets the charge that God is eternally vindictive, but it spells the defeat of God's purpose—that all shall be made to serve the King of kings and Lord of lords. Universalism loses sight of the paradox that God's love is universal, but only some open themselves to the full impact of this love. It ends in a denial of the biblical warnings of God's wrath against sin. Double-predestinarianism (or restrictivism) seeks to give a credible explanation of how the mystery of grace coexists with unbelief. If God's power is unlimited and if he predestines only some to salvation, it follows logically that he predestines others to damnation. This position results in a denial of the universality of God's love, though it preserves the absoluteness of God's power.

The doctrine of reincarnation is an earnest though misguided attempt to resolve rationally the mystery of why some people are in more dire straits than others in the pilgrimage of life. According to this view the unfortunate are placed in a precarious existence because they are working out the effects of misdeeds in a previous life. Reincarnationism constitutes a tacit denial of God's universal grace and a resolute embracing of works-righteousness.[79]

I propose an alternative which has been aptly called divine perseverance.[80] God loves all and pursues all into the darkness of sin and hell. The paradox is that God's grace accomplishes its goal but in and though human determination. This goal is never fully realized while there are some who live in defiance of grace. Yet even this defiance of grace could not take place without God's inscrutable sanction. God's love will not let us go—even when we use our freedom to resist this love.[81] The future is open rather than closed, for even beyond the pale of death God's grace is at work bringing all souls into subjection to the authority and lordship of Christ. How God's grace triumphs when sin persists is a mystery that is past human comprehension, but it is not a total conundrum, for Christian experience confirms that when we believe, we are moved to do so through Christ's Spirit working within us (cf. 1 Cor 15:10; Phil 2:12-13).[82] When we resist and defy God's plan of salvation, it is God who is withholding his grace, thereby preventing us from faith and obedience.

7. One of the major sources of erroneous thinking concerning the mystery of heaven and hell is the legacy of rationalism that has penetrated the fabric of both Catholicism and Protestant fundamentalism. We want to make things clear that will always remain somewhat obscure. It is incumbent on us to recognize that there are two strands in the Bible—one universalistic and the other particularistic. It is my firm conviction that we are closer to the truth when we read the particularistic texts in light of the more comprehensive or universalistic texts. The sheep will be separated from the goats (Mt 25), but at the same time God will ultimately be all in all; all things will be reconciled in him (cf. Eph 1:10; Col 1:19-20). Fundamentalists, who draw a rigid bifurcation between God's love and God's wrath, are guilty of a selective reading of holy Scripture in this area.

8. As Christians we should celebrate heaven but not hell. The way to hell should be spurned as the way that leads to oblivion and despair. Yet we should thank God for his presence in hell. Dante was right that those who are consigned to hell should abandon all hope, but we must

also insist that those on the way to heaven must retain hope for the whole of human creation, even for the lost and rejected. Hell like heaven can be made to glorify God, for hell is a tribute to God's justice. It is also a demonstration of God's love. We must not teach the wholesale emptying of hell, but we can hope that some, perhaps even many, might be reclaimed for salvation. Yet this is a personal hope, not a certain expectation. Hell is not a lingering evil but a lesser good. It too has a place in the panorama of sacred history in which darkness is finally overcome by light (cf. Jn 1:5).

9. Evangelical rationalism sometimes conveys the impression that if there is no heaven and hell "there simply is no persuasive reason to be moral."[83] But this reveals a legalistic understanding of salvation. As Christians we do good not primarily because we wish to satisfy a divine requirement or avoid divine retribution but to show our gratitude for God's gift of salvation in Jesus Christ. We seek to live the morally good life not in order to preserve our own souls but in order to glorify God through sacrificing ourselves for the welfare of others as Christ sacrificed himself on the cross for the sake of the whole world. Real love contains something of the heedless in it, as Reinhold Niebuhr astutely observed.[84] When love is reduced to a moral obligation that comports with human self-interest, it then becomes a law that binds rather than frees the human conscience for selfless service under the cross.

The gospel is not that hell can be avoided but that hell has been vanquished by the almighty God. This God, moreover, loves all equally, though he is more pleased when we respond to his love in faith than in unbelief. But even those who disbelieve are still the objects of his persevering love, and this accounts for their continuing misery as well as for their fleeting glimpses of a happiness that can never be theirs apart from faith in the risen Lord.

10. Christianity is primarily concerned not with the salvation of individual souls but with the salvation of the world. Christ came not just to set up oases of light in a world of darkness but to drive out the darkness so that all may see the light. The message of faith is not simply

that salvation is offered to all but that salvation has been effected for all, though it still seeks concrete realization in daily life and practice. It is up to us to ponder this glorious fact and rejoice. If we limit the efficacy of God's grace and give up on any part of the human race, we allow sin to regain some of its power, though it can be only for a time. The finality of evil does not belong to the message of redemption, for Christ makes all things new (Rev 21:5). May we go forward in the full assurance of hope that Jesus is victor over sin, death and the devil and that his kingdom will triumph as all others collapse.

·TWELVE·

THE DAWNING

OF HOPE

We exult in the hope of the divine glory that is to be ours.

ROMANS 5:2 REB

We are . . . looking forward to the happy fulfillment of our hope
when the splendour of our great God and Saviour Christ Jesus will appear.

TITUS 2:12-13 REB

In the judgment of fire the light of His salvation shines forth.

EBERHARD ARNOLD

The Christian hope is not hope in the human spirit,
in human goodness, in human endurance, in human achievement:
the Christian hope is in the power of God.

WILLIAM BARCLAY

Assurance of salvation is not salvation secured.
Faith always remains hope, even when earth seems to offer no hope.

ERNST KÄSEMANN

Hope in the Christian sense is not simply wishing that something will eventuate to our advantage, but inwardly knowing that God is acting to bring joy and peace into our lives and into the life of the whole world. Hope is looking forward to the movement of the Spirit of God throughout world history culminating in the coming again of Jesus Christ in power and glory to set up the kingdom that shall have no end. Hope is the glad expectation that Christ will be triumphant not only in our own lives but in the history of humanity.

Hope is not only individual but also corporate, not only personal but also social. Hope places us in contact with realities we do not see. Hope enables us to go forward on the basis of Christ's promise to be with all those who call upon his name in faith and expectation.

Hope sometimes entails giving up earthly hopes in order to grasp the heavenly promise. Paul said of Abraham: "In hope he believed against hope, that he should become the father of many nations" (Rom 4:18; cf. 8:24-25). Hope does not rule out earthly expectations, but it subordinates these lesser hopes to the blessed hope—Christ coming again in glory (cf. Mt 6:32-33).

We are not only animated by hope but also saved by hope, because hope means placing our confidence in God alone. According to Paul, "In hope we were saved. Now hope that is seen is not hope. For who hopes for what is seen? But if we hope for what we do not see, we wait for it with patience" (Rom 8:24-25 NRSV).

The Ground and Goal of Hope

For Christians the ground and content of our hope is Jesus Christ. It rests first of all upon his work in creation. It was through Christ that God created the world (Heb 1:2). It is also through Christ that God rules the world and restrains the powers of evil that have infiltrated the world. Again, it is through Christ that the Spirit of God brings gifts of hope and mercy to all who are contrite in spirit.

The source of our hope lies not only in God's creation but in God's decision to incarnate himself in human flesh and establish a kingdom of light in the midst of the darkness of a world devastated by sin. We can hope because God loved us so much that he condescended to take our sin upon himself in the person of his Son and set us free from the curse of sin and death. We can hope because of Christ's obedience unto death on a cross. It is on the basis of his obedience, not our own, that we can rest assured that we are adopted into the family of God and that our names are written in the book of life in heaven. We can hope because God has chosen to justify the ungodly out of his sheer mercy and love, not because of human merit or worthiness. Paul put it succinctly, "Through him we have obtained access to this grace in which we stand, and we rejoice in our hope of sharing the glory of God" (Rom 5:2).

It is not only the ministry of Christ culminating in his death on the cross that gives us assurance of salvation but also the resurrection of Christ from the dead, which reveals the powers of darkness as powerless in the face of the power of sacrificial love. This note is especially pronounced in 1 Peter 1:3-4: "In his great mercy by the resurrection of Jesus Christ from the dead, he gave us new birth into a living hope, the hope of an inheritance, reserved in heaven for you, which nothing can destroy or spoil or wither" (REB).

We must also consider Pentecost as a source of hope for victory—both in this life and in the life to come. Karl Barth regarded Pentecost as the second stage in the parousia of Christ—after the resurrection of Christ.[1] We can hope because Christ sent forth his Holy Spirit upon the company of the church in order to bring us the taste of heavenly redemption and the power to bear witness to this redemption in our words and deeds. In the words of the apostle, "Hope . . . will not let us down, because the love of God has been poured into our hearts by the Holy Spirit" (Rom 5:5 NJB). It is not only Christ on the cross that is the hope of glory but "Christ in you" (cf. Col 1:27; 2 Cor 13:5)—Christ residing within the depths of our souls through the power of his Spirit.

Finally, the Christian hope rests on the visible return of Jesus Christ at the end of the age in order to bring in the kingdom that shall have no end. As it is written in Titus 2:13, we await "our blessed hope, the appearing of the glory of our great God and Savior Jesus Christ." The rolling down of the curtain on world history is indeed the culmination of the Christian hope, for we see in this dramatic event or series of events the visible realization of the promises of God to his people that he will heed our cries and redress the wrongs we have suffered. By hope we are enabled to see through the subterfuges of the devil and be confirmed in our expectation that light shines in the darkness, and darkness is not able to overcome it (Jn 1:5). We can hope because Christ has come in the Jesus of history, he is coming in the power of the Spirit, and he will come again on the basis of the promises in holy Scripture. Then, paradoxically, hope will cease because we shall see Christ face to face, but only because God will reveal himself to us in an act of pure grace and mercy. I fully concur in this cogent observation of Hans Urs von Balthasar: "We shall never see God, even in the 'open vision' of eternity, otherwise than in his unutterably free revelation of himself, and so in a self-giving, a stepping forth from his inaccessible abyss of being, in his bridging over the infinite gulf separating us from him."[2]

Self-Transcending Hope

Hope does not leave us imprisoned in ourselves but takes us out of ourselves into the trials and dreams of others. Hope directs us first of all to Christ, then to our neighbor and last of all to ourselves. Hope does not arise out of egoism but challenges egoism, for it puts the glory of God and the welfare of others over the needs and concerns of the self. There is an unmistakable note of altruism in Christian hope. We hope not only for ourselves but also for all of humanity. As Pannenberg expresses it, "Christian hope is not just individual hope in God but hope for the world, for the kingdom of God, and only in this context hope for one's own salvation."[3]

Hope is not selfish, intent only on the self's realization, yet also not self-negating or self-denigrating. Hope excludes the deliberate promotion of personal happiness, but not the expectation of joy and delight in the service of others. Hope excludes the elevation of the self over all other concerns, but not the legitimate place for lesser concerns (cf. Mt 6:33). Hope includes what is best for the self, but only because what is best redounds to God's glory. Hope does not abrogate a concern for one's own salvation, but it does resist making this the overriding concern in the Christian life.

Hope is both a work of faith and a gift of grace. It is something to be seized as well as something to be celebrated (cf. Heb 6:18; 10:23). In

Roman Catholic tradition it is often denominated a theological virtue—
a moral quality of the soul that one can cultivate through habitual action. I prefer to speak of hope as a new attitude produced within us by
the Holy Spirit. Hope is cleaving to the promises of Christ in faith in the
knowledge that apart from his grace we can do nothing. The gift character of hope is admirably elucidated by Thomas Merton:

> Hope then is a gift . . . total, unexpected, incomprehensible, undeserved . . .
> but to meet it we have to descend into nothingness. It is the acceptance of
> life in the midst of death, not because we have courage, or light, or wisdom
> to accept, but because by some miracle the God of life himself accepts to
> live, in us, at the very moment when we descend into death.[4]

Hope does not simply wait upon God in patient resignation, but it
resolves to move forward in the confident expectation that God's grace
is more powerful than human sin, that divine perseverance is more potent than human obduracy. Jerome reminds us that hope, like faith, requires effort: "It is not without effort that we come to know the hope of
our calling and the riches of God's inheritance in the saints. This effort
in fact comes in response to that renewing gift which God himself
gives in the glorious resurrection of his own Son."[5]

Although hope requires human effort, it does not rest on human
merit. Grace empowers us to act in faith, but our actions do not compel God to give us grace. Our actions do not make us worthy in the
sight of God, but God's forgiving love makes our actions acceptable to
him. Augustine, especially in his conflict with Pelagius, was adamant
that grace always precedes human merit: "Unless the mercy of God in
calling precedes faith, no one can even believe and thus begin to be
justified and to receive the power to do good works. So grace comes
before all merit."[6]

This must not be taken to mean that the believer cannot look forward to rewards in heaven. These are rewards, however, that are
based on the work of the Holy Spirit in our lives rather than on works
that we can claim as our very own. God rewards us according to the

way Christ chooses to display within us his righteousness and love. In Augustine's theology God not only produces merit within us, but crowns our merits with his gifts. In Reformation theology it is considered highly unbiblical to speak of merits in connection with the realization of salvation, though we may still speak of rewards that are promised to all those who believe and obey in the power of the Spirit.

To summarize, hope enables us to lay hold of the glories that are yet to be revealed to us, glories intended not just for ourselves but for the whole world. Hope is not egocentric, but it is also not exclusively heterocentric. It seeks the conversion of the self as well as the transfiguration of society.

Hope is not an escape from the problems of the world but the assurance that we can deal with these problems in the light of God's grace. Karl Barth put it very poignantly: "The Christian hope does not lead us away from this life; it is rather the uncovering of the truth in which God sees our life. It is the conquest of death, but not a flight into the Beyond."[7]

Hope directs us to the eternal promises of God, but it also inspires us to apply these promises to our lives in the here and now. Hope is faith that looks toward the future, but only so that we can live meaningfully and purposefully in the present. Hope is anchored in what God in Christ has done for us in the past. It is animated by what the Holy Spirit is doing for us in the present. It is fulfilled in what Christ by his Spirit will do for us in the future—when all things will be reconciled in God.

The Certainty of Hope

The hope that springs from faith and is nurtured by faith is certain and confident. This note is especially striking in the epistle to the Hebrews: "Now faith is that which provides us with confident assurance with regard to things which we hope for; it serves by way of convincing us about things which cannot be seen" (Heb 11:1 GNC). Hope in Christ for the forgiveness of sins and life eternal is not equivocal but steadfast and unwavering. "We have that hope as an anchor for our lives, safe and secure" (Heb 6:19 REB).

Hope is not a blind leap in the dark but an inner conviction that is unshakable and enduring. Hope is certain because the God whom it exalts has the whole world in his hands. He is the director and shaper of human destiny. Yet this certainty needs to be renewed through daily repentance and obedience. In the words of Hebrews, "We desire each one of you to show the same earnestness in realizing the full assurance of hope until the end" (Heb 6:11).

In much modern theology it is held that faith contains doubt and hope contains risk. [8] In open theism even God is subject to risk: therefore his promises have no absolute guarantee of success.[9] Against this view evangelical theology is adamant that hope is certain because God's promises are certain. Doubt will indeed accompany faith and hope, but this is because we are never fully delivered from sin in this life. As our faith and hope grow, so our doubts will ebb and our fears recede.

Hope is animated by the experience of the glory of God, which is progressively realized in history. According to Jerome, this glory "abides, develops and increases."[10] It is beyond the reach of human perception, but not beyond the compass of human experience. We can know in part because we are known by God. We can hope because we are upheld by the Spirit of God.

We as Christians have eternal security because we rest our confidence in the God who will not let us go. We have eternal security because no power or force can separate us from the love of God (Jn 10:28; Rom 8:38-39). Yet if we turn again to the way of sin after having once been enlightened concerning the truth of the gospel, God is under no obligation to sustain us and bless us. We cannot escape from the hand of God, but God can let us fall into perdition. No earthly or creaturely power can take our eternal security from us, but God himself can take it from us if we flagrantly disregard his laws and spurn his gospel.[11]

According to Calvin, hope looks forward to the fulfillment of God's promises in the world to come:

Let us . . . learn . . . that the holy patriarchs under the Old Testament were aware how rarely or never God fulfills in this world what he promises to his servants; and that they therefore lifted up their hearts to God's sanctuary, in which they found hidden what does not appear in the shadows of the present life. This place was the Last Judgment of God, which, although they could not discern it with their eyes, they were content to understand by faith. Relying upon this assurance, they did not doubt that, whatever might happen in the world, the time would nevertheless come when God's promises would be fulfilled.[12]

What is missing in Calvin's rumination is the scriptural affirmation that the Christian hope also pertains to this life, that some of God's promises are indeed fulfilled in this life. I am thinking of extraordinary healings, corrections of injustices and the bringing of souls to salvation.

Relative and Ultimate Hopes

This brings us to both the contrast and the congruity between relative and ultimate hopes. Scripture is clear that hope relates to life in this world as well as in the world to come. Christ alone is the hope of the world, but Christ is active in human history bringing all things to completion. The Christian hope has both a this-worldly and an other-worldly dimension, and we need to include both of these in our gospel proclamation. Godly living inspired by faith "holds promise for the present life and also for the life to come" (1 Tim 4:8).

Against the dominant strand in liberal theology we must insist that relative or secular hopes not be allowed to overshadow or preempt the blessed hope—Christ coming again in glory to set up his eternal kingdom. Kierkegaard's injunction should be taken seriously: "You know well enough that there is a hope that should be put to death; that there is a lust and a desire and a longing that should be slain. Earthly hope should be put to death, for in just this way did man first come to be saved by the true hope."[13] Yet Kierkegaard should not be followed uncritically: the fuller biblical teaching is that earthly hopes can be tolerated so long as they remain below—so long as they are not confused with the eternal hope.

We must not cling to this-worldly hopes, but we can look forward to their partial realization through faith. Sometimes we have to surrender earthly pleasures and goals in order to carry the cross of discipleship. Hope that is directed primarily to gaining security and happiness in this world is a spurious hope and needs to be curtailed if not repudiated. Paul was quite firm in his relegation of earthly hope to a secondary status in the Christian life: "If it is for this life only that Christ has given us hope, we of all people are most to be pitied" (1 Cor 15:19 REB).

We should by no means give up the quest for human betterment in this world, but we must never confuse our feeble attempts to rectify social injustices with the dawning of the kingdom of God, which will come in God's own way and time. When our hope is anchored in eternity, we are then free to bring an eternal dimension to our efforts to further the cause of justice in this world. C. S. Lewis made this timely observation: "If you read history you will find that the Christians who did most for the present world were just those who thought most of the next. . . . It is since Christians have largely ceased to think of the other world that they have become so ineffective in this one."[14]

At the same time we know of groups and movements that encourage giving up the quest for a more equitable world order and simply wait for the second coming of Christ, which, they hope, will rectify social imbalances. These groups can be labeled escapist and in some cases gnostic. They flee from the world rather than seek to work within it as a leaven permeating society with the righteousness of the kingdom of God that is available to us now through the Holy Spirit. Christ came not to take us out of the world but to send us into the world as ambassadors of another world—life with Christ in eternity (cf. Jn 17:15-18).

Providence Versus Fate

Whereas the ancient world was bedeviled by fate, Christianity challenged this pessimistic outlook by positing a world being opened to new possibilities by the providence of God.[15] Fate envisions a world without hope for real change because everything is bound to an inexorable transcendent necessity. Providence on the other hand affirms a world that is brimming with hope because it is being directed by a moral governor who enables his subjects to act in freedom, that is, in conformity to their greatest good. Providence holds out hope for victory over life's circumstances; fate encourages endurance and resignation. Providence spurs us to action; fate bids us painfully accept what the gods have decreed. Providence is supremely personal and suprarational; fate is impersonal and irrational. Providence brings meaning into human effort and history; fate is a cosmic determinism that empties life of meaning or purpose. Providence brings the light of God to bear on human decision; fate is blind, inscrutable and inescapable. Providence carries a message of hope; fate carries a sense of doom.

Among the Greek tragedians the tragic flaw in personal life was fate, a shadow that casts a pall over all human existence. Fate ensures that something will happen regardless of our plans and efforts.[16] In Christianity the tragic flaw is sin, which does not happen to us necessarily but which is freely chosen though it leads us directly into bondage. Sin is inevitable but not necessary. It becomes inevitable because of the way we choose to live. Fate is being subjected to a destiny that is not freely chosen. It makes a mockery of human choice and planning. As Roger Hazelton phrases it, fate "denotes that strange and spectral something which controls, determines, hedges about the life of man, overriding our wishes and disregarding our needs."[17]

In the Christian worldview, providence sets us free from the spell of fate, which brings dread to human existence. Providence reveals that human destiny can be altered by divine intervention. It carries the hope that the person of faith can surmount the circumstances of life through divine empowering. It brings meaning to our labors and struggles, for "we have set our hope on the living God, who is the Saviour of all" (1 Tim 4:10 REB).

Fate must not be confounded with either determinism or indeterminism (chance). The point is not whether we are determined to act or behave in a certain way either by God or by the forces of history, but whether our actions are doomed to be fruitless and meaningless. In the fatalistic worldview our actions are devoid of meaning and purpose, notwithstanding what we do. They will eventuate in unwarranted suffering or untimely death, whether we defy or assent to the movement of world history.

Providence presents an alternative to determinism, indeterminism and fatalism. Life can be meaningful and fruitful because the living God of history is working within our decisions and indecisions to bring about a new world and a new humanity. We are set free by the Spirit of God to have a role in shaping our destiny. It is God's Spirit who enables us to live out our holy vocation. God is not the sole cause of all that happens, but he is the overriding cause. As scholastic theology has put it, God is the primary cause, but there are secondary causes by which God fulfills his purposes.[18] Human activity is one of these secondary causes. We are free to make our own decisions, but our decisions have no efficacy unless God concurs with them. We can act and believe in freedom through divine empowering. True freedom is not being guided by whim or caprice but being open to the infallible guidance of the living God. Providence does not mean being compelled by God to act in a particular way, but being liberated by God so that we will act according to his will and purpose. Providence is moral direction in a world of chaos, not divine ordination of whatever comes to pass.

The Christian worldview makes a place for contingency, that is, events that happen by unforeseen causes, events that are entirely unpredictable. Yet contingency is not absolute because every event is under the guidance of God, every event is made to serve the plan of God. We allow for possibilities in human life that may or may not be realized, but these possibilities are brought to actualization by God and humanity working together. Ideally human decision is subordinated to divine decision, and when this happens humans have true freedom.

In the discussion of this important theme in theology I seek to avoid the false alternatives of both compatibilism and incompatibilism. Can the exercise of human freedom be made compatible with divine foreordination and predestination? In my opinion we cannot resolve this mystery and must allow it to remain a paradox to human understanding. We need to affirm human freedom in answering and living out the call from God; yet at the same time we must insist that in our answer God is acting, enabling us to respond in faith and obedience. In this view, human freedom is not compromised but instead established. If we remain in the domain of human logic, we will either sacrifice human freedom in order to do justice to divine sovereignty or impose limitations on divine sovereignty in the interests of preserving human freedom.[19]

Providence itself can be misunderstood as a cosmic determinism. It can be reduced to a law of nature that bends human freedom toward immutable laws that make life meaningful but not challenging. In the biblical vision, providence is the interplay between the living God and his human subjects, which involves our struggling with God in order to realize the purposes that he has for us. Providence is the unfolding of the plan of God on the plane of history, but ordinarily through human instrumentality. We are made covenant partners with God, not in procuring our salvation but in fulfilling God's plan for our lives as ambassadors and servants of the Lord Jesus Christ. Providence brings hope to the human enterprise because we are given the knowledge that our destiny is in the hands of an all-powerful and all-loving God who unceasingly brings good out of evil, meaning out of chaos. We can therefore look forward to a future filled with promise in the conviction that Christ is more powerful than the principalities and powers of the world. His grace liberates us from the twin evils of chance and fate and allows us to live as free beings in a moral universe.

In this schema the universe is partly but not wholly open. Contingency is made to serve divine foreordination. Human freedom is made to serve the unfolding of the divine plan of salvation. We can hope because we know on the basis of divine revelation that our choices are undergirded and directed by divine providence. Even when we stumble and go astray, God is there ready to pick us up so that we can resume our pilgrimage of faith in this valley of the shadow of death.

Faith Versus Cynicism

Christianity struck a blow not only against fatalism but also against cynicism. Cynicism is derived from a sect of the same name that arose in ancient Greece in the fourth century B.C. and continued until the sixth century A.D.[20] In the context of this chapter, cynicism denotes an attitude toward life that stands in continuity with the ancient philosophical school of Cynics but is more comprehensive in meaning. Cynicism teaches that the essence of virtue is self-control and independence. It encourages one to live according to the rhythms of nature as opposed to social conventions. It promotes distrust of accepted standards of morality and of social institutions that shape the moral ethos. The goal is self-sufficiency, which can be achieved in the final analysis only through self-discipline.

Cynics are often scornful of the motives and virtues of others. They are prone to believe that all people are motivated by selfish desire. Their aim is to survive in a world where the stronger prey upon the weaker. They strive for authenticity in a world of guile and deception.

Cynicism is sometimes seen as similar to Christianity because it supposedly shares a low view of human nature. Actually cynicism stands in antithesis to the Christian life and worldview. Whereas the cynic holds humanity in contempt, the Christian takes pity upon humanity. From the Christian perspective humanity is corrupt but not beyond hope of redemption, because divine grace is more powerful than human sin. A cynic views the human race as irrevocably devious and undependable. A Christian views the human race as liberated by the grace of God even in its fallenness and therefore capable of acts of mercy and righteousness that transcend mere human potentiality. A cynic is inclined to give up on humanity. A Christian works to change humanity.

Both a cynic and a born-again Christian will distrust humankind, but for different reasons. For the first, the human person is generally too frail to withstand the pressures of life. For the second, the human person is a sinner, deliberately prideful and slothful, but one who is claimed for redemption by the very God himself.

Whereas cynicism consigns humanity to the unceasing struggle for survival, Christianity views humanity through the eyes of hope. This is so not because we mortals are endowed with infinite possibilities (the Renaissance view), but because we are elected by the living and mighty God for a vocation of meaning and purpose. We are called not simply to cultivate our own garden (as Voltaire recommended), but to tell others the good news of what God has done for us and the whole world in Jesus Christ. We can celebrate the attainments of humanity because they are given eternal significance by the Spirit of God who brings them into the service of the kingdom of righteousness. Cynics tend to be pessimistic because they sense the limitations of humanity. Christians are more apt to be optimistic because they believe in the grace of God that exceeds all human limitations (cf. Eph 3:20). They are not content merely to get along in the world: they are inspired to change the world so that the world will sing the praises of God's glory.[21]

Beyond Optimism and Pessimism
The Christian vision of life and the world transcends the polarity of optimism and pessimism. The Enlightenment view of inevitable progress in history is controverted by the persistence of wars and rumors of war. The existentialist view that human existence is always precarious and basically tragic is radically challenged by the unforeseen gift of conversions and revivals that literally alter the course of world history.[22] The gnostic depreciation of this world as irremediably evil stands in stark contrast to the biblical portrayal of the world as a battleground between good and evil in which the former finally prevails at the end of history.

Christians will have a tempered optimism because we believe in both the sovereignty of God and the intractability of sin. We can look forward to the future with hope not because of our faith in human ingenuity and wisdom, but because of our unwavering conviction that God is in control, even when the facts of history seem to indicate otherwise. Reinhold Niebuhr astutely observed that Christianity nurtures both a provisional pessimism and an ultimate optimism. We know that in the long term righteousness will conquer, though in the short term evil will continue to cast a shadow over all human achievements.

An attractive alternative to optimism and pessimism is meliorism, proposed by William James and a number of other modern philosophers.[23] Meliorism holds that the world is neither completely evil nor completely good, but that it can always be improved. The future is open, and this means that changes for the good can always occur. God is omni-benevolent but not all-powerful. "Humanity must work together with the forces of God in creating a universe with less evil and more good."[24] Meliorism is closer to a naïve optimism than to pessimism, for it builds on a faith in powers resident within the human psyche.

Another worldview that has its basis in both the Renaissance and the Enlightenment is utopianism—the claim that humanity is at the "arrival at that stage of history in which the ambiguities of life are conquered."[25] Utopianism often takes a revolutionary turn, fired by the belief that "present revolutionary action will bring about the final transformation of reality."[26] According to Tillich utopianism includes both threat and promise. While temporarily bringing meaning to history, it finally ends in disillusionment because progress toward justice within history is only partial, given humanity's existential alienation from the ground and source of its being.

In opposition to the utopianism spawned by the Enlightenment, Reinhold Niebuhr advocated a Christian realism that presses for changes in society that are within the parameters of human possibility. These changes fall abysmally short of the transcendent ideal of sacrificial love, but they nevertheless indicate approximations of this ideal. The most people can hope for in this life is a creative compromise that allows for a society that is moving toward a higher degree of justice; yet it remains a pale shadow of the perfect righteousness emblematic of the kingdom of God. While Niebuhr's ruminations contain much biblical wisdom, his compromise solution to social problems has been frequently though sometimes unfairly criticized as an evasion of the radical demands of discipleship under the cross.[27]

I believe the Christian approach to personal and social evil is best categorized as *undefeatism*—the power to move forward in the freedom of the Spirit. In contrast to meliorism our hope and trust is not in the resiliency of the human spirit but in the promises of God as revealed in holy Scripture. Christians will be resolute without being naïve. They will be unwavering in their commitment without slavish adherence to general principles that sometimes have to be set aside if mercy is to triumph over judgment.[28] Christians will be obedient to the divine commandment without resting on their laurels as agents of social change. They will experience defeat without being defeated. Through the power of the Spirit they will rise again to continue the battle on a new level. Their hope lies not in human strategies or programs but in the eschatological reality of the coming kingdom of God, which stands in judgment over all human claims and accomplishments while giving meaning and significance to all human striving.

Faith, Hope and Love

Faith, hope and love in Roman Catholic tradition are the theological virtues that give direction and meaning to Christian life. In Protestantism we prefer to speak of these virtues as manifestations of the Spirit as he works within us. We do not attain them with the assistance of grace, but they are instilled within us by the Spirit through the power of grace. They are human acts, but they carry divine efficacy.

What is of crucial importance is that these manifestations of the Spirit belong together and cannot be separated. The dawning of hope is at the same time the beginning of faith and the flowering of love.

Faith includes hope just as faith works through love. The inseparable union of faith and hope is attested in Hebrews, which defines faith as "the assurance of things hoped for, the conviction of things not seen" (Heb 11:1). Calvin put it this way: "Faith believes the veracity of God, hope expects the manifestation of it in due time."[29]

Hope is indissolubly linked with love as well as with faith. I cannot concur with the Quietist ideal of a "love without hope" (Fénelon). If love is envisioned as totally gratuitous, without any motivation (as with Nygren),[30] then it would seem that love does not require hope, at least for the individual. But in biblical thought, agape involves not the negation or abandonment of desire, but its conversion and transformation. Agape signals the rebirth of eros in a new form rather than its death. Hope does not rule out self-love, but it does entail the subordination of self-love to other-love. We hope not simply for the self but for the church and for the world. The glory of God and the welfare of our neighbor take priority over self-realization. But the paradox is that when we lose ourselves in the service of others, we gain the fulfillment of the self in the end. We find hope when we give of ourselves in love—to God and to our neighbor.

Faith, hope and love have their origin in Pentecost, for it is through the outpouring of the Holy Spirit that we are enabled to believe and obey. The Bruderhof theologian Eberhard Arnold gives poignant articulation to the vision of the new age of the Spirit:

> Whoever receives the spirit of the new creation which hastens on the end of all time, receives the eternal powers of the one God, who formed the first creation in the same spirit. The future strength of God, in its all-transforming expectation of the end, lives as the spirit of strength in the present aging creation. The new dawn has begun in it already. Everyone must see—a new creation is arising! Its Gospel is meant for every creature.[31]

And again from Eberhard Arnold: "Nothing but a last, deepest inward revival, a great, full awakening to God and to His all-determining rule, will be instrumental in carrying into the whole world the Gospel, the glad message of Christ and His unique importance."[32]

We can face the future with hope because we have already been given a foretaste of future glory in the power of the Spirit (2 Cor 1:22; 5:5; Eph 1:13-14). We can embark on a pilgrimage of faith because we are energized by the Spirit, who liberates our will for obedience in the name of Christ. We can give ourselves to the service of the kingdom in the power of love because the Spirit rekindles within us the hope of life everlasting.

AFTERWORD

This is an epilogue for the entire Christian Foundations series rather than for a single volume or chapter. I shall here reexamine the themes of theological method and authority, and show how they bear upon this modest venture in dogmatics.

In these volumes I have proposed a theology of Word and Spirit that strives to unite the objective and subjective poles of divine revelation. I have acknowledged an underlying affinity with the theology of the Word of God as elucidated by Karl Barth. It is true that Barth occasionally veers toward a revelational positivism, which reduces revelation to the outer word of Scripture and church proclamation.[1] While he does affirm the work of the Holy Spirit as the subjective possibility of revelation, he resists making a prominent place for the inner word, the divine light that shines within the person of faith and within the visible signs of Scripture and church tradition. Barth, it should be noted, rejects the designation of a positivism of revelation, and he does continue to affirm throughout his dogmatic system the hiddenness of revelation even in the face of Jesus Christ. Barth and I stand together in upholding the dynamic quality of revelation, but I make a more prominent place for the experience of faith in the realization of revelation on the plane of human history.

Just as my theology of Word and Spirit cannot be reduced to a theology of the Word of God, which is more cerebral than experiential, so it must be clearly differentiated from a theology of spiritual presence, which we find, for example, in Paul Tillich.[2] Tillich speaks of Jesus Christ as the final revelation but not as the only revelation. In the Tillichian brand of theology the Trinity itself is reduced to Spirit, in contrast to the rationalist penchant for viewing ultimate reality as logic or logos (as in Gordon Clark). The criterion that I employ in theology is not a creed or universal principle at our disposal. Neither is it an experiential awareness of the power of being. Instead it is the living Word of God, the Jesus Christ of faith and history, who remains always transcendent and inaccessible except as he reveals himself through the Spirit. Our appeal can never be to human wisdom but must always be to divine revelation—yet revelation united with visible signs and means, such as Scripture, sacraments and church proclamation.

I have presented in these volumes a systematic theology, but it does not make a claim to ontological or philosophical comprehensiveness (as we find in Hegel). It is systematic but not scholastic, since it does not set out to harmonize the axioms of Scripture or the guiding principles of church tradition. It prizes faithfulness over coherence, without disclaiming the latter. It holds that our knowledge of God is at the most analogical, not univocal. It is an open-ended theology, open to revision and correction in the light of the Word of God. Its affirmations are not irreformable as in much of the older dogmatics. The ideal in theology is a *theologia viatorum* (a theology of wayfarers).

I here acknowledge my preference for Kierkegaard over Hegel, a theology of paradox over a theology of synthesis. I uphold a theology that does not proceed to resolve paradox but begins with faith in the absolute paradox—the Word becoming flesh in Jesus Christ. At the same time, faith looks forward to the eschatological transcending of paradox—when we shall know even as we are known (1 Cor 13:12).[3]

With Barth I hold that we must be open to correction by Kierkegaard, but we must not remain with Kierkegaard. Paradox is only a means to greater understanding, not an end that defies understanding. Our goal as evangelical theologians is not the overthrow of rationality by faith but the harnessing of rationality in the service of faith. Yet even when we make progress in understanding our faith, we must continue to bow before the mysteries that animate faith.[4]

I seek to go beyond both the anti-foundationalism of postmodern theology and the biblicistic foundationalism of the old Protestant scholasticism. I espouse a markedly qualified foundationalism in which foundations are uncovered through submission to divine revelation. The foundations that theology is able to articulate are not identical with the ontological realities that they depict. But theology can claim a rough correspondence between human articulation and divine revelation. What I am proposing is a revised supernaturalism—one that acknowledges that truth in itself is not directly accessible to human reason but is partially hidden in the act of divine revelation.

A theology of Word and Spirit will be historical but not historicist. It repudiates the notion that historical knowledge can serve as the basis for faith, but it insists that we find divine revelation in a particular event or series of events within history, events testified to in holy Scripture. There is nothing within history itself that yields definitive truth regarding God and his plan of salvation, but history is the arena in which the living God discloses himself and his will to the community of faith.

Against narrative theology I maintain that theological insights cannot be contained within the confines of narrative history. Revelational truth rises above history just as it descends into history. Yet it never becomes part of the fabric of history, but always stands over and against history as a Word from the beyond.

I have called my theology sacramental because it postulates that the Spirit works through outward or visible signs in realizing his mission to the world. These outward signs, however, do not carry the Word of God through their own power. Instead they point to the Word of God through the power of the Holy Spirit.

I heartily acknowledge a certain congruity between my thought and that of T. F. Torrance.[5] But I am closer to Kierkegaard than to Torrance in elucidating the role of paradox and dialectic in theology. Torrance espouses a critical realism in which being is united with form. According to one critic he here tends to ignore Barth's warning that this method ends in confusing the proper object of theology with other objects.[6] Torrance recognizes but downplays Barth's insistence on a *"diastasis between the words of the text and the Word of the Spirit."*[7]

Both Torrance and Pannenberg from different perspectives question analogical predication of God and here show an affinity to the Greek apophatic tradition.[8] I believe we dare not surrender analogical language for God, for otherwise we end in the mire of subjectivism.[9] Pannenberg contends for doxological language for God, but doxology in the biblical sense encompasses commitment to truth. One can say with Pannenberg that God is beyond all analogy, but we must then immediately add that God wills to enter into an analogical relationship with his people in order to communicate with them. The word that the church proclaims is a bearer of meaning, not simply an utterance of praise.

While viewing the Trinity as the culmination of the theological enterprise, I do not begin with the dialectic within the trinitarian life of God because this tends to divorce truth from experience. I continue to maintain that the point of departure in a catholic evangelical theology is God's self-disclosure in Jesus Christ through the power of the Spirit. The content of this disclosure is the gospel of what God has done for us in Christ—in his sacrificial death on the cross and his glorious resurrection from the grave. Here it can be seen that soteriology is the core and center of a biblically based theology. Theology must be integrally related not only to the experience of faith but also to the living out of a Christian life that gives our faith credibility. The resurrection of Christ from the dead ignites the fire of regeneration that sweeps through world history, finally culminating in the glorious kingdom of God.

My purpose in offering these volumes is not simply to refine theology's reflection on the Word of God but to pave the way for the reform of the church in the light of the Word of God. The church today needs both revival and reform, but one cannot happen without the other. It is my hope that these volumes will play a part in restoring biblical teaching and preaching in the church as well as fostering a life of discipleship under the cross. It is also my prayer that these volumes will be used by the Spirit to instill a holy optimism in the people of God—based not on the potentialities of the human spirit, but on the invincibility of the Holy Spirit as he works through sacred Scripture and church proclamation in bringing sinners to repentance and thereby altering the face of world history.

Notes

Chapter 1: Introduction

[1]For my earlier discussion of the social forms of Christianity, see Donald Bloesch, *The Church* (Downers Grove, Ill.: InterVarsity Press, 2002), pp.189-203.

[2]See Ernst Troeltsch, *The Social Teaching of the Christian Churches*, trans. Olive Wyon (1931; reprint, London: George Allen & Unwin, 1950), pp. 326-445; 993-1013.

[3]Ibid., p. 996.

[4]Ibid., p. 993.

[5]See Charles E. Moore, ed., *Provocations: Spiritual Writings of Kierkegaard* (Farmington, Penn.: Plough Publishing House, 1999), p. 227.

[6]I am indebted to Troeltsch in my typology, but there are some important differences. I include types of religious formation that do not fit into Troeltsch's schema.

[7]My use of "cult" approaches but is not equivalent to Troeltsch's "mystical society."

[8]In actual practice a cult is often intolerant and manipulative.

[9]A cult basically signifies a new religion, whereas a sect indicates a truncated form of traditional religion.

[10]H. Richard Niebuhr has this insightful observation: "Denominationalism . . . is a compromise, made far too lightly, between Christianity and the world. Yet it often regards itself as a Christian achievement and glorifies its martyrs as bearers of the Cross. It represents the accommodation of Christianity to the caste-system of human society." See Niebuhr, *The Social Sources of Denominationalism* (1929; reprint, Hamden, Conn.: Shoe String Press, 1954), p. 6.

[11]See Emil Brunner, *The Misunderstanding of the Church*, trans. Harold Knight (Philadelphia: Westminster Press, 1953).

[12]See Donald G. Bloesch, *Centers of Christian Renewal* (Philadelphia: United Church Press, 1964) and *Wellsprings of Renewal* (Grand Rapids: Eerdmans, 1974).

[13]See Samuel Emerick, ed., *Spiritual Renewal for Methodism* (Nashville: Methodist Evangelistic Materials, 1958).

[14]See Walter Houston Clark, *The Oxford Group: Its History and Significance* (New York: Bookman Associates, 1951); and Garth Lean, *Frank Buchman: A Life* (London: Constable, 1985).

[15]Troeltsch, *Social Teaching*, pp. 993-97.

[16]For my earlier discussion of heresy, heterodoxy and apostasy, see Bloesch, *The Holy Spirit: Works and Gifts* (Downers Grove, Ill.: InterVarsity Press, 2000), pp. 144-46, 176-78.

[17]Mark J. Edwards, ed., *Galatians, Ephesians, Philippians,* Ancient Christian Commentary on Scripture (Downers Grove, Ill.: InterVarsity Press, 1999), p. 118, emphasis in original.

[18]Gerald Bray, ed., *Romans,* Ancient Christian Commentary on Scripture (Downers Grove, Ill.: InterVarsity Press, 1998), p. 279.

[19]To be sure, the Pauline writer describes the church as "the pillar and bulwark of the truth" (1 Tim 3:15), but this is the church in its unity with the kingdom. He is here speaking not simply of the church as a social institution but of the "the church of the living God," the church as the vessel of the Spirit. The church in this sense is not only supported by the truth of the Word of God but is itself supportive of this truth.

[20]Nicolas Berdyaev, *The Destiny of Man,* trans. Natalie Duddington (London: Geoffrey Bles, 1937), pp. 160-61.

[21]For my critique of Troeltsch see Donald G. Bloesch, *The Church: Sacraments, Worship, Ministry, Mission* (Downers Grove, Ill.: InterVarsity Press, 2002), pp. 240-44.

[22]Troeltsch, *Social Teaching,* pp. 1005-6.

[23]Kierkegaard, in Moore, *Provocations,* p. 227.

[24]A communitarian vision does not necessarily imply life in a religious community, though it may call for this on some occasions. It does imply that the local congregation become a fellowship of love in which every member looks out for the material as well as the spiritual needs of every other.

[25]See, for example, Stanley J. Grenz, *Theology for the Community of God* (Nashville, Tenn.: Broadman & Holman Publishers, 1994).

[26]John A. Mackay, *His Life and Our Life* (Philadelphia: Westminster Press, 1964), pp. 26-27.

[27]The Spirit is working everywhere but primarily in order to drive people to Jesus Christ, and in this sense the Spirit works in conjunction with the Word. His preservative work is always in the service of his redemptive work, his work in relating people to Jesus Christ as Lord and Savior.

Chapter 2: Controversial Themes in Eschatology

[1]Of particular significance are Johannes Weiss, *Jesus' Proclamation of the Kingdom of God,* ed. and trans. R. H. Hiers and D. L. Holland (Philadelphia: Fortress, 1971); and Albert Schweitzer, *The Quest of the Historical Jesus* (1910; reprint, New York: Macmillan, 1956).

[2]The more thoroughgoing preterists include Edward E. Stevens, Max R. King, John Bray and John Noë. See John L. Bray, *Matthew 24 Fulfilled* (Lakeland, Fla.: John L. Bray Ministry, 1996); John Noë, *Beyond the End Times: The Rest of . . . the Greatest Story Ever Told* (Bradford, Penn.: Preterist Resources, 1999); and Marti Mikl, *Understanding God's Israel* (Phoenix, Ariz.: Triple M. Publishing, 1999). Most thoroughgoing preterists still affirm a future consummation of the kingdom.

[3]Paul Tillich, *Systematic Theology* (Chicago: University of Chicago Press, 1963), 3:359-61, 392.

[4]Reinhold Niebuhr, *An Interpretation of Christian Ethics* (New York: Harper & Bros., 1935), p. 58.

[5]See Rudolf Bultmann, *The Presence of Eternity: History and Eschatology* (New York: Harper, 1957); and H. W. Bartsch, ed., *Kerygma and Myth*, trans. R. H. Fuller, 2 vols. (London: SPCK, 1953-1962).

[6]See Emil Brunner, *The Christian Doctrine of the Church, Faith, and the Consummation*, trans. David Cairns (Philadelphia: Westminster Press, 1962), pp. 362-74; 394-400. Also see John Knox, *Christ and the Hope of Glory* (Nashville: Abingdon, 1960).

[7]See my extensive discussion on the millennium on pp. 87-113.

[8]See T. A. Kantonen, *The Christian Hope* (Philadelphia: Muhlenberg, 1954); Iain Murray, *The Puritan Hope* (London: Banner of Truth, 1971); J. Marcellus Kik, *An Eschatology of Victory* (Phillipsburg, N.J.: Presbyterian & Reformed, 1971); and John Jefferson Davis, *Christ's Victorious Kingdom* (Grand Rapids: Baker, 1986).

[9]See Walter Rauschenbusch, *A Theology for The Social Gospel* (Nashville: Abingdon, 1945).

[10]See James H. Moorhead, *World Without End: Mainstream American Protestant Visions of the Last Things, 1880-1925* (Bloomington, Ind.: Indiana University Press, 1999), pp. 48-169.

[11]Jürgen Moltmann, *Theology of Hope*, trans. James W. Leitch (New York: Harper & Row, 1967), p. 329.

[12]Moltmann readily acknowledges that his schema of the three stages of an advancing kingdom of freedom draws upon the eschatological vision of Joachim of Flora. See Moltmann, *The Trinity and the Kingdom*, trans. Margaret Kohl (San Francisco: Harper & Row, 1981), pp. 203-22. For a fuller discussion see pp. 101-2, 106-7.

[13]See David Chilton, *Paradise Restored* (Tyler, Tex.: Reconstruction Press, 1985); *Theonomy: A Reformed Critique*, ed. William S. Barker and W. Robert Godfrey (Grand Rapids: Zondervan, 1990); and Rousas John Rushdoony, *The Institutes of Biblical Law* (Tyler, Tex.: Craig, 1973). For books on dispensationalism see p. 276 in the notes to chapter five.

[14]Karl Barth too can be listed as an amillennialist, but at the same time his theology contains a strong postmillennial dimension.

[15]Emmy Arnold, ed., *Inner Words* (Rifton, N.Y.: Plough, 1975), pp. 90-91.

[16]See Stanley J. Grenz, *The Millennial Maze* (Downers Grove, Ill.: InterVarsity Press, 1992), pp. 91-125. For my fuller discussion of dispensationalism see pp. 94-98 in this volume.

[17]Arnold, *Inner Words*, p. 126.

[18]For the preterist position see Noē, *Beyond the End Times*; and John Noē, *The Apocalypse Conspiracy* (Brentwood, Tenn.: Wolgemuth & Hyatt/Word, 1991). Also see R. C. Sproul, *The Last Days According to Jesus* (Grand Rapids: Baker, 1998).

[19]Arnold, *Inner Words*, pp. 178-79.

[20]See Joseph Ratzinger, *Eschatology, Death and Eternal Life*, trans. M. Waldstein and A. Nichols (Washington D.C.: Catholic University of America Press, 1988), pp. 6-7.

²¹Neonaturalists include those who affirm the reality of God but not as independent of nature. Among scholars in the age of modernity who adhere to a fundamentally naturalistic understanding of God are Theodore Munger, Ralph Waldo Emerson, William James, Theodore Parker, Shailer Mathews, Edward Scribner Ames, Pierre Teilhard de Chardin, C. Lloyd Morgan, Gordon Kaufman, Charles Hartshorne, Bernard E. Meland, Henry Nelson Wieman, Daniel Day Williams, John Cobb Jr., Peter Hodgson, Schubert Ogden, David Griffin, Bernard Loomer, Philip Heffner and Lewis Ford.

²²See Heinrich Quistorp, *Calvin's Doctrine of the Last Things*, trans. Harold Knight (Richmond, Va.: John Knox Press, 1955), pp. 79-81. For my further discussion of postmortem salvation see pp. 143-48 in this volume.

²³See Quincy Howe Jr., *Reincarnation for the Christian* (Philadelphia: Westminster Press, 1974); Geddes MacGregor, *Reincarnation in Christianity* (Wheaton, Ill.: Quest Books, 1978); MacGregor, *Reincarnation as a Christian Hope* (Totowa, N.J.: Barnes & Noble Books, 1982); Matthew Fox, *One River, Many Wells* (New York: Jeremy P. Tarcher/Putnam, 2000), pp. 335-73; and Sylvia Cranston, "Reincarnation: The Lost Chord of Christianity?" in *Immortality and Human Destiny*, ed. Geddes MacGregor (New York: Paragon House, 1985), pp. 143-60. For critiques of reincarnation see Hans Küng, *Eternal Life?* trans. Edward Quinn (New York: Doubleday, 1984), pp. 59-66; Mark Albrecht, *Reincarnation: A Christian Appraisal* (Downers Grove, Ill.: InterVarsity Press, 1982); Robert A. Morey, *Reincarnation and Christianity* (Minneapolis: Bethany Fellowship, 1980); Hans Schwarz, *Eschatology* (Grand Rapids: Eerdmans, 2000), pp. 301-7; Jürgen Moltmann, *The Coming of God*, trans. Margaret Kohl (Minneapolis: Fortress, 1996), pp. 110-16; and Roger E. Olson, *The Mosaic of Christian Belief* (Downers Grove, Ill.: InterVarsity Press, 2002), pp. 316-19.

²⁴John Hick holds to reincarnation into higher, more spiritual realms rather than the return of the soul to earth. See Hick, *Death and Eternal Life* (Louisville, Ky.: Westminster John Knox, 1994), pp. 391-92; 412-14; 417-19.

²⁵From my perspective, eternal death begins with sin.

²⁶Karl Barth, *Prayer*, trans. Sara F. Terrien (Philadelphia: Westminster Press, 1952), p. 20.

²⁷Pierre-Yves Emery, *The Communion of Saints*, trans. D. J. Watson and M. Watson (London: Faith Press, 1966), p. 111.

²⁸The term *restrictivism* is used widely in the circles of open theism (John Sanders, Clark Pinnock, etc.).

²⁹See Gabriel Fackre, Ronald H. Nash and John Sanders, *What About Those Who Have Never Heard?* (Downers Grove, Ill.: InterVarsity Press, 1995). Also see Edward William Fudge and Robert A. Peterson, *Two Views of Hell: A Biblical and Theological Dialogue* (Downers Grove, Ill.: InterVarsity Press, 2000).

³⁰Someone like John Hick is better classified as a pluralist than as an inclusivist in that he sees the world religions as independent sources of salvation rather than being connected with Jesus Christ in any way. On the differences between inclusivism, pluralism and restrictivism see Dennis L. Okholm and Timothy R. Phillips, eds., *More Than One Way? Four Views on Salvation in a Plural-*

istic World (Grand Rapids: Zondervan, 1995). For my earlier discussion of pluralism and inclusivism see Bloesch, *Jesus Christ: Savior and Lord* (Downers Grove, Ill.: InterVarsity Press, 1997), pp. 229-49; and Bloesch, *The Church* (Downers Grove, Ill.: InterVarsity Press, 2002), pp. 235-51.

[31]For a credible defense of universalism based on the actual scriptural testimony, see Jan Bonda, *The One Purpose of God: An Answer to the Doctrine of Eternal Punishment*, trans. Reinder Bruinsma (Grand Rapids: Eerdmans, 1998).

[32]Neal Punt, *Unconditional Good News* (Grand Rapids: Eerdmans, 1980), p. 30.

[33]According to Weber, Barth's position on the final destiny of human beings is based not on "a law of universal atonement" but on the freedom of God's grace. Otto Weber, *Karl Barth's Church Dogmatics,* trans. Arthur C. Cochrane (Philadelphia: Westminster Press, 1953), p. 102.

[34]For my fuller discussion of divine perseverance, see p. 240 in this volume.

[35]Norman Pittenger, *After Death—Life in God* (New York: Seabury, 1980).

[36]Quoted in Kenneth Woodward, "Death in America," *U.S. Catholic and Jubilee* 36, no. 1 (1971): 13.

[37]See George Hunsinger, "Hellfire and Damnation: Four Ancient and Modern Views," *Scottish Journal of Theology* 51, no. 4 (1998): 406-34. Another theologian who tries to avoid unnecessary speculation in this area of theology is Robert W. Jenson. See his *Systematic Theology* (New York: Oxford University Press, 1999), 2:364-65.

[38]For both Calvin and Barth it is the Spirit who makes Christ's work efficacious in human life. It is the Spirit who creates faith, but faith can erode when God witholds his Spirit from us. Neither theologian teaches a hypothetical salvation that Christ merely offers to humankind; instead they uphold an actual salvation that Christ effects through his cross and resurrection, and the outpouring of his Spirit at Pentecost. When the Spirit acts upon us, we are enabled to respond positively to God's gracious initiative and thereby to be included in the salvific process.

[39]Karl Barth, *Church Dogmatics*, ed. G. W. Bromiley and T. F. Torrance (Edinburgh: T & T Clark, 1957), 2(2):306-506. Also see Weber, *Karl Barth's Church Dogmatics*, pp. 93-103.

[40]See Donald G. Bloesch, *Jesus Is Victor! Karl Barth's Doctrine of Salvation* (Nashville: Abingdon, 1976).

[41]Herman H. Ridderbos, *The Epistle of Paul to the Churches of Galatia* (Grand Rapids: Eerdmans, 1953), p. 227.

[42]See Raymond Stamm, "The Epistle to the Galatians," in *Interpreter's Bible*, ed. G. A. Buttrick (Nashville: Abingdon, 1953), 10:590-91; and Hendrikus Berkhof, "Israel as a Theological Problem in the Christian Church," *Journal of Ecumenical Studies* 6, no. 3 (1969): 335-38.

[43]Berkhof, "Israel as a Theological Problem," pp. 330, 344-45.

[44]Ibid., p. 334.

[45]Ibid.

[46]Ibid., p. 344.

[47]For my further discussion of Israel see pp. 197-212 in this volume.

Chapter 3: Light Against Darkness

[1]Quoted in "The Ecumenical Century," *Time* 78, no. 23 (1961): 79-80.

[2]Eduard Thurneysen, *A Theology of Pastoral Care*, trans. Jack Worthington and Thomas Wieser (Richmond: John Knox, 1962), p. 321.

[3]"Angel" in *The Oxford Dictionary of the Christian Church*, ed. F. L. Cross, rev. ed. (New York: Oxford University Press, 1983), p. 52.

[4]Origen *Against Celsus* 6,43. *The Ante-Nicene Fathers*, ed. Alexander Roberts and James Donaldson (Grand Rapids: Eerdmans, 1956), 4:592.

[5]See G. Vermes, "Dead Sea Scrolls," in *Interpreter's Dictionary of the Bible*, supp. vol. (Nashville: Abingdon, 1976), pp. 216-17.

[6]See my discussion of the demonic in Bloesch, *Essentials of Evangelical Theology* (1978; reprint, San Francisco: Harper & Row, 1982), 2:131-35. For my later discussion, see Bloesch, *The Holy Spirit* (Downers Grove, Ill.: InterVarsity Press, 2000), pp. 209-21.

[7]Paul Tillich, *Systematic Theology* (Chicago: University of Chicago Press, 1963), 3:102.

[8]Paul Tillich, *The Protestant Era*, ed. and trans. James Luther Adams (Chicago: University of Chicago Press, 1948), p. 304.

[9]Luther, "A Mighty Fortress Is Our God," *The Worshiping Church: A Hymnal* (Carol Stream, Ill.: Hope Publishing, 1990), no. 43.

[10]See Edwin Lewis, *The Creator and the Adversary* (New York: Abingdon-Cokesbury, 1948), pp. 128-47.

[11]James Luther Adams, *Paul Tillich's Philosophy of Culture, Science and Religion* (New York: Harper & Row, 1965), p. 231.

[12]See Anton Fridrichsen, "The Conflict of Jesus with Unclean Spirits," trans. Hugo Odeberg, *Theology* 22, no. 129 (1931): 122-35.

[13]Emmanuel Mounier, *Personalism*, trans. Philip Mairet (Notre Dame, Ind: University of Notre Dame Press, 1952), p. 82.

[14]Nathan Söderblom, *Religion of Revelation*, quoted in Gustaf Aulén, "Nathan Söderblom as Theologian," *Una Sancta* 24, no. 1 (1967): 18.

[15]Philip S. Watson, *The Concept of Grace* (Philadelphia: Muhlenberg, 1959), p. 45.

[16]See Rudolf Otto, *The Kingdom of God and the Son of Man*, trans. Floyd V. Filson and Bertram Lee Woolf, rev. ed. (1943; reprint, Boston: Starr King, 1951).

[17]See Rudolf Bultmann, *Theology of the New Testament*, trans. Kendrick Grobel (New York: Charles Scribner's Sons, 1951), 1:41, 48.

[18]See *Interpreter's Bible* (Nashville: Abingdon, 1955), 4:397; and Derek Kidner, *Psalms 73—150* (London: Inter-Varsity Press, 1975), pp. 268-69. Also see J. Clinton McCann Jr., "The Book of Psalms," in *The New Interpreter's Bible* (Nashville: Abingdon, 1996), 4:974.

[19]*New Jerusalem Bible* (Garden City, N.Y.: Doubleday, 1985), p. 1627, notes.

[20]Ibid.

[21]For my further discussion see pp. 62-64.

[22]Gustaf Wingren, *The Living Word* (London: SCM Press, 1960), p. 94.

[23]Dietrich Bonhoeffer, *Ethics*, trans. Neville Horton Smith (New York: Macmillan, 1965), p. 204.

[24]Helmut Thielicke, *Man in God's World*, ed. and trans. John W. Doberstein (New York: Harper & Row, 1963), p. 195.

[25]The kingdom of Christ transcends the boundaries of the empirical church, but the fulcrum of its power is within the church, or more properly, within the Holy Spirit who builds up the church.

[26]*Luther's Works,* ed. Jaroslav Pelikan (St. Louis: Concordia, 1961), 24:417.

[27]For my further discussion of the millennium in this volume see pp. 87-113.

[28]These denizens of the underworld include the demonic hosts and reprobate human beings. See the discussion in Robert Johnstone, *The Epistle of Paul to the Philippians* (1875; reprint, Grand Rapids: Baker, 1955), pp. 157-59.

[29]Emmanuel Mounier, "Christian Faith and Civilization," trans. Erwin W. Geissman, *Cross Currents* 1, no. 1 (1950): 3-23.

[30]For my further discussion of heaven and hell see pp. 219-232 in this book.

[31]See Jaroslav Pelikan, *The Christian Tradition* (Chicago: University of Chicago Press, 1971), 1:136.

[32]Karl Barth, *Prayer*, trans. Sara F. Terrien (Philadelphia: Westminster Press, 1952), p. 73.

[33]A New Age tinge is detectable in Geoffrey Hodson's remark: "The Devil is the shadow of himself which a man sees when he turns his back to the light." Hodson, *The Kingdom of the Gods* (Wheaton, Ill.: Theosophical Publishing House, 1952), p. 177.

[34]See Thomas Aquinas *Summa Theologica* 1, Questions 50-64.

[35]See Karl Barth, *Church Dogmatics,* trans. G. W. Bromiley and R. J. Ehrlich (Edinburgh: T & T Clark, 1960), 3(3):369-531.

[36]Paul Tillich, *Systematic Theology* (Chicago: University of Chicago Press, 1951), 1:260.

[37]Indicative of the new interest in angels by the mainstream church is the splendid essay by Gabriel Fackre, "Angels Heard and Demons Seen," *Theology Today* 51, no. 3 (1994): 345-58.

Chapter 4: The Day of the Lord

[1]See George Eldon Ladd, *Jesus and the Kingdom* (New York: Harper & Row, 1964), pp. 101-17; 303-24.

[2]Karl Barth, *Church Dogmatics,* ed. G. W. Bromiley and T. F. Torrance, trans. G. W. Bromiley (Edinburgh: T & T Clark, 1961), 4(3):293-95, 315-17.

[3]M. Rist, "Apocalypticism," in *The Interpreter's Dictionary of the Bible* (Nashville: Abingdon, 1962), 1:157.

[4]P. D. Hanson, "Apocalypticism," in *The Interpreter's Dictionary of the Bible,* supp. vol. (Nashville: Abingdon, 1976), pp. 28-34.

[5]Quoted in Robert Gleason, *The World to Come* (New York: Sheed & Ward, 1958), p. 159.

[6]Hendrikus Berkhof, *Well-Founded Hope* (Richmond, Va.: John Knox Press, 1969), p. 44.

[7]Gleason, *World to Come*, p. 83.

[8]Alois Winklhofer, *The Coming of His Kingdom*, trans. A. V. Littledale (New York:

Herder & Herder, 1963), p. 45.

[9]W. Stewart McCullough concludes that in light of the fact that Israel developed a belief in immortality, one acceptable exegesis is that "the verse expresses the psalmist's hope that God's guidance of him will continue after death." *Interpreter's Bible* (Nashville: Abingdon, 1955), 4:391. Also see Derek Kidner, *Psalms 73—150* (London: Inter-Varsity Press, 1975), pp. 262-63.

[10]Sherman E. Johnson in *Interpreter's Bible* (Nashville: Abingdon, 1951), 7:553.

[11]Cited in Paul Althaus, *The Theology of Martin Luther*, trans. Robert C. Schultz (Philadelphia: Fortress, 1966), p. 416. See pp. 410-25. Also see *Luther's Works,* ed. Jaroslav Pelikan (St. Louis: Concordia, 1967), 30:196-99. It should be noted that Luther did not wish to separate the judgment at the time of death and the last judgment. They are one and the same seen from different perspectives. Lutheran orthodoxy, on the other hand, made a clear distinction between the general or final judgment and "the *particular judgment* by which, at the hour of death, a state of glory or of ignorance is awarded every man" (David Hollatz). Cited in Heinrich Schmid, ed., *The Doctrinal Theology of the Evangelical Lutheran Church* (Minneapolis: Augsburg, 1961), p. 644.

[12]James P. Martin, *The Last Judgment in Protestant Theology from Orthodoxy to Ritschl* (Grand Rapids: Eerdmans, 1963), pp. 69-70, 74.

[13]John Calvin, *Commentary on a Harmony of the Evangelists Matthew, Mark and Luke,* trans. William Pringle (Edinburgh: Calvin Translation Society, 1845), 1:320.

[14]See John Dillenberger, *God Hidden and Revealed* (Philadelphia: Muhlenberg, 1953).

[15]See my further discussion on pp. 197-212 of this volume.

[16]See Thomas F. Torrance, *Kingdom and Church* (Edinburgh: Oliver & Boyd, 1956), pp. 118-19.

[17]Ladd, *Jesus and the Kingdom*, p. 333.

[18]F. F. Bruce, *The Epistle to the Hebrews* (Grand Rapids: Eerdmans, 1964), p. 256.

[19]Thomas S. Kepler, ed., *The Table Talk of Martin Luther* (New York: World, 1952), p. 117.

[20]With a significant number of higher critical scholars, Frederick Grant holds that chapter 13 of Mark is composite, including "material of a general apocalyptic nature, not necessarily to be attributed to Jesus, along with sayings which probably belonged in the authentic tradition of his words" (*Interpreter's Bible* [Nashville: Abingdon, 1951], 7:854). Some scholars argue that the Gospel writers were guided by catechetical interests in adapting material drawn from various sources in the service of Jesus' proclamation and mission. See the discussion in Vincent Taylor, *The Gospel According to St. Mark* (London: Macmillan, 1955), pp. 498-524. Interestingly, Taylor points out that the respected critical scholar Johannes Weiss "renounced the hypothesis of a small Jewish apocalypse, to which he formerly had adhered, preferring to trace the discourse to the sayings-source," the idea that the sayings of Jesus were already available to the apostolic writer in "a fixed literary form" (p. 499). On the grounds that this was not Mark's practice, William Lane disputes the com-

monly held assumption in critical scholarship that "elements of Jewish apocalyptic, authentic sayings of Jesus and pronouncements of Christian prophets . . . have been forged into a unified discourse by Marcan redaction." William L. Lane, *The Gospel According to Mark* (Grand Rapids: Eerdmans, 1974), pp. 449-50.

[21]John L. Bray, *Matthew 24 Fulfilled* (Lakeland, Fla.: John L. Bray Ministry, 1996), p. 220.

[22]David Chilton, *Paradise Restored* (Tyler, Tex.: Reconstruction Press, 1985), p. 224.

[23]W. F. Albright and C. S. Mann voice their reservations concerning the preterist interpretation: "It is simply not possible to refer this saying to the fall of Jerusalem, as do some writers, who then attempt to make sense of a *proclamation . . . throughout the world*." W. F. Albright and C. S. Mann, trans. and ed., *Matthew*, Anchor Bible (1971; reprint, New York: Doubleday, 1987), pp. 292-93.

[24]See Eduard Schweizer: "The image of lightning stresses the universal scope of Jesus' coming; the picture is that of a horizontal lightning bolt, conceived by the ancient world as illuminating the whole earth, east to west, at the same moment. Such will the 'presence' of Jesus be on 'his day' (Lk 17:24)." *The Good News According to Matthew*, trans. David E. Green (Atlanta: John Knox Press, 1975), p. 454.

[25]*Interpreter's Bible*, 7:552.

[26]Robert H. Gundry, *Matthew: A Commentary* (Grand Rapids: Eerdmans, 1982), p. 490.

[27]*NIV Study Bible* (Grand Rapids: Zondervan, 1985), p. 1477.

[28]J. Stuart Russell, *The Parousia* (1887; reprint, Grand Rapids: Baker, 1983), p. 545.

[29]Schweizer, *Good News According to Matthew*, p. 458.

[30]*NIV Study Bible*, p. 1521. Also see p. 1581.

[31]Daniel J. Lewis, *Three Crucial Questions About the Last Days* (Grand Rapids: Baker, 1998), p. 113.

[32]S. MacLean Gilmour, "The Gospel According to St. Luke," *Interpreter's Bible* (Nashville: Abingdon, 1952), 8:370.

[33]Robert H. Mounce, *Matthew* (Peabody, Mass.: Hendrickson, 1991), p. 228.

[34]Joseph A. Fitzmyer, trans. and ed., *The Gospel According to Luke (x-xxiv)*, Anchor Bible (New York: Doubleday, 1985), p. 1329.

[35]*New Jerusalem Bible* (New York: Doubleday, 1985), p. 1649.

[36]Ibid., p. 1679.

[37]Bray, *Matthew 24 Fulfilled*, pp. 221ff.

[38]From my perspective the aim should be to show how every text serves to elucidate the overall message of the Bible. To assert that every single text can be harmonized with every other is to claim the possibility of a synoptic or absolute perspective that belongs only to God.

[39]Mounce, *Matthew*, p. 222.

[40]J. Heinrich Arnold, *Discipleship* (Farmington, Penn.: Plough, 1994), p. 270.

[41]Ibid., p. 277.

[42]In Emmy Arnold, ed., *Inner Words* (1963; reprint, Rifton, N.Y.: Plough, 1975), p. 169.

Chapter 5: The Millennial Hope

[1]Martin Rist, "The Revelation of St. John the Divine," *Interpreter's Bible* (Nashville: Abingdon, 1957), 12:519.

[2]Bruno Forte, *The Trinity as History*, trans. Paul Rotondi (Staten Island: Alba House, 1989).

[3]See Stanley J. Grenz, *The Millennial Maze* (Downers Grove, Ill.: InterVarsity Press, 1992).

[4]Raymond F. Bulman, "Paul Tillich and the Millennialist Heritage," *Theology Today* 53, no. 4 (1997): 467-68.

[5]Jürgen Moltmann, *The Coming of God*, trans. Margaret Kohl (Minneapolis: Fortress, 1996), p. 193.

[6]Grenz, *Millennial Maze*, p. 27.

[7]Karl Barth, *The Word of God and the Word of Man*, trans. Douglas Horton (New York: Harper & Row, 1957), p. 160.

[8]Ibid., p. 158.

[9]Paul Tillich, *Systematic Theology* (Chicago: University of Chicago Press, 1963), 3:298.

[10]Paul Tillich, *Theology of Peace*, ed. Ronald H. Stone (Louisville, Ky.: Westminster John Knox, 1990), p. 43.

[11]Augsburg Confession, Article 17.

[12]James P. Martin, *The Last Judgment* (Grand Rapids: Eerdmans, 1963), p. 26.

[13]Ibid., p. 27.

[14]See Anthony A. Hoekema, *The Four Major Cults* (Grand Rapids: Eerdmans, 1963), pp. 137-43.

[15]Quoted in Hans Schwarz, *On the Way to the Future* (Minneapolis: Augsburg, 1972), p. 154.

[16]Adrio König, *The Eclipse of Christ in Eschatology* (Grand Rapids: Eerdmans, 1989), p. 137.

[17]For a premillennialist who seeks to maintain the social relevance of the faith, see Vernon C. Grounds, *Revolution and the Christian Faith* (Philadelphia: J. B. Lippincott, 1971).

[18]James Leo Garrett Jr., *Systematic Theology* (Grand Rapids: Eerdmans, 1995), 2:759.

[19]See Bloesch, *Essentials of Evangelical Theology* (1978; reprint, San Francisco: Harper & Row, 1982) 2:190-91. Also see Charles E. Hill, *Regnum Caelorum: Patterns of Millennial Thought in Early Christianity*, 2nd ed. (Grand Rapids: Eerdmans, 2001).

[20]See Robert G. Clouse, "Johann Heinrich Alsted and English Millennialism," *Harvard Theological Review* 62, no. 2 (1969): 189-207; and Clouse, "Views of the Millennium," in *Evangelical Dictionary of Theology*, ed. Walter A. Elwell (Grand Rapids: Baker, 1984), pp. 714-18. See also R. G. Clouse, "The Rebirth of Millenarianism," in *Puritans, the Millennium and the Future of Israel: Puritan Eschatol-

ogy 1600-1660, ed. Peter Toon (Cambridge: James Clarke, 1970), pp. 42-65.

[21]See my earlier discussion of dispensationalism (pp. 33-34). Also see Bloesch, *The Holy Spirit: Works and Gifts* (Downers Grove, Ill.: InterVarsity Press, 2000), pp. 169-73.

[22]For a perceptive analysis of dispensationalism, see Grenz, *Millennial Maze,* pp. 91-125. For a lucid discussion of the role of the Plymouth Brethren in shaping modern dispensationalism, see Robert Baylis, *My People: The Story of Those Christians Sometimes Called Plymouth Brethren* (Wheaton, Ill.: Harold Shaw, 1995), pp. 3-79. The author addresses the problem of schism in the Brethren movement and offers biblical solutions.

[23]Hal Lindsey, *The Late Great Planet Earth* (New York: Bantam, 1973). See also his *Apocalypse Code* (Palos Verdes, Calif.: Western Front, 1997). Another book that popularizes dispensational themes is Tim F. LaHaye and Jerry B. Jenkins, *Left Behind: A Novel of the Earth's Last Days* (Wheaton, Ill.: Tyndale House, 1995).

[24]This position is a marked departure from classical Reformed theology, which speaks of one covenant of grace with two dispensations. See Donald K. McKim, ed., *Encyclopedia of the Reformed Faith* (Louisville: Westminster John Knox, 1992), pp. 73-74, 84-87.

[25]*Scofield Reference Bible,* new ed. (New York: Oxford University Press, 1917), p. 1115.

[26]See Robert L. Saucy, *The Case for Progressive Dispensationalism* (Grand Rapids: Zondervan, 1993). Also see Grenz, *Millennial Maze,* pp. 122-25. Grenz raises pertinent questions about the biblical credibility of progressive dispensationalism. At the same time he finds promise for evangelical rapprochement in the progressive movement. A more reserved appraisal of progressive dispensationalism is given by Charles C. Ryrie, *Dispensationalism* (Chicago: Moody Press, 1995), pp. 161-81.

[27]See Edwin McNeill Poteat's helpful exposition of Psalm 87 in *The Interpreter's Bible* (Nashville: Abingdon, 1955), 4:468-72.

[28]Charles Ryrie allows for the view that the dispensations are different ways of salvation but only because the content of the faith is different. *Dispensationalism,* p. 121.

[29]Philip Edgcumbe Hughes, *Interpreting Prophecy* (Grand Rapids: Eerdmans, 1976), p. 130.

[30]Hans K. LaRondelle, *The Israel of God in Prophecy* (Berrien Springs, Mich.: Andrews University Press, 1983), p. 141.

[31]See John H. Gerstner, *A Primer on Dispensationalism* (Phillipsburg, N.J.: Presbyterian & Reformed, 1982); and Gerstner, *Wrongly Dividing the Word of Truth: A Critique of Dispensationalism* (Brentwood, Tenn.: Wolgemuth & Hyatt, 1991).

[32]See D. H. Kromminga, *The Millennium in the Church* (Grand Rapids: Eerdmans, 1945), pp. 30-40; and Grenz, *Millennial Maze,* pp. 40-41.

[33]According to one biblical scholar, "Revelation's structure is not linear; it does not tell us a simple story in a straight line. At times the vision circles back and tells us the same thing it has already told us but in a different way." Paul Spils-

bury, *The Throne, the Lamb and the Dragon* (Downers Grove, Ill.: InterVarsity Press, 2002), p. 35.

[34]König, *Eclipse of Christ*, p. 132.

[35]G. C. Berkouwer, *The Return of Christ*, ed. Marlin J. Van Elderen, trans. James Van Oosterom (Grand Rapids: Eerdmans, 1972), p. 307.

[36]Grenz, *Millennial Maze*, p. 214.

[37]See Greg L. Bahnsen, *Theonomy in Christian Ethics*, 2nd ed. (Phillipsburg, N.J.: Presbyterian and Reformed, 1984); Rousas John Rushdoony, *The Institutes of Biblical Law* (Tyler, Tex.: Craig, 1973); and James B. Jordan, *The Law of the Covenant* (Tyler, Tex.: Institute for Christian Economics, 1984). For a Reformed response to what has come to be known as reconstructionism, see William S. Barker and W. Robert Godfrey, eds., *Theonomy: A Reformed Critique* (Grand Rapids: Zondervan, 1990).

[38]David Chilton, *The Days of Vengeance: An Exposition of the Book of Revelation* (Fort Worth, Tex.: Dominion, 1987), p. 502.

[39]At the same time postmillennialists anticipate the conversion of Israel into the family of the church. In this sense they tend to be pro-Israel.

[40]See Kromminga, *Millennium in the Church*, pp. 77-88.

[41]See Paul Tillich, *A History of Christian Thought*, ed. Carl E. Braaten (New York: Harper & Row, 1968), pp. 175-80, 182, 205-6, 286.

[42]See Iain H. Murray, *The Puritan Hope* (Edinburgh: Banner of Truth, 1971).

[43]T. A. Kantonen, *The Christian Hope* (Philadelphia: Muhlenberg, 1954).

[44]J. Marcellus Kik, *The Eschatology of Victory* (Phillipsburg, N.J.: Presbyterian & Reformed, 1971).

[45]Loraine Boettner, *The Millennium* (Philadelphia: Presbyterian & Reformed, 1957).

[46]John Jefferson Davis, *Christ's Victorious Kingdom* (Grand Rapids: Baker, 1986).

[47]*Inner Words*, ed. Emmy Arnold (Rifton, N.Y.: Plough, 1975), p. 178.

[48]Cf. Christoph Blumhardt: "Our whole spirit demands that we speak up and say, 'And yet—the night is far spent, the day is at hand!' This became true in the hour when Jesus was born on earth. . . . It must become true on earth also; and because it must become true, it will become true" (*Inner Words*, p. 177). Also see R. Lejeune, ed., *Christoph Blumhardt and His Message* (Woodcrest, Rifton, N.Y.: Plough, 1963), pp. 196-97; Christoph Blumhardt, *Action in Waiting* (Farmington, Penn.: Plough, 1998), pp. 57-68; and Vernard Eller, ed., *Thy Kingdom Come: A Blumhardt Reader* (Grand Rapids: Eerdmans, 1980), pp. 40-43.

[49]Kantonen, *Christian Hope*, p. 68.

[50]Shirley Jackson Case, *The Millennial Hope* (Chicago: University of Chicago Press, 1918), p. 238.

[51]Ibid., p. 232.

[52]Loraine Boettner, "Postmillennialism" in *The Meaning of the Millennium*, ed. Robert G. Clouse (Downers Grove, Ill.: InterVarsity Press, 1977), p. 125.

[53]Norman Cohn, *The Pursuit of the Millennium* (1957; reprint, London: Paladin, 1970), p. 29.

[54]Robert S. Ellwood Jr., *Alternative Altars* (Chicago: University of Chicago Press,

1979), pp. 84-91.

[55]Harry R. Boer, "The Reward of the Martyrs," *The Reformed Journal* 25, no. 2 (1975): 8.

[56]Shailer Mathews, *The Social Teaching of Jesus* (New York: Macmillan, 1897), p. 54.

[57]Reinhold Niebuhr, *Beyond Tragedy* (New York: Charles Scribner's Sons, 1937), p. 277.

[58]Reinhold Niebuhr, *Faith and History* (New York: Charles Scribner's Sons, 1949), p. 239.

[59]Ibid., p. 235.

[60]Ibid., pp. 235-43.

[61]See Reinhold Niebuhr, *The Nature and Destiny of Man* (1941; reprint, New York: Charles Scribner's Sons, 1951), 2:204-12.

[62]Niebuhr astutely perceives the danger of making the kingdom nonhistorical: "The realm of redemption is never, as in rational and mystical religion, above the realm of living history, but within and at the end of it." Niebuhr, *An Interpretation of Christian Ethics* (1935; reprint, New York: Seabury, 1979), p. 18. At the same time he can say: "In one sense the Kingdom of God remains outside the world," for it is always something different from worldly attainments (*Beyond Tragedy*, p. 262). It is "relevant to every moment of history as an ideal possibility and as a principle of judgment upon present realities." (*Beyond Tragedy*, pp. 285-86).

[63]Niebuhr can also use the language of *telos* and *finis*, but he does not see the kingdom as a transforming leaven within history. He describes himself as "provisionally pessimistic" and "ultimately optimistic."

[64]See Richard Bauckham, ed., *God Will Be All in All: The Eschatology of Jürgen Moltmann* (Edinburgh: T & T Clark, 1999).

[65]Moltmann, *Coming of God*, p. 192.

[66]Moltmann fails to give adequate recognition to the eternal reign of Christ in the absolute future.

[67]Moltmann, *Coming of God*, p. 159.

[68]Ibid., p. 153.

[69]Ibid., p. 195.

[70]Ibid.

[71]Bauckham, *God Will Be All in All*, p. 139.

[72]Ibid., p. 231.

[73]The humanist bent in Moltmann's thought is especially evident in his *Religion, Revolution and the Future*, trans. M. Douglas Meeks (New York: Charles Scribner's Sons, 1969).

[74]Jürgen Moltmann, *The Source of Life: The Holy Spirit and the Theology of Life*, trans. Margaret Kohl (Minneapolis: Fortress, 1997), pp. 19-22.

[75]See Moltmann, *The Power of the Powerless*, trans. Margaret Kohl (San Francisco: Harper & Row, 1983).

[76]Moltmann does not use this Jamesian terminology, but his overall position comports with American transcendentalism and pragmatism. For my further

discussion of meliorism see pp. 257-58.

[77]Moltmann, *Coming of God*, p. 234.

[78]See Richard Bauckham, "The Millennium," in *God Will Be All in All*, pp. 123-47. Also see Bauckham's cogent appraisal of Moltmann in Kent E. Brower and Mark W. Elliott, eds., *Eschatology in Bible and Theology* (Downers Grove, Ill.: InterVarsity Press, 1997), pp. 263-77.

[79]Reinhold Niebuhr, *Faith and History*, p. 233.

[80]Quoted in Richard Curtis, *They Called Him Mister Moody* (Garden City, N.Y.: Doubleday, 1962), p. 266.

[81]Grenz, *Millennial Maze*, p. 214. While Grenz chooses amillennialism, he could just as well be placed in my category—transmillennialism.

[82]I concur with Christoph Blumhardt that the Savior has come, the Savior is coming and the Savior will come to consummate all things. Cf. R. Lejeune, ed., *Christoph Blumhardt and His Message*, pp. 78-80, 131, 220-27; and Christoph Blumhardt, *Action in Waiting*, pp. 7, 37-44, 205. Blumhardt's emphasis is that the Savior is on the way and is at work now in nature and history.

[83]Hans Urs von Balthasar, *Prayer*, trans. Graham Harrison (San Francisco: Ignatius, 1986), p. 105.

[84]See C. Norman Kraus, *Dispensationalism in America* (Richmond, Va.: John Knox Press, 1958), p. 132.

[85]Ibid.

[86]I am not implying that Christians do not really know the mysteries of faith but that their knowledge is dimmed, and therefore these mysteries remain such even to faith.

Chapter 6: The Resurrection of the Dead

[1]Origen, *On First Principles*, trans. G. W. Butterworth (New York: Harper Torchbook, 1966), p. 247.

[2]John Dominic Crossan, *Jesus: A Revolutionary Biography* (San Francisco: Harper, 1994), p. 95.

[3]Millard J. Erickson, *The Word Became Flesh* (Grand Rapids: Baker, 1991), p. 487.

[4]See Willi Marxsen, *The Resurrection of Jesus of Nazareth*, trans. Margaret Kohl (Philadelphia: Fortress, 1970).

[5]Gerd Lüdemann, *What Really Happened to Jesus*, trans. John Bowden (Louisville, Ky.: Westminster John Knox, 1995).

[6]John Shelby Spong, *Resurrection: Myth or Reality?* (San Francisco: Harper Collins, 1994).

[7]See Edward Schillebeeckx, *Jesus: An Experiment in Christology*, trans. Hubert Hoskins (New York: Crossroad, 1981). See esp. pp. 526-27; 538-41; 626-74.

[8]Ibid., pp. 644-50.

[9]I here concur with Carl E. Braaten in his "The Resurrection Debate Revisited," *Pro Ecclesia* 8, no. 2 (1999): 147-58. See esp. p. 155.

[10]Quoted in Alan Sell, *Christ Our Saviour* (Shippensburg, Penn.: Ragged Edge, 2000), p. 34.

[11]See I. John Hesselink, *Calvin's First Catechism* (Louisville: Westminster John Knox, 1997), pp. 125-28.

[12]Blaise Pascal, *Pensées and the Provincial Letters*, trans. W. F. Trotter and Thomas M'Crie (New York: Modern Library, 1941), nos. 586-87, p. 192.

[13]*Provocations: Spiritual Writings of Kierkegaard*, ed. Charles E. Moore (Farmington, Penn.: Plough, 1999), p. 67.

[14]Karl Barth, *The Faith of the Church*, ed. Jean-Louis Leuba, trans. Gabriel Vahanian (New York: Meridian Books, 1958), p. 108.

[15]Michael Horton, *We Believe* (Nashville: Word, 1998), p. 250.

[16]Ibid., p. 255.

[17]Ibid., p. 250.

[18]Hesselink, *Calvin's First Catechism*, p. 126.

[19]Quoted in Sell, *Christ Our Saviour*, p. 35.

[20]T. F. Torrance, *Reality and Evangelical Theology* (Philadelphia: Westminster Press, 1982), p. 37.

[21]See Geza Vermes, *Jesus the Jew* (London: Collins, 1973), p. 41.

[22]Martin Luther, *On the Councils and the Church*, 3, W.A. 50:627. Quoted in T. F. Torrance, *Kingdom and Church* (Edinburgh: Oliver & Boyd, 1956), p. 49.

[23]Pierre-Yves Emery, *The Communion of Saints*, trans. D. J. Watson and M. Watson (London: Faith Press, 1966), pp. 34-35.

[24]Karl Rahner and Herbert Vorgrimler, *Theological Dictionary*, ed. Cornelius Ernst, trans. Richard Strachan (New York: Herder & Herder, 1968), p. 234.

[25]C. H. Dodd, *The Epistle of Paul to the Romans* (1932; reprint, London: Hodder & Stoughton, 1954), p. 125.

[26]Romano Guardini, *The Last Things*, trans. Charlotte E. Forsyth and Grace B. Branham (Notre Dame, Ind.: University of Notre Dame Press, 1954), p. 72.

[27]Cf. *Catechism of the Catholic Church* (United States Catholic Conference, 1994): "The obedience of Jesus has transformed the curse of death into a blessing." No. 1009.

[28]See *Heidelberg Catechism*, Question 42.

[29]See Dietrich Bonhoeffer, *Letters and Papers from Prison*, enlarged edition, ed. Eberhard Bethge (New York: Macmillan, 1972), p. 376.

[30]Aristotle *Nicomachean Ethics* 3.6.

[31]Jean-Paul Sartre, *Being and Nothingness*, trans. Hazel E. Barnes (New York: Philosophical Library, 1956), p. 539.

[32]Cited in Robert Gleason, *The World to Come* (New York: Sheed & Ward, 1958), p. 75.

[33]Baruch Spinoza, *The Ethics of Spinoza: The Road to Inner Freedom*, ed. Dagobert D. Runes (Secaucus, N.J.: Citadel, 1976), p. 151.

[34]T. A. Kantonen, *The Christian Hope* (Philadelphia: Muhlenberg, 1954), p. 33.

[35]See Gleason, *World to Come*, pp. 68-69.

[36]See John Bunyan, *The Pilgrim's Progress* (Philadelphia: John C. Winston, 1933), pp. 159-69.

[37]For my further discussion of these interim realms see pp. 133-53.

[38]Cf. Norval Geldenhuys, *Commentary on the Gospel of Luke* (1951; reprint,

Grand Rapids: Eerdmans, 1966), pp. 510-14; and Joseph A. Fitzmyer, *The Gospel According to Luke x-xxiv* (New York: Doubleday, 1985), pp. 1298-1307.

[39]See Oscar Cullmann, *Immortality of the Soul or Resurrection of the Dead?* (New York: Macmillan, 1958).

[40]W. D. Davies, *Paul and Rabbinic Judaism*, 2nd ed. (London: SPCK, 1955), pp. 309-24.

[41]*Catechism of the Catholic Church*, no. 966.

[42]See Alois Winklhofer, *The Coming of His Kingdom*, trans. A. V. Littledale (New York: Herder & Herder, 1963), pp. 213-33.

[43]See H. A. A. Kennedy, *St. Paul's Conceptions of the Last Things* (London: Hodder & Stoughton, 1904), p. 247.

[44]Luther, W.A. 36:673. Quoted in Torrance, *Kingdom and Church*, p. 50.

[45]Alan Richardson, ed., *A Theological Word Book of the Bible* (1950; reprint, New York: Macmillan, 1962), p. 108.

[46]Robert E. Bailey, "Is 'Sleep' the Proper Biblical Term for the Intermediate State?" *Zeitschrift für die Neutestamentliche Wissenschaft und die Kunde der Alteren Kirche* 55, no. 3/4 (1964): 161-67.

[47]Jeremias, *Theol. Woerterbuch z. N.T.*, 1, p. 148. Cited in Kantonen, *Christian Hope*, p. 98.

[48]See Winklhofer, *Coming of the Kingdom*, pp. 216-22. Winklhofer is willing to affirm a material identity between the earthly and heavenly body, though he prefers to speak of a substantial identity.

[49]Cited in Gleason, *The World to Come*, p. 162.

[50]Ernst Käsemann, *Commentary on Romans*, trans. and ed. Geoffrey W. Bromiley (1980; reprint, Grand Rapids: Eerdmans, 1990), p. 237.

[51]For my earlier discussion on metaphorical or poetic language, see Bloesch, *A Theology of Word & Spirit* (Downers Grove, Ill.: InterVarsity Press, 1992), pp. 67-106; and *Holy Scripture* (InterVarsity Press, 1994), pp. 255-77.

[52]K. E. Kirk, *The Epistle to the Romans* (Oxford: Clarendon, 1937), p. 213.

[53]Gerald R. Cragg in *Interpreter's Bible* (Nashville: Abingdon, 1954), 9:521.

[54]Käsemann, *Commentary on Romans*, p. 238.

[55]Braaten, "Resurrection Debate Revisited," p. 158.

[56]Ibid.

[57]According to G. B. Caird the first *"Come!"* in Revelation 22:17 "is addressed not to Christ but to all comers; and, since it is spoken by *the Spirit* that inspires the prophets and by *the bride*, the new Jerusalem, it is a summons both to join the ranks of the Conquerors and to enter into the Conquerors' reward." See G. B. Caird, *The Revelation of St. John the Divine* (New York: Harper & Row, 1966), pp. 286-87. Robert W. Wall by contrast sees the first *Come* as directed to Christ and the third in Revelation 22:17 as directed to believers who need renewal in faith. See Robert W. Wall, *Revelation* (Peabody, Mass.; Hendrickson, 1991), pp. 267-68. Revelation 22:17 needs to be related to Revelation 22:20, where the focus is unmistakably on the return of Jesus Christ to the embattled church on earth.

Chapter 7: The Interim State

[1]See Ralph V. Turner, *"Descendit Ad Infernos,"* Journal of the History of Ideas 27, no. 2 (1966): 173-94.

[2]See Philip S. Johnston, *Shades of Sheol: Death and Afterlife in the Old Testament* (Downers Grove, Ill.: InterVarsity Press, 2002).

[3]See H. A. Guy, *The New Testament Doctrine of the "Last Things"* (London: Oxford University Press, 1948), p. 23.

[4]Calvin R. Schoonhoven, *The Wrath of Heaven* (Grand Rapids: Eerdmans, 1966), p. 57.

[5]Cf. Gerald C. Studer, *After Death, What?* (Scottdale, Penn.: Herald, 1976), pp. 26-41.

[6]See Charles V. Pilcher, *The Hereafter in Jewish and Christian Thought* (New York: Macmillan, 1940), pp. 90-92.

[7]For my further discussion of the church militant and the church triumphant see p. 161.

[8]Luther, W.A. XXV: 321. Quoted in Walter Martin, *The Kingdom of the Cults* (Grand Rapids: Zondervan, 1965), p. 385.

[9]P. T. Forsyth, *The Justification of God* (1917; reprint, Blackwood, South Australia: New Creation Publications, 1988), p. 153.

[10]See Loraine Boettner, *Immortality* (Grand Rapids: Eerdmans, 1956), pp. 95-96.

[11]See the discussion in T. Francis Glasson, *Greek Influence in Jewish Eschatology* (London: SPCK, 1961), pp. 38-45.

[12]Note that 4 Maccabees is not included in the wider canon of Scripture known as the apocrypha. See *The Old Testament Pseudepigrapha*, ed. James H. Charlesworth (New York: Doubleday, 1985), 2:531-64.

[13]Cited in Glasson, *Greek Influence in Jewish Eschatology*, p. 44.

[14]*The Message of the Wesleys*, ed. Philip S. Watson (New York: Macmillan, 1964), p. 238.

[15]I am not here affirming the dogma of Mary's assumption. I am only trying to find the kernel of truth in this dogma.

[16]Notes on Wisdom of Solomon 3:7 in *New Jerusalem Bible* (New York: Doubleday, 1985), p. 1049.

[17]Georges Crespy, "Fatigue and Rest According to the Bible" in Paul Tournier, ed., *Fatigue in Modern Society*, trans. James H. Farley (Richmond, Va.: John Knox, 1965), p. 67.

[18]Words of an unnamed English poet quoted by Elam Davies, *This Side of Eden* (Westwood, N.J.: Fleming H. Revell, 1961), p. 126.

[19]Quoted in Harald Lindström, *Wesley and Sanctification* (Wilmore, KY: Francis Asbury, 1980), p. 121. See Wesley's sermon *Of Hell*, 1788, W., 6, p. 384.

[20]Sermon for the Feast of All Saints, 3. Quoted in Pierre-Yves Emery, *The Communion of Saints* (London: Faith Press, 1966), p. 38.

[21]Emery, *Communion of Saints*, p. 126.

[22]See J. A. MacCulloch, "Eschatology," in *Encyclopaedia of Religion and Ethics*, ed. James Hastings (New York: Charles Scribner's Sons, 1914), 5:387-88.

[23]Ibid., p. 388.

[24]On my evaluation of the normativeness of the apocrypha see Bloesch, *Holy Scripture* (Downers Grove, Ill.: InterVarsity Press, 1994), pp. 161-70.

[25]See notes in *New Jerusalem Bible*, p. 1659.

[26]The harrowing of hell in this context means the despoiling or plundering of hell, the emptying of hell.

[27]J. A. MacCulloch, *The Harrowing of Hell* (Edinburgh: T & T Clark, 1930), p. 251.

[28]Ibid.

[29]Ibid., p. 94.

[30]Ibid., pp. 255-56.

[31]See P. Verdier, "Descent of Christ into Hell" in *New Catholic Encyclopedia* (New York: McGraw-Hill, 1967), 4:789.

[32]Note that Thomas Aquinas also believed in the salvation of righteous pagans, but not of the damned.

[33]MacCulloch, *The Harrowing of Hell*, pp. 149-51.

[34]I prefer "nether world of spirits" to "sheol-hades" or "hades" because the last two are associated too closely with the ancient Greek cultural ethos.

[35]In a letter to Hansen von Rechenberg in 1522. Quoted in Harry Buis, *The Doctrine of Eternal Punishment* (Grand Rapids: Baker, 1957), p. 74.

[36]P. T. Forsyth, *This Life and the Next* (1918; reprint, London: Independent Press, 1953), p. 34.

[37]Gerald Studer, *After Death, What?*, pp. 34-37.

[38]Benjamin Warfield took vigorous exception to some of the later Lutherans who were attracted to the idea of postmortem salvation. See his *The Plan of Salvation*, rev. ed. (Grand Rapids: Eerdmans, 1942), pp. 81-84.

[39]For Calvin's views see Calvin, *Institutes of the Christian Religion* 2.16.9-10, trans. Ford Lewis Battles, ed. John T. McNeill (Philadelphia: Westminster Press, 1960). Also see Heinrich Quistorp, *Calvin's Doctrine of the Last Things*, trans. Harold Knight (Richmond, Va.: John Knox Press, 1955), pp. 80-81.

[40]Friedrich Loofs, "Descent to Hades" in *Encyclopaedia of Religion and Ethics*, ed. James Hastings, 4:657.

[41]Luther's emphasis was always on the resurrection of the body on the last day, not on the immortality of the soul. Yet he made a place for immortality in the form of resurrection.

[42]*The Oxford Dictionary of the Christian Church*, ed. F. L. Cross and E. A. Livingstone (1974; reprint, Oxford: Oxford University Press, 1983), p. 1144.

[43]Edward J. Hanna, "Purgatory" in *Catholic Encyclopedia* (New York: Robert Appleton, 1911), 12:577.

[44]*Catechism of the Catholic Church* (United States Catholic Conference, 1994), no. 1032 (p. 269).

[45]Ibid., no. 1031.

[46]See Jaroslav Pelikan, *The Christian Tradition* (Chicago: University of Chicago Press, 1971) 1:355.

[47]Elmar Klinger, "Purgatory" in Karl Rahner, ed., *Encyclopedia of Theology: The Concise Sacramentum Mundi* (New York: Seabury, 1975), p. 1319.

[48]For my earlier discussion of purgatory see Bloesch, *The Church* (Downers

Grove, Ill.: InterVarsity Press, 2002), pp. 165-66.

[49]Karl Rahner and Herbert Vorgrimler, *Theological Dictionary*, ed. Cornelius Ernst, trans. Richard Strachan (1965; reprint, New York: Herder & Herder, 1968), p. 227.

[50]*Oxford Dictionary of the Christian Church*, p. 1145.

[51]Mother Mary of St. Austin, *The Divine Crucible of Purgatory* (New York: P. J. Kenedy & Sons, 1940), p. 9. Note that she is quoting from Maurice de La Taille, *Contemplative Prayer* (London: Burns, Oates & Washbourne, 1926), p. 23.

[52]Ladislaus Boros, *The Mystery of Death* (New York: Herder & Herder, 1965), pp. 139-41.

[53]Bernhard Bartmann, *Purgatory*, trans. Dom Ernest Graf (London: Burns, Oates & Washbourne, 1936), p. 186.

[54]In evangelical theology all Christians have the power of binding and loosing, but this power resides in the Word of God, not in human proclamation as such. Moreover, as messengers of God we can communicate the assurance of salvation, but we do not impart salvation itself. God may speak, however, through our feeble and broken witness, thereby making this witness a means of grace to despairing sinners.

[55]Rahner, *Theological Dictionary*, pp. 391-92.

[56]Ludwig Ott, *Fundamentals of Catholic Dogma*, 4th ed. (Rockford, Ill.: Tan Books, 1974), p. 485. See also pp. 441-45.

[57]Jerry L. Walls, *Heaven: The Logic of Eternal Joy* (New York: Oxford University Press, 2002). See Steven Webb's cogent review of this book in *The Christian Century* 119, no. 25 (2002): 41-43. For my further interaction with Jerry Walls see chapter 11, pp. 241, 299.

Chapter 8: The Communion of Saints
[1]Quoted in Henry Barclay Swete, *The Holy Catholic Church: The Communion of Saints* (London: Macmillan, 1915), p. 222.

[2]For my earlier discussion of Mary's role and significance in Christian faith and thought, see Bloesch, *Jesus Christ: Savior & Lord* (Downers Grove: InterVarsity Press, 1997), pp. 107-20; and *The Church* (Downers Grove: InterVarsity Press, 2002), pp. 64-68.

[3]Bengt R. Hoffman, *Luther and the Mystics* (Minneapolis: Augsburg, 1976), p. 185.

[4]Cited in ibid., p. 186.

[5]Joseph Hall, *The Invisible World* (London: John Place, 1659), pp. 110-11, 122-24, 206-7.

[6]See *The Message of the Wesleys*, ed. Philip S. Watson (New York: Macmillan, 1964), pp. 224-25; 228-30.

[7]P. T. Forsyth, *This Life and the Next* (1918; reprint, London: Independent Press, 1953), p. 37.

[8]P. T. Forsyth, *The Justification of God* (1917; reprint, Blackwood, South Australia: New Creation Publications, 1988), p. 153.

[9]Emmy Arnold, ed., *Inner Words* (Rifton, N.Y.: Plough, 1975), p. 165.

[10]Ibid.

[11]Gabriel Fackre makes this point in "Jesus Christ in Bloesch's Theology" in *Evangelical Theology in Transition*, ed. Elmer M. Colyer (Downers Grove, Ill.: InterVarsity Press, 1999), p. 113.

[12]Gerhard Tersteegen, "God Himself Is Present," *Service Book and Hymnal* (1958; reprint, Minneapolis: Augsburg, 1961), no. 164.

[13]*Service Book and Hymnal*, no. 144.

[14]Ibid., no. 149.

[15]Ibid., no. 145.

[16]Ibid., no. 437.

[17]Ibid.

[18]Watson, *Message of the Wesleys*, pp. 230-31.

[19]Second Helvetic Confession, Ch. 17, *Book of Confessions* (Louisville, Ky.: Office of the General Assembly, Presbyterian Church [U.S.A.], 1991), 5:127.

[20]Ibid.

[21]Scholars differ regarding the identity of "the spirits of the righteous made perfect" (Heb 12:23 NRSV). The JB renders the text in question this way: "You have come to God himself, the supreme Judge, and have been placed with the spirits of the saints who have been made perfect." Some see these spirits as Christians in the NT period who have fallen asleep in Christ and who now reside in the intermediate state between death and the resurrection. Others view them as the OT people of God who have arrived at their goal—the city of God. Still others lean toward an inclusive designation referring to all people of faith who "await the culminating moment of the resurrection and the clothing of their spirits with glorified bodies." See the discussion in Philip Edgecumbe Hughes, *A Commentary on the Epistle to the Hebrews* (Grand Rapids: Eerdmans, 1977), pp. 549-55. Also see F. F. Bruce, *Commentary on the Epistle to the Hebrews* (Grand Rapids: Eerdmans, 1964), p. 378; Donald A. Hagner, *Hebrews* (1983; reprint, Peabody, Mass.: Hendrickson, 1990), pp. 226-28.

[22]See Adela Yarbro Collins, "The Apocalypse," in *The New Jerome Biblical Commentary* (Englewood Cliffs, N.J.: Prentice Hall, 1990), pp. 1005-6.

[23]It should be remembered that the departed in sheol or hades constitute those still without faith. They do not share in the communion of saints. At the same time, I do not discount the possibility that on occasion the Spirit of God might lead us to pray for them. We cannot reach them through our own powers and acumen, nor can they reach us, but the Spirit of God can reach them, for Christ descended into hades and led many of those in captivity into heaven (cf. Eph 4:8).

[24]Van Baalen believes that demonic spirits impersonated Samuel and therefore Samuel did not really appear. He acknowledges, however, that a significant number of evangelical exegetes hold that God interrupted the séance and permitted the real Samuel to appear, thereby shocking and upsetting the medium who had not anticipated such a thing. J. K. Van Baalen, *The Chaos of Cults* (1938; 2nd rev. ed., Grand Rapids: Eerdmans, 1956), pp. 40-42.

[25]"For the Beauty of the Earth," *Service Book and Hymnal*, no. 444.

[26]See Robert W. Jenson's insightful reflections on the communion of saints in his *Systematic Theology* (New York: Oxford University Press, 1999), 2:353-68. See esp. p. 368.

[27]Following Augustine, Roman Catholic tradition adheres to a typology of visions of the supernatural: corporeal, imaginative and intellectual. The first is a vision "in which the bodily eyes perceive an object . . . normally invisible to the sense of sight;" the second is "the representation of an image supernaturally produced in the imagination and presented to the intellect with as much clarity as are externally existing objects in the physical order;" the last is "a simple intuitive knowledge supernaturally effected without the aid of any sensible image or impressed species in the internal or external senses." Jordan Aumann, *The Theology of Christian Perfection* (Dubuque, Ia.: Priory, 1962), pp. 655-56. See Augustine, *De Gen ad lett.*, Lib. 2, c.7, n.16.

[28]*Samuel Rutherford and Some of His Correspondents* (London: Oliphant, Anderson & Ferrier, 1894), pp. 81-82.

[29]J. B. Phillips, *Ring of Truth* (New York: Macmillan, 1967), pp. 117-19.

[30]John F. Sullivan, *The Externals of the Catholic Church* (New York: P. J. Kenedy & Sons, 1959), p. 328.

[31]Philip Melanchthon, *Apology of the Augsburg Confession,* Article 21. In *The Book of Concord*, trans. and ed. Theodore G. Tappert (Philadelphia: Fortress, 1959), pp. 229-36.

[32]On Luther's acknowledgment of the role of Mary and the saints in our salvation, see *Luther's Works*, ed. Jaroslav Pelikan (St. Louis: Concordia, 1956), 21:295-358.

[33]*The Message of the Wesleys*, ed. Watson, p. 224.

[34]See E. R. Hardy, "The Blessed Dead in Anglican Piety," *Sobornost* 3, no. 2 (1981): 173.

[35]Ibid., p. 168.

[36]*Book of Common Prayer* (New York: Church Hymnal Corporation, 1979), p. 504. Note that the Anglican Catechism also endorses prayers for the dead "because we still hold them in our love, and because we trust that in God's presence those who have chosen to serve him will grow in his love, until they see him as he is" (p. 862).

[37]In *Prayer and the Departed: A Report of the Archbishops' Commission on Christian Doctrine* (London: n.p., 1971), p. 90. Cited in Kallistos Ware, "'One Body in Christ': Death and the Communion of Saints," *Sobornost*, 3, no. 2 (1981): 191.

[38]Ware, "One Body in Christ," p. 191.

[39]Forsyth, *This Life and the Next*, p. 34.

[40]The "coming ages" in Ephesians 2:7 might well refer to the ages of eternity—after the second advent of Christ. Cf. Leon Morris, *Expository Reflections on the Letter to the Ephesians* (Grand Rapids: Baker, 1994), pp. 52-53.

[41]See the discussion in Herman Bavinck, *The Last Things: Hope for This World and the Next*, ed. John Bolt, trans. John Vriend (Grand Rapids: Baker, 1996), pp. 73-74.

[42]See ibid., p. 72. Also see my discussion on pp. 281-82.

[43]Ware, "One Body in Christ," p. 190.

[44]See p. 1947 in New Jerusalem Bible. This commentary is significant, since Catholic tradition has used this text to support its doctrine of penance, which entails Christians making reparation for their sins that supplements Christ's reparation. See Ludwig Ott, *Fundamentals of Catholic Dogma* (Rockford, Ill.: Tan Books, 1974), pp. 316-17, 485.

[45]*The Heidelberg Catechism with Commentary*, ed. Allen O. Miller and M. Eugene Osterhaven (Philadelphia: United Church Press, 1963), Q55, p. 98.

[46]Dietrich Bonhoeffer, *Sanctorum Communio*, trans. R. Gregor Smith (London: Collins, 1963), p. 133.

[47]See Zinzendorf, *Twenty-one Discourses on the Augsburg Confession*, trans. F. Okeley (London, 1753), 19:243. One interpreter writes: "The blissful dead were not believed to be inactive: they regularly interceded with the Saviour on behalf of their living Brethren and Sisters on earth who, it was implied, directly benefited from these activities." Geoffrey Stead, "Moravian Spirituality and Its Propagation in West Yorkshire During the Eighteenth-Century Evangelical Revival," *The Evangelical Quarterly* 71, no. 3 (1999): 237.

[48]*Worship and Service Hymnal* (Chicago: Hope Publishing, 1968), no. 458.

[49]Loraine Boettner, *Immortality* (Grand Rapids: Eerdmans, 1956), p. 92.

[50]Quoted in J. Paterson-Smyth, *The Gospel of the Hereafter* (Toronto: Musson, 1910), p. 121.

[51]Paterson-Smyth, *Gospel of the Hereafter*, p. 122.

[52]E. Allison Peers, *Mother of Carmel: A Portrait of St. Teresa of Jesus* (New York: Morehouse-Gorham, 1948), p. 178.

[53]Quoted in Hans Urs von Balthasar, *Two Sisters in the Spirit: Thérèse of Lisieux and Elizabeth of the Trinity* (San Francisco: Ignatius, 1992), p. 201.

[54]Ida Friederike Goerres, *The Hidden Face*, trans. Richard and Clara Winston (New York: Pantheon, 1959), p. 2. See *Autobiography of St. Thérèse of Lisieux*, ed. & trans. Ronald Knox (New York: P. J. Kenedy & Sons, 1958), pp. 237-38.

[55]See Dietrich Bonhoeffer, *Sanctorum Communio*, ed. Joachim von Soosten and Clifford J. Green, trans. Reinhard Krauss and Nancy Lukens (Minneapolis: Fortress, 1998), pp. 180-81. Note that the first statement is an interpretation of Luther by Bonhoeffer, not an exact translation. The second is from one of Luther's treatises in 1519. See *Luther's Works*, 42:163 and 35:54-55.

[56]Quoted by Douglas Steere, "Common Frontiers in Catholic and Non-Catholic Spirituality" in *Protestants and Catholics on the Spiritual Life*, ed. Michael Marx (Collegeville, Minn.: Liturgical Press, 1965), p. 52.

[57]Pierre-Yves Emery, *The Communion of Saints* (London: Faith, 1966), p. 126.

[58]For my earlier discussion of the tension between scriptural and ecclesiastical authority see Bloesch, *Holy Scripture: Revelation, Inspiration & Interpretation* (Downers Grove, Ill. InterVarsity Press, 1994), pp. 141-70.

Chapter 9: Predestined to Glory

[1]Within the framework of biblical faith, election can have three meanings. First, it refers to the intention of God to bring the whole world into submission to

Christ. Second, it refers to the adoption of those who believe into the family of God. Third, it refers to the designation of some believers for special kinds of witness and service.

[2]The consensus of Christian tradition is that God brings about physical disaster because of human sin, but God is not the cause of moral evil.

[3]For my in-depth discussion of Israel's salvation see chapter 10 of this volume.

[4]Wolfhart Pannenberg, *Systematic Theology*, trans. Geoffrey W. Bromiley (Grand Rapids: Eerdmans, 1998), 3:442.

[5]See Martin Luther, *The Bondage of the Will*, trans. J. I. Packer and O. R. Johnston (Old Tappan, N.J.: Fleming H. Revell, 1957).

[6]See Ivor J. Davidson, "*Crux Probat Omnia*: Eberhard Jüngel and the Theology of the Crucified One," *Scottish Journal of Theology* 50, no. 2 (1997):168.

[7]See Gordon Rupp, *The Righteousness of God* (1953; reprint, London: Hodder & Stoughton, 1963), p. 283. Also see Pannenberg, *Systematic Theology*, 3:446. It should be noted that the personalist side of Luther's theology was already palpably evident in his earliest writings.

[8]See Roger E. Olson's perceptive discussion in his *The Story of Christian Theology* (Downers Grove, Ill.: InterVarsity Press, 1999), pp. 456-60. Also see James Daane's incisive and provocative study *The Freedom of God* (Grand Rapids: Eerdmans, 1973).

[9]It could be argued that Calvin's predestinarian bent, more obvious in his later than in his earlier writings, represented not so much a shift of emphasis in his thinking as a change in rhetoric. According to Thomas F. Torrance and James B. Torrance, when Calvin was more polemical he became more predestinarian; when the accent was on devotion he was more biblical and existential. Benjamin Reist maintains that the mature Calvin subsumed predestination under the rubric of Christian experience. See Reist, *A Reading of Calvin's Institutes* (Louisville, Ky: Westminster John Knox, 1991), pp. 75-77, 80-81, 86, 89.

It should be noted that Calvin frequently echoed the universal themes of the gospel despite his commitment to the doctrine of reprobation. This is evident not only in his sermons and commentaries but also in his *Institutes*. See my reflections on p. 236.

[10]T. F. Torrance, *Calvin's Doctrine of Man* (Grand Rapids: Eerdmans, 1957), p. 7. T. F. Torrance joins Karl Barth in accusing Protestant orthodoxy of reducing divine revelation to "propositional truths" that "can be arranged logically into rigid systems of belief." Thomas F. Torrance, *Karl Barth, Biblical and Evangelical Theologian* (Edinburgh: T & T Clark, 1990), p. 227. James Torrance presents a credible case that the scholastic Calvinists made divine election prior to grace and thereby posited an inscrutable, impassible God behind Christ. See J. B. Torrance, "The Incarnation and 'Limited Atonement,'" *Evangelical Quarterly* 50, no. 2 (1983): 83-94. For a more sympathetic portrayal of the orthodoxy that followed the Reformation, see Michael S. Horton, *Covenant and Eschatology: The Divine Drama* (Louisville, Ky.: Westminster John Knox Press, 2002), pp. 2-4, 184, 188, 248-49. Also see my later discussion in this volume, pp. 191-92.

[11]Pannenberg, *Systematic Theology*, 3:452-53.

[12]See John Dillenberger, *God Hidden and Revealed* (Philadelphia: Muhlenberg, 1953), pp. 100-143.

[13]In the Barthian perspective the right knowledge of the law of God is subsequent and not prior to the knowledge of the gospel. See my discussion of law and gospel in Bloesch, *Jesus Christ: Savior & Lord* (Downers Grove, Ill.: InterVarsity Press, 1997), pp. 198-209.

[14]See Hans Schwarz, *On the Way to the Future* (Minneapolis: Augsburg, 1972), p. 149.

[15]See pp. 234-38.

[16]See p. 302 n. 4.

[17]David Basinger holds that all human language presupposes the law of non-contradiction. See Basinger, "Biblical Paradox: Does Revelation Challenge Logic?" *Journal of the Evangelical Theological Society* 30, no. 2 (1987): 213.

[18]A scholarly case can be made that "paradox" is integral to the theology of Paul. See Ernst Käsemann, *Commentary on Romans*, trans. and ed. Geoffrey W. Bromiley (Grand Rapids: Eerdmans, 1980), pp. 117, 227, 277. Käsemann's focus is on the unfolding of salvation history.

[19]Augustine, *Nature and Grace* (415). Cited in Michael Marshall, *The Restless Heart: The Life and Influence of St. Augustine* (Grand Rapids: Eerdmans, 1987), p. 135.

[20]Augustine, *Sermons*, 169.13. Cited in Marshall, *Restless Heart*, p. 135.

[21]See Søren Kierkegaard, *Philosophical Fragments*, trans. David Swenson and Howard V. Hong (1936; 2nd ed., Princeton, N.J.: Princeton University Press, 1962), pp. 46-67.

[22]P. T. Forsyth, *The Church and the Sacraments,* 2nd ed. (London: Independent Press, 1947), p. 89.

[23]Emil Brunner, *The Philosophy of Religion*, trans. A. J. D. Farrer and Bertram Lee Woolf (New York: Charles Scribner's Sons, 1937), p. 55. Cf. Brunner, *The Christian Doctrine of God*, trans. Olive Wyon (1950; reprint, Philadelphia: Westminster Press, 1974), pp. 336-39.

[24]Paul Tillich, *Systematic Theology* (Chicago: University of Chicago Press, 1951), 1:57.

[25]Bernard Ramm, *A Handbook of Contemporary Theology* (Grand Rapids: Eerdmans, 1966), p. 96.

[26]Paul K. Jewett, *Election and Predestination* (Grand Rapids: Eerdmans, 1985), p. 108.

[27]See my discussion in chapter 2 of this volume, pp. 41-43. For my earlier discussion see Bloesch, *Jesus Christ: Savior & Lord*, p. 258; and Bloesch, *The Holy Spirit* (Downers Grove, Ill.: InterVarsity Press, 2000), pp. 388-89. In contradistinction to a rationalistic theology, which allows for only two options in interpreting the mysteries of faith, a dialectical theology presses toward a third option—beyond thesis and antithesis.

[28]G. C. Berkouwer, *The Church*, trans. James E. Davison (Grand Rapids: Eerdmans, 1976), p. 205.

[29]On double agency in Karl Barth see George Hunsinger, *How to Read Karl Barth* (New York: Oxford University Press, 1991), pp. 185-224. Interestingly Hunsinger does not include the role of paradox in his discussion.

[30]See James Luther Adams, *Paul Tillich's Philosophy of Culture, Science, and Religion* (New York: Harper & Row, 1965), pp. 149-155, 190-91.

[31]For a perceptive discussion of Luther's concept of the freedom and bondage of the human will, see Harry J. McSorley, *Luther: Right or Wrong?* (Minneapolis: Augsburg, 1969).

[32]Vocation is also ipso facto grounded in the action of God, yet the human role is much more evident. It is God who *calls* us to bear witness to Christ, but it is up to us to respond, and we can do so through the power of the Spirit. We are not co-workers with God in accomplishing our redemption, but we are co-workers in spreading the good news of the coming kingdom of God.

[33]Quoted by Daniel Day Williams, *The Demonic and the Divine* (Minneapolis: Fortress, 1990), p. 25.

[34]Edward John Carnell, *A Philosophy of the Christian Religion* (Grand Rapids: Eerdmans, 1952), p. 450. Also see L. Joseph Rosas III, "The Theology of Edward John Carnell," *Criswell Theological Review* 4, no. 2 (1990): 351-71.

[35]Hugh Ross, *The Genesis Question* (Colorado Springs: NavPress, 1998), p. 184.

[36]Vincent Brümmer, *Speaking of a Personal God* (Cambridge: Cambridge University Press, 1992), pp. 25-27, 37-38. Brümmer is adamant that "we cannot accept an explicit contradiction and maintain that we have still made a meaningful statement" (p. 38).

[37]Basinger, "Biblical Paradox," p. 213.

[38]See Elmer M. Colyer, *How to Read T. F. Torrance* (Downers Grove, Ill.: InterVarsity Press, 2001), pp. 322-74.

[39]See James Daane, *The Freedom of God* (Grand Rapids: Eerdmans, 1973), pp. 14-44.

[40]*Luther's Works*, ed. E. Theodore Bachmann (Philadelphia: Muhlenberg, 1960), 35:378.

[41]See Charles E. Hambrick-Stowe, *Charles G. Finney and the Spirit of American Evangelicalism* (Grand Rapids: Eerdmans, 1996), pp. 81-82. Note that I have embellished this illustration.

[42]John Polkinghorne, *Science and Providence* (Boston: Shambhala, 1989), p. 84.

[43]Forsyth, *The Church and the Sacraments*, p. 89.

[44]John Sanders, *The God Who Risks* (Downers Grove, Ill.: InterVarsity Press, 1998), p. 289.

[45]Ibid. For a credible alternative to John Sanders's position on God and reason, see Terrance Tiessen, *Providence and Prayer* (Downers Grove, Ill.: InterVarsity Press, 2000). Tiessen can perhaps be faulted for giving a purely rational resolution of this controversy and thereby underplaying the elements of mystery and paradox in Christian faith. This book can nevertheless be welcomed as an earnest attempt to throw light on an imponderable and vexing question.

[46]See the appendix to this chapter.

[47]See p. 185 in this chapter.

[48]Mark J. Edwards, ed., *Galatians, Ephesians, Philippians,* Ancient Christian Commentary on Scripture (Downers Grove, Ill.: InterVarsity Press, 1999), p. 134.

[49]Ibid., p. 133.

[50]Liberal theology shows the impact of Kantian skepticism, whereas modern evangelical theology bears the imprint of the empiricism of John Locke and Thomas Reid. See my earlier discussion in Bloesch, *The Holy Spirit* (Downers Grove, Ill.: InterVarsity Press, 2000), pp. 34-47.

[51]See Rudolf Otto, *The Idea of the Holy,* trans. John W. Harvey (2nd ed. 1950; reprint, New York: Oxford University Press, 1964), pp. 1-30. Note that Otto calls orthodoxy "the mother of rationalism" (p. 3).

[52]A number of conservative evangelicals appeal to Thomas Aquinas in their methodology. Yet Thomas insisted that we mortals can have at the most an analogical knowledge of God, never one that is literal or univocal.

[53]Jean-Alphonse Turretin exemplifies the "enlightened orthodoxy" that placed its faith in reason as the corroborator of divine revelation. In Turretin we see the collapse of the older scholastic orthodoxy, which still held on to mystery in faith, and the rise of modern evangelical rationalism. In the Christian rationalist mind-set, faith becomes intellectual assent to the basic truths that are clearly presented in holy Scripture. See Martin I. Klauber, *Between Reformed Scholasticism and Pan-Protestantism: Jean-Alphonse Turretin (1671-1737) and Enlightened Orthodoxy at the Academy of Geneva* (Cranbury, N.J.: Associated University Presses, 1994). Also see my earlier discussion in this volume, pp. 112-13, 117-19.

[54]Conservative evangelicals have been divided between evidentialists, who appeal to evidences to confirm the truth of faith, and presuppositionalists, who appeal to the consistency and inherent truthfulness of the biblical revelation. See Bruce C. Meyer and J. Budziszewski, "Evidentialists and Presuppositionalists," *First Things* 103 (May 2000): 5; and James Emery White, *What Is Truth?* (Nashville: Broadman & Holman, 1994). White gives a perceptive but not always convincing analysis of the methodologies of Cornelius Van Til, Francis Schaeffer, Carl Henry, Millard Erickson and Donald Bloesch.

[55]See Ronald Nash, ed., *The Philosophy of Gordon H. Clark* (Philadelphia: Presbyterian & Reformed, 1968).

[56]See Otto, *Idea of the Holy,* pp. 12-30.

[57]See Carl F. H. Henry, *God, Revelation and Authority,* 6 vols. (Waco, Tex.: Word, 1976-1983).

[58]For a vigorous defense of Carl Henry's position on faith and reason, see Chad Owen Brand, "Is Carl Henry a Modernist? Rationalism and Foundationalism in Post-war Evangelical Theology," *Trinity Journal* 20, no. 1 (1999): 3-21. For a more reserved—but still mainly appreciative—appraisal of Carl Henry see Ray S. Anderson, "Evangelical Theology," in *The Modern Theologians,* ed. David F. Ford, 2nd ed. (Oxford: Blackwell Publishers, 1997), pp. 489-98. For a keen rebuttal of Henry and of evangelical rationalism by a Pentecostal scholar, see Terry L. Cross, "A Proposal to Break the Ice: What Can Pentecostal Theology Offer Evan-

gelical Theology?" *Journal of Pentecostal Theology* 10, no. 2 (2002): 44-73. The danger in Pentecostalism is that it tends to subordinate the Word to the Spirit.

[59]Henry, *God, Revelation and Authority*, 1:229-30.

[60]See John Dillenberger, *God Hidden and Revealed* (Philadelphia: Muhlenberg, 1953).

[61]In his dialogue with Hans Frei, Henry acknowledges that narration can also be a means of revelation. Yet for him revelation is essentially propositional. See Carl F. H. Henry, "Narrative Theology: An Evangelical Appraisal," *Trinity Journal* 8, no. 1 (1987): 3-19. Also see Hans Frei, "Response to 'Narrative Theology: An Evangelical Appraisal,'" *Trinity Journal* 8, no. 1 (1987): 21-24.

[62]Henry resists higher criticism, though following Warfield he allows for textual or lower criticism.

[63]According to Henry, "The Bible is a propositional revelation of the unchanging truth of God." He also considers revelation "universally accessible" in the form of the inspired Scriptures (*God, Revelation and Authority*, 1:229; 3:457).

[64]Henry regards Kierkegaard as suspect because of his supposed irrationalism. See my critique of Kierkegaard in Bloesch, *A Theology of Word and Spirit* (Downers Grove, Ill.: InterVarsity Press, 1992), pp. 61-66.

[65]Charles E. Moore, ed., *Provocations: Spiritual Writings of Kierkegaard* (Farmington, Penn.: Plough, 1999), p. 258.

[66]Because I do not identify God's self-revelation in Jesus Christ with the scriptural witness, I do not quite fit into the category of a scriptural foundationalist (a designation that Chad Brand applies to Henry). The only enduring and incorrigible foundation for faith is not a book but a person—the living Jesus Christ. Yet Christ remains hidden until he makes himself known in the event of decision and faith. This is a foundation that cannot be discovered by rational reflection and therefore is not at our immediate disposal in the building of a systematic theology. It is a foundation to which holy Scripture introduces us through the power of the Holy Spirit. For my previous discussion of foundationalism see Bloesch, *Theology of Word and Spirit*, pp. 21-22, 275; *Holy Scripture* (Downers Grove, Ill.: InterVarsity Press, 1994), pp. 20-21; *God the Almighty* (Downers Grove, Ill.: InterVarsity Press, 1995), pp. 12-13; and *The Holy Spirit* (Downers Grove, Ill.: InterVarsity Press, 2000), pp. 27-28.

[67]See Kierkegaard's discussion in Søren Kierkegaard, *Philosophical Fragments*, trans. David Swenson and Howard V. Hong, 2nd ed. (Princeton, N.J.: Princeton University Press, 1962), pp. 28-60.

[68]Henry resolutely rejects myth as a category to apprehend the ultimate, and rightly so. But cannot myth be a literary form in which ultimacy discloses itself?

[69]For my previous and more extensive critique of open theism, see Bloesch, *God the Almighty: Power, Wisdom, Holiness, Love* (Downers Grove, Ill.: InterVarsity Press, 1995), pp. 254-60.

[70]See Clark H. Pinnock, *Most Moved Mover: A Theology of God's Openness* (Grand Rapids: Baker, 2001). Pinnock acknowledges a striking affinity between open theism and process theology, but he does not wish to make God ontologically

dependent on the creation (see pp. 140-51). Also see Christopher A. Hall and John Sanders, *Does God Have a Future? A Debate on Divine Providence* (Grand Rapids: Baker, 2003).

[71]J. I. Packer, *Evangelism and the Sovereignty of God* (Downers Grove, Ill.: Inter-Varsity Press, 1961), p. 16.

[72]Emil Brunner mounts a brilliant argument for the necessity of holding together the polarities of faith, including universal reconciliation and divine judgment. In his view "all 'symmetrical' logically satisfying knowledge of God is fatal." *The Christian Doctrine of the Church, Faith, and the Consummation*, trans. David Cairns (Philadelphia: Westminster Press, 1962), p. 424.

Chapter 10: Israel's Salvation: The Supersessionist Controversy

[1]Michael B. McGarry, *Christology After Auschwitz* (New York: Paulist, 1977), pp. 7-8.

[2]Franklin H. Littell, *The Crucifixion of the Jews* (New York: Harper & Row, 1975), p. 30.

[3]Johannes Aagaard, "The Church and the Jews in Eschatology," *Lutheran World* 2 (1964): 270-78.

[4]H. H. Rowley, *The Biblical Doctrine of Election* (London: Lutterworth, 1950), p. 149.

[5]A. Roy Eckardt, *Elder and Younger Brothers* (New York: Charles Scribner's Sons, 1967), p. 104.

[6]The idea of merit frequently intrudes into rabbinic Judaism, though many scholars continue to hold to the priority of grace. Steinberg contends that the Jews were chosen by God "in part because of the merits of the first fathers, whose righteousness was so great as to win this high calling for their descendants." Milton Steinberg, "Questions Christians Ask," in *Face to Face: A Primer in Dialogue*, ed. Lily Edelman (Washington, D.C.: B'nai B'rith, 1967), p. 22.

[7]"In the end, Paul comes to understand Jewish disbelief as a mission of mercy entrusted to Israel by God in the last days (Rom 11:30-32). Paradoxically, Israel fulfills its ancient calling to enlighten the Gentiles *by means of its own blindness!*" John Koenig, *Jews and Christians in Dialogue* (Philadelphia: Westminster Press, 1979), p. 56.

[8]See Iain H. Murray, *The Puritan Hope* (London: Banner of Truth, 1971), pp. 39-82, and Robert M. Healey, "The Jew in Seventeenth-Century Protestant Thought," *Church History* 46, no. 1 (1977): 63-79.

[9]Karl Barth, *A Shorter Commentary on Romans*, trans. D. H. van Daalen (London: SCM, 1963), p. 145.

[10]This is also made strikingly clear in Ephesians 2:11-22, where the desolation of the Gentiles is attributed to their alienation from the commonwealth of Israel (v. 12).

[11]Franz Rosenzweig sagaciously observed: "Whenever the pagan within the Christian soul rises in revolt against the yoke of the Cross, he vents his fury on the Jew." This is because to strike at the Jews is also to strike at the Messiah of Israel and the Savior of the world. Quoted in *Jews and Christians*, ed. George A. F.

Knight (Philadelphia: Westminster Press, 1965), p. 163.

[12]Franz Mussner, *Tractate on the Jews: The Significance of Judaism for Christian Faith*, trans. Leonard Swidler (Philadelphia: Fortress, 1984), pp. 196-97.

[13]Herbert Danby, quoted in Donald A. Hagner, *The Jewish Reclamation of Jesus* (Grand Rapids: Zondervan, 1984), p. 183.

[14]Joseph Klausner, *Jesus of Nazareth: His Life, Times, and Teaching*, trans. Herbert Danby (London: George Allen & Unwin, 1925), pp. 377-97.

[15]See Eckardt, *Elder and Younger Brothers*, p. 160.

[16]It can be shown that when Christianity is divorced from its Jewish roots, it either blends into a kind of Enlightenment rationalism or verges on an ahistorical mysticism.

[17]Peter von der Osten-Sacken, *Christian-Jewish Dialogue*, trans. Margaret Kohl (Philadelphia: Fortress, 1986), pp. 166-68; 173-75.

[18]Paul M. van Buren, *Discerning the Way* (New York: Seabury, 1980), pp. 180-96.

[19]Markus Barth, *Israel and the Church* (Richmond, Va.: John Knox Press, 1969), p. 111.

[20]Karl Barth, *Shorter Commentary on Romans*, pp. 140-41.

[21]Karl Barth contends that the key to missions to the Jews lies in making the Jews jealous (cf. Rom 11:14), and this can happen only when the church leads an authentic existence characterized by caring and mercy. For Barth, true witness entails the union of *kerygma* and *diakonia* (service). For Karl Barth's unique contribution to the Jewish-Christian dialogue and the role of missions to the Jews in this dialogue, see Katherine Sonderegger, *That Jesus Christ Was Born a Jew: Karl Barth's "Doctrine of Israel"* (University Park, Penn: Pennsylvania State University Press, 1992). See esp. pp. 100-102, 140-42.

[22]Markus Barth, *Israel and the Church*, p. 113.

Chapter 11: The Triumph of Grace

[1]Count Nicholaus Ludwig von Zinzendorf, *Nine Public Lectures on Important Subjects in Religion*, trans. and ed. George W. Forell (Iowa City: University of Iowa Press, 1973), p. 62.

[2]This was also the position of Charles Hodge and Benjamin Warfield. A strong emphasis on the sovereignty of God's grace invariably leads to a holy optimism concerning the destiny of the human race. See esp. Benjamin B. Warfield, *The Plan of Salvation*, rev. ed. (Grand Rapids: Eerdmans, 1942), pp. 98-104.

[3]Ralph G. Turnbull, ed., *Devotions of Jonathan Edwards* (Grand Rapids: Baker, 1959), p. 17.

[4]For my much earlier discussion see Bloesch, *Essentials of Evangelical Theology* (1978; reprint, San Francisco: Harper & Row, 1982), 2:211-34.

[5]See my earlier discussion in this book on pp. 38-43.

[6]Quoted in Hans Küng, *Justification*, trans. Thomas Collins, Edmund E. Tolk and David Granskou (New York: Thomas Nelson & Sons, 1964), p. 163.

[7]François Fénelon, *Christian Perfection*, trans. Mildred Whitney Stillman (New York: Harper & Bros., 1947), p. 128.

[8]Peter T. Forsyth, *The Work of Christ* (London: Hodder & Stoughton, 1910), p. 168.

[9]Augustine, *The Confessions*, in *Basic Writings of Saint Augustine*, ed. Whitney J. Oates (New York: Random House, 1948), 1:4.

[10]Jürgen Moltmann, *Jesus Christ for Today's World*, trans. Margaret Kohl (Minneapolis: Fortress, 1994), p. 142.

[11]See my review of John Paul's *Fides et Ratio* in *The Princeton Theological Review* 6, no. 4, issue 19 (1999): 30-31. Also see my delineation of the biblical-classical synthesis in Bloesch, *God the Almighty* (Downers Grove: InterVarsity Press, 1995), pp. 205-40.

[12]Nicolas Berdyaev, *Truth and Revelation*, trans. R. M. French (New York: Collier, 1962), p. 138.

[13]Cited in Vladimir Lossky, *The Mystical Theology of the Eastern Church* (Crestwood, N.Y.: St. Vladimir's Seminary Press, 1976), p. 234. Cf. Kallistos Ware, *The Orthodox Way* (Crestwood, N.Y.: St. Vladimir's Orthodox Theological Seminary, 1979), pp. 181-82.

[14]See Dante Alighieri, *The Divine Comedy*, trans. H. R. Huse (New York: Rinehart, 1954), pp. 16-17.

[15]See endnote 72 in this chapter.

[16]Donald Baillie, *God Was in Christ* (New York: Charles Scribner's Sons, 1948), p. 173.

[17]Hans Urs von Balthasar, *Prayer*, trans. A. V. Littledale (New York: Paulist, 1961), p. 177.

[18]Thomas Merton, *Seeds of Contemplation* (Norfolk, Conn.: New Directions, 1949), p. 75.

[19]Paul Tillich, *Systematic Theology* (Chicago: University of Chicago Press, 1951), 1:283-84.

[20]Ibid., p. 283.

[21]Richard J. Neuhaus, *Death on a Friday Afternoon* (New York: Basic Books, 2000), p. 143.

[22]*The New Confraternity Edition of the Revised Baltimore Catechism*, no. 3, ed. Francis J. Connell (New York: Benziger Bros., 1949), no. 185, p. 106.

[23]While the immediate reference is to Israel, the fuller meaning of this text is that sin does not cancel out the love of God.

[24]See James Daane's penetrating critique of the decretal theology of Herman Hoeksema in Daane, *The Freedom of God* (Grand Rapids: Eerdmans, 1973), pp. 24-33, 92-93.

[25]See Paul Althaus, *Die letzten Dinge* (4th ed. 1933), p. 183. Cited in J. A. T. Robinson, *Honest to God* (Philadelphia: Westminster Press, 1963), p. 80.

[26]Karl Barth, *Church Dogmatics*, ed. G. W. Bromiley and T. F. Torrance (Edinburgh: T & T Clark, 1957), 2(2):27.

[27]Ewald Plass, ed., *What Luther Says* (St. Louis: Concordia, 1959), 2:628.

[28]See David Manning White, ed., *The Search for God* (New York: Macmillan, 1983), p. 287.

[29]*Luther's Works,* ed. Jaroslav Pelikan (St. Louis: Concordia, 1958), 14:143.

[30]Ibid., p. 144.

[31]Cited in James Breig, "Hell: Still a Burning Question?" *U.S. Catholic* 43, no. 11 (1977): 8.

[32]An older Catholic Catechism in France depicted a hell that surely contravenes the deepest insights of biblical faith:

> A devouring fire is the suffering common to all the damned, but each one of them suffers the pains appropriate to the sins he has committed. The impure are cruelly beaten by demons or torn by wild beasts. The envious are encoiled, bitten, eaten, by monstrous reptiles; gluttons and drunkards are devoured by cruel hunger and thirst and fed upon the gall of dragons and the venom of asps. The wrathful and the vindictive tear each other to pieces and wrench each other's hair out. The slothful are stabbed with flaming needles, stung by scorpions, clamped into everlasting braziers . . . etc.

Quoted in Emmanuel Mounier, *The Spoil of the Violent*, trans. Katherine Watson (West Nyack, N.Y.: Cross Currents reprint, 1961), p. 35.

Equally repugnant is the description of hell in Father Furniss, *Books for Children*, a series that enjoyed wide circulation among English Catholics in the nineteenth century:

> A little child is in this red-hot oven. Hear how it screams to come out! See how it turns and twists itself about in the fire! It beats its head against the roof of the oven. It stamps its little feet on the floor. You can see on the face of this little child what you see on the faces of all in hell—despair, desperate and horrible.

Quoted in George H. Smith, *Atheism: The Case Against God* (Los Angeles: Nash, 1974), p. 300. Note that the catechism cited by Mounier never received official church approbation.

[33]Cited in Edward Fudge, "Putting Hell in Its Place," *Christianity Today* 20, no. 22 (1976): 14.

[34]Richard Wurmbrand, "We Have One Choice: To Be Smugglers or Murderers" (a pamphlet, n.d.).

[35]The metaphor of hell as a sanatorium for the spiritually deranged has an indisputable biblical basis: the close association of sin and sickness (Mt 9:5-6; Mk 5:34); the practical equation of salvation and health (Jer 8:22; 30:17; Is 53:5; 1 Pet 2:24); and the depiction of God or Jesus as physician (Mt 9:12; Mk 2:17; Lk 4:23; 5:31-32). Yet this metaphor should not be pressed too far, for it could take away the horror of hell and thereby mute the reality of God's wrath. The truth in this metaphor is that the gates of hell have been penetrated by the grace of God, and this means that hell is given a positive role in the plan of salvation.

[36]See John Milton, *Paradise Lost and Paradise Regained*, ed. Christopher Ricks (New York: New American Library, 1968), Book 6, p. 179.

[37]In his *The Pilgrim's Regress* C. S. Lewis describes hell and its fixed pains as God's last "mercy" to those who will let him do no other. See *The Pilgrim's Re-*

gress (1950; reprint, London: Geoffrey Bles, 1965), p. 180.

[38]In the biblical perspective hell is not infinite but age-long. See the discussion of *aiōnios* in J. Paterson-Smyth, *The Gospel of the Hereafter* (Toronto: Musson, 1910), pp. 182-83. Also see Vernard Eller, *The Most Revealing Book of the Bible: Making Sense Out of Revelation* (Grand Rapids: Eerdmans, 1974), p. 142.

[39]Cited in Markus Barth, *Ephesians 4—6* (1974; reprint, New York: Doubleday, 1982), p. 585.

[40]See the discussion in Markus Barth, *Ephesians 4—6*, pp. 487-89.

[41]See Alfred North Whitehead, *Process and Reality* (New York: Macmillan, 1929), pp. 518, 531. A biblical Christian will take strong exception to Whitehead's naturalistic perspective.

[42]See Eduard Thurneysen, *Dostoevsky*, trans. Keith R. Crim (Richmond, Va.: John Knox Press, 1964), p. 66.

[43]Daniel Day Williams, "Tragedy and the Christian Eschatology," *Encounter* 24, no. 1 (1963): 75.

[44]See C. S. Lewis, *The Great Divorce* (London: Geoffrey Bles, 1946), pp. 61-67. It should be noted that Lewis's emphasis in this book is on the divorce between heaven and hell, not on the commerce between them.

[45]Technically these are misunderstandings rather than heresies, but they become heresies when they function as all-determining concepts that shape the life and thought of the church. When they become part of the gospel, they then pose a threat to the church's understanding of its mission. Predestination itself belongs to the gospel, but when it takes the form of predestination to damnation in the sense of excluding an undetermined segment of the human race from the very possibility of salvation, it creates a misleading vision of God's purposes for humanity. For the ongoing debate between inclusivists and exclusivists, see Gabriel Fackre, Ronald H. Nash and John Sanders, *What About Those Who Have Never Heard?* (Downers Grove, Ill.: InterVarsity Press, 1995).

[46]See Jonathan L. Kvanvig, *The Problem of Hell* (New York: Oxford University Press, 1993), pp. 155-59.

[47]At the same time we cannot categorically deny the possibility of a universal restoration, but this can never be a dogma of faith because of the repeated scriptural warnings against disobedience and apostasy.

[48]Quoted in Friedrich Loofs, "Descent to Hades (Christ's)," in *Encyclopaedia of Religion and Ethics*, ed. James Hastings (New York: Charles Scribner's Sons, 1914), 4:660.

[49]Paul Tillich, *Systematic Theology* (Chicago: University of Chicago Press, 1963), 3:321.

[50]Austin Farrer, *Saving Belief* (London: Hodder & Stoughton, 1964), pp. 140-57.

[51]Charles Hodge, *Systematic Theology* (New York: Charles Scribner's Sons, 1898), 3:879-80.

[52]Bonhoeffer acutely perceived that the Christian faith does not deprive its followers of "treasures in the literal sense of the word, treasures accumulated by the disciples for themselves," *Cost of Discipleship*, trans. R. H. Fuller, rev. ed.

(London: SCM, 1959), p. 156.

[53]Cf. R. T. France, *The Gospel According to Matthew* (Grand Rapids: Eerdmans, 1985), pp. 111, 116-17, 272-73.

[54]See Ware, *Orthodox Way*, p. 185.

[55]Cited in ibid.

[56]Ibid., p. 184.

[57]The classic doctrine of the atonement, which depicts victory over all the powers that afflict and enslave the human race, including death, sin and hell, is admirably delineated by Gustaf Aulén in his *Christus Victor*, trans. A. G. Hebert (New York: Macmillan, 1951).

[58]D. James Kennedy, "Sermon on Grace," Trinity Broadcasting Network (June 15, 1999).

[59]Matthew Fox, ed., *Breakthrough: Meister Eckhart's Creation Spirituality in New Translation* (New York: Doubleday, 1980), p. 107.

[60]"To the man who persistently tries to change the truth into untruth, God does not owe eternal patience and therefore deliverance" (Barth, *Church Dogmatics* 4(3):477).

[61]See note 35 in this chapter.

[62]See Wilhelm Vischer, *The Witness of the Old Testament to Christ*, trans. A. B. Crabtree (London: Lutterworth, 1949), 1:68-81.

[63]Paul Tillich, *Love, Power, and Justice* (New York: Oxford University Press, 1954), p. 114.

[64]Philip Watson, ed., *The Message of the Wesleys* (New York: Macmillan, 1964), p. 129.

[65]James Russell Lowell, "Once to Every Man and Nation," *The Hymnal*, 2nd ed. (St. Louis: Eden, 1942), no. 399.

[66]Hans Urs von Balthasar, *Prayer*, p. 239. Cf. C. S. Lewis: "In all discussions of hell we should keep steadily before our eyes the possible damnation, not of our enemies nor our friends . . . but of ourselves." *The Problem of Pain* (New York: Macmillan, 1962), p. 128. In the evangelical theology that draws its spiritual vision from the Reformation, Christians can have assurance of salvation through the gift of faith, which never deceives. We have the promise that we shall never perish, for no one can snatch the company of the faithful from the hand of Christ (Jn 10:27-30). We are not to take God's grace for granted, but we can be sure that his grace will see us through every difficulty.

[67]A. W. Tozer, *The Knowledge of the Holy* (New York: Harper & Row, 1961), p. 95.

[68]Quoted in DeVern Fromke, *Unto Full Stature* (Mt. Vernon, Mo.: Sure Foundation Publishers, 1965), p. 214.

[69]Nothingness in this context carries connotations of destruction and perdition.

[70]See Karl Barth, *Credo*, trans. J. Strathearn McNab (London: Hodder & Stoughton, 1936), pp. 171-72.

[71]John Calvin, *Commentaries on the Epistles to the Philippians, Colossians, and Thessalonians*, trans. John Pringle (Edinburgh: Calvin Translation Society, 1851), p. 148.

[72]Calvin, *Institutes of the Christian Religion*, trans. Ford Lewis Battles, ed. John T.

McNeill (Philadelphia: Westminster Press, 1960), 3.20.38 (2:901). The particularist strain in Calvin persists in his continuing remarks: "Yet we ought to be drawn with a special affection to those, above others, of the household of faith, whom the apostle has particularly commended to us in everything."

[73]Bernard Ramm, *The Evangelical Heritage* (Waco, Tex.: Word, 1973), pp. 136-37.

[74]To be sure, sheol does not directly correspond to the eschatological hell, but it is the forecourt of hell. Church tradition tends to support the view that Christ's descent into hades includes the harrowing of hell.

[75]In working out his version of the classic theory of the atonement, Luther sees the words of Hosea fulfilled in Christ's overthrow of the powers of death, hell and destruction. See Aulén, *Christus Victor*, pp. 103-111.

[76]On the salient differences between Barth's view and several other positions see George Hunsinger, "Hellfire and Damnation: Four Ancient and Modern Views," *Scottish Journal of Theology* 51, no. 4 (1998): 406-34.

[77]Victor Strandberg, "A Hell for Our Time," *The Christian Century* 85, no. 36 (1968): 1105.

[78]Dante, *The Divine Comedy*.

[79]See chapter 2, note 23.

[80]I acknowledge my indebtedness to Gabriel Fackre for this propitious term. From my perspective this term does not imply that world history has a single outcome, i.e., universal salvation. In articulating his eschatology Fackre draws upon the Andover Theologians of the late nineteenth century. See Fackre et al., *What About Those Who Have Never Heard?* pp. 87-88.

[81]See George Matheson, "O Love That Wilt Not Let Me Go," in *The Hymnal*, no. 278.

[82]See Bloesch, *Essentials of Evangelical Theology*, 1:201-8.

[83]Jerry L. Walls, "Can We Be Good Without Hell?" *Christianity Today* 41, no. 7 (1997): 23. Also see Walls, *Hell: The Logic of Damnation* (Notre Dame, Ind.: University of Notre Dame Press, 1992).

[84]See Reinhold Niebuhr, *An Interpretation of Christian Ethics* (1935; reprint, New York: Seabury Press, 1979), pp. 65-83; and Niebuhr, *Christian Realism and Political Problems* (New York: Charles Scribner's Sons, 1953), pp. 147-73.

Chapter 12: The Dawning of Hope

[1]Karl Barth, *Church Dogmatics*, trans. G. W. Bromiley, ed. G. W. Bromiley and T. F. Torrance (Edinburgh: T & T Clark, 1961), 4(3):292-96.

[2]Hans Urs von Balthasar, *Prayer*, trans. A. V. Littledale (New York: Paulist, 1961), p. 125.

[3]Wolfhart Pannenberg, *Systematic Theology*, trans. G. W. Bromiley (Grand Rapids: Eerdmans, 1998), 3:178.

[4]Cited by Martin Marty in *Context* 3, no. 12 (1998): 8.

[5]Mark J. Edwards, ed., *Galatians, Ephesians, Philippians,* Ancient Christian Commentary on Scripture (Downers Grove, Ill.: InterVarsity Press, 1999), p. 121.

[6]Gerald Bray, ed., *Romans,* Ancient Christian Commentary on Scripture (Downers Grove, Ill.: InterVarsity Press, 1998), p. 251.

[7]Karl Barth, *Dogmatics in Outline*, trans. G. T. Thomson (New York: Harper, 1959), p. 154.

[8]There is some truth in this allegation, but the point is that in hope risk is being overcome. Risk is present not in the sense that the object of our hope is uncertain but in the sense that the commitment of faith entails risk to human life and security.

[9]See John Sanders, *The God Who Risks: A Theology of Providence* (Downers Grove, Ill.: InterVarsity Press, 1998); and Gregory A. Boyd, *God of the Possible* (Grand Rapids: Baker, 2000). For an opposing view see Paul Helm, *The Providence of God* (Downers Grove, Ill.: InterVarsity Press, 1993), pp. 39-68; and John M. Frame, *No Other God: A Response to Open Theism* (Phillipsburg, N.J.: Presbyterian & Reformed, 2001). For my critique of open theism in this volume see pp. 195-96. For my earlier and more extensive appraisal of open theism see Bloesch, *God the Almighty* (Downers Grove, Ill.: InterVarsity Press, 1995), pp. 254-60.

[10]Edwards, *Galatians, Ephesians, Philippians,* p. 157.

[11]See my earlier discussion in Bloesch, *Essentials of Evangelical Theology* (1978; reprint, San Francisco: Harper Collins, 1982), 1:235-42.

[12]Calvin, *Institutes of the Christian Religion*, trans. Ford Lewis Battles, ed. John T. McNeill (Philadelphia: Westminster Press, 1960), 2.10.17 (1:443).

[13]Søren Kierkegaard, *Purity of Heart*, trans. Douglas Steere (1938; reprint, New York: Harper & Brothers, 1956), p. 169.

[14]Quoted by Cal Thomas in "Not of This World," *Newsweek* 133, no. 13 (1999): 60.

[15]See my earlier discussion in Bloesch, *God the Almighty*, pp. 211-13.

[16]See A. Dorner and St. George Stock, "Fate" in *Encyclopaedia of Religion and Ethics*, ed. James Hastings (New York: Charles Scribner's Sons, 1914), 5:771-78, 786-90.

[17]Roger Hazelton, *Providence: A Theme with Variations* (London: SCM Press, 1958), p. 35.

[18]See Richard A. Muller, *Dictionary of Latin and Greek Theological Terms* (Grand Rapids: Baker, 1985), pp. 61-64. This theme is also present in Calvin. See McNeill's edition of *Institutes of the Christian Religion,* 1.16-18 (1:197-237).

[19]Calvin, *Institutes of the Christian Religion,* 1.18.3 (1:234). Ford Lewis Battles rightly shows that in Calvin's exposition of God's promises logic is "subordinated to Scripture" and "is rejected as a device for understanding what is beyond the limits of the revealed mysteries" (see translator's note at *Institutes,* 1.18.3).

[20]See Wilhelm Windelband, *A History of Philosophy* (1901; reprint, New York: Harper Torchbooks, 1958), 1:82-86.

[21]This optimistic note is captured in Colin Sterne's hymn "We've a Story to Tell to the Nations." *Elmhurst Hymnal* (St. Louis: Eden, 1921), no. 276.

[22]As Karl Barth developed his theology, he became an avowed opponent of existentialism, whereas he was often classified as an existentialist in his earlier years.

²³See Frederick Copleston, *A History of Philosophy* (New York: Doubleday Image, 1985), 8:343-44.

²⁴Peter A. Angeles, "Meliorism (Theology)," in *Dictionary of Philosophy* (New York: Harper & Row, 1981), p. 167.

²⁵Paul Tillich, *Systematic Theology* (Chicago: University of Chicago Press, 1963), 3:354.

²⁶Ibid.

²⁷See, for example, John Howard Yoder, *The Politics of Jesus* (Grand Rapids: Eerdmans, 1972), pp. 16, 111-12. For a credible defense of Niebuhr as a prophet of social righteousness upholding the demands of Christian discipleship, see Charles C. Brown, *Niebuhr and His Age: Reinhold Niebuhr's Prophetic Role and Legacy,* 2nd ed. (Harrisburg, Penn.: Trinity Press International, 2002).

²⁸See Bloesch, *Freedom for Obedience* (San Francisco: Harper & Row, 1987), pp. 48-69.

²⁹Calvin, *Institutes of the Christian Religion,* ed. and trans. John Allen (Philadelphia: Presbyterian Board of Christian Education, 1936), 3.2.42 (1:646).

³⁰See Anders Nygren, *Agape and Eros,* trans. Philip S. Watson (Philadelphia: Westminster Press, 1953), pp. 61-159.

³¹Emmy Arnold, ed., *Inner Words* (Rifton, N.Y.: Plough, 1975), p. 48.

³²Ibid., p. 106.

Afterword

¹Revelational positivism in the sense that Bonhoeffer used it to categorize Barth's theology carries the implication of an authority imposed on the self from on high, that is, a heteronomous authority. Against revelational positivism I prefer to say that theological authority is both external and internal to the self. It is not imposed upon the self from without, but it leads the self out of its interiority to an authority that both transcends and encompasses the self.

One must be careful not to link Barth too closely with revelational positivism. While he does affirm the definitiveness associated with divine revelation, this is the kind that engenders humility, since we are reminded that the knowledge of revelation eludes rational comprehension. It is well to note that Barth warned against both mysticism and dogmatism; the latter would imply what current theology means by revelational positivism. He also resolutely resisted the proclivity of orthodoxy to identify the sign and the thing signified in the event of revelation.

²Other prominent theologians who have subordinated Word to Spirit include Friedrich Schleiermacher, Ernst Troeltsch, Wilhelm Herrmann, Horace Bushnell, Theodore Parker, Rudolf Otto, Bernard E. Meland, Henry Nelson Wieman, Daniel Day Williams, J. A. T. Robinson, Rosemary Radford Ruether, Gordon D. Kaufman and Peter Hodgson.

³For my earlier discussion of Kierkegaard see Bloesch, *A Theology of Word and Spirit* (Downers Grove, Ill.: InterVarsity Press, 1992), pp. 61-66.

⁴On how Pannenberg deals with "paradox" see his *Jesus—God and Man*, trans. Lewis L. Wilkins and Duane A. Priebe (Philadelphia: Westminster Press, 1968),

pp. 157-58. Pannenberg is less comfortable with "paradox" than I am.

[5]See my critical appraisal of Torrance in *Theology of Word and Spirit*, pp. 178-83.

[6]See Gary Dorrien, *The Barthian Revolt in Modern Theology* (Louisville: Westminster John Knox, 2000), pp. 160-63. Elmer Colyer makes a credible case that Torrance readily acknowledges the element of mystery in divine revelation. See Colyer, *The Nature of Doctrine in T. F. Torrance's Theology* (Eugene, Ore.: Wipf and Stock, 2001), pp. 179-211; and Colyer, *How to Read T. F. Torrance* (Downers Grove, Ill.: InterVarsity Press, 2001), pp. 322-74.

[7]Dorrien, *Barthian Revolt*, p. 163.

[8]On Pannenberg's critique of analogy as a means of describing God, see Wolfhart Pannenberg, *Basic Questions in Theology*, trans. George H. Kehm (1970; reprint, Philadelphia: Westminster Press, 1983), 1:212-38; and F. LeRon Shults, *The Postfoundationalist Task of Theology: Wolfhart Pannenberg and the New Theological Rationality* (Grand Rapids: Eerdmans, 1999), pp. 127-34.

[9]I endorse analogical knowledge that stems from God's self-revelation in Christ (*analogia fidei*), not from the human endeavor to rise up to God (*analogia entis*). Torrance could relate positively to this statement, but Pannenberg would have difficulty with it.

Bibliography of Writings
By and About Donald G. Bloesch

Entries are organized chronologically, unless otherwise noted, into five categories: books of which Donald G. Bloesch is the author or editor, books to which Dr. Bloesch has contributed one or more essays, articles and book reviews written by Dr. Bloesch, books and articles written about Dr. Bloesch and his works, and works by Dr. Bloesch that have been translated into languages other than English.

Books Authored or Edited by Donald G. Bloesch

Centers of Christian Renewal. Philadelphia: United Church Press, 1964.

The Christian Life and Salvation. Grand Rapids: Eerdmans, 1967.

The Crisis of Piety. Grand Rapids: Eerdmans, 1968.

The Christian Witness in a Secular Age. Minneapolis: Augsburg, 1968.

Christian Spirituality East and West. Chicago: Priory Press, 1968. (coauthor)

The Reform of the Church. Grand Rapids: Eerdmans, 1970.

The Ground of Certainty: Toward an Evangelical Theology of Revelation. Grand Rapids: Eerdmans, 1971.

Servants of Christ: Deaconesses in Renewal. Minneapolis: Bethany Fellowship, 1971. (editor)

The Evangelical Renaissance. Grand Rapids: Eerdmans, 1973; London: Hodder & Stoughton, 1974.

Wellsprings of Renewal: Promise in Christian Communal Life. Grand Rapids: Eerdmans, 1974.

Light a Fire. St. Louis: Eden, 1975.

The Invaded Church. Waco, Tex.: Word, 1975.

Jesus Is Victor! Karl Barth's Doctrine of Salvation. Nashville: Abingdon, 1976.

The Orthodox Evangelicals. Nashville: Thomas Nelson, 1978. (coeditor)

Essentials of Evangelical Theology 1: God, Authority and Salvation. San Francisco: Harper & Row, 1978.

Essentials of Evangelical Theology 2: Life, Ministry and Hope. San Francisco: Harper & Row, 1979.

The Struggle of Prayer. San Francisco: Harper & Row, 1980. 2nd ed. Colorado Springs: Helmers & Howard, 1988.

Faith and Its Counterfeits. Downers Grove, Ill.: InterVarsity Press, 1981.

Is the Bible Sexist? Westchester, Ill.: Crossway, 1982.

The Future of Evangelical Christianity. New York: Doubleday, 1983.

Crumbling Foundations. Grand Rapids: Zondervan, 1984.

The Battle for the Trinity. Ann Arbor: Servant Books, 1985.

A Hermeneutics of Ultimacy: Peril or Promise? Lanham, Md.: University Press of America, 1987. (coauthor)

Freedom for Obedience. San Francisco: Harper, 1987.

Theological Notebook. 1. Colorado Springs: Helmers & Howard, 1989.

Theological Notebook. 2. Colorado Springs: Helmers & Howard, 1991.

A Theology of Word and Spirit: Authority and Method in Theology. Christian Foundations, vol. 1. Downers Grove, Ill.: InterVarsity Press, 1992.

Holy Scripture: Revelation, Inspiration and Interpretation. Christian Foundations, vol. 2. Downers Grove, Ill.: InterVarsity Press, 1994.

God the Almighty: Power, Wisdom, Holiness, Love. Christian Foundations, vol. 3. Downers Grove, Ill.: InterVarsity Press, 1995.

Jesus Christ: Savior and Lord. Christian Foundations, vol. 4. Downers Grove, Ill.: InterVarsity Press, 1997.

Evangelical Theology in Transition. Downers Grove, Ill.: InterVarsity Press, 1999. (coauthor)

The Holy Spirit: Works and Gifts. Christian Foundations, vol. 5. Downers Grove, Ill.: InterVarsity Press, 2000.

The Church: Sacraments, Worship, Ministry, Mission. Christian Foundations, vol. 6. Downers Grove, Ill.: InterVarsity Press, 2002.

Reinhold Niebuhr's Apologetics. Eugene, Ore.: Wipf and Stock, 2002.

The Last Things: Resurrection, Judgment, Glory. Christian Foundations, vol. 7. Downers Grove, Ill.: InterVarsity Press, 2004.

Books Featuring Contributions by Donald G. Bloesch

"Rethinking the Church's Mission." In *Vocation and Victory: An International Symposium in Honour of Erik Wickberg*, edited by J. W. Winterhager and Arnold

Brown. Basel: Brunnen Verlag, 1974, pp. 251-62.

"The Basic Issue." In *Christ Is Victor*, edited by W. Glyn Evans. Valley Forge, Penn.: Judson Press, 1977, pp. 27-30.

"A Call to Spirituality." In *The Orthodox Evangelicals*, edited by Robert Webber and Donald Bloesch. Nashville: Thomas Nelson, 1978, pp. 146-64.

"Scriptural Primacy." In *Issues in Sexual Ethics*, edited by Martin Duffy. Souderton, Penn.: United Church People for Biblical Witness, 1979, pp. 27-35.

"The Challenge Facing the Churches." In *Christianity Confronts Modernity*, edited by Peter Williamson and Kevin Perrotta. Ann Arbor, Mich.: Servant Books, 1981, pp. 205-23.

"Pietism." In *Beacon Dictionary of Theology*, edited by Richard S. Taylor. Kansas City, Mo.: Beacon Hill, 1983, pp. 400-402.

"Sin, Atonement, and Redemption." In *Evangelicals and Jews in an Age of Pluralism*, edited by Marc H. Tannenbaum, Marvin R. Wilson and A. James Rudin. Grand Rapids: Baker, 1984, pp. 163-82.

"Conversion." In *Evangelical Dictionary of Theology*, edited by Walter Elwell. Grand Rapids: Baker, 1984, pp. 272-73.

"Descent into Hell (Hades)." In *Evangelical Dictionary of Theology*, 1984, pp. 313-15.

"Fate, Fatalism." In *Evangelical Dictionary of Theology*, 1984, pp. 407-8.

"Moral Re-Armament." In *Evangelical Dictionary of Theology*, 1984, pp. 733-34.

"Peter T. Forsyth." In *Evangelical Dictionary of Theology*, 1984, pp. 422-23.

"Prayer." In *Evangelical Dictionary of Theology*, 1984, pp. 866-68.

"Sin." In *Evangelical Dictionary of Theology*, 1984, pp. 1012-16.

"A Christological Hermeneutic." In *The Use of the Bible in Theology: Evangelical Options*, edited by Robert Johnston. Atlanta: John Knox Press, 1985, pp. 78-102.

"A Typology of Marriage" and "Voices in the United Church of Christ: Theological Reflections on Family Life." In *The Family Album*. St. Louis: Church Leadership Resources, 1985, pp. 5-8.

"Christian Faith and Twentieth-Century Ideologies." In *Christianity in Conflict*, edited by Peter Williamson and Kevin Perrotta. Ann Arbor, Mich.: Servant Books, 1986, pp. 43-61.

"Karl Barth: Appreciation and Reservations." In *How Karl Barth Changed My Mind*, edited by Donald K. McKim. Grand Rapids: Eerdmans, 1986, pp. 126-30.

"Process Theology and Reformed Theology." In *Process Theology*, edited by Ronald H. Nash. Grand Rapids: Baker, 1987, pp. 31-56. Republished in *Major Themes in the Reformed Tradition*, edited by Donald K. McKim. Grand Rapids: Eerdmans, 1992, pp. 386-99.

"God the Civilizer." In *Christian Faith and Practice in the Modern World*, edited by Mark A. Noll and David F. Wells. Grand Rapids: Eerdmans, 1988, pp. 176-98.

"No Other Gospel: 'One Lord, One Faith, One Baptism.'" In *Courage in Leadership,* edited by Kevin Perrotta and John C. Blattner. Ann Arbor, Mich.: Servant Books, 1988, pp. 83-94.

"Ethics/Spiritual Life." In *The Best in Theology 4*, edited by J. I. Packer. Carol Stream, Ill.: Christianity Today, 1990, pp. 177-221.

"Evangelicalism." In *Harper's Encyclopedia of Religious Education*, edited by Iris V. Cully and Kendig Brubaker Cully. San Francisco: Harper & Row, 1990, pp. 234-36.

"A Faithful Church: Concerns of the Biblical Witness Fellowship." In *Theology and Identity: Traditions, Movements, and Polity in the United Church of Christ*, edited by Daniel L. Johnson and Charles Hambrick-Stowe. New York: Pilgrim, 1990, pp. 132-38.

"Niebuhr, Karl Paul Reinhold (1892-1971)." In *Dictionary of Christianity in America*, edited by Daniel G. Reid et al. Downers Grove, Ill.: InterVarsity Press, 1990, pp. 825-26.

"Expiation." In *Holman Bible Dictionary,* edited by Trent C. Butler. Nashville: Holman Bible Publishers, 1991, pp. 458-60.

"Sanctification." In *Encyclopedia of the Reformed Faith*, edited by Donald K. McKim. Louisville, Ky.: Westminster John Knox, 1992, pp. 336-38.

"Evangelicalism." In *A New Handbook of Christian Theology*, edited by Donald W. Musser and Joseph L. Price. Nashville: Abingdon, 1992, pp. 168-73.

"Is Spirituality Enough?" In *Roman Catholicism*, edited by John Armstrong. Chicago: Moody Press, 1994, pp. 142-60.

"Counterfeit Spirituality." In *The Christian Educator's Handbook of Spiritual Formation*, edited by Kenneth O. Gargel and James C. Wilhoit. Wheaton, Ill.: Victor, 1994, pp. 60-73.

"Barth, Karl." In *New Dictionary of Christian Ethics and Pastoral Theology*, edited by David J. Atkinson et al. Downers Grove: InterVarsity Press, 1995, pp. 184-85.

"Spirit and Word." In *PFR Reform: The Nature and Use of Scripture.* Louisville, Ky.:

Presbyterians for Renewal, 2001, pp. 23-27.

"Reclaiming the Gospel." In *Story Lines,* edited by Skye Fackre Gibson. Grand Rapids: Eerdmans, 2002, pp. 12-15.

"Penetrating the World with the Gospel." In *The Conviction of Things Not Seen,* edited by Todd E. Johnson. Grand Rapids: Brazos Press, 2002, pp. 183-97.

"Prayer, Mysticism, Faith, and Reason." In *Indelible Ink*, edited by Scott Larsen. Colorado Springs: Waterbrook, 2003, pp. 99-109.

"Clark Pinnock's Apologetic Theology." In *Semper Reformandum: Studies in Honour of Clark H. Pinnock*, edited by Stanley E. Porter and Anthony R. Cross. Carlisle, U.K.: Paternoster, 2003, pp. 247-60.

Articles and Book Reviews by Donald G. Bloesch

"Theology and Philosophy." *Quest* (spring 1952): 1-10. Published by the University of Chicago.

"The Flight from God." *Witness* 1, no. 1 (1953): 6-7.

"Theology and Psychotherapy." *Witness* 2, no. 1 (1953): 7-10.

"The Bible, Plato, and the Reformers." Review of *The Rise and Fall of the Individual,* by W. P. Witcutt. *Interpretation* 13, no. 2 (1959): 219-21.

"Creation as Event." Review of *The Doctrine of Creation,* vol. 3, part 1 of *Church Dogmatics,* by Karl Barth. *The Christian Century* 76, no. 37 (1959): 1055-56.

"The Christian and the Drift Towards War." *Theology and Life* 2, no. 4 (1959): 318-26.

Review of *Fundamentalism and the Church,* by A. Gabriel Hebert, and *"Fundamentalism" and the Word of God,* by J. I. Packer. *Religion in Life* 29, no. 1 (1959-60): 154-55.

"Defender of Free Grace." Review of *Autobiography of St. Thérèse of Lisieux* and *The Hidden Face,* by Ida F. Goerres. *The Christian Century* 77, no. 11 (1960): 318.

Review of *The Objective Society,* by Everett Knight. *The Presbyterian Outlook* 142, no. 13 (1960): 15.

"Billy Graham: A Theological Appraisal." *Theology and Life* 3, no. 2 (1960): 136-43.

"Biblical Religion vs. Culture Religion." *Theology and Life* 3, no. 3 (1960): 175-76.

"Nothing Ventured." Review of *Reasons for Faith,* by John H. Gerstner. *The Christian Century* 77, no. 42 (1960): 1217-18.

Review of *Reasons for Faith,* by John H. Gerstner. *Theology and Life* 3, no. 4

(1960): 331-32.

"Love Illuminated." Review of *The Four Loves,* by C. S. Lewis. *The Christian Century* 77, no. 50 (1960): 1470.

Review of *The Providence of God,* by Georgia Harkness. *Interpretation* 15, no. 1 (1961): 106-7.

"Syncretism: Its Cultural Forms and Its Influence." *Dubuque Christian American* 36, no. 2 (1961): 2.

"World-Relatedness." Review of *Images of the Church in the New Testament,* by Paul S. Minear. *The Christian Century* 78, no. 32 (1961): 958-59.

"Vain Hope for Victory." *The Pulpit* 32, no. 11 (1961): 9-11.

Review of *The Word of God in the World Today,* by Hilda Graef. *The Presbyterian Outlook* 143, no. 45 (1961): 15.

"The Christian Life in the Plan of Salvation." *Theology and Life* 5, no. 4 (1962): 299-308.

Review of *A Kierkegaard Critique,* edited by Howard Johnson and Niels Thulstrup. *The Presbyterian Outlook* 144, no. 40 (1962): 15.

"Virgin Birth Defended." Review of *The Virgin Birth,* by Thomas Boslooper. *The Christian Century* 80, no. 16 (1963): 493-94.

Review of *The Restored Relationship,* by Arthur B. Crabtree. *The Pulpit* 35, no. 3 (1964): 27-28.

"A Name for Your Church." *United Church Herald* 7, no. 10 (1964): 18-19.

Review of *How the Church Can Minister to the World Without Losing Itself,* by Langdon Gilkey. *The Presbyterian Outlook* 147, no. 14 (1965): 15.

"The Divine Sacrifice." *Theology and Life* 8, no. 3 (1965): 192-202.

Review of *Christ's Church: Evangelical, Catholic, and Reformed,* by Bela Vassady. *Theology and Life* 8, no. 3 (1965): 238-40.

"Spiritual Ecumenism." Review of *Protestantism in an Ecumenical Age,* by Otto Piper. *The Christian Century* 82, no. 47 (1965): 1450-51.

"A Theology of Christian Commitment." *Theology and Life* 8, no. 4 (1966): 335-44.

Review of *Ultimate Concern: Tillich in Dialogue,* edited by D. MacKenzie Brown. *Christian Advocate* 10, no. 1 (1966): 20.

"Prophetic Preaching and Civil Rights." *The Pulpit* 37, no. 2 (1966): 7-9.

Review of *Secular Salvations,* by Ernest B. Koenker. *The Presbyterian Outlook* 148, no. 7 (1966): 15.

"The Confession and the Sacraments." *Monday Morning* 31, no. 6 (1966): 6-8.

"The Charismatic Revival: A Theological Critique." *Religion in Life* 35, no. 3 (1966): 364-80.

"The Secular Theology of Harvey Cox." *The Dubuque Seminary Journal* 1, no. 2 (1966): 1-4.

Review of *On the Boundary* and *The Future of Religions,* by Paul Tillich. *Christian Advocate* 10, no. 19 (1966): 19.

"The Crisis of Piety." *The Covenant Quarterly* 25, no. 1 (1967): 3-11.

"The Pilgrimage of Faith." *Encounter* 28, no. 1 (1967): 47-62.

Review of *Christ the Center,* by Dietrich Bonhoeffer. *The Presbyterian Outlook* 149, no. 11 (1967): 15.

"The Constitution of Divine Revelation." Reader response in *Journal of Ecumenical Studies* 4, no. 3 (1967): 550-51.

"Catholic Theology Today." Review of *Theological Investigations* vol. 4, by Karl Rahner. *Christianity Today* 12, no. 3 (1967): 38-39.

Review of *Salvation in History,* by Oscar Cullmann. *Christian Advocate* 11, no. 25 (1967): 16.

"An Exposé of the New Factory Farms." *The Catholic Worker* 33, no. 11 (1967). Republished in *NCSAW Report,* February 1968.

"What's Wrong with the Liturgical Movement?" *Christianity Today* 12, no. 7 (1968): 6-7.

Review of *The Sacraments: An Ecumenical Dilemma,* edited by Hans Küng. *Journal of Ecumenical Studies* 5, no. 2 (1968): 391-92.

Review of *Glossolalia: Tongue Speaking in Biblical, Historical, and Psychological Perspective,* by Frank Stagg et al. *Religion in Life* 37, no. 2 (1968): 308-9.

"Intensive Farming." *Lutheran Forum* 2, no. 7 (1968): 4-6.

"The Meaning of Conversion." *Christianity Today* 12, no. 17 (1968): 8-10.

"Thielicke's Ethics: A Review Article." *The Lutheran Quarterly* 20, no. 3 (1968): 309-13.

"Church Funds for Revolution?" An editorial in *Christianity Today* 12, no. 15 (1968): 27-28.

"This Immoral War." A pamphlet. University of Dubuque, 1968.

Review of *The Way to Unity After the Council,* by Augustin Cardinal Bea, and *Our Dialogue with Rome,* by George Caird. *Journal of the American Academy of Religion* 36, no. 3 (1968): 287-89.

"The Need for Biblical Preaching." *The Reformed Journal* 19, no. 1 (1969): 11-14. Published by Eerdmans.

"Fractured Theology." *The Reformed Journal* 19, no. 2 (1969): 14-16.

"Why People Are Leaving the Churches." *Religion in Life* 38, no. 1 (1969): 92-101.

Review of *Is the Last Supper Finished: Secular Light on a Sacred Meal,* by Arthur Vogel. In *The Presbyterian Outlook* 151, no. 13 (1969): 15.

"Historicist Theology." Review of *Systematic Theology: A Historicist Perspective,* by Gordon Kaufman. *Christianity Today* 13, no. 20 (1969): 16-17.

"Can Gospel Preaching Save the Day?" *Eternity* 20, no. 7 (1969): 6-8, 33.

"Martyred for Christ." *Presbyterian Life* 22, no. 15 (1969): 34-35.

Review of *The Reality of Faith,* by H. M. Kuitert. *Encounter* 30, no. 3 (1969): 272-74.

"Syncretism and Social Involvement." Review of *The Protest of a Troubled Protestant,* by Harold Brown. *Eternity* 20, no. 10 (1969): 44.

"Evangelical Confession." *Dialog* 9, no. 1 (1970): 26-34.

"Is Christianity a Comedy?" Review of *The Feast of Fools,* by Harvey Cox. *Eternity* 21, no. 4 (1970): 59-60.

Review of *In Pursuit of Dietrich Bonhoeffer,* by William Kuhns. *Religious Education* 65, no. 3 (1970): 279-80.

"True and False Ecumenism." *Christianity Today* 14, no. 21 (1970): 3-5.

Review of *Power Without Glory,* by Ian Henderson. *Encounter* 31, no. 3 (1970): 283-84.

"A Catholic Theologian Speaks." Review of *Theological Investigations* 6, by Karl Rahner. *Christianity Today* 14, no. 20 (1970): 26-28.

"Decision and Risk." Review of *Put Your Arms Around the City,* by James Angell and *Habitation of Dragons,* by Keith Miller. *The Christian Century* 88, no. 4 (1971): 133-35.

Review of *To Will and To Do,* by Jacques Ellul. *Eternity* 22, no. 4 (1971): 50.

"The Meaning of Salvation." *Good News* 4, no. 4 (1971): 53-57.

"Heaven's Warning to Earth's Pride." *Eternity* 22, no. 5 (1971): 12-13, 45-47.

"Burying the Gospel, Part I." *Christianity Today* 15, no. 25 (1971): 8-11.

"Burying the Gospel, Part II." *Christianity Today* 16, no. 1 (1971): 12-14.

"'Christian' Radical?" Review of *Schweitzer: Prophet of Radical Theology,* by Jackson Lee Ice. *The Christian Century* 88, no. 44 (1971): 1296.

"The Misunderstanding of Prayer." *The Christian Century* 88, no. 51 (1971):

1492-94.

"New Wind Rising." Review of *Theology of the Liberating Word*, edited by Frederick Herzog. *Christianity Today* 16, no. 9 (1972): 17.

"Child Communion as a Means of Cheap Grace." *Monday Morning* 37, no. 5 (1972): 3-5.

"Unrestricted Communion." *The Presbyterian Journal* 30, no. 50 (1972): 12-13. Reprint of March 6 *Monday Morning* article.

"Salvation as Justice." Review of *The Message of Liberation in Our Age,* by Johannes Verkuyl. *The Christian Century* 89, no. 26 (1972): 751-52.

"The Ideological Temptation." *Listening* 7, no. 1 (1972): 45-54.

"The New Evangelicalism." *Religion in Life* 41, no. 3 (1972): 327-39.

"Key 73: Pathway to Renewal?" *The Christian Century* 90, no. 1 (1973): 9-11.

"What Kind of Bread Do We Give Them?" *Eternity* 24, no. 3 (1973): 37-40, 49. An expansion and revision of the essay on salvation published in *Good News* 4, no. 4. Republished under the title "Significato Di Salvezza" in the Italian ecumenical journal, *Vivere In, Anno 1, N. 4* (1973): 20-22.

"The Missing Dimension." *Reformed Review* 26, no. 3 (1973): 162-68, 179-88.

"The Wind of the Spirit." *The Reformed Journal* 23, no. 8 (1973): 11-16.

"Catholic Ferment." A review of *Revolution in Rome,* by David F. Wells. *The Christian Century* 90, no. 6 (1973): 184-86.

"Ramm Reaffirms Our Great Heritage." Review of *The Evangelical Heritage,* by Bernard Ramm. *Eternity* 25, no. 1 (1974): 36.

"Hardness of Heart." *Cross Talk* 3, no. 3, pt. 10 (1974). Adult Sunday School Curriculum of the United Methodist Church.

"Whatever Became of Neo-Orthodoxy?" *Christianity Today* 19, no. 5 (1974): 7-12.

Review of *The Christian Tradition* 1, by Jaroslav Pelikan. *Journal of Ecumenical Studies* 10, no. 4 (1974): 801-3.

Review of *Concepts of Deity,* by H. P. Owen, and *The Freedom of God*, by James Daane. *The Reformed Journal* 24, no. 2 (1974): 23.

"Rethinking Mission." Review of *Liberal Christianity at the Crossroads,* by John Cobb, and *Frontiers for the Church Today,* by Robert McAfee Brown. *The Christian Century* 91, no. 7 (1974): 211-12.

"A New Tribalism." Review of *The Restless Heart,* by Robert Harvey. *Christianity Today* 19, no. 8 (1975): 32.

"To Build Bridges." Review of *Models of the Church,* by Avery Dulles. *The Chris-*

tian Century 92, no. 4 (1975): 89-91.

"New Enlightenment." Comparative review of *Atheism: The Case Against God,* by George H. Smith, and *Without Burnt Offerings,* by Algernon D. Black. *The Christian Century* 92, no. 12 (1975): 339.

"What Troubles Christendom?" *His* 35, no. 5 (1975): 18-24.

"Where the Church Touches the World." *His* 35, no. 6 (1975): 12-14.

"Moltmann's Crucified God." *Communio* 2, no. 4 (1975): 413-14. Originally published as a book review in *Christianity Today* 19, no. 19 (1975): 28. Correction made in *Christianity Today* 19, no. 21 (1975): 23. For corrected and revised essay see *Communio.*

"The Basic Issue." *Decision* 16, no. 11 (1975): 3-4.

Review of *The Evangelical Faith*, by Helmut Thielicke. *Eternity* 26, no. 11 (1975): 51-52.

"What's Behind the Manson Cult?" Review of *Our Savage God,* by R. C. Zaehner. *Christianity Today* 20, no. 5 (1975): 35.

"A Righteous Nation." *Crosstalk* 5, no. 1, pt. 1 (1976).

"Wind of the Spirit." Review of *Aspects of Pentecostal-Charismatic Origins,* edited by Vinson Synan, and *Jesus and the Spirit,* by James D. G. Dunn. *The Review of Books and Religion* 5, no. 5 (1976): 11.

"Options in Current Theology." Review of *Thinking About God*, by John Macquarrie. *Christianity Today* 20, no. 14 (1976): 39-40.

"Prayer and Mysticism (1): Two Types of Spirituality." *The Reformed Journal* 26, no. 3 (1976): 23-26.

"Prayer and Mysticism (2): Divergent Views on Prayer." *The Reformed Journal* 26, no. 4 (1976): 22-25.

"Prayer and Mysticism (3): Towards Renewed Evangelical Prayer." *The Reformed Journal* 26, no. 5 (1976): 20-22.

Review of *The New Demons,* by Jacques Ellul. *Eternity* 27, no. 9 (1976): 53-54.

Review of *The Evangelicals,* edited by David F. Wells and John D. Woodbridge. *Christian Scholar's Review* 6, no. 1 (1976): 81-83.

"An Evangelical Views the New Catholicism." *Communio* 3, no. 3 (1976): 215-30.

"True Spirituality." Review of *The Inward Pilgrimage*, by Bernhard Christensen. *Christianity Today* 21, no. 2 (1976): 44-45.

Review of *Catholicism Confronts Modernity*, by Langdon Gilkey. *Eternity* 28, no. 1 (1977): 56-58.

"Christian Humanism." Review of *On Being a Christian,* by Hans Küng. *Christianity Today* 21, no. 15 (1977): 50-51.

"Defender of Evangelicalism." Review of *The Evangelical Faith* 2, by Helmut Thielicke. *The New Review of Books and Religion* 1, no. 10 (1977): 6.

"The Mystical Side of Luther." Review of *Luther and the Mystics*, by Bengt R. Hoffman. *Christianity Today* 21, no. 20 (1977): 30.

"The Pilgrimage of Karl Barth." Review of *Karl Barth: His Life from Letters and Autobiographical Texts*, by Eberhard Busch. *Christianity Today* 22, no. 2 (1977): 35-36.

"Breakthrough into Freedom." *The Presbyterian Journal* 36, no. 29 (1977): 7-8, 19-20.

"The Church: Catholic and Apostolic." Review of *The Church*, by G. C. Berkouwer. *Christianity Today* 22, no. 5 (1977): 46-47.

"Creative Transcendence." Review of *Historical Transcendence and the Reality of God,* by Ray Sherman Anderson. *The Reformed Journal* 27, no. 12 (1977): 30.

"Biblical Piety vs. Religiosity." *Religion in Life* 46, no. 4 (1977): 488-96.

"A Subversive Act." Review of *Thy Will Be Done: Praying the Our Father as Subversive Activity*, by Michael H. Crosby. *The Christian Century* 95, no. 6 (1978): 195-96.

Review of *God, Revelation and Authority,* vols. 1-2, by Carl F. H. Henry. *Reformed Review* 31, no. 9 (1978): 93-95.

"Tensions in the Church." Review of *The Church in the Power of the Spirit*, by Jürgen Moltmann. *Christianity Today* 22, no. 14 (1978): 36-39.

Review of *Final Testimonies*, by Karl Barth. *New Oxford Review* 45, no. 5 (1978): 21-22.

"A Bleak Outlook." Review of *The Betrayal of the West,* by Jacques Ellul. *The Christian Century* 95, no. 27 (1978): 801-2.

"Toward a Catholic Evangelical Understanding of the Lord's Supper." *Spirituality Today* 30, no. 3 (1978): 236-49.

"Crisis in Biblical Authority." *Theology Today* 35, no. 4 (1979): 455-62.

Review of *The Grammar of Faith*, by Paul Holmer. *Eternity* 30, no. 3 (1979): 50-52.

"Donald G. Bloesch Replies." *New Oxford Review* 46, no. 4 (1979): 10-11. A response to Canon Francis W. Read on The Chicago Call.

Review of *Historical Theology: An Introduction*, by Geoffrey W. Bromiley. *Theol-*

ogy Today 36, no. 3 (1979): 452-53.

"Process Theology in Reformed Perspective." *Listening* 14, no. 3 (1979): 185-95. Published in a slightly altered version in *The Reformed Journal* 29, no. 10 (1979): 19-24.

"A Catholic Examination of the Basics." Review of *Foundations of Christian Faith*, by Karl Rahner. *Christianity Today* 23, no. 25 (1979): 50.

Review of *Understanding Pietism,* by Dale Brown. *TSF News and Reviews* 3, no. 2 (1979): 11.

Response to "Theological Education and Liberation Theology," by Frederick Herzog et al. *Theological Education* 16, no. 1 (1979): 16-19.

"Postmodern Orthodoxy." Review of *Agenda for Theology,* by Thomas C. Oden. *Christianity Today* 24, no. 6 (1980): 37. Republished in *Pastoral Renewal* 5, no. 5 (1980): 38-39.

"The Sword of the Spirit: The Meaning of Inspiration." *Reformed Review* 33, no. 2 (1980): 65-72. Also published in *Themelios* 5, no. 3 (1980): 14-19.

"Rationalism." Review of *God, Revelation and Authority,* vols. 3 and 4, by Carl F. H. Henry. *The Christian Century* 97, no. 13 (1980): 414-15.

"Hartshorne, Barth, and Process Theology." Review of *Becoming and Being*, by Colin E. Gunton. *The Reformed Journal* 30, no. 5 (1980): 31-32.

"Liturgical Sexism: A New Dispute," *Eternity* 31, no. 6 (1980): 13.

"To Reconcile the Biblically Oriented." *The Christian Century* 97, no. 24 (1980): 733-35.

"What Think Ye of Christ? A Test." *Christianity Today* 24, no. 15 (1980): 25.

"How the Twentieth Century Is Eroding the Christian Message." Review of *The Secularist Heresy*, by Harry Blamires. *Pastoral Renewal* 5, no. 5 (1980): 38-39.

Review of *A Critical Faith*, by Gerd Theissen. *Interpretation* 35, no. 1 (1981): 102-3.

"Soteriology in Contemporary Christian Thought." *Interpretation* 35, no. 2 (1981): 132-44.

"Traditional Roles Defended." Review of *Man and Woman in Christ*, by Stephen Clark. *Christianity Today* 25, no. 7 (1981): 56.

"Karl Barth and the Life of the Church." *Center Journal* 1, no. 1 (1981): 65-77.

"Reflections on Intercommunion." *Living Faith* 1, no. 4 (1981): 13-17.

"What Kind of People?" *A.D.* 10, no. 5 (1981): 18-20. Two separate essays for United Church of Christ and United Presbyterian editions.

Review of *Essentials of Wesleyan Theology,* by Paul A. Mickey. *Eternity* 32, no. 7-8

(1981): 33-34.

"The Reformers Shed the Shackles of Legalism." *Christianity Today* 25, no. 18 (1981): 18-20.

"Peril and Opportunity in the Church Today." *Center Journal* 1, no. 1 (1981): 14-17. Published concurrently in *Living Faith* 2, no. 3 (1981): 3-5. Republished in *The Presbyterian Layman* 15, no. 2 (1982): 11-12.

"Is Concern over Heresy Outdated?" *Eternity* 32, no. 11 (1981): 16-17. Republished in *Good News* 16, no. 2 (1982): 67-70.

"A Discussion of Hans Küng's *Does God Exist?*" *Dialog* 20, no. 4 (1981): 317-21.

Review of *Historical Theology: An Introduction*, by Geoffrey Bromiley. *Living Faith* 2, no. 3 (1981): 3-5. Note: This is a fresh review of this book and not the same review published in *Theology Today* (1979).

"Rethinking Monotheism." Review of *The Trinity and the Kingdom*, by Jürgen Moltmann. *The Reformed Journal* 31, no. 11 (1981): 29-30.

"Karl Barth Speaks Again on Piety and Morality, Logos and Praxis." Review of *Ethics*, by Karl Barth. *The Review of Books and Religion* 10, no. 3 (1981): 9.

"Secular Humanism—Not the Only Enemy." *Eternity* 33, no. 1 (1982): 22.

Review of *The Fundamentalist Phenomenon*, edited by Jerry Falwell et al. *New Oxford Review* 49, no. 3 (1982): 24.

"Encountering Systematics as an Evangelical." *Catalyst* 2, no. 2 (1982): 1-3.

"The Struggle of Prayer." *Presbyterian Communiqué* (Summer/Fall 1982): 24-25, 31.

Review of *The Atoning Gospel*, by James E. Tull. *TSF Bulletin* 6, no. 2 (1982): 23. Published concurrently in *Intepretation* 37, no. 1 (1983): 106-7.

Review of *The Analogical Imagination*, by David Tracy. *TSF Bulletin* 6, no. 3 (1983): 23-24.

Review of *The Faith of the Church*, by M. Eugene Osterhaven. *The Presbyterian Outlook* 165, no. 7 (1983): 14.

Review of *By What Authority*, by Richard Quebedeaux. *New Oxford Review* 50, no. 4 (1983): 31-32.

"Apocalyptic and Last Things." Review of *The Open Heaven: A Study of Apocalyptic in Judaism and Early Christianity*, by Christopher Rowland. *The Review of Books and Religion* 12, no. 1 (1983): 6.

"Many Barth Letters." Review of *Letters 1961-1968,* by Karl Barth, and *Karl Barth and Rudolf Bultmann Letters, 1922-1966,* edited by Bernd Jaspert, translated by Geoffrey W. Bromiley. *The Review of Books and Religion* 11, no. 8 (1983): 9.

"But Should We Be Ordained?" Review of *Ordination: A Biblical-Historical View*, by Marjorie Warkentin. *Eternity* 34, no. 7 (1983): 38.

"Donald Bloesch Responds." Reply to Clark Pinnock. *Evangelical Newsletter* 10, no. 20 (1983): 3.

Review of *Models of Revelation*, by Avery Dulles. *The Christian Century* 100, no. 34 (1983): 1057-58.

"Evangelical: Integral to Christian Identity? An Exchange Between Donald Bloesch and Vernard Eller." *TSF Bulletin* 7, no. 2 (1983): 5-10.

Review of *After Fundamentalism: The Future of Evangelical Theology*, by Bernard Ramm. *Christianity Today* 27, no. 19 (1983): 55-56.

Review of *Creation, Science, and Theology*, by W. A. Whitehouse. *Zygon* 18, no. 4 (1983): 480-82.

Review of *Here Am I!* by Adrio König. *Spirituality Today* 35, no. 4 (1983): 369-70.

"The Catholic Bishops on War and Peace." *Center Journal* 3, no. 1 (1983): 163-76.

"The Integrity of the Gospel." *Pastoral Renewal* 8, no. 7 (1984): 94, 96. Part of this is an excerpt from *The Future of Evangelical Christianity*.

Review of *The Divine Feminine*, by Virginia Ramey Mollenkott. *Eternity* 35, no. 2 (1984): 43-45.

Review of *An Introduction to Protestant Theology*, by Helmut Gollwitzer. *TSF Bulletin* 7, no. 3 (1984): 32-33.

"Sanctity." *Pastoral Renewal* 9, no. 1 (1984): 15-16.

"Living God or Ideological Construct?" Comparative review of *Sexism and God-Talk*, by Rosemary Ruether, and *Metaphorical Theology*, by Sallie McFague. *The Reformed Journal* 34, no. 6 (1984): 29-31.

"Concerns and Hopes for the United Church of Christ." *Living Faith* 5, nos. 1 and 2 (1984): 41-45, 60.

"In Defense of Biblical Authority." Review of *Scripture and Truth*, edited by D. A. Carson and John D. Woodbridge. *The Reformed Journal* 34, no. 9 (1984): 28-30.

"The Need for a Confessing Church Today." *The Reformed Journal* 34, no. 11 (1984): 10-15.

Review of *Christian Spirituality*, by Wolfhart Pannenberg. *Spirituality Today* 36, no. 4 (1984): 366-68.

"Forecast '85: Theology." *Eternity* 36, no. 1 (1985): 32.

"Cause for Rejoicing." *Pastoral Renewal* 9, no. 5 (1984): 79-80.

"Christ and Culture: Do They Connect?" *Christianity Today* 28, no. 10 (1984): 54-58.

"Sanctity." *Renewal News* no. 91 (1985): 13.

"Everybody's Favorite Symbol." *Christianity Today* 29, no. 18 (1985): 29-32.

"Toward the Recovery of Our Evangelical Heritage." *Reformed Review* 39, no. 3 (1986): 192-98.

"An Evangelical Perspective on Authority." *Prism* 1, no. 1 (1986): 4-22.

"The Legacy of Karl Barth." *TSF Bulletin* 9, no. 5 (1986): 6-9.

"Bloesch Replies to Finger." *TSF Bulletin* 10, no. 1 (1986): 43.

Review of *Ethics from a Theocentric Perspective,* vols. 1 and 2, by James M. Gustafson. *TSF Bulletin* 10, no. 2 (1986): 34.

"Be Wise as Serpents." *Eternity* 37, no. 11 (1986): D12-D15.

Review of *Christian Theology: An Eschatological Approach,* by Thomas Finger. *TSF Bulletin* 10, no. 5 (1987): 36-37.

Review of *Created in God's Image,* by Anthony Hoekema. *Interpretation* 41, no. 3 (1987): 328-29.

"Jacques Ellul, *The Humiliation of the Word.*" Review article in *Theological Education* 24, no. 1 (1987): 140-43.

"No Other Gospel." *Presbyterian Communiqué* 11, no. 2 (1988): 8-9. Republished in *Channels* 6, no. 2 (1989): 6-8.

"What's to Come." Review of *Knowing the Truth About Heaven and Hell,* by Harry Blamires. *Eternity* 39, no. 12 (1988): 41-42.

"Changing People, Changing Nations." Review of *On the Tail of a Comet: The Life of Frank Buchman,* by Garth Lean. *Christianity Today* 33, no. 4 (1989): 60-61.

"Reply to Randy Maddox." *Christian Scholar's Review* 18, no. 3 (1989): 281-84.

"All Israel Will Be Saved: Supersessionism and the Biblical Witness." *Interpretation* 43, no. 2 (1989): 130-42.

"A Reply to Paul Quackenbush." *On the Way* 6, no. 2 (1989): 41-45. On the church and homosexuality.

"A Plan for Unity." *Christianity Today* 34, no. 3 (1990): 17.

"Beyond Patriarchalism and Feminism." *Touchstone* 4, no. 1 (1990): 9-11.

"The Father and the Goddess." Review of *Women and Early Christianity* and *Matriarchs, Goddesses, and Images of God*, by Susanne Heine. *Christianity Today* 34, no. 14 (1990): 74-76. Republished in *Partnership* (1991): 18-19.

"The Lordship of Christ in Theological History." *Southwestern Journal of Theology*

33, no. 2 (1991): 26-34.

"Twenty-five Years Later." Review of *Vatican II and Its Documents: An American Reappraisal*, by Timothy E. O'Connell. *Perspectives* 6, no. 2 (1991): 24.

"Lost in the Mystical Myths." *Christianity Today* 35, no. 9 (1991): 22-24.

"The Finality of Christ and Religious Pluralism." *Touchstone* 4, no. 3 (1991): 5-9. Republished in *Cross Point* 4, no. 4 (1991): 22-28, and in abridged form in *Mission and Ministry* 9, no. 2 (1992): 4-9.

"Law and Gospel in Reformed Perspective." *Grace Theological Journal* 12, no. 2 (1991): 179-87.

Review of *Tracking the Maze: Finding Our Way Through Modern Theology from an Evangelical Perspective*, by Clark Pinnock. *Interpretation* 46, no. 1 (1992): 106.

"Our Vocation to Holiness." *Faith and Renewal* 17, no. 2 (1992): 20-25.

"Salt and Light." *Touchstone* 5, no. 4 (1992): 25-28, 48.

Review of *The Variety of American Evangelicalism*, edited by Donald W. Dayton and Robert K. Johnston. *Interpretation* 47, no. 1 (1993): 105-6.

Review of *Doing Theology in Today's World*, edited by John D. Woodbridge and Thomas Edward McComisky. *Theology Today* 49, no. 4 (1993): 579-82.

"Liberation Confession." Review of *Loyalty To God: The Apostles' Creed in Life and Liturgy*, by Theodore Jennings. *The Christian Century* 110, no. 8 (1993): 275-76.

Review of *No Other Gospel! Christianity Among the World's Religions*, by Carl E. Braaten. *The Christian Century* 110, no. 27 (1993): 950-51.

"Theologian Donald Bloesch Speaks on Justice, Morality." *The Presbyterian Layman* 27, no. 6 (1994): 15.

"A Fellowship of Love." Review of *Theology for the Community of God*, by Stanley J. Grenz. *Christianity Today* 39, no. 2 (1995): 64-66.

"On Natural Law: Carl F. Henry and Critics." *First Things* no. 52 (April 1995): 3-4.

Review of *Ecumenical Faith in Evangelical Perspective*, by Gabriel Fackre. *Interpretation* 49, no. 2 (1995): 218, 220.

"A Theology for the Twenty-first Century." Review of *Systematic Theology* 2, by Wolfhart Pannenberg. *Christianity Today* 39, no. 4 (1995): 106.

"A Jesus for Everyone, a Christ for None." Review of *Christianity: Essence, History, and Future*, by Hans Küng. *Christianity Today* 39, no. 11 (1995): 40, 42.

"The Demise of Biblical Preaching." *Touchstone* 8, no. 4 (1995): 13-16.

Review of *The Scandal of the Evangelical Mind*, by Mark A. Noll. *The Princeton Seminary Bulletin* 16, no. 3 (1995): 375-77.

"Hymns for the Politically Correct." Review of *The New Century Hymnal*. *Christianity Today* 40, no. 8 (1996): 49-50.

Review of *Resist the Powers with Jacques Ellul,* by Charles Ringma. *The Ellul Forum* no. 17 (July 1996): 14.

"An Evangelical Response." Review of *Faith Alone*, by R. C. Sproul. *Christianity Today* 40, no. 11 (1996): 54-55.

Review of *In the Face of God: The Dangers and Delights of Spiritual Intimacy*, by Michael Horton. *The Christian Century* 114, no. 29 (1997): 952-54.

"Two Patterns of Discipleship." *Cross Point* 10, no. 4 (1997): 6-11.

"The Paradoxical Love of the Cross." *Reformation and Revival* 6, no. 4 (1997): 133-47.

"Knowing Jehovah: What the Old Testament Teaches Us About Spirituality." Review of *The Friendship of the Lord: An Old Testament Spirituality*, by Deryck Sheriffs. *Christianity Today* 42, no. 2 (1998): 72-74.

"Evangelical Rationalism and Propositional Revelation." *Reformed Review* 51, no. 3 (1998): 169-81.

"There's More to Church Than Proclamation: Wolfhart Pannenberg's Sacramental Theology," Review of *Systematic Theology* 3, by Wolfhart Pannenberg. *Christianity Today* 42, no. 9 (1998): 69-70.

"Accepting the Cross." *Cross Point* 12, no. 1 (1999): 29-33.

Review of *God-Mystery-Diversity: Christian Theology in a Pluralistic World*, by Gordon D. Kaufman. *International Bulletin of Missionary Research* 23, no. 2 (1999): 80-81.

Review of *Restoring the Center: Essays Evangelical and Ecumenical*, by Gabriel Fackre. *Interpretation* 53, no. 3 (1999): 323-24.

Review of *Justice the True and Only Mercy: Essays on the Life and Theology of Peter Taylor Forsyth*, edited by Trevor Hart. *Scottish Journal of Theology* 52, no. 2 (1999): 238-40.

Review of *Fides et Ratio,* by Pope John Paul II. *The Princeton Theological Review* 6, no. 4, issue 19 (1999): 30-31.

"Toward a Consistent Pro-Life Ethic." *The Princeton Theological Review* 7, nos. 2 and 3, (2000): 40-41.

"Whatever Happened to God?" *Christianity Today* 45, no. 2 (2001): 54-55.

Review of *Retrieving the Tradition and Renewing Evangelicalism: A Primer for Suspicious Protestants,* by D. H. Williams. *Interpretation* 55, no. 2 (2001): 220.

"Taking the Bible Seriously." *The Witness* 22, no. 1 (2001): 6-7.

"A Response to Frank Macchia." *Journal of Pentecostal Theology* 10, no. 2 (2002): 18-24.

Books and Articles About Donald G. Bloesch

Several of these books and articles deal only cursorily with Bloesch's theology. This is not an exhaustive list and contains only a small sample of the numerous reviews and appraisals of Bloesch's works.

Holmer, Paul. "Pro Piety." Review of *The Crisis of Piety,* by Donald G. Bloesch. *The Christian Century* 85, no. 45 (1968): 1407.

Nash, Ronald H. *The Word of God and the Mind of Man.* Grand Rapids: Zondervan, 1982, pp. 95-96, 121-32.

Noll, Mark. Foreword to *The Future of Evangelical Christianity* by Donald G. Bloesch. New York: Doubleday, 1983. Reprint, Colorado Springs: Helmers & Howard, 1988.

————. "The Surprising Optimism of Donald Bloesch." *Center Journal* 3, no. 3 (Summer 1984): 95-104.

Van Essen, R. "A Theological Portrait: Dr. Donald G. Bloesch." Translated by Daniel W. Bloesch. *Soteria: Evangelical Theological Reflection* 3, no. 3 (1986).

Hall, Christopher Alan. *The Source and Significance of Paradoxical Elements in the Thought of Donald Bloesch.* Master's thesis, Regent College, Vancouver, British Columbia, 1987.

Gier, Nicholas F. *God, Reason and the Evangelicals.* Lanham, Md.: University Press of America, 1987.

Keylock, Leslie R. "Meet Donald G. Bloesch." *Moody Monthly* 88, no. 7 (1988): 61-63.

Herzog, Frederick. *God-Walk: Liberation Shaping Dogmatics.* Maryknoll, N.Y.: Orbis, 1988, pp. 252, 255-56, note 35.

Nessan, Craig L. *Orthopraxis or Heresy.* Atlanta: Scholars, 1989, pp. 702-7.

Mohler, Richard Albert, Jr. "Evangelical Theology and Karl Barth: Representative Models." Ph.D. diss., Southern Baptist Theological Seminary, 1989.

Perry, Ronald Mark. "A Holistic Model of Church Renewal in Light of a Critical

Evaluation of the Contributions of D. Elton Trueblood, Donald G. Bloesch and Leonardo Boff." Ph.D. diss., New Orleans Baptist Theological Seminary, 1992.

McKim, Donald K. "Donald G. Bloesch." In *A Handbook of Evangelical Theologians,* edited by Walter Elwell. Grand Rapids: Baker, 1993, pp. 388-400.

Bell, Richard. Review of *Holy Scripture,* by Donald G. Bloesch. *Journal of Religion* 77, no. 4 (1994): 636-38.

White, James Emery. *What Is Truth? A Comparative Study of the Positions of Cornelius Van Til, Francis Schaeffer, Carl F. H. Henry, Donald Bloesch and Millard Erickson.* Nashville: Broadman & Holman, 1994.

Meyers, Jeffrey J. "Evangelical Meltdown." *Contra Mundum* 12 (summer 1994): 1-24.

Deddo, Gary W. "Shapers of Modern Evangelical Thought: Donald Bloesch." *Religious and Theological Studies Fellowship Bulletin* 6 (Jan.-Feb. 1995): 17-19.

Hasel, Frank M. *Scripture in the Theologies of W. Pannenberg and D. G. Bloesch: An Investigation and Assessment of Its Origin, Nature, and Use.* Frankfurt and New York: Peter Lang, 1995, esp. the fairly comprehensive list of doctoral dissertations on Bloesch's theology on p. 171.

Crampton, W. Gary. "The Neo-Orthodoxy of Donald Bloesch." *The Trinity Review* 126 (Aug. 1995): 1-4.

Toon, Peter. *The End of Liberal Theology: Contemporary Challenges to Evangelical Orthodoxy.* Wheaton: Crossway Books, 1995.

Cameron, Charles M. Review of *Holy Scripture* by Donald G. Bloesch. *Scottish Bulletin of Evangelical Theology* 13, no. 2 (1995): 148-50.

Review of *God the Almighty* by Donald G. Bloesch. *Publishers Weekly* 242, no. 46 (1995): 38.

Smith, David L. *All God's People.* Wheaton, Ill.: Victor Books, 1996, pp. 170-73.

Gill, David W. "God, in His Own Words." Review of *God the Almighty* by Donald G. Bloesch. *Christianity Today* 40, no. 6 (1996): 37-40.

Olson, Roger. "Donald G. Bloesch." In *A New Handbook of Christian Theologians,* edited by Donald W. Musser and Joseph L. Price. Nashville: Abingdon, 1996, pp. 67-73.

Lindbeck, George. Review of *Holy Scripture* by Donald G. Bloesch. *Interpretation* 50, no. 3 (1996): 324-26.

Colyer, Elmer M. "A Theology of Word and Spirit: Donald Bloesch's Theological Method." *The Journal for Christian Theological Research* 1, no. 1 (1996):

<http://home.apu.edu/~CTRF/articles/1996_articles/colyer.html>.

Murphy, Nancey. *Beyond Liberalism and Fundamentalism: How Modern and Postmodern Philosophy Set the Theological Agenda.* Valley Forge, Penn.: Trinity Press International, 1996.

Houts, Margo G. "Is God Also Our Mother?" *Perspectives* 12, no. 6 (1997): 8-12.

Adams, Daniel J., ed. *From East to West: Essays in Honor of Donald G. Bloesch.* Lanham, Md.: University Press of America, 1997. See esp. pp. v-x, 1-22, 211-32.

Andersen, Carlton. Review of *God The Almighty* by Donald G. Bloesch. *Dialog* 36, no. 4 (1997): 312-14.

Dorrien, Gary. *The Remaking of Evangelical Theology.* Louisville: Westminster Press, 1998.

Brand, Chad Owen. *Donald George Bloesch's Contribution to Theological Method.* Ph.D. diss., Southwestern Baptist Theological Seminary, Fort Worth, 1998.

McCurdy, Leslie. *Attributes and Atonement: The Holy Love of God in the Theology of P. T. Forsyth.* Carlisle, U.K.: Paternoster Press, 1999, pp. 257-59.

Brand, Chad Owen. "Is Carl Henry a Modernist? Rationalism and Foundationalism in Post-War Evangelical Theology." *Trinity Journal* 20 new series, no. 1 (spring 1999): 3-21.

Colyer, Elmer M., ed. *Evangelical Theology in Transition: Theologians in Dialogue with Donald Bloesch.* Downers Grove, Ill.: InterVarsity Press, 1999.

Callahan, James. "Bloesch, Donald G." In *Evangelical Dictionary of Theology*, edited by Walter Elwell. Second edition. Grand Rapids: Baker, 2001, p. 175.

Yurs, Mark E. "The Evangelical Homiletics of Donald G. Bloesch." *The Journal of the American Academy of Ministry* 7, no. 1 (2001): 31-37.

Husbands, Mark. "Donald Bloesch." In *Biographical Dictionary of Evangelicals,* edited by Timothy Larsen. Downers Grove, Ill.: InterVarsity Press, 2003, pp. 58-59.

Translations of Works by Donald G. Bloesch

Essentials of Evangelical Theology (Korean, Russian, Serbo-Croatian, Polish)

The Crisis of Piety (Korean)

The Ground of Certainty (Korean)

Wellsprings of Renewal (Korean)

Faith and Its Counterfeits (Korean, Chinese, Japanese)

The Reform of the Church (Japanese, Korean)

"A Christological Hermeneutic" (Chinese)

"The Meaning of Salvation" (Italian)

The Evangelical Renaissance (Spanish)

The Christian Life and Salvation (Korean)

The Struggle of Prayer (Korean, Turkish, Spanish)

A Theology of Word & Spirit (Korean)

"Evangelical Rationalism & Propositional Revelation" (Japanese)

Subject Index